8th Australian Edition

MYOB®
Software

FOR
DUMMIES®

A Wiley Brand

8th Australian Edition

**MYOB®
Software**

FOR

DUMMIES®

A Wiley Brand

by Veechi Curtis

FOR

DUMMIES®

A Wiley Brand

MYOB Software For Dummies®

8th Australian Edition published by
Wiley Publishing Australia Pty Ltd
42 McDougall Street
Milton, Qld 4064
www.dummies.com

Copyright © 2015 Wiley Publishing Australia Pty Ltd

The moral rights of the author have been asserted.

National Library of Australia
Cataloguing-in-Publication data:

Author:	Curtis, Veechi, author.
Title:	MYOB Software For Dummies / Veechi Curtis
Edition:	8th Australian Edition
ISBN:	9780730315377 (pbk.)
	9780730315384 (ebook)
Series:	For Dummies
Notes:	Includes index.
Subjects:	M.Y.O.B. (computer file)
	Accounting — computer programs
	Small business — accounting — computer programs
Dewey Number:	657.0285536

Cover image: © MYOB, 2015. MYOB® is a registered trademark of MYOB Technology Pty Ltd.

Typeset by diacriTech, Chennai, India

Printed in Singapore by
C.O.S. Printers Pte Ltd

10 9 8 7 6 5 4 3 2 1

Contents at a Glance

Table of Contents

Introduction

. . . .

*N*ot many people will talk to you in the dead of night, listen without answering back, offer advice whenever asked, and not take up more than their fair share of the bed. It's these qualities (and many more besides) that make MYOB such a perfect companion.

I admit that reaching this comfortable state of cohabitation can take a while. Lots of people feel totally overwhelmed by MYOB at first but, fortunately, the sensation is always temporary. You can do it! I've taught MYOB to hundreds of people over the years and I'm yet to meet someone who hasn't gotten their head around the whole deal in the end.

In fact, it's often the very people who are the most unsure in the beginning who end up being the best bookkeepers. That's because being cautious pays off in the long run — it's a quality that brings great rewards when it comes to number-crunching. So, however anxious you feel, you can cast your cares to the wind. Be brave, be confident and read on.

About This Book

This book is a bit different from other books about MYOB, not least because this book is part of the *For Dummies* series. Dummies books aren't about thinking that you're a 'dummy' — far from it. What the Dummies series is all about is sharing a 'can-do' attitude and a fresh approach. I talk less about old-school ways of doing simple tasks, and more about how to get stuff done quickly and easily. Similarly, I tend to steer clear of pedantic explanations, and instead suggest that you adapt MYOB to work the way you do, depending on the kind of business you have.

I've written this book with the latest version of MYOB AccountRight in mind, including AccountRight Basics, AccountRight Standard, AccountRight Live, AccountRight Plus and AccountRight Premier. (This book doesn't include info about MYOB Essentials.) If you have AccountRight Basics or Standard, you may come across references to features that don't exist, such as inventory or payroll. I point out these differences wherever possible.

One more thing. Throughout this book you'll see *sidebars* — text that sits in a separate box with grey shading. Think of sidebars as the chocolate topping on your ice-cream: Nice to have, but not essential. Feel free to skip these bits.

Foolish Assumptions

Over the years, I've learnt to assume as little as possible. However, to write this book, I did have to make two small assumptions about you, the reader:

- ✔ Your knowledge of computers and how they work is a little more advanced than knowing where to find the on/off switch.
- ✔ You either plan to purchase MYOB software in the near future, or you already have MYOB software installed on your computer.

Icons Used in This Book

What use is a *For Dummies* book without the little icons pointing you in the right direction? Here's a brief description of the icons used in this book:

Want to be streets ahead of the competition? Then look for this handy icon.

You guessed it! This icon marks content relating to everyone's favourite topic — the beloved Goods and Services Tax.

This icon flags information about storing your company file in the cloud, and highlights both the pros and the cons of working in this way.

Don't forget these little pearls of wisdom. Remember, remember, remember!

The Technical Stuff icon highlights technical information not suitable for the faint-hearted.

Tips are the little ways to make life easier, including shortcuts and handy brainwaves.

This icon flags information specific to upgrading from one version of MYOB to another.

Every time you see a Warning icon, you can be sure I'm sharing a hard-earned lesson from personal experience!

Beyond the Book

I've written a few additional articles about MYOB-related topics that you can find at www.dummies.com/extras/myobsoftwareau. In one article, I write about importing and exporting data, and in another I talk about tips to speed the way you work. A third article talks about generating payment summaries for employees at the end of each payroll year.

At www.dummies.com/extras/myobsoftwareau you can also find a bonus Part of Tens list, which lists 10 perilous pitfalls — 10 things to avoid doing in MYOB if you want to keep both your hair and your sanity.

I like to think of my books as a conversation with readers, rather than a one-way monologue. If you have any comments, questions or feedback, I'd love to hear from you. Please feel free to email me at veechi@veechicurtis.com.au or visit my webpage at www.veechicurtis.com.au.

Where to Go From Here

MYOB Software For Dummies is no great work of fiction (something that would be a tad tricky given the subject matter) and so doesn't require you to start at the beginning and follow through to the end. Instead, feel free to jump in and start reading from whatever section is most relevant to you:

> ✔ **New to MYOB and trying to get a company file set up from scratch?**
> I suggest you read Chapters 1, 2 and 3 to get your company file started. A clean start takes a bit of planning and, hopefully, these early chapters help you do just that.

✔ **New to MYOB but the company file is already up and running?**
Maybe you're starting a new job and, although the business has been
using MYOB for a while, you're new to the whole deal. In this situation,
I suggest you start by reading the last half of Chapter 1 and all of
Chapter 2 to familiarise yourself with the basics. Then browse through
Chapter 4 to 8 to discover how to do everyday tasks.

✔ **Familiar with MYOB but you want to take advantage of new
technology to do things faster?** Then head to Chapter 5 to read about
bank feeds, Chapter 13 for info about electronic payments, Chapter 14
for advanced reporting, and Chapter 16 for how to shift to working in
the cloud.

✔ **Want to know that your accounts are as clean as a whistle and your
figures make sense?** Wonderful. Head to Chapter 9 to discover how
to reconcile your bank account, Chapter 15 to check your codings
and calculations, Chapter 17 to review your financial statements,
and Chapter 18 to put your company file through the health check
from hell.

Part I
The Building Blocks

getting started
with

MYOB

In this part ...

- ✔ Get familiar with MYOB and build a mental picture of the tasks that lie ahead, setting a plan of action into place.

- ✔ Discover how to set up accounts, and learn the difference between assets and liabilities, costs of sales and expenses.

- ✔ Add customers and suppliers, set up credit terms, and keep your lists looking shipshape.

- ✔ Nurture your inner bean counter and get those opening balances spot on.

Chapter 1

Starting from Scratch

· ·

In This Chapter

▶ Drawing up an action plan

▶ Navigating through the Easy Setup Assistant

▶ Finding your way around — picking up the local lingo

▶ Opening and closing your company file

▶ Inviting other folk to join the party

· ·

MYOB transforms the usually quite technical process of bookkeeping into a relatively straightforward activity. Within a couple of hours of installing the software, you can be invoicing customers, entering bank transactions and looking at your profit.

In this chapter, I share my ideas about the best way to get started with MYOB, highlighting what's important (and ignoring what's not), and providing a bit of a road map so you can find your way around.

If you've recently purchased MYOB and you want to set up your first company file, I suggest you start from the beginning and read through the first half of this chapter, which explains what information you'll need, the best time to start, and the basics of setting up customers, suppliers and accounts.

If you're new to MYOB but a company file is already up and running — maybe you're starting a new job as a bookkeeper — I suggest you skip straight to the second half of this chapter. Start reading from the section 'Getting to Know Each Other', which explains how to find your way around MYOB.

Planning for What Lies Ahead

I've done literally hundreds of accounting software setups over the years, taking anything from 15 minutes to several days to complete the process. How long the setup for your business takes depends on the complexity of your business, the amount of time you've got on your hands and, last but not least, the kind of person you are.

Understanding what's involved

How many times have you volunteered for something without understanding what was really involved, and later lived to regret your actions? (To volunteer to become treasurer of our local soccer club was one such moment in my life.) With such innocence in mind, and because I don't want you to feel unhappy, I'm going to outline exactly what's involved with this whole MYOB caper:

1. **Decide on a start date.**

   If you're not sure what your start date should be, skip to the sidebar 'When is the best time to start?', later in this chapter.

2. **If you haven't done so already, install MYOB.**

   The only tricky question you may encounter during this process is whether you want to install the PC Edition or the Server Edition. Only choose the AccountRight Server Edition if you want other computers on your network to access your company files, or if you're installing AccountRight on Windows XP (versions 2014.4 and below).

3. **Follow the prompts to complete the New Company File and Easy Setup Assistant interviews.**

   These interviews walk you through setting up your first MYOB company file and entering opening balances for accounts, customers and suppliers. See 'Creating your company file' and 'Introducing the Easy Setup Assistant' a little later in this chapter.

4. **If you're new to MYOB, take the time to have a good old stickybeak.**

   In the thick of this chapter, in the section 'Getting to Know Each Other', I take you on a grand tour.

5. **Go to the Accounts command centre area and click Accounts List. Customise this list to fit your business.**

   I always recommend tweaking your Accounts List to fit your business, adding accounts, changing account names or deleting accounts that you don't need. I explain how to add and edit accounts in Chapter 2, and to record opening balances in Chapter 3.

6. Sign up for bank feeds.

I talk lots more about bank feeds in Chapter 5 where I explain not only how to sign up for bank feeds, but also how bank feeds can cut data-entry time by up to 80 per cent. Bank feed applications can take up to 14 days for MYOB to approve, so I suggest you lodge your bank feed forms as soon as possible.

7. Invite others to work with you.

If you have employees who are going to work in MYOB, set them up with User IDs and passwords right from the start. Similarly, if you plan to work with your company file in the cloud, invite your accountant to join the fun. (I talk more about user roles later in this chapter in 'Setting Up User Roles'.)

8. Enter some sales transactions.

If you create invoices to send to customers, recording sales is a great way to get to know MYOB. (I explain how to add customers in Chapter 2, how to enter opening balances in Chapter 3, and how to record sales in Chapter 4.)

9. Start designing your forms (invoices, purchase orders and so on).

Chapter 12 covers all you need to know.

10. Record a few expenses.

From the moment you start recording expenses, you can start looking at your profit and how business is faring. For more about recording expenses, see Chapters 5 and 6.

11. If you buy or sell items (rather than services), set up your inventory.

It's strange, but inventory isn't mentioned anywhere in the Easy Setup Assistant. Fear not. Progress to Chapter 10, read it faithfully, and set up your inventory before going any further.

12. If you have employees, set up payroll.

If you're going to use payroll, you should do so from the very beginning of the payroll year (July). When you've completed the rest of your setup, hop to Chapter 11, which covers payroll in depth.

13. Decide whether or not you want to store your company file in the cloud.

For more about this momentous decision, see Chapter 16.

14. Decide on a backup system and put it in place.

Backing up is important, even if you're planning to work in the cloud, so be sure to establish a backup system. See Chapter 16 to find out more.

Gathering your wits about you

You wouldn't set off across the Nullarbor Plain without water or fuel, would you? Nor should you attempt to set up MYOB without a couple of essentials close to hand. Here's what you need:

- ✔ **If you're setting up the books for an established business, the most recent set of tax returns or final accounts you have available:** Previous Profit & Loss reports and even tax returns come in handy, helping you to work out what accounts to include in your Accounts List.

- ✔ **Bank statements and credit card statements:** You need bank statements so that you can enter the opening balance of your bank account for the date that you start using MYOB. Depending on whether or not you already have bank feeds activated, you may also need bank statements as a reference for recording transactions.

- ✔ **A list of who owes you money:** It's always cheering when you realise that if everyone coughed up tomorrow, you'd actually be quite rich.

- ✔ **A list of everyone you owe money to:** If you intend to record supplier bills (I talk lots more about this decision in Chapter 8), make a list of everyone you owe money to.

TIP

When is the best time to start?

The very best time of year to start recording your accounts is the start of the financial year (that's 1 July for 99 per cent of Australian businesses). Even if July is long gone by the time you're ready to get started, it's still probably best to start by entering accounts from the beginning of that financial year.

Why? If you start on the first day of a new financial year, the transition from your old accounting system to your new one is a cinch. That's because accounts are always finalised at the end of each financial year. These final accounts provide the opening balances for the following year and save you

paying your accountant to draw up interim accounts.

With suitably religious overtones, MYOB refers to the month that you start recording transactions as your *conversion month*. So if you're entering information from July onwards, your conversion month is July.

Don't be tricked into thinking that this conversion month is the current month. Even if it's February when you install MYOB software, if you want to go back later and enter transactions from July in the previous year, your conversion month should be July.

Creating your company file

Assuming you've already installed MYOB software, you're ready to create your first company file. Here goes.

1. Fire up MYOB and click Create to start a new company file.

Double-click the MYOB software icon on your desktop. When the Welcome window appears, click Create a Company File.

If you're upgrading from a previous version of MYOB, you don't need to create a new company file. Instead, all you need to do is ensure you have the latest version of MYOB installed. With this complete, you can open your company file and run the upgrade process when prompted.

2. Select the correct version of AccountRight.

As you can see in Figure 1-1, you can select any one of four versions when creating a new file (AccountRight Basics, Standard, Plus or Premier), regardless of what version of MYOB you installed. If you select the wrong AccountRight product and you choose a product that's higher up the family tree than the product you subscribed to, you won't be allowed to activate your file. Instead, you either have to start again from scratch (using the correct version this time) or you will have no choice but to upgrade (and, in the process, be compelled to pay a higher monthly fee).

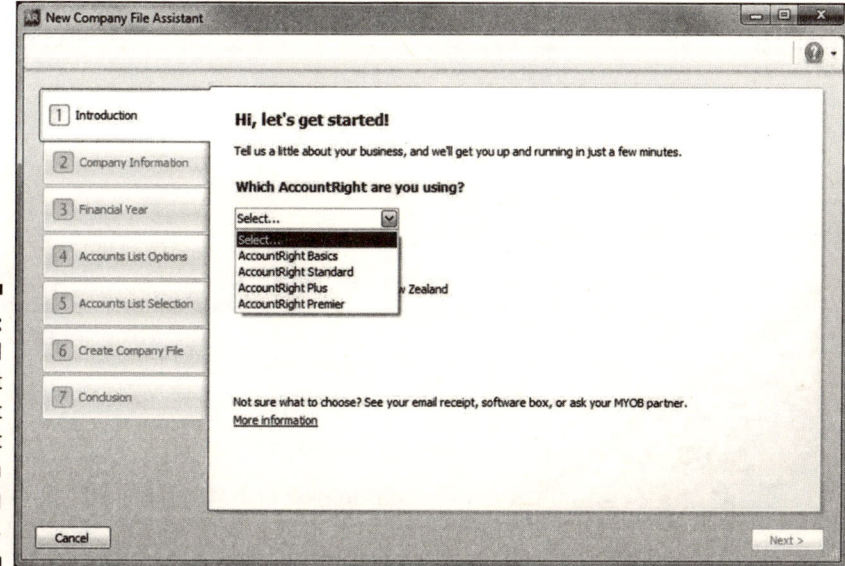

Figure 1-1: Be careful to select the correct AccountRight version when getting started.

So the moral of my tale? Be extremely careful when selecting what version of AccountRight you want to use. Given that you have a 30-day grace period before you need to activate your file, you could end up doing a whole heap of work in the wrong version, and then have to start again from scratch.

3. **Click Next and, when prompted, fill in your serial number, business name, ABN, address and so on.**

   You can find your serial number on the software CD sleeve or, if you purchased MYOB via a download, on a confirmation email from MYOB.

4. **Set the Financial Year and confirm when this year ends.**

   To answer this question, ask yourself what year it will be when the current financial year ends. For example, if it's July 2015 now, it will be June 2016 by the time you're next due to complete a tax return. Therefore, type **2016** as your Current Financial Year.

   Be careful to set the financial year correctly, because once you've selected a year, you can't change it!

5. **Specify your conversion month.**

   July is almost always the best bet for your conversion month. (For more info, check out the sidebar 'When is the best time to start?', earlier in this chapter.)

6. **Create your Accounts List.**

   You have a choice to start with a ready-made list, import a list from another file or build your own list from scratch. Unless you have an accounting background, you're best to start with one of the ready-made lists.

7. **Review your company file name.**

   Keep your company file name short but distinctive, and avoid ampersands (&), asterisks and full stops.

8. **Consider the location of your file.**

   MYOB saves your company file in a special folder called a *library*. Libraries are very similar to folders on your computer, but come with some extra bells and whistles so that it's easier to search through data and organise stuff. (Windows comes with four Libraries: Documents, Music, Pictures and Videos.) When you install MYOB on your computer, you automatically create a new library called — you guessed it — MYOB.

   If you install the Server Edition of MYOB, you can also choose to store your file on a different computer, such as the office server or on another networked computer in your office. To do this, click Change Location, click Network Libraries, and click Add a Network Library.

Your last option is not to store your company file locally at all, but instead to store your file online. I talk lots about working online in Chapter 16, but at this point, even if you plan to work in the cloud, I suggest you start with a local copy. After you've set up your company file, you can make a decision about whether you want to work locally, online, or a combination of the two.

9. **Click Create Company File.**

   This process may take a minute or so.

10. **Click Easy Setup Assistant.**

    Ah, now the fun really begins. Read on to find out more.

Introducing the Easy Setup Assistant

So, you've created your company file. Now you need to customise it to fit your particular business. The Easy Setup Assistant makes this process as straightforward as possible, as follows:

✔ If you just created your first company file, clicking the Setup Assistant button that appears at the end of the introduction automatically takes you to the Easy Setup Assistant.

✔ Did it last week? Open up your company file and select Easy Setup Assistant from the Setup menu.

Getting MYOB to work the way you do

Your first stop on the Easy Setup Assistant menu is the Customise button. This little baby lets you call the shots; you set your preferences so that MYOB works the way you want it to.

As far as most settings are concerned, I suggest you pretty much accept all that's on offer. However, I list here a couple of the preferences which you may want to change:

✔ **Record selection:** If you're no good at remembering numbers and account codes, tick the option Select and Display Account Name, Not Account Number. This means instead of entering account numbers when recording income and expenses, you can just type the account name.

✔ **Contact logs:** Don't tick any of the contact log boxes — unless you've already thought of a good reason to maintain contact logs on all financial transactions (and I can't think of one!). All they do is make your company file larger, which in turn may make it run slower. You can switch contact logs back on later if you come across some special situation where you need them.

Setting up your accounts

After you finish your journey through the Customise section of the Easy Setup Assistant, click the Accounts button. You arrive at the Accounts List you built when creating your company file (refer to 'Creating your company file', earlier in this chapter, for more details).

If you're in a hurry, you don't have to make any changes to your Accounts List right now. However, if you have the time, you're best to start by customising your Accounts List properly, so that it has all the accounts you need for your business. Go to Chapter 2 to find out how to add new accounts, change accounts or delete accounts, and head for Chapter 3 to find out how to add account opening balances.

I find the Accounts List in the Easy Setup Assistant rather squishy and difficult to work with. It's much clearer if you go to the Command Centres menu at the top and choose Accounts followed by Accounts List.

Preparing for sales

The next part of the Easy Setup Assistant is the Sales button. Here, MYOB prompts you to select default sales layouts, default tax codes, payment information and so on, as shown in Figure 1-2. Remember that you only need to set up customers and sales in the Easy Setup Assistant if you plan to use MYOB to create invoices for your customers.

Again, I don't need to bore you by explaining every little itsy bit, but instead clarify the stuff most likely to cause you strife, as follows:

✔ **Layout.** If you're not sure what layout to select, I suggest you click the Item layout. This layout works well not just for items, but for services too. (For more on this topic, see Chapter 4.)

Figure 1-2:
The Sales
section of
the Easy
Setup
Assistant.

✔ **Selling Details.** Select the Income Account that you plan to use for most of your sales. Don't worry if this income account won't apply to all customers; simply choose the account you know you'll use most frequently.

✔ **Tax Codes.** Choose the Tax Code you use most often for sales (this code is usually GST, unless you're in the business of selling GST-free food, childcare or medical services). However, if you're not registered for GST (maybe you're turning over less than $75,000 a year), select N-T (standing for No Tax) as your Tax Code.

✔ **Linked Accounts.** The Account for Customer Receipts should be your regular business bank account and the Account for Undeposited Funds should be a special account called Undeposited Funds. (For more about Undeposited Funds accounts, see Chapter 7.)

✔ **Customer Cards.** Before entering sales, you need to build your customer list. If you're in a hurry, it's okay to enter customer names only — you can return later to fix up the address and phone details. If you're in a *real* hurry, you can get away with only entering names for those customers who owe you money at the moment, and add the remaining names and details later when you have more time.

If you already have your customer list stored in another program, such as Microsoft Excel or Access, you can import this information directly into your company file, without having to retype a single thing. Click the Import button and follow the prompts to bring this information across.

✔ **Historical Sales.** For more information about entering historical sales and customer opening balances, make your way to Chapter 3.

Conduct your own experiment

Every time you start MYOB, can you see the hyperlink right at the bottom (in very small letters, admittedly) called Explore a Sample Company? Click here for a list of four sample companies: Clearwater Basics, Clearwater Plus, Clearwater Premier and Clearwater Standard. Select the Clearwater file that corresponds to the version that you're using, and click Open. (If you have had multiple versions of MYOB installed, you may need to click the Samples folder, followed by the AU folder, followed by the version number folder, in order to view the list of sample files.)

Accept the User ID of Administrator (this ID comes up automatically), leave the password blank, and click OK. You can now go ahead and explore this sample file, adding or deleting transactions, experimenting with reports.

Talking about suppliers

The fourth part of the Easy Setup Assistant is the Purchases button. You only need to complete this section if you plan to use MYOB to create purchase orders or record supplier invoices (see Chapter 8 for my words of wisdom regarding this decision). This part of the Easy Setup Assistant has eight steps, but here I only talk about the bits that could trip you up, as follows:

- **Buying Details.** Click the Buying Details button to select the Expense Account that applies to most of your purchases. Don't worry if this expense account won't apply to all suppliers; simply choose the account that you think you'll use most often.

- **Tax Codes.** When it comes to Tax Codes, choose the Tax Code that you use most often for purchases (this code is usually GST, unless you're in the business of buying GST-free food, goods from overseas or medical equipment). However, if you're not registered for GST (maybe you're turning over less than $75,000 a year), select N-T (standing for No Tax) as your Tax Code.

- **Linked Accounts.** The Account for Paying Bills should default to your general business bank account.

- **Supplier Cards.** If you're pressed for time, you can get away with entering names only for those suppliers who you owe money to, and add the remaining supplier details later on.

- **Opening Balances.** For more information about entering historical purchases and supplier opening balances, make your way to Chapter 3.

Bracing for payroll

If you're using a version of MYOB that includes payroll features, Payroll forms the last stage of your Easy Setup Assistant.

Payroll is the most complex part of any accounting software setup, especially if you have several employees with different rates of pay. Make your way over to Chapter 11, where I cover setting up payroll in detail.

Getting to Know Each Other

Before leaping into the deep end and entering transactions, how about a whistlestop tour? It helps to know what MYOB calls things (after all, do ordinary mortals instinctively understand the difference between a command centre and a menu bar?) and to get a feeling for what sits where.

Discovering the lingo

When you first open up your company file, you arrive at a window similar to Figure 1-3. See the icons along the top (Accounts, Banking, Sales, Time Billing and so on)? Each one of these icons takes you to a different *command centre*, with a neat little flowchart displaying the major tasks associated with that centre. For example, when you click the Sales icon, you arrive at the *Sales command centre*, and the flowchart displays a bunch of sales-related tasks, such as the Sales Register and the Enter Sales command.

Next is the *menu bar*, which is the technical name for the list of commands that runs along the top. Not a regular three-course meal; rather, the same kind of menu you find in any software program (File, Edit, Lists and so on). Click each command and read the options that appear below.

At the bottom of each command centre is a set of four *quick analysis menus* or shortcuts to key tools: The To Do List, the Find Transactions menu, the Reports menu and the Business Insights menu:

- ✔ **To Do List:** The To Do List displays tasks that need your attention, such as overdue accounts, outstanding sales orders, or stock that needs re-ordering. (All sounds good in theory but, in practice, I find most people don't use their To Do List much.)

- ✔ **Find Transactions:** This menu is an essential part of your accounting-software-survival kit. Here's where you go to view transaction details on any account, customer, supplier or employee.

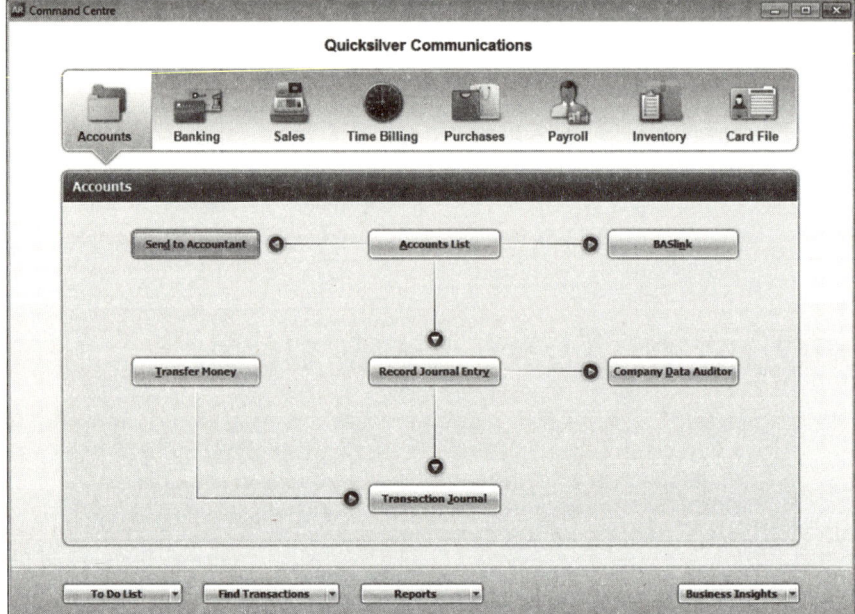

Figure 1-3:
The MYOB
command
centres are
your central
reference
point.

✔ **Reports:** The Reports menu offers a report for every occasion. Explore what's available — you'll be pleasantly surprised. (Chapters 14 and 17 look at reports in more detail.)

✔ **Business Insights:** The Business Insights menu is your trusty in-house management adviser, highlighting key aspects of your business, such as profitability reports, sales analysis, and a list of who owes you money (and how much).

Understanding what goes where

MYOB stores most information about your company in three different ways: Lists, registers and forms.

A *list* in MYOB software stores key data relevant to your business. Each list is essentially a database or folder in a filing system. You can access these lists by selecting Lists from the top menu bar. The list options are as follows:

✔ **Cards List:** Stores info about customers, suppliers and employees. You usually need to set up card information before you record transactions. For example, in order to record a sale for a customer, you first need to set up the customer's details in your Cards List. Chapter 2 explains how to add, edit and delete cards.

✔ **Accounts List:** A list of asset, liability, income and expense accounts relevant to your business. Chapter 2 explains how to add, edit and delete accounts.

✔ **Items List:** A list of items that you buy, inventory or sell. You can use this list to store details for services that you sell, not just physical items. Chapter 10 explores your Items List in detail.

All transactions are stored in *registers*, which list relevant transactions in date order. The register options are as follows:

✔ **Sales Register:** Lists sales, quotes, orders and unpaid invoices.

✔ **Bank Register:** Lists bank deposits, transfers and withdrawals.

✔ **Purchases Register:** Lists purchases, orders and unpaid bills.

✔ **Items Register:** Displays all sales, purchases and inventory movements for any selected item.

Forms enable you to customise what prints out of MYOB, including sales invoices, purchase orders, remittance advices or mailing labels. (I find it makes more sense to think of the word 'templates' rather than 'forms'.) Chapter 12 explains everything you need to know about forms.

Setting priorities

Earlier in this chapter, in 'Understanding what's involved', I provide a summary of the steps you need to take when getting started. This summary provides a good overview of all the steps that are involved but, in real life, time pressures may mean that you can't work through everything step by step.

If I'm setting up MYOB for a client and time is in short supply, I tend to prioritise certain activities over others, as follows:

1. **I usually start by setting up customers, figuring out how to record customer sales, and customising customer invoices. (See Chapters 2, 4 and 12.) I also start recording customer payments so I know who owes me money. (Chapter 7.)**

2. **I like to get bank feeds set up as soon as possible, and start record all transactions going out of business bank accounts. (See Chapters 5 and 6.)**

3. **If a business has employees, I set up payroll and start recording employee pays. (See Chapter 11.)**

4. **After two or three weeks has passed, I do the first bank reconciliations, and check everything has been recorded correctly. (Chapter 9.)**

If you're coming into a business as a new bookkeeper and MYOB is already up and running, your priorities are going to be slightly different. In this situation, I suggest that you focus on ensuring day-to-day transactions are up to date, that bank reconciliations are complete and accurate (see Chapter 9), and that payroll has been set up correctly (see Chapter 11).

Once you're sure the basics are in place, you can check that GST reports are working properly (see Chapter 15) and that the financial reports make sense (Chapter 17). You can then give the company file a thorough health check from head to toe (Chapter 18).

Opening Up, Closing Down

The most straightforward activities sometimes seem confusing when everything is new. Read on to find out how to close your company file when you've had enough, and to open it up again when you're ready for more.

Getting back in

A new day has dawned and you want to reopen your company file? Here's what to do:

1. **Open up MYOB.**

   When you install MYOB on your computer, a lurid purple icon complete with the letters AR appears on your computer's desktop. Double-click this icon to fire up your MYOB application.

   You arrive at a list of recently opened files.

2. **Click the name of your company file to open this file.**

   If you can't see your company file listed here, the problem may be that you're trying to access your company file from a different computer or from a backup. Chapter 16 provides lots more detail about opening and locating company files in these kinds of tricky situations.

3. **Enter your User ID and password.**

   If you haven't yet set up user roles and passwords (see 'Setting Up User Roles', later in this chapter, to find out more), enter Administrator as your User ID and leave the password blank. Click OK and you're in.

Back-to-front dates

Back-to-front dates can be very confusing: You type in a date and it's rejected. You try and try again, and then suddenly it dawns on you that your dates are back to front. That is, when you type 1/7/15, MYOB thinks you're talking about the seventh day of the first month, 2015 — not the first day of the seventh month, 2015. In fact, the problem isn't anything to do with MYOB; rather in the settings of your computer's Control Panel.

To remedy this situation, go to the Clock, Language and Region settings within your Control Panel. Under the Date, Time & Number Formats, select English (Australia) as the Format.

If I'm working on a PC, I can't be bothered minimising other programs just to get to my desktop, so I prefer to add MYOB to my taskbar. (Your taskbar is the list of programs that appears when you click your Windows Start button.) Want to give this a go? Click your Start button, open your Programs folder followed by your MYOB folder, and then rest your mouse on the MYOB application itself. Right-click with your mouse, and select the Pin to Taskbar button.

Activating your file

The first time you open up your new company file, a message appears asking you to activate it. Don't panic, you have 30 days in which to do the deed.

You can choose to activate your software online or by phone. Either method works fine; take your pick. This being the first time, you'll also have to register your software in the same hit. You're asked a few questions — your business name, contact details, industry type and so on — and, as a reward, you receive a confirmation number. Type this number when prompted and you're away.

If you don't activate your software within the timeframe, your company file changes to read-only status on the 31st day, at which point you can still view your transactions, but you won't be able to change transactions or add more.

Packing up and going home

You're tired and want to go home — it's time to quit. To close MYOB, simply head for the File on the top menu bar and select Exit.

Depending on your preference settings, you may also see a message asking if you want to back up. In almost all situations, the right thing to do is click Yes, and back up onto an external drive, such as a CD, external hard disk or flash drive. Chapter 16 has lots more information on backing up and how often you need to do it.

Setting Up User Roles

If you're the only person who is ever going to work in your company file (maybe you're a sole trader with no employees and you do your own bookkeeping), you don't need to add any more user names. Simply type 'Administrator' as the User ID every time you open your company file, and leave the password blank.

However, if you want to have other people work in your company file, I strongly recommend you set up a different user name for each person. This way, you can keep track of who entered what (very useful when a mistake gets made and nobody wants to own up).

Creating an Administrator password

Before setting up different users, each with their own password, you're best to create a password for the Administrator User ID. (If you don't, people can just log in as the Administrator, which misses the whole point of setting up users.)

Here's what to do:

1. **Open your company file, typing Administrator as the User ID.**

2. **Leave the Password field blank and click Change Password.**

3. **Enter your password in the New Password field and again in the Confirm Password field. Leave the Existing Password field blank.**

   Try to avoid using the names of your pets or children, it's sooo obvious.

4. **Click Record.**

   Your company file should open.

5. Remember this password!

Next time you open up your company file, you'll need this password. So guess what? Don't forget it! By the way, if you're going to manage security effectively, only the business owner or manager should know the password that's associated with the Administrator ID.

Adding new users and assigning roles

Every time you create a new user, MYOB asks you to assign a role, or roles, to that user. A role specifies what things this person is allowed to do. For example, if you assign the Sales role to a new user, this person will only be able to access the features in Sales and Time Billing. They won't be able to access other functions such as financial reports or payroll.

Here's how to add a new user and assign roles:

1. **Ensure that you are logged on either with Administrator as the User ID or with a User ID that has an Administrator role.**

   The User ID of 'Administrator' is automatically assigned the Administrator role. However, you can create other users with different names and assign them the Administrator role also.

2. **Select User Access from the Setup menu and click New User in the top-left corner.**

3. **Enter a User ID and Password for this person.**

   For User IDs, I usually just use the person's first name. I usually use the first name as the password too at this point, and then tell this person to change their password to something that they can remember (and which is secure) when they first log on.

4. **Click the Manage Roles tab and think about how these roles could apply to your business.**

   I found this window confusing at first, but here's how it works: The first column lists the different roles, the second column lists the names of each command centre with a tick against whatever command centres the selected role can access, the third column lists each function within the command centre, and the fourth column shows whether the person assigned this role can view data only, or whether they can record transactions also. (Figure 1-4 shows these four columns in action.)

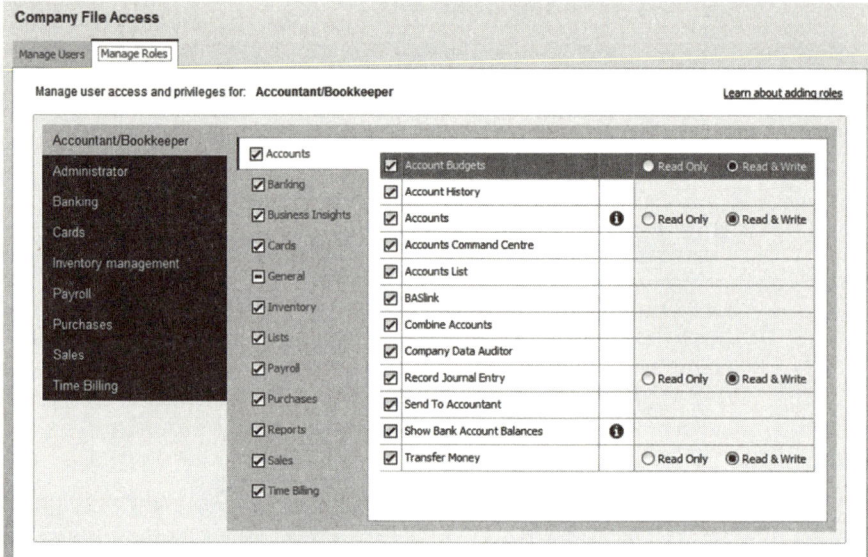

Figure 1-4:
For each user, you can choose one or more out of nine different roles.

5. **Return to the Manage Users tab and click against the role or roles you want to assign to this user.**

   For example, if I'm setting up a role for someone in the warehouse who is responsible for placing purchase orders and managing stock, I'd click both the Inventory Management role and the Purchases role.

6. **Click Save to save your changes.**

   Note that what you've done so far is add a new user. If you plan to store your company file in the cloud, you also need to invite this user to work online. Read on to find out more.

Inviting users to work online

If you store your company file in the cloud, you not only need to set up users in your company file (as I describe in the previous section), but you also need to set up each user for online access. Here's how:

1. **Follow the steps explained in the previous section to add new users, but instead of clicking Save when complete, click the Online Access button.**

Your internet browser opens, with a prompt to log in to the my.myob website. This website is where you go to view your account details, subscription details and so on.

2. **Enter your email address and password.**

At this point, you need the email address and password you used when first registering with MYOB.

Rather confusingly, the User ID and password you use to open your company file are almost certainly different from the email address and password you use to log into the my.myob website. If you're not sure what the correct details are, I suggest you wing it by entering your email address and clicking the Forgot Your Password link.

3. **Click Sign In.**

The Manage Online Access window appears, listing all the current users who you've already added for this company file.

4. **Choose between Invite New Online User and Invite New Online Administrator.**

In the kind of mind-numbing complexity that only IT folk could dream up, inviting someone to be an Online Administrator is completely different to giving someone the Administrator role within your company file. Online files have two levels of security. The first login is for online access and online functions, and the second login is for the processes within the data file.

In practical terms, the big deal about giving someone the Administrator role within your company file is that this role has access to everything, including payroll and financial reports. In contrast, when you assign someone the role of Online Administrator, this has nothing to do with what bookkeeping tasks or reports someone can access, but instead is about being able to shift files in and out of the cloud, and update bank feeds.

You may well find that you invite someone to be an Online Administrator so that this person can update bank feeds (often an essential part of day-to-day bookkeeping) but that you don't give this person an Administrator role within your company file (because you want to restrict access to other things such as payroll or financial reports).

5. **Enter the email address for this user, along with their first and last name, and click Invite.**

The Manage Online Access screen appears and then MYOB sends an invitation email to the lucky person.

What to do if you forget your password

In the same way as the sun will rise in the morning and set in the evening, sooner or later you — or someone else — will forget the password.

Unless the person who has forgotten their password is the only person with an Administrator role, the easy solution is to get someone who does have that role to log on and reset that person's password. (Go to Setup and select User Access.)

However, the blues come calling if the person who has forgotten their password is the only one with an Administrator role. In this scenario, more drastic action is required.

Start by trying every password you can think of — unlike banking passwords, MYOB doesn't lock you out if you guess wrong a few times. Try every password that you've ever used, including the names of your kids, pets or obscure lost lovers. It's amazing what people can retrieve from the dark and dusty shadows of their brain.

If guesswork fails, you may need to send your company file to MYOB to have your password reset. Phone 1300 555 123 to ask about this service. (At the time of writing, if you have a support plan the cost is $55.)

An alternative is to jump online and visit www.password-service.com, a slightly naughty kind of website that sells utilities for recovering lost passwords. The price for the full version, which cracks into all passwords in the blink of an eye, is US$29.95. You can also download a free trial version that cracks the first character only of the Administrator password, which is often all you need to trigger your memory.

By the way, if you've never created a password in your MYOB company file, and you've found your way to this part of the book because you're desperately trying to open up your file, try logging in with the user ID 'Administrator' (and leave the password blank).

Chapter 2

Accounts, Customers and Suppliers

- -

In This Chapter

▶ Understanding life's mysteries: Birth, death and your MYOB accounts

▶ Keeping your Accounts List trim, taut and terrific

▶ Adding customers and customer details

▶ Setting up suppliers

▶ Taming lists so they do what you want them to do

▶ Tracking down transactions on accounts, customers and suppliers

- -

*L*ife is full of lists. Lists of things you need to do before you die, lists of lingering regrets, lists of things you suspect you did while under the influence (surprisingly similar to that list of regrets) and lots of other lists besides.

This chapter is all about lists. First, I talk about your Accounts List — the list of assets, liabilities, income and expense accounts that reflects the inner workings of your business. Then I talk about your customer and supplier lists, explaining how to set up new customers and suppliers.

Designing Your Accounts List

The first thing I do when setting up MYOB for a new client is sit down with them and chat about how they'd like to organise their Accounts List. That's because the Accounts List affects everything else that happens, including how you record income and expenses, and the format of your Profit & Loss reports.

Put simply, your Accounts List is a list of categories describing what your business owns and owes, where money comes from and where money goes.

To see what I mean, go to the Accounts command centre and click the Accounts List button. A list of accounts appears, similar to the one shown in Figure 2-1. Although you could probably make do with this list just as it is, I suggest you take the time to tailor the Accounts List specifically for your business.

Start by looking at every account in your Accounts List and thinking about what it's doing there. If you don't need an account, you can get rid of it. If you need an extra account, add it in. You can even rename accounts if you want to. (I explain how to do all these things later in this chapter.)

If you've been in business for more than a year or so, an easy way to tailor your Accounts List is to dig out the most recent reports from your accountant and compare your accountant's list of accounts with those in MYOB. If you need to add more accounts in MYOB to make the two match, do so.

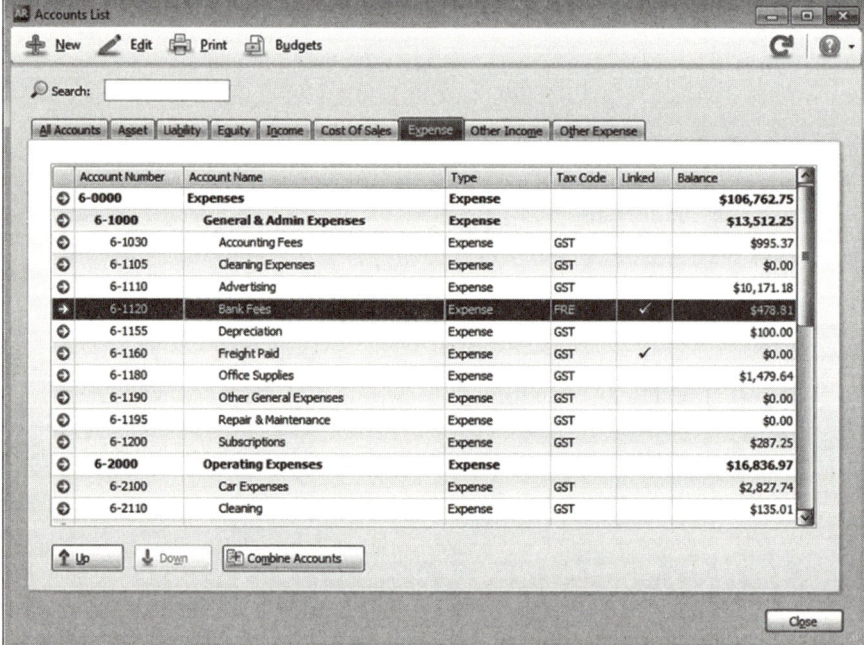

Figure 2-1:
The Accounts List describes every asset, liability, income and expense in your business.

Looking at account classifications

Whenever you do anything to your Accounts List — be it adding, deleting or changing an account — you have to decide which kind of account you're dealing with. I explain each account classification in Table 2-1.

By the way, asset, liability and equity accounts are the accounts that appear on your Balance Sheet; income, cost of sales and expense accounts show up on your Profit & Loss report.

Table 2-1	Account Classifications Used in the Accounts List
Account Classification	*When to Use It*
Assets	Assets are the good stuff — anything you own, such as money in bank accounts, computers, office equipment, motor vehicles and cash. **Asset account numbers start with 1**.
Liabilities	Liabilities are what keep you awake at night — that's everything you owe to other people. Liabilities include credit card debts, loans, GST, other taxes owing and outstanding supplier accounts. **Liability account numbers start with 2**.
Equity	Equity is a fancy term for the owner's stake in the business, made up of money invested initially, and accumulated profit/loss built up over time. Equity accounts include owner drawings, capital contributions, retained earnings and share capital. **Equity account numbers start with 3**.
Income	Income is all the money you earn and includes everything you invoice or sell to your customers. **Income account numbers start with 4**.
Cost of Sales	Cost of Sales is the direct cost of selling goods or providing your service. This account classification includes purchases, raw materials, freight, commissions, production labour and subcontract labour. **Cost of Sales account numbers start with 5**.
Expenses	Expenses are the day-to-day running costs of your business and include advertising, bank charges, rent, telephone and wages. **Expense account numbers start with 6**.
Other Income	Other Income is probably better described as non-trading income. It includes income that's not really part of your everyday business, such as interest income, one-off capital gains or gifts from mysterious benefactors (if only). **Other Income account numbers start with 8**.
Other Expenses	Again, think of Other Expenses as abnormal expenses that are not part of your everyday business, such as lawsuit expenses, capital losses or entertaining aliens from outer space. **Other Expense account numbers start with 9**.

Other terms sometimes used to describe Cost of Sales accounts include *variable expenses*, *direct costs* or *cost of goods sold*; other terms for Expense accounts include *fixed expenses*, *indirect costs* or *overheads*. Different words, same concepts.

Cost of sales or an expense?

No matter what type of business you run, you probably have some outgoings that directly relate to sales. In your Accounts List, any outgoings that relate directly to sales should have Cost of Sales as the account classification. The idea is that when sales go up, cost of sales goes up, and when sales go down, cost of sales goes down.

Think about your business and figure out which expenses are truly cost of sales accounts. For example, if you're a manufacturer, your cost of sales accounts probably include things like raw materials, electricity, production labour and factory rental. If you're a tradesperson, your cost of sales accounts

will include materials and subcontract labour. If you're a retailer, your cost of sales accounts are the goods that you buy to sell again, usually called Purchases. On the other hand, if you're a consultant, you probably don't have any cost of sales accounts, because you're not actually producing or selling anything except your time.

Expenses that aren't cost of sales accounts include things like accounting fees, bank fees, computer gear, depreciation, electricity, interest, motor vehicles, rent, stationery and telephone. These business expenses don't change much from month to month, regardless of whether your sales go up or down.

Understanding account types

If you create a new account that's either an asset or a liability, you're prompted to select an Account Type. For those anxious to get everything picture perfect, read on to find out what type to choose.

When creating an asset account:

- ✔ Choose Bank as the Account Type if you're creating a new bank account (such as a cheque account, savings account or term deposit). Obvious really.

- ✔ Choose Accounts Receivable as the Account Type if you plan to use this account for tracking how much money customers owe you.

- ✔ Choose Other Current Asset as the Account Type for anything that isn't a bank account, but is a short-term asset. Examples include Prepaid Insurance, Employee Advances or Inventory.

- ✔ Choose Fixed Asset as the Account Type for anything material that you can touch, feel and see. Sounds kind of sensual but I'm talking about relatively mundane things such as Plant & Equipment, Land & Buildings and Fixtures & Fittings.

✔ Choose Other Asset as the Account Type for those odd things that accountants like to describe as 'intangibles'. Examples include Goodwill and Formation Expenses.

When creating a liability account:

✔ Choose Credit Card as the Account Type not only for your credit cards, but also for any bank accounts that are always in the red, such as bank overdrafts or line of equity accounts.

✔ Choose Accounts Payable as the Account Type if you plan to use this account to track how much money you owe suppliers.

✔ Choose Other Current Liability as the Account Type for any money you owe that's relatively short term. Examples include Loans from Directors, Customer Deposits, PAYG Payable, GST accounts and Superannuation Payable.

✔ Choose Long Term Liability as the Account Type for Hire Purchase accounts, Bank Loans and long-term Loans from Directors.

✔ The last Account Type is described as Other Liability. Do send me an email if you figure out when you would use this Account Type — I'm blowed if I can find a good use for it — so I can illuminate all readers in the next edition.

Adding your first new account

So you want to create a new account? Here's how:

1. **Go to the Accounts command centre and click Accounts List.**

2. **Decide the classification of account you're creating, and then click the appropriate tab.**

   Here's where you decide whether the account you want to create is an asset or a liability account, an income or an expense account, a Desiree potato or a rotting pumpkin. When you've made up your mind, click the correct tab.

   (Refer to Table 2-1 if you're not sure.)

3. **Decide how to number your new account.**

   Decide where you'd like this new account to appear in the list, and pick a number so that this account falls in the right spot. (MYOB sorts accounts in numeric order, not alphabetical order.) So, if your

Advertising Expense account is numbered 6-1000 and your Cleaning Expense account is numbered 6-3000, and you want to insert a new Bank Charge Expense account between these two, then choose a number between 6-1000 and 6-3000 — say, 6-2000.

Now, jot down the number on a scrap of paper.

4. **Click New (you find this button in the top-left corner).**

5. **Choose whether the new account is a Header Account or a Detail Account.**

   If this new account is to be a heading that appears in bold with other accounts listed below it, select Header Account. If you want it to be an account that you add transactions to, select Detail Account.

   (For more about header and detail accounts, see 'Grouping apples with apples', later in this chapter.)

6. **Pick an Account Type (for asset and liability accounts only).**

   If this new account is an asset or liability, you need to pick the appropriate Account Type, such as Bank, Fixed Asset, Credit Card or Accounts Payable. If you're not sure which Account Type to select, refer to the preceding section. In particular, make sure you select Bank as the Account Type for cheque, savings or investment accounts, and Credit Card as the Account Type for credit cards or overdrafts.

7. **Type in the Account Number and Account Name.**

   Now you can type in the account number you decided on at Step 3. Then, press the Tab or Enter key and type in the name of your new account. Your new account should now look similar to Figure 2-2.

8. **Click the Details tab then choose a Tax Code for the new account.**

   When you reach the Details tab, select the most appropriate default Tax Code. Most income and expense accounts should have GST as the Tax Code (unless you sell GST-free supplies), although some expenses, such as bank charges and donations, should have FRE as the Tax Code. Asset, liability and equity accounts almost always have N-T as the Tax Code, although fixed assets usually have CAP as the Tax Code. See Chapter 15 for more about GST, or talk to your accountant if you're not sure.

9. **Click OK and you're done.**

   Fantastic! You just created your first new account.

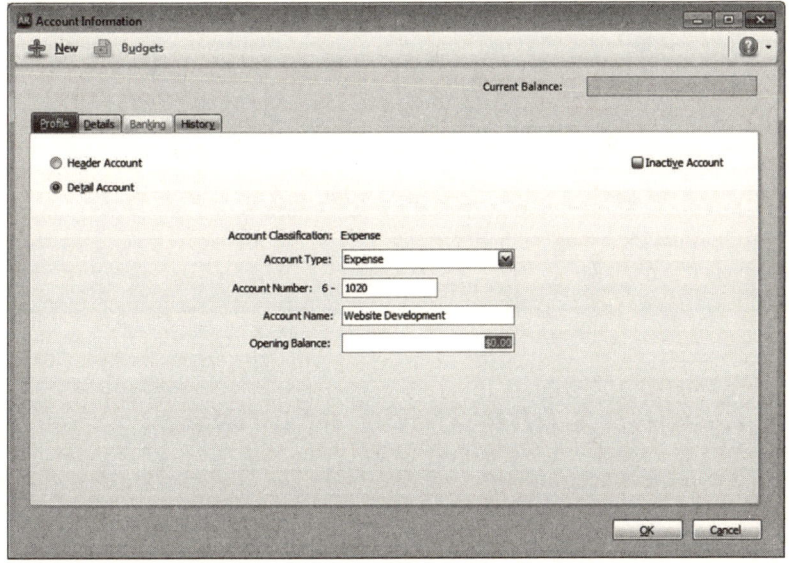

Figure 2-2:
Creating a new account.

Thinking about that pot of gold

As part of tidying up your Accounts List, it's a good idea to tweak your list of income accounts. If you have fewer than five income accounts, have a think about how you could describe your income in more detail. Each major source of income needs a separate income account.

Maybe you're a builder who earns money from new houses, as well as renovations and extensions. Maybe you're like me and earn money from a combination of journalism, consulting and teaching. No matter how you earn a crust, try to split your income into at least five different categories. That way, you can generate regular Profit & Loss reports that reflect how your business generates revenue.

Alternatively, maybe your business doesn't just have different sources of income but is actually several businesses bundled under the one name — like the newsagent that doubles as a post office, or a chain of hairdressing salons at several different locations. In other words, you not only have different sources of income, but also have specific costs which relate to each of these sources. If so, don't be tempted to create separate expense accounts for each source of income. Instead, use a single set of expense accounts, but set up either job or category tracking to look after your cost centre reporting. For details on how to do this, see Chapter 17.

Do words mean more to you?

If you're not a numbers person, you may prefer to refer to account names, rather than account numbers, when you record transactions. For example, instead of typing 6–2189 as the account code when recording a telephone bill, you type Telephone Expense.

To experiment with this preference and see what suits you best, go to Setup⇨Preferences and click the Windows tab. Tick the option to Select and Display Account Name, Not Account Number.

Deleting unwanted accounts

If you have accounts in your Accounts List that you know you'll never use, waste no time in getting rid of them. (I assume here that you're deleting an account you haven't used yet, and which has no transaction history. To hide or get rid of an account that has transactions in it, see 'Making accounts, customers or suppliers inactive' and 'Merging two into one (ah, young love)', later in this chapter.)

Here's how to delete an unused account:

1. **Go to your Accounts List and double-click that unwanted beastie.**

2. **Go up to Edit (on the top menu bar) and select Delete Account.**

   Poof! It's gone. Alternatively, if you get a message saying that you can't delete this account because it's a linked account, read on.

3. **Click the Details tab for the account you want to delete.**

4. **Click the arrow next to the words Linked Account.**

   When you click on the arrow, a list of linked accounts appears, including the one you're trying to delete.

5. **Remove the tick against the account you want to delete.**

   For example, if you're trying to delete your Freight Income account, remove the tick from the option that lists its account number and is labelled 'I charge freight on sales'.

WARNING!

Although it's okay to delete or change most linked accounts for things like freight, late fees and discounts, don't be tempted to change the linked accounts for the Asset Account for Tracking Receivables, or the Liability Account for Tracking Payables.

6. **Click OK**.

   You're returned to the Edit Accounts window. You can now go ahead and delete the account.

7. **On the top menu bar, choose Edit⇨Delete Account.**

Keeping Your Accounts List Looking Good

After you've done the initial Accounts List clean-up — deleting unwanted accounts and creating new ones as you see fit — it's time to submit your Accounts List to a little cosmetic surgery. Read on to find out more.

Putting things in order

I'm a bit of a pedant about making sure my income and expense accounts are listed in alphabetical order in my Accounts List (within each sub-heading, that is), because the format of my Accounts List flows directly through to my financial reports.

However, MYOB sorts accounts in numeric order, not alphabetical order. This means that if you're not careful with numbering when you're creating new accounts, your Accounts List can soon get out of alphabetical order. To reorganise your accounts, you simply need to change some of your account numbers.

For example, earlier in this chapter in Figure 2-1, Cleaning Expenses (account 6-1105) is out of alphabetical order: It appears before Advertising (account 6-1110) and Bank Fees (6-1120) in the Accounts List. To make this account appear in the correct position, I change its number; for example, changing the number of Cleaning Expenses from 6-1105 to 6-1130.

Now it's your turn:

1. **Go to your Accounts command centre, click on Accounts List, and then double-click on the account that's out of order.**

2. **Edit the account's number.**

3. **Click OK.**

Grouping apples with apples

If you have many accounts that belong together, you can further categorise them into groups in your Accounts List using header and detail accounts. For example, you can create a group for your wages accounts, motor vehicle expense accounts or different kinds of marketing expense accounts.

Header accounts are the headings (surprisingly enough) and appear in bold in the list. Detail accounts are the accounts that belong under each header. For example, if you create a header account and name it Motor Vehicle Expenses, you can then add lots of detail accounts to sub-categorise your motor vehicle expenses, such as Fuel, Rego, Insurance and Repairs.

You can create groups of accounts within other groups if you're really enthusiastic. For example, you could create a header account called Payroll Expenses, along with several detail accounts, and within this header you could add another header called Wages & Salaries, with detail accounts relating to different kinds of wages below that (see Figure 2-3).

	6-3000	Payroll Expenses	Expense	
	6-3050	**Wages & Salaries**	**Expense**	
	6-3100	Wages Management	Expense	N-T
	6-3105	Wages Front Desk Staff	Expense	N-T
	6-3110	Wages Finance Staff	Expense	N-T
	6-3120	Superannuation	Expense	N-T

Figure 2-3: Creating headers to group accounts.

Here are some things you can do after you've set up header and detail accounts:

✔ You can choose at any time between displaying a highly detailed report (for example, a Profit & Loss report that itemises every expense) and a less detailed report that just shows the subtotals of each group.

✔ You can view a Profit & Loss report showing different levels of detail. Display your Profit & Loss report (found under the Accounts tab of your Reports menu) and select your Report Level from the report filters — 1, 2, 3 or 4. Level 1 shows the least detail; Level 4 shows the most.

✔ You can tell when detail accounts belong to header accounts because they're indented and sit in a bunch below the header account. However, sometimes things get muddled and detail accounts appear immediately below their header account without any indentation. This is easy to fix: Highlight the detail account and click the Down button until it sits in the right spot.

Setting Up New Customers

To view your customers, head up to Lists (tucked away on the top menu bar) and select Cards. (If you're working on a new company file, you may find you arrive at a completely blank list.) Alternatively, go to the Card File command centre, and click the Cards List button. MYOB refers to your customer records as *cards*, a rather quaint term harking back to when people used to store handwritten records in little cards on their desk.

Defining credit terms

Before you set up too many new customers, I recommend you first define your *default credit terms* — namely, the payment terms you offer to the majority of your customers. (Don't worry if some customers have different terms; you can override the defaults for individual customers later on.)

Here's how to set up your default credit terms:

1. **From the main menu, choose Setup⇨Preferences and then click the Sales tab.**
2. **Click the Terms button in the top-left corner.**

   This takes you to the Default Customer Terms window.
3. **From the Payment is Due drop-down box, choose when you want your customers to pay, using Table 2-2 as a guide.**

Table 2-2	Default Credit Terms
Payment Method	*Payment Terms*
C.O.D.	Cash, glorious cash. Payment must be made at the time of delivery.
Prepaid	All orders should be prepaid in advance (if you can get it, why not?).
In a Given No. of Days	The given number of days is the time between the invoice date and the payment due date. Use the Balance Due Days field to fill in the number of days.
On a Day of the Month	The due date is calculated by combining this day with the month on the invoice.
No. of Days after EOM	Payment is due a certain number of days after the end of the month (EOM).
Day of Month after EOM	The due date is a certain number of days following the end of the month. Use this option if the due date is always the last day of the following month.

4. Select the default Tax Codes.

If you charge GST on most or all of your sales, choose GST as both the default Tax Code and the Freight Tax Code.

If you sell a mix of taxable and non-taxable items, don't sweat. Simply select either GST or FRE — depending on which code applies most often in your business — for the Default Tax Code. Then select GST as the Freight Tax Code, assuming you're shipping most goods within Australia. Later, when you set up individual items in MYOB, you can specify individual tax codes for each one.

By the way, I don't recommend you check the box called Use Customer's Tax Code. Why not? Because if you do, MYOB then refers to the customer's tax code for every sale, rather than to the tax codes of the individual items that the customer is buying. Unless you predominantly sell to overseas customers, charging GST based on the customer's tax status is incorrect.

5. Enter a Credit Limit, if desired.

If you don't want to set a default credit limit for all customers, that's fine — simply leave this field blank. Later on, you can set individual limits by going to the Selling Details tab for each customer.

Importing lists from other software

I often meet new clients who already have a customer or supplier listing set up on their computer, before they start using MYOB. They don't want

Can MYOB be your customer database?

Yes. Because you can store so much information about your customers in your MYOB company file, you probably won't need a separate database to track customer details.

However, sometimes I come across a business that needs to maintain loads of very specific information about its customers. The business may be a club that wants to keep a record of golf scores for each member, a vet who wants to record every animal's vaccination history or an acupuncturist updating a client's treatment records. In these situations, you're probably best to maintain an independent database in addition to the cards in MYOB.

If you do decide to maintain a separate customer database, make sure you're not duplicating information by typing customer details first into a database and again into your MYOB company file. Lots of software companies can help you integrate your database with MYOB so that information flows automatically between applications. Visit the MYOB Add-Ons page at my website (www.veechicurtis.com.au) for details about different software providers.

to type in the information again, but don't know how to get the information into their MYOB company file.

The solution is to use MYOB's Import/Export Assistant feature to bring your customer data into your new company file automatically. Although, at first, importing data seems quite easy, you do need to be careful — after all, you don't want to import 1,000 customers and then discover each one has a fundamental error. So, for some tips and warnings about importing data, I suggest you first read my online article 'Importing Data into MYOB', available at www.dummies.com/extras/myobsoftwareau.

Entering contact details

When creating a new customer, the first step is to enter all contact details (you know, name, address and so on). Although you can get away with just whacking in a name and nothing else if you're in a hurry, I go the whole hog here and explain every step:

1. **From the main menu, choose Lists⇨Cards.**

   Alternatively, you can go to the Card File command centre and click the Cards List button.

2. **Select the card type and then click New.**

   Along the top are tabs labelled All Cards, Customer, Supplier, Employee and Personal. Click the Customer tab, and then click the New button in the top-left corner.

3. **Indicate whether the card is a Company or an Individual and fill in the name.**

   Click Individual if this card is for a person with a first name and a last name. Why? If you enter a name, such as Jemima Puddleduck, and select Company, her name always appears under J, not under P, and she'll be forever hard to find.

4. **If you want, fill in a Card ID.**

   MYOB sorts cards by referring to names, not numbers. However, if you prefer to allocate numbers to cards (to issue customer numbers or membership numbers), then use the Card ID field.

5. **Press the Enter or Tab key, then fill in the Address, City, State and Postcode.**

6. **Complete additional addresses, if necessary**.

   If a customer or supplier has an alternative location or shipping address that's different to the billing address, select Address 2 as the Location and record the details.

7. **Fill in phone numbers, fax, email and website details**.

   You have three fields for phone numbers, one for a fax, one for email and one for a website address. Fill in whatever info you have handy (you can always return and complete the rest of the details later).

8. **If you like, enter a Salutation and Contact**.

   A salutation is the name that MYOB uses as the addressee if you ever create a mail merge file. If you don't intend to use mail merge, ignore this field. But if you think you may use mail merge in the future, stick in your contact's first name as the Salutation and their full name as the Contact.

9. **Click OK to save these details**.

   Well done!

If you make a mistake when you create a new customer, or if someone's details change, it's easy enough to fix. From the Lists menu, choose Cards, and then highlight the card in question. Click Edit, change any details that you need to, and then click OK. You're done.

Adding other kinds of details

In the previous section, I explain how to record contact details under the Profile tab of each customer. Next, I suggest you check out the other tabs available for each customer card. Go to your Cards List, double-click any customer name, and you'll see seven tabs running along the top: Profile, Card Details, Selling Details, Payment Details, Contact Log, Jobs and History.

In particular, check out the Selling Details tab, as shown in Figure 2-4, where you can record additional info about invoice formats, price levels, credit limits and so on.

Don't worry if you're not sure what information to fill in — here's the low-down on what's hot (and what's not):

✔ **Select repeating invoice information.** If you intend to invoice a customer regularly, fill in the information that stays the same every time — such as the Sale Layout, the Shipping Method, Salesperson or Customer Billing Rate. If this information changes from invoice to invoice, simply leave these fields blank.

✔ **Review customer credit terms.** Credit details for customers default to whatever terms you set up in your Preferences (see 'Defining credit terms', earlier in this chapter). If a customer has different credit terms from your default, record the changes in the Customer Terms Information fields.

✔ **Get the Tax Codes right.** Usually you can ignore the Tax Code and Freight Tax Code fields, because when you're creating a sale, GST information comes either from your Accounts List or from your Items List. However, if a customer is an overseas customer and you don't charge GST, change the Tax Code fields to EXP and check the box Use Customer's Tax Code.

✔ **Don't worry too much about recording ABN info for customers.** The law doesn't require that you keep a record of your customer's ABN. The only time you require a customer's ABN is if you make a sale for $1,000 or more and you *don't* have the customer's full address details.

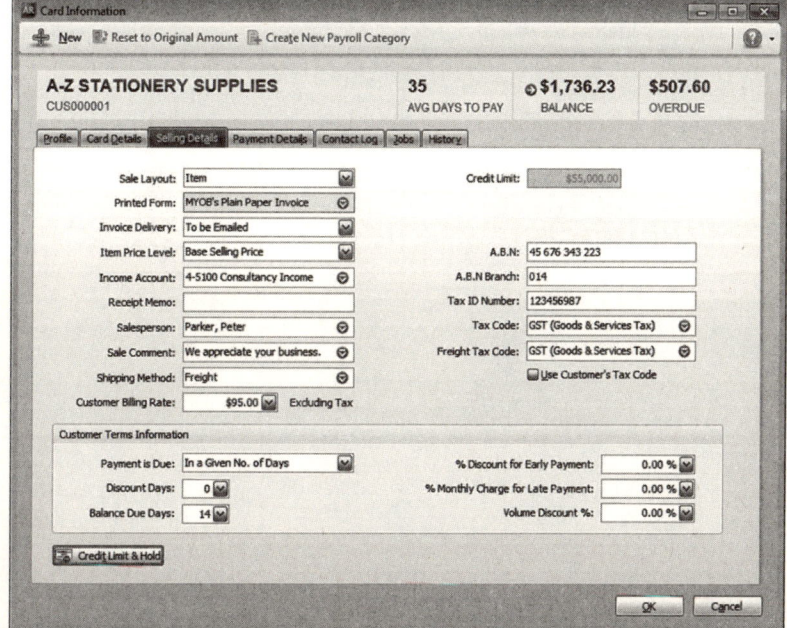

Figure 2-4:
The Selling Details tab allows you to detail the kind of sales you make to particular customers.

Dig Deeper with Customer Analysis

For some larger businesses, you may find it's a good idea to split your customers into *groups*. You can analyse customer demographics (for example, male versus female, age groups and socioeconomic backgrounds). Or you can group customers in ways that are specific to your business, such as a gym that groups its members according to the classes they attend.

To set up groups for your customers, follow these steps:

1. **Decide how to group your customers or clients.** Without knowing your business, I can't tell you how to do this. But to give you an idea, I group my clients according to the software they use, their location and what type of client they are.

2. **Set up labels for each customer group.** Head for the Lists menu and select Custom List & Field Names. Select Customers. Change the titles of Custom List #1, List #2 and List #3 so that they become the labels for each customer group. For example, the title for Custom List #1 may be Software Type and the title for Custom List #2 may be Location.

3. **Set up lists for each customer group.** From the main menu, choose Lists⇨Custom Lists⇨Customers. Now decide what you want to appear under each custom list. For example, under Client Type in my customer list, I have Books, Consulting, Freelance and Publishing.

4. **Allocate each customer to their group.** For each customer, click the Card Details tab. Select the group that applies. In the following figure, you can see an example of how this works.

You'll note that you can also store customer information in Custom Fields rather than Custom Lists. Custom Fields work best for information that is unique to each customer, such as birthdays, renewal dates, security codes or serial numbers.

A-Z STATIONERY SUPPLIES	35	$1,736.23	$507.60
CUS000001	AVG DAYS TO PAY	BALANCE	OVERDUE

Profile | Card Details | Selling Details | Payment Details | Contact Log | Jobs | History

Click on picture area to add the picture

Notes: Serial Number: 1600 723 4042

Identifiers.. | S

Software: | MYOB

Location: | Blue Mountains

Client Type: | Small Business

Birthday: | 5 June 1967

Support Details: | High Maintenance

Custom Field #3:

OK   Cancel

Adding New Suppliers

To add a new supplier, go to the Card File command centre, click the Cards List button followed by the Supplier tab, and then click New in the top-left corner. If you're in a hurry, you can get away with just adding the supplier name and nothing more. However, if you want to do a thorough job, you may want to add a few more details.

From your Cards List, double-click any supplier's card and click the Buying Details tab. Here's what you can do next:

- ✔ **Pick the Purchase Layout.** You only have to worry about this field if you print Purchase Orders — in which case, select your Purchase Order layout here.

- ✔ **Select the Expense Account.** Here you find the wonder tip for this chapter. If you take the time to complete the expense account that normally applies to the supplier (for example, choosing Rent Expense for your landlord), every time you record a transaction for this supplier, the account is selected automatically.

- ✔ **Check supplier credit terms.** The credit terms appear as whatever default terms you set up in Preferences under the Purchases tab. If a supplier offers different terms, change these now. (For more details about credit terms, refer to Table 2-2, earlier in this chapter.)

- ✔ **Select the tax code.** If a supplier's GST status differs from the norm (maybe the supplier has an ABN but isn't registered for GST), complete the Tax Code field and click the box Use Supplier's Tax Code.

- ✔ **Enter the supplier's ABN.** The Tax Office requires that you verify that the ABN on a supplier's invoice is both correct and current. This verification process used to be horribly time-consuming, but with the latest versions of MYOB, all you have to do is enter the ABN in the ABN field of the supplier's card (or hover your mouse over the ABN if an ABN has already been entered). So long as you're connected to the internet, MYOB automatically runs a check against the Australian Business Register website to validate ABN details, and instantaneously flags any incorrect or out-of-date ABNs in red.

Now, with the essentials of the supplier's Buying Details complete, you're ready to finalise the payment details. Go to the Payment Details tab of the supplier's card and complete the supplier's account details. This information is essential if you want to be able to record payments in MYOB and then create an electronic payments batch file that you can open up in your internet banking. (Chapter 13 talks more about this process.)

Looking After Your Lists

Housekeeping has to be one of life's most tedious activities. What's worse is that there's never any escaping it. Your MYOB company file is no different. After a few weeks pass, you'll find that a bit of housekeeping is already required in order to keep your lists in tip-top condition.

Here I explain how to locate customer or supplier details, delete unwanted list items, make list items inactive and combine two entries in one.

Viewing customer and supplier details

After you add a few customers and suppliers, go to your Cards List and check out your work. Make life easier by trying out the following tips:

✔ **Alter your view settings**. For example, you can sort each column simply by clicking the column label at the top. So, if you click the Name column label, cards are sorted alphabetically so that cards starting with the letter 'A' appear at the top. Click the Name label a second time and cards starting with the letter 'A' appear at the bottom. Or you can click the Current Balance column so that customers who owe you the most appear at the top.

✔ **Remove columns that you don't want.** Try right-clicking with your mouse on a column that you don't need to see (ensuring you click the label at the top of the column itself), then left-click Remove This Column. Similarly you can add new columns by right-clicking on any column header, selecting Column Chooser, and dragging any columns that are currently hidden back to your main list.

✔ **Experiment with searches.** Can you see the Search field in the top-left next to the magnifying glass icon? Try searching by name, phone number or postcode. For example, if all I can remember is that my customer lives in Blackheath, I can type '4787' into the search field of my Cards List (every Blackheath phone number starts with 4787) and in the blink of an eye, I get a list of all customers living in Blackheath.

✔ **View by postcode.** To view all customers by a particular postcode or range of postcodes, click the Advanced button and then enter the postcode or postcode range you're looking for.

Deleting customers or suppliers

Having customers or suppliers in your list that you don't use is like littering your lounge room with old socks. Time to get rid of the mess:

1. **Go to your Cards List and double-click the unwanted customer or supplier name.**

2. **Go up to Edit (on the top menu bar) and select Delete Card.**

   Done. Alternatively, if you get a message saying that the card can't be deleted, because journal entries or job history are attached, then read on . . .

Note: Deleting accounts is a similar process as outlined in the preceding steps (except you select Delete Account rather than Delete Card). However, you often hit the problem of not being able to delete an account because it's linked. Refer to 'Deleting unwanted accounts', earlier in this chapter, for more details.

Making accounts, customers or suppliers inactive

What a drag. You try to delete an account, a customer or a supplier, but a warning message says you can't go ahead because journal entries are attached, there's associated job history or a supplier is linked with a particular account.

You have two alternatives: You can either merge the account or card, or you can make it inactive, as follows:

- ✔ To merge two accounts or two cards, skip ahead to the following section.

- ✔ To make an account inactive, double-click the offending account, and then tick the Inactive Account box.

- ✔ To make a customer or supplier card inactive, double-click the card, and then tick the Inactive Card box.

When you make an account or a card inactive, it still appears in the Accounts List and Cards List, almost as if nothing has happened. However, if you're in the middle of a transaction and you call up a list of accounts or names, the account or card doesn't show up.

Merging two into one (ah, young love)

After you've been using MYOB for a while, chances are you'll want to tweak your lists. Maybe you realise that you accidentally created two separate accounts called Advertising Expense or two customers with the same name; maybe you realise that you've got too many accounts and you want to have a slightly less detailed Accounts List. However, you can't delete a card or an account if you've already allocated transactions to it.

The solution is to combine duplicate accounts or cards. Here's how:

1. **Go to your list and first highlight the account, customer or supplier that you want to keep.**

2. **Click on Combine Accounts or Combine Cards.**

   You arrive either at the Combine Accounts or Combine Cards window. The account or card that you want to keep shows up as Primary.

3. **For the Secondary account or card, select the item you want to get rid of.**

   Remember, you're going to get rid of the account or the card; you won't be getting rid of any transactions, because what you're actually doing is merging two into one. Ah, that romance stuff rears its head again.

4. **Click the Combine Accounts or Combine Cards button.**

   A message of great portent appears, announcing that yes, two are about to combine into one. In Figure 2-5, you can see how I'm merging my regular Bank Charges account with an unwanted Bank Fees account.

5. **Click OK.**

   In a blink of an eye, the two accounts or cards are merged.

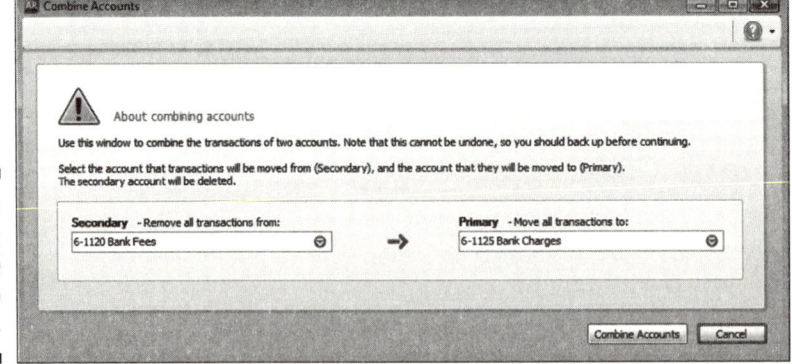

Figure 2-5: Combining (merging) two accounts.

Looking Up Transactions for Accounts, Customers or Suppliers

Want to look up transactions for an account, customer or supplier? I talk about finding transactions in lots of spots throughout this book:

- ✔ Chapter 4 provides details about finding customer invoices.

- ✔ Chapter 5 explains how to look up bank account transactions.

- ✔ Chapter 7 talks about locating customer payments.

- ✔ Chapter 8 explores how to find supplier bills or payments.

- ✔ Chapter 10 explains how to look up transactions relating to specific items of inventory.

- ✔ Chapter 19 gives tips on advanced searches, including searching for particular words or amounts.

Don't get muddled between looking up *transactions* for a particular customer or supplier, and looking up *contact details*. To view contact details — maybe to look up a phone number or check a contact name — go to your Cards List, highlight the customer or supplier in question, and then click Edit.

Chapter 3

Setting Up Opening Balances

. . . .

In This Chapter

▶ Setting up opening balances for customers

▶ Doing the same thing for your suppliers

▶ Sorting out account opening balances

▶ Making sure inventory opening balances are okay

. . . .

In this chapter, I explain how to record opening balances for customers, suppliers and inventory, as well as how to set up opening balances for all asset, liability and equity accounts. Although some of these activities can be a little daunting if you don't have bookkeeping experience, don't be anxious; I walk you through each stage, step by step.

You only need to read this chapter if your business was already up and running before you started using MYOB. If your business is new and you're using MYOB right from the word 'go', you don't have any opening balances to carry forward. You can happily ignore this entire chapter.

Customer Opening Balances

In the first part of this chapter, the aim of the game is to tell MYOB about all the customers who owed you money at the point you started using MYOB — which for most businesses, will be the first day of the current financial year. By entering opening balances, you stay on top of who owes you money, and just how much, right from the start.

Recording how much customers owe you

Start by listing all customers who owed you money at your start date. Make sure this list includes invoice numbers, invoice amounts and the total GST for each invoice. Then, with this list in your sticky hand, you're ready to record customer opening balances.

The first step is to tell MYOB the total amount that customers owe you:

1. **Go to Setup⇨Balances⇨Account Opening Balances.**

2. **Enter the total amount that customers owe you in the Opening Balances column next to Trade Debtors.**

   Refer to the list of customers with amounts owing, and add up the total that you're owed at the point you started using MYOB. This is the amount you enter next to Trade Debtors.

3. **Click OK.**

   Great. You've completed the first step.

You're now ready to enter information about individual outstanding invoices:

1. **Go to Setup⇨Balances⇨Customer Opening Balances.**

2. **Click Add Pre-Conversion Sale.**

3. **For each customer who owes you money, enter the Customer Name, the invoice number and the date.**

   As the Date, enter the original date of the outstanding invoice. Also with the Memo, simply accept the default description of 'Pre-conversion sale'. Figure 3-1 shows what a typical pre-conversion sale looks like.

   If you have a customer who owes you for several separate invoices, you may be tempted simply to add one invoice for the whole amount. Don't. Although it takes longer to enter your opening balances sale by sale than to enter one lump sum, this extra detail is useful later on when you need to match customer payments against specific invoices.

4. **Complete the Tax Code and double-check that the tax amount comes up correctly.**

   If you sell a mixture of taxable and non-taxable items, GST won't calculate correctly. To fix this, click the arrow next to the word Tax, and

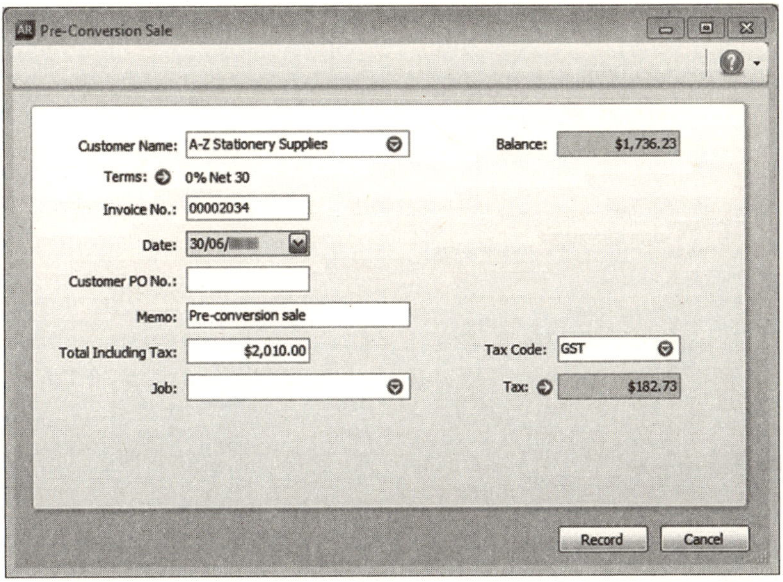

Figure 3-1:
Recording
a pre-
conversion
sale for a
customer
who owed
you money
before you
started
using
MYOB.

edit the tax amount. (See also the sidebar 'GST hiccups' a little later in this chapter.)

5. Repeat this process for every outstanding amount.

After you've recorded every invoice, you're ready to check that everything balances. Read on to find out more . . .

Checking your totals

Have you recorded every single invoice that customers owed you at the point you started using MYOB? Great. Go to Customer Balances one more time (Setup⇨Balances⇨Customer Opening Balances) and check out the figure for Total Sales in the bottom-right corner. In the perfect world, this amount should equal the amount of the Linked Receivables Account Balance, and the Out of Balance Amount should be $0.00. You can see how this looks in Figure 3-2.

If your Out of Balance amount isn't zero, don't fret. Look for your mistake by hopping to Reports on the top menu bar. Click Index to Reports, followed by the Sales tab, and then select the Receivables Reconciliation [Detail] report. Display this report and compare each line with your original list of outstanding invoices. Try to spot the difference, keeping a keen eye out for credit notes. (It's easy to forget to stick a minus sign in front of credit notes when you enter them as pre-conversion sales.) You should be able to spot the difference between this report and the list you were working from when entering opening balances.

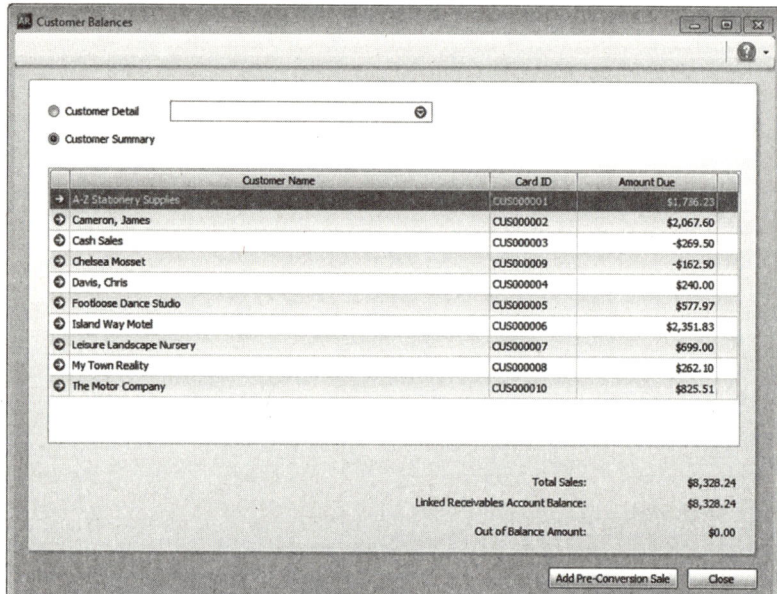

Figure 3-2:
The Out of
Balance
Amount for
Customer
Balances
should
be zero.

GST hiccups

When you recorded opening balances for customers or suppliers, did you end up editing the GST amount on any pre-conversion sales or purchases? (You would have had to do this if you had an invoice or bill with a mixture of taxable and non-taxable goods.)

If you edit GST amounts on pre-conversion sales or purchases *and* you report for GST on a cash basis, you will find that the GST calculates incorrectly the first couple of times you generate your Business Activity Statement from MYOB. This problem will continue to occur until all your opening balances have been paid.

One solution is to go to the GST tab of your Reports menu and complete your Business Activity Statement using the GST [Summary Cash] report as your reference. You may need assistance from your accountant or an MYOB Certified Consultant with this process. Alternatively, you can enter two pre-conversion transactions for each mixed tax invoice or bill — one with GST and the other without.

Supplier Opening Balances

The idea of entering opening balances for suppliers is that you tell MYOB about all the suppliers to whom you owed money at the point you started using MYOB. However, before worrying about this step, ask yourself whether you need to do anything at all:

✔ If you always pay suppliers by cash, EFTPOS or credit card, and you don't buy any goods on credit, you don't need to worry about supplier opening balances.

✔ If you don't purchase much from suppliers on credit, and you don't want to use MYOB to track how much you owe, you don't need to worry about recording opening balances. Instead, you can simply record bills at the point of payment, either by working directly from bank feeds or by recording transactions in Spend Money.

If you're not sure whether you want to record supplier bills in MYOB or not, make your way to Chapter 8, where I talk about this decision in more detail.

If you decide that you definitely do want to record supplier opening balances, return to the beginning of the chapter and follow my instructions under the heading 'Customer Opening Balances' except adapt these instructions for suppliers. The principles are exactly the same, but bear the following in mind:

✔ Where I say 'Customer', simply substitute the word 'Supplier'.

✔ Where I say 'Sale', substitute the word 'Purchase'.

✔ Where I refer to 'Trade Debtors', look for 'Trade Creditors'.

✔ Where I refer to 'Receivables', look for 'Payables'.

Once complete, don't forget to ensure your opening supplier balances are correct. After entering all outstanding supplier bills, you should find that Total Purchases in the Supplier Balances window equals the amount you entered for Trade Creditors in the Account Opening Balances window. The Out of Balance Amount should be zero.

Account Opening Balances

If your accountant has already finalised last year's accounts, you can record account opening balances by referring to your closing Balance Sheet report as at 30 June. This report is the perfect reference for entering opening balances, and means you can skip straight to the section 'Balancing the whole deal'. However, if you don't yet have a complete Balance Sheet report for the previous financial year, read on.

Entering opening account balances is a pretty technical process, and if you're at all unsure about what to do, you're probably best to ask for assistance from your accountant or MYOB Certified Consultant. The easiest approach — if you haven't done so already — is to shift your company file into the cloud and invite your adviser to log in and review these balances. For more information about working in the cloud, see Chapter 16.

Entering a few balances to get started

You don't need to record all opening balances in order to get going with MYOB. Indeed, you can get away with simply entering the bare essentials. To enter these figures, go to your Setup menu (on the top menu bar) and select Account Opening Balances from the Balances menu. You can see in Figure 3-3 what this menu looks like.

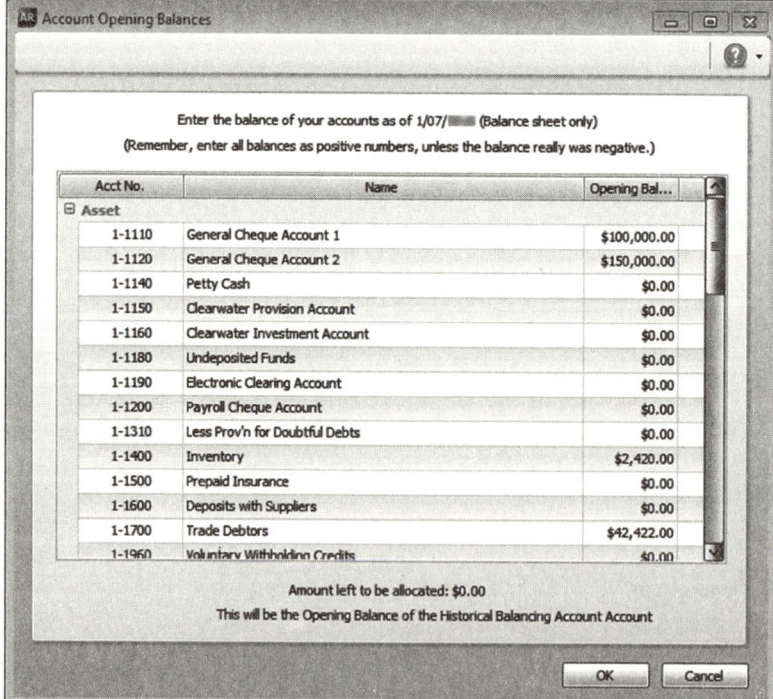

Figure 3-3: Recording account opening balances.

The most important opening balances to enter are as follows:

- ✔ **Your opening bank account balance:** Simply look at the opening balance on your bank statement for the day you started using MYOB. (If you're in any doubt about what figure to enter, I talk a little more about opening bank balances in Chapter 9.) Enter this amount against the Business Bank Account balance at the top of your Account Opening Balances.

- ✔ **Any other bank account balances:** Ideally, enter the opening balances for all other business accounts, such as online savings accounts and credit cards.

- ✔ **Opening balance of Trade Debtors:** Did you have any customers who owed you money at the point you started using MYOB? If so, enter the total amount owed to you by these customers on that date. Refer to 'Recording how much customers owe you' earlier in this chapter for more detail.

- ✔ **Opening balance of Trade Creditors:** Whether or not you want to enter a balance for Trade Creditors depends on a few factors. Refer to 'Supplier Opening Balances', earlier in this chapter, for more detail.

You'll notice that when you only enter a few balances, MYOB shows an Amount Left to Be Allocated in the bottom-right corner. Don't worry about this amount. Either your accountant can fix your opening balances later or, if you're keen, you can try to do so yourself. Read on to the next section to find out how.

Balancing the whole deal

If you want to have a stab at entering all the opening balances, feel free. In order to do so, ask your accountant for a copy of your Balance Sheet for the date from which you started using MYOB. Then, with this document to hand, you're ready to begin.

1. **Return to your Setup menu (on the top menu bar) and select Account Opening Balances from the Balances menu.**

   Working from your Balance Sheet report, enter opening balances one by one.

   Sharp-eyed pedants (something you could fairly accuse me of, most days) may note that a Balance Sheet only lists asset, liability and equity accounts, but the Opening Balances menu lists income and expense accounts also. Don't worry. You can safely ignore opening balances for income and expense accounts.

2. **When you've entered all the amounts from your Balance Sheet, check that the Amount Left to be Allocated is now zero.**

   Can you see how earlier in this chapter, the Amount Left to be Allocated in Figure 3-3 is $0.00? This state of affairs is the name of the game.

   One of the satisfying things about accounting work is that everything has to balance. However, if you have no luck on this front, read on.

If the Amount Left to be Allocated doesn't return to zero, here are some ideas to fix the problem:

✔ **Have you entered all minus figures correctly?** Anything appearing in brackets on your Balance Sheet, such as Accumulated depreciation accounts, should be entered as minus amounts in your opening balances.

✔ **Have you entered an incorrect amount somewhere?** Spot this at a glance by going to the Reports menu on the top menu bar, clicking Index to Reports and then the Accounts tab. Highlight the Balance Sheet report and select your start date as the Date. Compare this report with your accountant's Balance Sheet and then try to spot the difference.

✔ **Is your Amount Left to be Allocated a multiple of nine?** If so, you have probably reversed a figure — for example, typing $63 instead of $36.

If you can't get your opening balances to balance, don't worry. Your best bet is to ask your accountant to have a look at your company file and spot what you've done wrong.

The mystery of Historical Balancing

Whenever you create a new company file, MYOB automatically creates an equity account called Historical Balancing. This account acts like a holding account for setting up new balances, or storing out-of-balance amounts.

When you enter just a few opening balances to get started, in the way that I recommend in this chapter, MYOB dumps the other side of these entries into your Historical Balancing Account.

If you have an amount in this account, this indicates that your opening balances are incomplete, or that you've made a mistake when recording opening balances. Don't worry too much — your accountant can easily fix this problem.

However, if you've been running MYOB for more than a year and you still have an amount in your Historical Balancing Account, I suggest you provide a gentle reminder to your accountant that this account needs some attention.

Opening Inventory Balances

You only need to worry about adding opening inventory quantities and costs if you plan to use the inventory features in MYOB. Chapter 10 talks all about this decision. Chapter 10 also explains how to set up numbers and descriptions for inventory items, and you'll need to have this information in place before you can record your opening inventory.

Counting is as easy as 1, 2, 3 . . .

In order to enter your opening inventory balances, you need to know the opening counts and costs for each item. With this information in hand, get ready . . . get set . . .

1. **Go! Head for the Inventory command centre and click Count Inventory.**

   A list of all your items appears.

2. **In the Counted column, enter stock counts for the first 20 or so items in your list.**

   I recommend you enter opening inventory counts in short batches, rather than all at once, because if you accidentally press the wrong key, you won't lose a whole heap of work.

   After you've entered the first 20 or so items, you should end up with a list of items and counts, as shown in Figure 3-4.

3. **Click Adjust Inventory.**

4. **Select your Inventory account as your Default Adjustment Account, and then click Continue.**

   At this point, the rather complicated-looking Default Expense Account window pops up. Don't stress out about the fine print; simply enter the number of your Inventory asset account as the Default Adjustment Account. (Inventory always starts with the number 1.)

5. **Click Opening Balances and, when prompted, click Adjust Balances.**

   MYOB gets terribly psychic at this point and asks if you're entering opening inventory balances. Indeed, this is exactly what you're doing, so just click Opening Balances to continue.

   An extra window also appears asking if you want to adjust your balances so that your asset accounts match with inventory balances. This is a good idea, so click Adjust Balances.

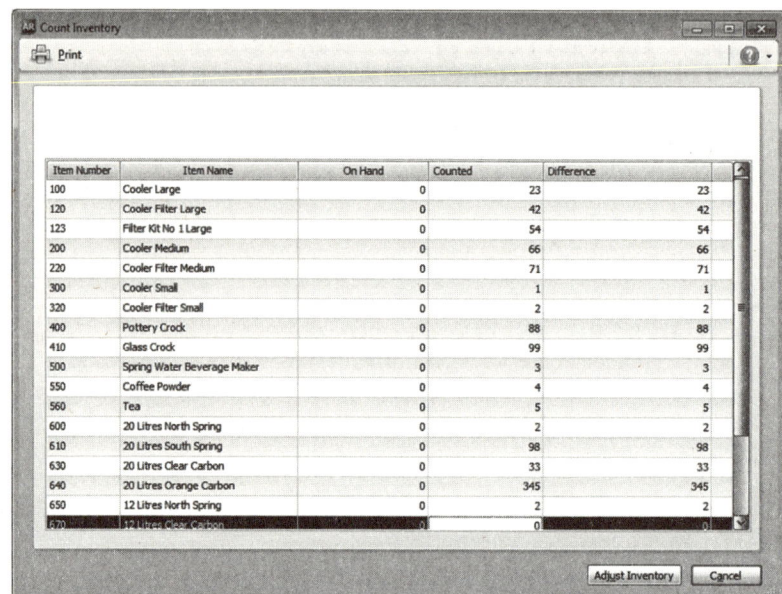

Figure 3-4:
Recording
opening
inventory
counts.

6. **Check the Date and write a suitable memo**.

   Aha! You've arrived at the Adjust Inventory window. Check the Date (it should be the date of stocktake, not the current date) and put something short and sweet in the Memo field (for example, 'Opening stock counts').

7. **Complete the Unit Cost column for each item**.

   One by one, fill in the item costs for each line of this window, as I do in Figure 3-5.

   Remember that you're entering costs, not selling prices, and that these cost prices should be tax-exclusive, before GST.

8. **Click Record**.

   After you click Record, repeat the entire process again and again, in batches of 20 or so items, until you've entered opening quantities and costs for all your items.

If you view the Buying Details of an item after recording the item's opening balance, you may be surprised to see that the Last Purchase Price shows up as zero. Don't worry — this is because you haven't recorded a purchase for this item yet! If you click the Profile for that item instead, you'll be able to see the Average Cost, which should be the cost price that you entered when doing the opening stock count.

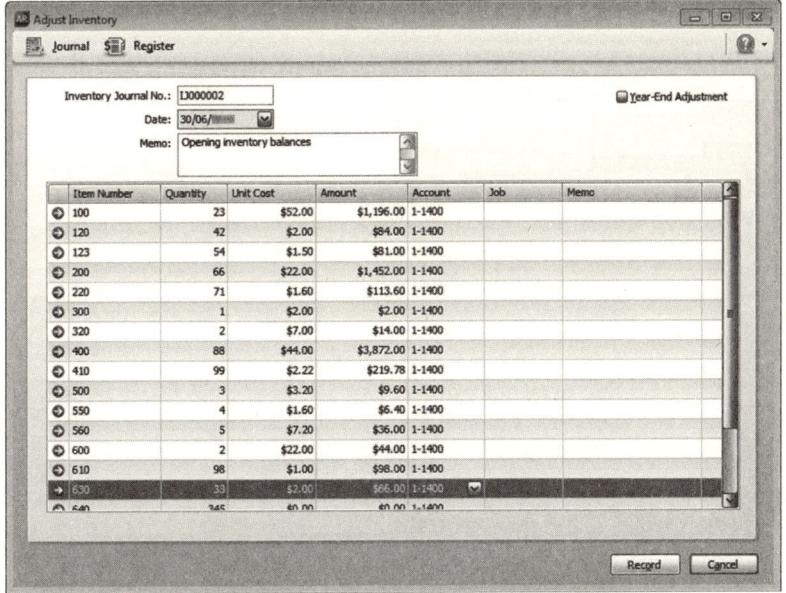

Figure 3-5:
Recording
how much
each item
costs.

Reviewing inventory totals

As you know by now, entering inventory counts and unit costs is a fairly involved process. That's why it's a good idea to check your work before you record any item sales or purchases.

Here's how to do so:

1. **Go to Reports, click the Inventory tab, and display the Items List report**.

   For the Date, choose the date that was correct when you counted your stock counts. If you're just getting started, this date is probably the first day of your financial year.

2. **Check that this report makes sense**.

   Check through each line of this report, particularly the Units on Hand and Average Cost columns.

Part II
Everyday Activities

Five Ways to Spend Less Time Working in MYOB (and More Time at the Beach)

- **Sign up for bank feeds.** When you sign up for bank feeds, your bank obligingly 'feeds' your MYOB file with a list of transaction details direct from your bank account. These transaction details appear in MYOB, complete with the date, the amount and, in most cases, name details. Safe as houses, quick as a robber's dog, and saves you hours of typing.

- **Configure allocation rules wherever possible.** Allocation rules are to bank feeds what pickles are to a cheese sandwich — the perfect partner. The idea is you first get bank feeds to supply MYOB with the basic detail of each transaction. Then you set up rules so MYOB automatically codes these transactions to the correct accounts.

- **Separate your business and personal bank accounts.** Every time you put personal transactions through a business account, either you or your bookkeeper waste valuable time and energy. Besides, having a bookkeeper trawl through bank statements and ask you about your purchases of groceries/wine/lingerie is always fairly depressing.

- **Ditch cheques completely.** If you still write cheques, stop. Cheques are expensive in bank fees, time-consuming for the person who receives payment this way and painful for bookkeepers. (Instead of being able to see from the bank feed whom a payment was for, the bookkeeper needs to find the chequebook, look through the cheque stubs, and decipher your hieroglyphics.)

- **Try not to pay for anything with cash.** I can't think of a worse way to spend my time than sorting through receipts, figuring out what I paid for with cash, and then writing up painful little summaries of every cash payment. Instead, use your bank card to pay for anything to do with the business, no matter how large or small.

Visit www.dummies.com/extras/myobsoftwareau for a free article and more tips about everyday activities in MYOB.

In this part ...

- ✔ Discover how to create invoices to send to your customers from wherever you may be (in your office, on a desert island or busking on the city streets).

- ✔ Find out why bank feeds are such a big deal, and why you can't afford not to sign up.

- ✔ Harbour no illusions about the costs of business. Look at how to record expenses, keep track of bank accounts, and deal with petty cash.

- ✔ Record customer payments, see how much customers owe you, and use MYOB to help you chase overdue accounts.

- ✔ Generate purchase orders, keep tabs on how much you owe to suppliers, and learn how to record supplier payments.

- ✔ Know your accounts are picture perfect by reconciling your bank account, every time.

Chapter 4

Making Sales

*F*inding your way through your first invoice is like finding your way through a foreign city for the first time. Although it's possible to reach your destination by sheer animal instinct, it's much easier if you have a map with detailed street directions. So, with the aim of finishing your first invoice by the shortest possible route, I suggest you provide the animal instinct and let me, in this chapter, provide the street directions.

Recording Your First Sale (Yippee!)

Producing your very first sale in MYOB can be a pretty amazing experience: Type in your customer's details, describe what you're selling and click Send to email this invoice to your customer.

The process is mostly pretty intuitive, but one thing that many people miss is that you can actually choose between five quite different invoice layouts:

✔ **Item:** The item layout is the best layout for most things. You use the item layout not only for selling items, but also for selling services — where, for example, you set up your hourly rate as an item, or your monthly membership fee as an item.

✔ **Service:** The service layout is best if you want to include lots of descriptive information about the service you provide.

✔ **Professional:** The professional layout is pretty much the same as the service layout, except you get a Date column as well. This layout is perfect for professionals who charge out for services over a period of time.

✔ **Time Billing:** The Time Billing layout is good if you bill in fine detail for your working hours, itemising each date, activity, the time spent on that activity and the relevant rate. You can use Time Billing invoices to log not just time, but also phone calls, photocopies, postage and other out-of-pocket expenses.

✔ **Miscellaneous:** You only use this layout for account adjustments.

I explain each of these layouts in the next few pages, as well as how to create your very first invoice.

Setting up services in your Items List

I'm going to leap straight into the thick of things and ask you to think of a service you provide to customers, such as a service fee, an hourly fee, a consulting charge, delivery fee or callout fee. With this in mind, I suggest you jump in and create this service as your first item:

1. **Go up to your Lists menu and select Items.**

2. **Click New.**

3. **Enter an Item Number and Name for this item.**

Keep your numbering logical and consistent, and make the Name meaningful — after all, this is what customers are going to see on their sales invoices. For example, if you're setting up an item to bill for your labour, the Item Name could be something simple like 'ServFee', and the Name could be more detailed, such as 'Hourly Onsite Service Fee'.

4. **Click I Sell This Item.**

Don't click I Buy This Item or I Inventory This Item.

5. **Select an income account as the Income Account for Tracking Sales.**

Note: In Chapter 2, I talk about designing your Accounts List so that your income accounts reflect the different kinds of revenue your business generates. Now that you're setting up items for the purpose of billing customers, link each item to the most relevant income account.

In Figure 4-1, notice how I link the 'ServFee' item to an income account called Service — Other Income.

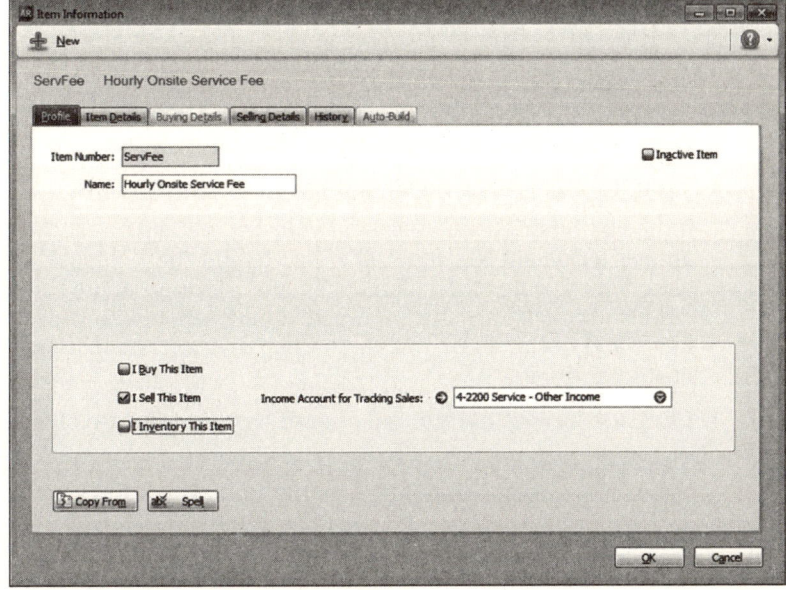

Figure 4-1:
Creating
items
for each
service you
provide (or
each item
you sell).

6. **Click the Selling Details tab.**

7. **Enter the Base Selling Price, the Selling Unit of Measure and the Tax Code When Sold.**

   The Base Selling Price is how much you charge for this service. If the Rate you enter includes GST, don't forget to tick the Inclusive checkbox.

8. **Click OK.**

   Well done, you've created your first service item. Now you're ready to send someone an invoice!

Take the short road home

Why go on the back roads when you can take the expressway? Hop straight to Sales from anywhere in MYOB by holding down the Ctrl key and at the same time pressing the letter J.

(For a complete list of all the shortcut keys available in MYOB, download the cheat sheet for this book, available at www.dummies .com/extras/myobsoftwareau.)

Billing for hours worked or items sold

Ready to create your first invoice? Then here you go:

1. **From the Sales command centre, click Enter Sales.**

2. **Type the customer's name and click Use Customer.**

   If the customer already exists in your list, details about the customer appear automatically. If not, it's time to add them to your list. Either click New to enter the customer's name, address and a thousand other details, or click Easy Add to create a new listing with the customer's name and nothing else. (Refer to Chapter 2 for lots more info on adding customers.)

3. **Click the Layout button and choose Item as your invoice type.**

   The item layout isn't only for selling items, but also for units of time, service fees, membership fees or anything with a fixed price.

4. **Accept the invoice number and check the date.**

   Most of the time, you're fine to accept whatever invoice number MYOB suggests. (The invoice number automatically goes up by one with every new invoice.) However, if you want to change the invoice number, you can.

5. **If you have a customer purchase order number, type the number in the Customer PO No field.**

6. **Enter the quantity of the item you're selling in the Ship column.**

   Yes, the Ship column refers to quantities for services as well as items. For example, if you're billing this customer for two hours at $80/hr, enter **2** in the Ship column.

7. **Type the item code in the Item Number column.**

   For info on setting up items that you buy and sell, go on a spin to Chapter 10. For more on setting up your services as items, refer to the preceding section.

8. **Review the Item Description and the Price.**

   The Item Description and Price come up automatically, based on whatever you entered when you created this item. However, it's fine to override the standard description or the price if you need to.

   Mates' rates? Edit the customer's payment terms (go to the Selling Details tab of the customer's card) to include a Volume Discount. This percentage then appears automatically in the Discount column.

9. **If you're using jobs, enter a Job number now**.

   If you want to track job income and expenses, enter the job number now. (For more about jobs, and to discover how to track the profit from any job, project, venture or cost centre, see Chapter 17.)

10. **Check the tax code in the Tax column**.

    Skip ahead to 'Picking your poison' later in this chapter for more info on selecting tax codes.

    While you're here, take a squiz at the top-right corner of your invoice. See that box called Tax Inclusive? If this box is ticked, enter the sale amount *including* GST. If this box isn't ticked, enter amounts *excluding* GST. Do whatever suits you best.

11. **Fill in any other information that you reckon would be handy**.

    The other fields in an invoice are all optional, such as comments, shipping details or promised delivery date.

    By this time, your invoice probably looks pretty similar to Figure 4-2 (assuming you're in the business of providing appliance repair services).

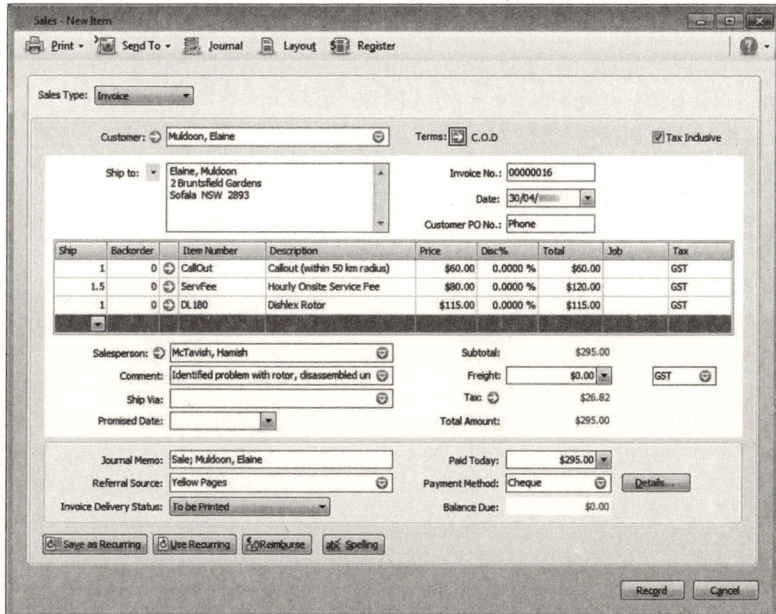

Figure 4-2:
A typical invoice, with an Item layout.

12. **Leave the Journal Memo as is**.

    Use the Journal Memo for additional notes only if you're really stuck (the Comment field is a better spot).

13. **If the customer is making a payment with this invoice, record the payment in Paid Today**.

    The Paid Today field is really handy if the customer has already paid (maybe you received this order online), or if the customer pays cash on the spot. Feed the amount into the Paid Today field and click the Details button next to the Payment Method field to select the account.

14. **Click Print or Send To Email**.

    Either click the Print button or click Send To followed by Email. (If this is your first invoice, enter your own email address as the customer's invoice address so that you can check what the invoice looks like first.)

If you're like me, you'll find that the standard invoice format in MYOB leaves a bit to be desired. Never mind. In Chapter 12, I explain more about customising templates and how to get your invoices looking good.

Providing a service

Service invoices give you plenty of room to include a detailed description in the body of the invoice about the excellent goods or services you have just provided for your customer.

To select Service as your layout, simply enter the customer's name and then, before you record any other information, click the Layout button at the top and select Service as your layout type.

Service invoices are very similar to Item invoices (and to skim through the instructions for creating an Item invoice, refer to the preceding section), but with two easy-to-spot differences:

⯈ **You can enter a description rather than select an Item code.** Let your creativity run wild. Don't just type 'Service of washing machine'. Tell the customer what you really did, down to every drop of sweat, drip of oil or minuscule spare part.

⯈ **You need to choose the income account every time you record a sale.** Next to the Description column is a narrow column headed Account No. Browse through your income accounts and take your pick of the one that fits best.

Taking a professional bent

Professional invoices are almost the same as Service invoices, but include an additional column on the left side for listing dates. This format comes in really handy if you charge by the hour and take several days, or even weeks, to complete a job. You can show the client precisely what dates you worked and how much time you spent on the work each day.

People who use Professional invoices include accountants, barristers and consultants. For an example, see Figure 4-3, which shows a consultant's Professional invoice, billing for onsite training, meetings and parking.

Creating a Professional invoice is almost exactly the same as creating a Service invoice. The only difference is that after you enter the customer's name but before you enter any data, click the Layout button at the top and select Professional as your layout type, instead of Service.

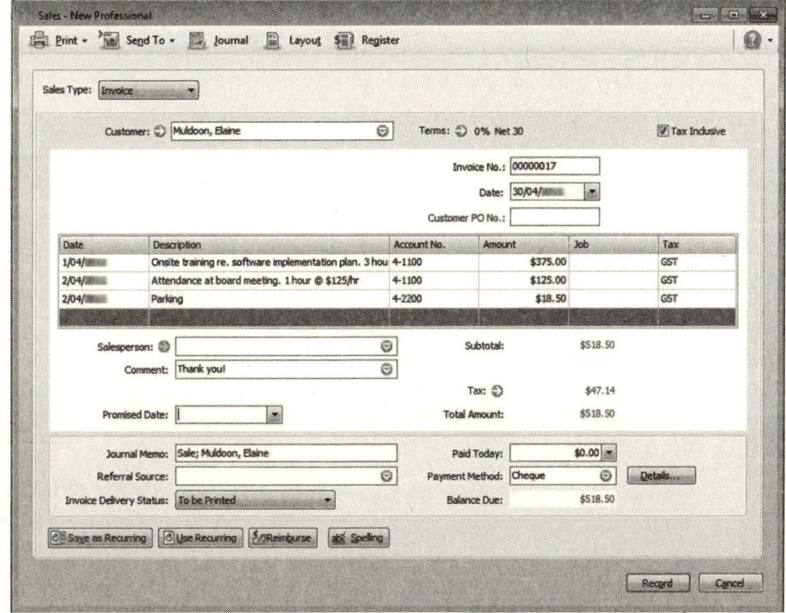

Figure 4-3:
A typical
Professional
invoice.

Billing for every split second

The most exclusive invoice template, Time Billing, exists in AccountRight Plus and AccountRight Premier, but not in AccountRight Basics or AccountRight Standard.

Time Billing works best if you like to bill in detail for your working hours, itemising each date, activity, the time spent on that activity and the relevant rate. You can use Time Billing invoices to log not just time, but phone calls, photocopies, postage and other out-of-pocket expenses.

With Time Billing, you make a list of your different activities in the Activities List and then record how long you spend doing these activities in the Enter Activity Slips window. When you're ready to bill the client, here's what to do:

1. **From the Time Billing command centre, click Prepare Time Billing Invoice.**

2. **Select your customer's name from the Work in Progress window.**

   The Work in Progress window shows the list of customers for whom you've already recorded activity slips. (To enter an activity slip, go to Enter Activity Slips from the Time Billing command centre.)

3. **Enter the amount for the invoice in the Bill column.**

   The Billable column shows the amount you're billing the customer if you're charging for all the hours logged at your normal rate. You can leave the Bill column as is if you're satisfied with this amount, or you can alter the amount to deduct a discount or add extra costs.

   If the bill looks a bit steep, enter the amount you want to write off as a minus figure in the Adjustment column. If you want to increase the bill, enter the adjusting amount as a positive figure. Figure 4-4 shows a Work in Progress window where a consulting charge has been adjusted downwards by $40.

4. **Click Prepare Invoice.**

   A customer invoice comes up automatically, showing all the time that you've logged, with any adjustments that you've made. If you like, you can change the invoice further at this point, adding descriptions, comments or additional items.

5. **Complete this invoice as you would any other kind of invoice, and then click Record.**

   In other words, check that the amounts are right, add job codes or memos if required, and so on.

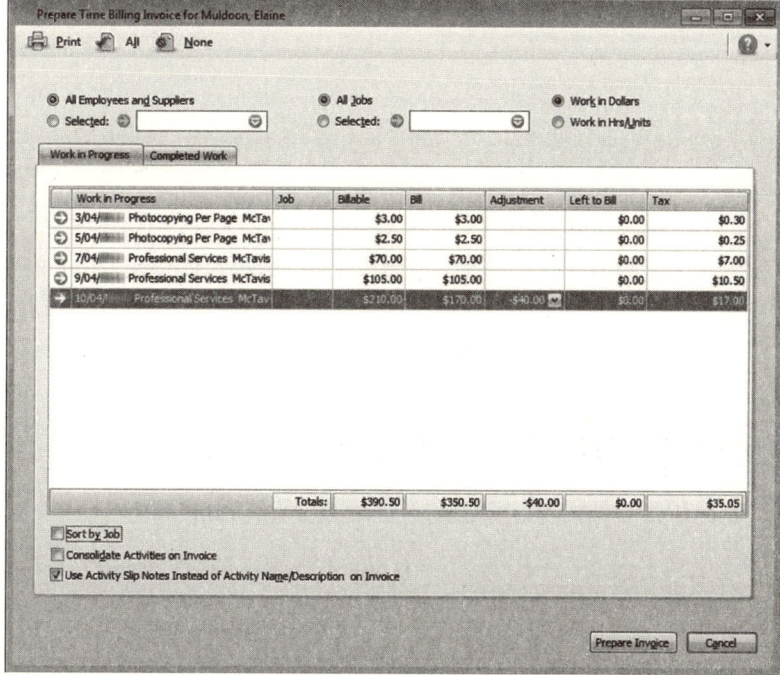

Figure 4-4:
You can adjust Time Billing invoices upwards or downwards.

Getting invoices how you want 'em

I mention earlier in this chapter that the format of the standard invoice that comes out of MYOB isn't that crash hot. For information about *customising forms* (in other words, changing fonts and colours, adding logos and so on), flip over to Chapter 12. After you've creating a customised form, you can select this form from the Print menu whenever you generate an invoice.

Tracking sales back to their source

Notice how every sale includes a field called Referral Source? If you can, use this field to record how this customer found out about you (via your website, print advertising, word of mouth or whatever). Later on, when you've recorded a few sales, you can print a Referral Source sales report and analyse what value of sales came from each source.

However, as well as customising forms, here are a few layout tricks you can try within the invoice itself:

- ✔ To insert a blank line in an invoice, choose Edit⇨Insert Line.

- ✔ To insert a header or subtotal in an invoice, choose Edit⇨Insert Header or Edit⇨Insert Subtotal. *Note:* You can't change the font of headers, and they don't display in bold, so you're usually best to type headers in capital letters.

- ✔ For more information about setting default formats and selecting different forms for different customers, see 'Selecting the right form for each occasion' later in this chapter.

Invoicing on the Move

If you or any of your employees work away from the office, you may want to raise invoices while you're on the move. Depending on your personal preferences, you can choose to create an invoice direct from your smartphone, or you can shift your company file into the cloud (if it isn't stored there already) and log in using a laptop or Windows PC.

Billing from your smartphone

To bill a customer direct from your smartphone, you need to complete the following:

- ✔ **Download the free app MYOB OnTheGo from the app store.** What is it about software developers that they feel the need to delete the spaces between words when naming products?

- ✔ **Shift your MYOB company file into the cloud.** Chapter 16 talks lots about working in the cloud and how to do this.

- ✔ **If you want to bill a customer for items, ensure these items are set up in your company file.** I talk about setting up items at the beginning of this chapter.

With these three requirements complete, I suggest you simply fire up the app on your smartphone and follow the prompts to create an invoice. You can see what the app looks like in Figure 4-5.

Figure 4-5:
MYOB
OnTheGo
enables you
to create
invoices
direct
from your
smartphone.

(Screenshot of smartphone showing New Invoice screen)

5:48 pm — 34%

Cancel — New Invoice — Save

John Wiley & Sons — *Item*

Item

#Consult75 Consultation

Description

Consultation

Quantity — **Unit Price** — **Total**

2 — $120.00 — **$240.00**

Tax

GST 10%

You'll find that the functionality of MYOB OnTheGo is simple, but provides all the essentials for creating invoices when you're out and about. Not only can you add new invoices and email these invoices to customers, but you can also add new customers and review outstanding customer balances.

When I first started using MYOB OnTheGo I found the whole process to be pretty intuitive, with the exception of a couple of little things:

✔ Unless you have already selected Item as the Sale Layout on a customer's card (which you do by opening up the full version of MYOB and going to the Selling Details tab for this customer), MYOB OnTheGo chooses a Service invoice as the default layout.

✔ In order to use your own customised forms, rather the standard MYOB templates, you need to select a standard Sale Layout and Printed Form for each customer. (Again, you need to do this in the full version of MYOB.)

MYOB OnTheGo also hooks up with a pretty impressive mobile payments service called MYOB PayDirect. PayDirect enables you to add a device to your smartphone so that you can accept customer payments by EFTPOS or credit card on the spot. (Ideal for any mobile business such as appliance repairs, electricians, fitness coaches, plumbers or tutoring services.)

Logging into MYOB when out in the field

Although I find MYOB's smartphone app to be pretty nifty, I find typing on my smartphone screen to be a bit fiddly. Like me, you may find that if you have more than one or two invoices to create, you prefer to work in the full version of MYOB.

For a business with employees on the move, the best approach is to store your company file in the cloud. This means that you (or anyone else you nominate) can access your MYOB data from wherever you are, so long as you have an internet connection and a laptop or computer with MYOB software loaded on it.

You may be concerned by the idea of allowing field technicians or other employees access to your accounting data. Don't worry — you can set up user profiles to limit employees so that they can only add and view invoices, and can't view any other business data. (Chapter 1 talks about setting up users and roles, and Chapter 16 explains how to shift your account to the cloud.)

The other thing to remember about working with AccountRight in the cloud is that your monthly subscription allows you to work with an unlimited number of users. So even if you have 15 employees and all of these employees need to raise invoices from their laptops, each of these employees could have MYOB software on their machine. (Whenever you invite somebody to become a user, MYOB sends that person an email along with a link to download the software.)

You can't run the full version of AccountRight on a smartphone or a tablet — you can only run AccountRight on a computer that has Windows as its operating system.

Meeting GST Requirements

Although MYOB handles GST perfectly, it can't guarantee that you produce legit tax invoices every time. You have to complete your part of the deal as well.

Ensuring your invoice is up to scratch

In order for your invoice to meet Tax Office requirements, you need to ensure the following appears on your invoices:

✔ **Your Australian Business Number (ABN).** This is the number that the Australian Taxation Office gives you when you register your business, or when you register for GST. (If you haven't done so already, go to Setup and fill in your ABN details in the Company Information window.)

✔ **If you're registered for GST, the words 'Tax Invoice'.** These words appear automatically in the standard MYOB templates. Of course, if you're not registered for GST, you'll need to customise your invoice so that it says 'Invoice' at the top rather than 'Tax Invoice'.

✔ **If you charge GST, either the total amount of GST payable or a comment saying that the total price includes GST.** Also, if the invoice is for a mix of taxable and non-taxable goods, you need to clearly identify each item that's taxable and show exactly how much GST you're charging on each item.

✔ **For invoices for more than $1,000 (including GST), either the customer's name and address or the customer's name and ABN.** For invoices of this value or above, you're also meant to specify the quantity or volume of whatever it is you're supplying, such as the number of hours charged or the number of units supplied.

Keep in mind that GST isn't just a tax, but also an exercise in psychology. If you prefer to show prices *before* GST, so that arguably your prices look cheaper, choose a tax-exclusive invoice template when customising your invoice. If you prefer to show prices *after* GST, so there can be no possible confusion about how much is owed, select a tax-inclusive invoice template when customising your invoice. (Chapter 12 talks more about invoice customisation.)

Picking your poison

For every line on every invoice, you have to enter a code in the Tax column. Short of closing your eyes, clicking your mouse at random and accepting whatever tax code first appears, you're going to have to get a grip on which code to pick when.

Here are some pointers:

✔ If you're registered for GST, and charge GST on your sales, select GST as your tax code.

✔ If your business sells GST-free goods such as childcare or medical services, choose FRE as your tax code.

✔ If your business sells a mixture of goods, some attracting GST and some GST-free, choose the appropriate code (either GST or FRE) as your tax code.

✔ If your turnover is less than $75,000 annually, and you have chosen not to register for GST, select N-T (for Not Reportable) as your code.

✔ If this is a sale to an overseas customer, select EXP as your tax code.

Want the tax code to come up correctly every time? No worries:

✔ For service or professional sales, make sure that every income account in your Accounts List has the correct tax code in the Details tab of the account. Refer to Chapter 2 to find out more.

✔ For item sales, make sure every item has the correct tax code in the Selling Details tab.

✔ For sales to overseas customers, when you want to override these defaults, go to the customer's card, click the Selling Details tab, select EXP as the Tax Code and click the option Use Customer's Tax Code.

Toggling how you view prices

The introduction of GST heralded a major shift in the education system. Forget multiplying by two, dividing by five or understanding fractions. Cast algebra to the wind, and speak not of spelling or grammar. To get by in the world of GST, kids today need to be wizards at multiplying by ten and dividing by eleven.

Fortunately, MYOB can divide by eleven sooner than you can say 'knife'. When you record a new sale, you can display prices including or excluding GST. Simply click the Tax Inclusive button in the top-right of the sales window to toggle this preference on or off.

Digging Yourself Out of a Hole

Admit it! You rarely spend a day at work when something doesn't go amiss. It happens to everyone. So in the next couple of pages I explain how to change, delete and reverse invoices — *reversing* is when you create a new transaction that's the opposite of the transaction that you got wrong, so that the right and the wrong cancel one another out.

I also rave on about one of accounting's other little mysteries: Credit notes.

Looking things up

Assuming you know the invoice number, the quickest and easiest way to find an invoice is to go to your Find Transactions menu (found on the bottom of every command centre) and click the Invoice tab. Enter the invoice number and the invoice details appear in a flash. From here, you can click the arrow next to the invoice number to view the invoice in detail.

Here are a few more tips for finding stuff quickly and easily:

- ✔ **Search for all invoices belonging to a particular customer.** Go to your Sales Register, click the All Sales tab and select the customer's name from the Search By field.

- ✔ **Don't forget to change the dates.** MYOB always defaults to displaying the current month's transactions only, so if you need to, change the dates that come up in the Dated From and To boxes.

- ✔ **Try sorting the columns in different ways.** Did you know that you can sort any of the columns simply by clicking the column label? For example, if you want to sort by invoice number, simply click the Invoice No column label. Or if you want to sort by the amount owed, click the Amt Due column.

- ✔ **Cut to the chase using a smart search.** A super-handy tip is to click anywhere on the Sales Register grid and then type Ctrl-Shift-F. Up pops a Search field where you can search using any name, number or amount.

By the way, in the Sales Register you can see the Status listed for every invoice. For the uninitiated, *Open* means unpaid and *Closed* means paid. (Software programmers speak a different kind of English to you and me.)

Changing or deleting invoices

So you've just recorded a customer invoice when you realise that you've messed up. You have to move quickly if you're going to stop Madame Gautier in Paris receiving the assignment of haggis intended for Mrs MacDonald in Edinburgh.

If you haven't sent the invoice yet, all you have to do is find it in your Sales Register, double-click the sale to open it, and then fix your mistake. Click Record when you're done.

Alternatively, if you completely blew it with this invoice, you can always choose to delete it. To do this, first find the invoice in your Sales Register and double-click to display it. Then go to Edit (on the top menu bar) and select Delete Sale. Close your eyes and ... whoosh, the invoice is gone forever.

Of course, if you've already sent the botched invoice to your customer, you shouldn't make any changes at all, no matter how bad your mistakes. Instead:

✔ If you overcharged the customer, create a credit note for the difference (see 'Raising credit notes').

✔ If you undercharged the customer, create an additional invoice for the difference.

✔ If you stuffed things up completely, reverse the invoice and start afresh (see the following section for details).

If you have employees who are responsible for invoicing, and you have some customers who pay by cash, then consider setting internal controls so that the person receiving cash doesn't have the authority to access sales functions in MYOB. That way, nobody can be tempted to pocket the cash payment and then hop into your MYOB company file and simply delete the sale.

Reversing invoices

An alternative to deleting an invoice is to reverse it. In many situations, I prefer reversing invoices to deleting them, because reversals provide a complete audit trail of what took place. For example, maybe you invoiced the wrong customer by accident, and that customer has already received a statement showing the mistake. If you reverse this incorrect invoice, rather than simply delete it, the customer has the satisfaction of being able to look at their statement and see that everything has been fixed up.

To reverse an invoice, first check your preferences. Go to Setup➪Preferences and click the Security tab. Make sure this option is ticked: Transactions CAN'T be Changed; They Must be Reversed.

Now, find the invoice you want to reverse and display it. Then head up to the Edit menu and select Reverse Sale. MYOB generates a new

Speed dating

When typing dates on invoices — actually, this tip applies to dates anywhere in MYOB — only type in the numbers that require changing. For example, if the date reads 07/09/15 and you need to change it to 10/09/15, all you have to do is highlight the date, type the number '10', press the Tab key and the rest of the date fills in automatically.

Alternatively, to move the date forward by one day, press the + button on your keyboard. To move back one day, press the – button.

transaction that's exactly the opposite of your original sale, the only difference being that all amounts or quantities are negative, not positive. All you have to do is change the date (usually the current date makes most sense) and click Record.

Oh, one important thing. When you've finished recording this reversal, don't forget to return to your preferences and remove the tick from the option Transactions CAN'T be Changed; They Must be Reversed.

Raising credit notes

In principle, creating a credit note is just the same as creating an invoice; the only difference is you use negative quantities in the Ship column (if it's an Item invoice) or negative amounts in the Amount column (if it's any other kind of invoice).

Here's what to do:

1. **Click Enter Sales to create a new sale for this customer.**

2. **Enter the customer's name, and then press the Tab key.**

3. **Enter the details of this credit.**

   If this is an Item invoice, use negative figures in the Ship column, followed by the items you're crediting in the Item Number column.

   If this is a Service or Professional invoice, stick negative figures in the Amount column.

For the credit note's tax code, use whatever tax code you had on the original invoice.

4. Enter a brief explanation for this credit in the Description field.

Your credit note should look something like the one shown in Figure 4-6.

5. Click Print, Send to Email or Record.

Note that because the total is a negative amount, MYOB knows to put the words Adjustment Note at the top, rather than Tax Invoice.

6. Go to Returns & Credits and apply the credit to the original invoice.

Go to your Sales Register and click the Returns & Credits tab. Find your credit in the list and click Apply to Sale. Apply the negative balance of this credit invoice against the original invoice.

Alternatively, to issue a refund for this credit, skip to Chapter 7.

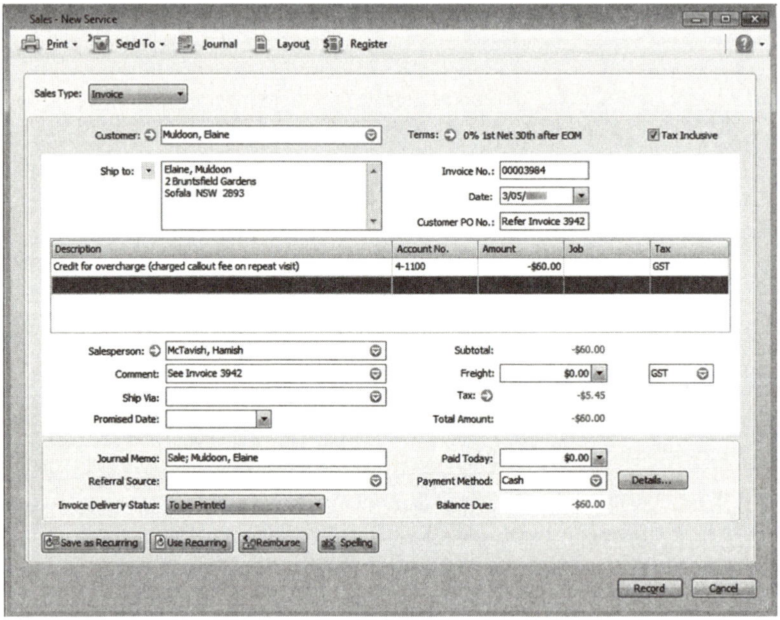

Figure 4-6:
Creating a
credit note.

No more trubl wid spelin

Are you the world's worst speller? Never mind, because MYOB comes complete with an in-built spellchecker.

To switch spellchecking on, head to the Windows tab of your Preferences menu and click the option to Automatically Check Spelling in Text Fields. Then return to whatever you're doing. Next time you go to record a transaction, any mistaches (oops, I mean mistakes) appear in the Spelling window, with helpful suggestions on how to reform your ways.

If you then click the Spelling button in the top-left corner of the Windows tab of your

Preferences, you can select your preferred language (always select English Australia rather than English United States) and refine how picky you want the spellchecker to be. You can also add words to the dictionary, and change various other spellcheck options.

The spellcheck preference is what's known as a *system-wide preference*. In other words, if a few people are working in the same company file and one person switches on spellchecking, then everybody else gets spellchecking too. Some folk hate spellcheckers, so if you share your company file with others, ask around first.

Working with Quotes and Sales Orders

The good news is, if you know how to create a sale, you already know how to create a quote or a sales order. Simply go to the Sales command centre and choose Enter Sales. Now, can you see the drop-down box in the top-left corner? Click here to toggle between Quote, Order and Invoice.

Sometimes novices get a little bamboozled by quotes and sales orders, so here are a few pointers to help you use them:

✔ To see a list of all outstanding quotes or sales orders, go to the Sales command centre and click the Sales Register button, followed by either the Orders or the Quotes tab.

✔ If a customer accepts your quote and you want to convert this quote into an invoice when the job is complete, go to your Sales Register and click the Quotes tab. Highlight the quote and then click Change to Invoice. The quote comes up, ready for you to update as necessary and record as a final invoice.

✔ If you want to keep a record of quotes, even after you've converted them to invoices, you can. Go to Setup⇨Preferences, click the Sales tab and deselect the preference Delete Quotes upon Changing to an Invoice.

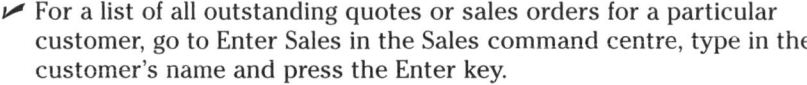

✔ For a list of all outstanding quotes or sales orders for a particular customer, go to Enter Sales in the Sales command centre, type in the customer's name and press the Enter key.

✔ To email or print quotes or orders from the Print/Email Invoices menu, click Advanced Filters and change the Sales Status (which normally defaults to Open) to Quotes or Orders.

✔ You can create a special invoice layout for quotes, basing it on your normal invoice but adding comments at the bottom about the conditions that apply (for example, 'This quote is only valid for 30 days'). See Chapter 12 for lots more on creating customised forms.

✔ Orders are a neat way of keeping track of 'pending' sales. For example, sometimes I'll do some phone consulting for a client. I don't want to bill them for a measly ten minutes of time, so I record this time as an 'order'. At some point in the future, when I go to invoice this client for some regular consulting, MYOB offers a prompt that an order exists. I simply call up the order, add the extra time, convert the order to an invoice, and everything is sweet.

✔ If you receive a sales order but don't have enough stock on hand to fill the order, a neat way of ordering the required goods is to first enter the sales order, but just before recording it, click Create PO ('PO' stands for purchase order). At this point, the sales order is recorded, and a purchase order appears automatically, ready for your review.

Setting up Shortcuts for Repeating Sales

Do you send some customers the same invoice month after month or year after year? Maybe you're a music teacher and you send out tuition fees every term, or a security firm with a set monthly fee, or an air-conditioning technician with a standard monthly service retainer.

The good news is you can set things up so that you don't have to wear out your fingers typing the same invoice every month — you can create the invoice automatically.

Setting up templates

The first step is to create a recurring invoice, just like a template that you use to produce identical products again and again. Here's how:

1. **Create your customer's invoice, but instead of clicking Record, click Save as Recurring**.

   Go to the Sales command centre, click Enter Sales and create your customer's invoice as explained earlier in this chapter. Then, just before you click Record, say to yourself, 'No, no, no — don't!' and instead find the Save as Recurring button (one of those buttons in a row at the bottom of the invoice), and then hit it with abandon.

2. **Give your recurring sale a name**.

   When prompted, type a name for your recurring sale. Call this sale whatever you like, as long as it's something you can recognise (the customer's name usually works pretty well).

3. **Select how often the sale happens and on what day of the month**.

   In the Schedule window that pops up (see Figure 4-7 for a preview of what you're in for), indicate whether you make this sale every week, every month, every quarter, or whenever. Specify when you next want this sale to occur (this date has to be at some point in the future; you can't travel back in time). You can even say how many times you want this sale to be recorded.

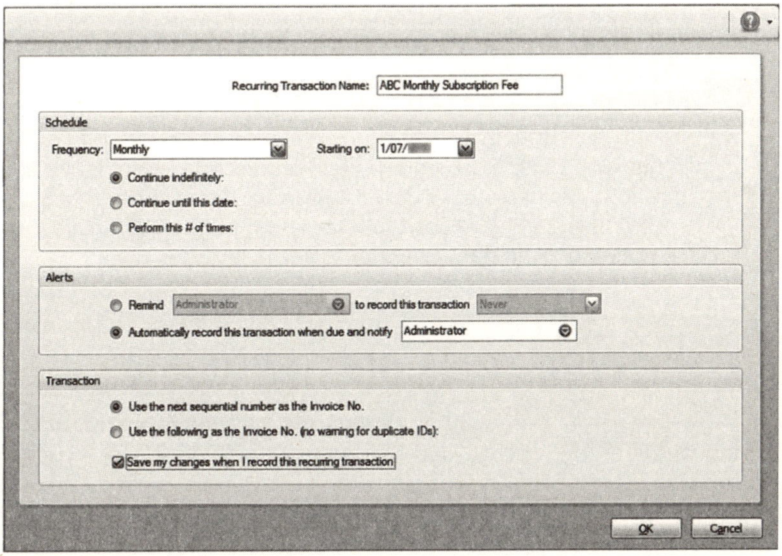

Figure 4-7: Setting up a recurring invoice.

4. **Decide whether you want software to record this transaction automatically, or whether you'd prefer to receive reminders.**

In the Alerts section, you can ask to be reminded when this transaction falls due (you'll see a reminder whenever you open your company file). Reminders are your best bet if this transaction changes or needs regular review. Alternatively, you can choose to get MYOB to record this transaction automatically. The automatic method works well for sales that proceed like clockwork, such as monthly subscriptions.

If you don't open your company file every working day, setting sales to record automatically probably won't work well for you, because automatic transactions only record when you open your company file, and MYOB dates them with the current system date. For example, if you schedule a whole swag of sales to record automatically on the first day of the month, but you don't open your company file until the fifth day, then they'll be dated a few days late.

5. **Decide whether you want your changes to be saved every time you record this transaction**.

Ah, this is such an innocent looking question. However, getting this one right is crucial. Imagine you bill a customer a set fee every month but, from time to time, you increase your rate. If you select the box Save My Changes When I Record This Recurring Transaction, MYOB knows to update the template if you ever edit the value of the sale, so that future invoices automatically come up at your new rate.

6. **Click Save**.

When you click Save, you're flicked back to your original invoice. Don't get confused and think that nothing has happened. It has. All you have to do now is click Record one last time to record the sale and save this template for the next time you want to bill this customer.

Recording sales automatically

So you've created an invoice, saved it as a template so that you can use it again, and you've recorded the invoice itself. Now, close your eyes and imagine time ticking by. Tick, tick, tick … Aha! You've arrived at the future, and now you're ready to bill your customer again.

What you need to do next depends on what options you selected when setting up the template, as follows:

✔ If MYOB records this sale automatically, you don't have to do much at all. Just sit back and relax.

✔ If you receive a reminder, all you have to do is zoom in on the reminder, change anything you want to change, and then click Record.

✔ If you don't receive a reminder but you're now ready to record that recurring sale again, go to Enter Sales and click Use Recurring. Find your recurring sale in the list, double-click it, make any necessary changes and click Record.

Copying and changing recurring invoices

From time to time you'll want to edit your sales template, maybe fixing up schedules, changing billing amounts or deleting old templates. To do any of these things, make your way to the Lists menu and select Recurring Transactions.

✔ To change the name, frequency or dates of a recurring transaction, highlight the transaction and click the Edit Schedule button in the bottom left.

✔ To change the details within a recurring transaction, such as the billing amount or the items billed, click the Edit button in the bottom right of the Recurring Transactions window. (If you double-click on the sale itself, you won't change the details; you just end up recording a new sale.)

✔ To copy a template from one customer to another (or to a whole batch of customers), click Create Copy and then choose the customer/s from the list. For example, a membership organisation would create one recurring sale for membership dues and then copy this template across to all customers.

✔ To delete a template, highlight the template and click Delete. This only deletes the template, and doesn't delete any transactions you recorded in the past using that template.

Sending Customer Invoices

So you're ready to send a customer your first invoice? Read on to find out how to select different forms for different customers, as well as how to print and email invoices.

Selecting the right form for each occasion

In Chapter 12, I explain how to customise your invoice template so that you get your invoice to look just right, with your business logo, colour/scheme and so on. However, once you've completed this process, you still need to tell MYOB that you want use this template in the future. (If you don't, MYOB continues to default to the standard template every time you record a sale, which is a total pain.)

Setting default forms

Here's how to configure MYOB so it picks the correct form every time:

1. **From the Sales command centre, click Print/Email Invoices.**

2. **Click the Advanced Filters button.**

3. **For each sale layout that you use, select your default form preference.**

   For example, you first select your Sales Type (Service, Professional or Item) and then select your preferred form from the Selected Form for Sale menu underneath (see Figure 4-8).

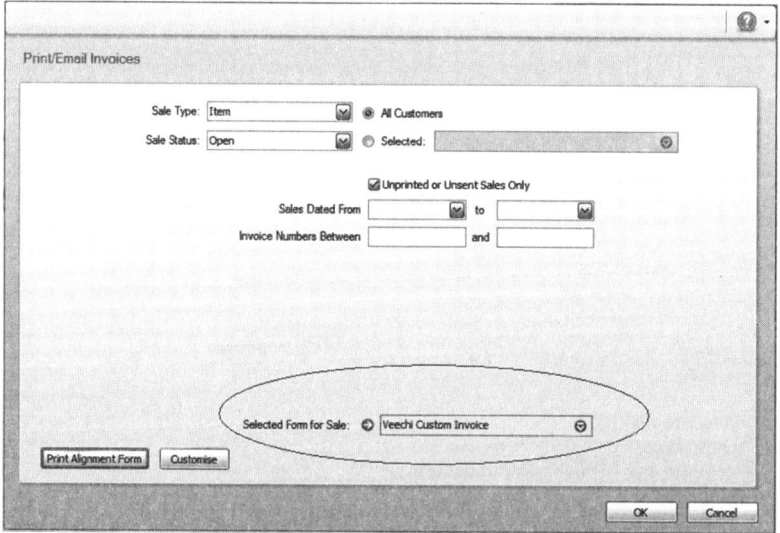

Figure 4-8:
Selecting your default form in the Advanced Filters menu.

4. **Click OK.**

You need to repeat this process for every person who uses MYOB in your business or organisation, and also every time you add a new user.

Setting different layouts for different customers

If the choice of form depends on the type of customer (maybe you have one form for cash sales, another for overseas customers and another for standard sales), the best approach is to go to the Selling Details tab of each customer's card and select a default Sale Layout and default Printed Form. That way, the correct layout and form appear automatically whenever you create a sale.

Printing your first invoice

After you get MYOB up and running, you'll probably rarely need to print an invoice, as most businesses find it much easier to send invoices by email. However, when you're first getting going, I recommend you start by printing the first few invoices so you can check they look just right.

To print an invoice, simply click the Print button in the top-left of the Sales window just before you record the sale. Alternatively, go to the Sales command centre and click Print/Email Invoices. A list of unprinted invoices appears. Select the invoice or invoices you want and click Print.

If you've already printed an invoice and you want to reprint it, head to Print/Email Invoices as normal but click the Advanced Filters button that appears on the right. Unclick the button that says Unprinted or Unsent Sales Only, select a date range or invoice number range, and then click OK.

Emailing invoices

To email a customer invoice, do the following:

1. **Create a sale as normal but instead of clicking Record, go to the Send To button at the top, and then select the Email option.**

You may see a message saying this sale is going to be recorded first. That's fine; just click OK to go ahead.

2. **Check the customer's email address is correct, change the message if you fancy, choose a different template if you need to, and then click Send.**

   If you like, you can change the default message to include a bit more info.

3. **Review the message that's going appear on all your emails.**

   To change this default message to something a little more exciting, click the Email Defaults button that appears in the top-right. From here, you can see how to edit the message defaults for both the subject and the body of your emails.

4. **Click Send.**

   Things go quiet for a few seconds as MYOB radiates a 'please-don't-hassle-me-I'm-working-really-hard' kind of message. And, if you're using Outlook, you may get a security message asking you to Allow or Deny this event.

   When the job's done, you arrive back at the Sales command centre, ready to continue your day. (And, assuming you're online, your email will already have been sent off into the ether.)

If you'd rather just email invoices in one big batch at the end of your session, you can. Go to Print/Email Invoices, click the To Be Emailed tab and change the Sales Type if necessary. You should see a list of all invoices that haven't yet been emailed to customers. Select the invoices you want to email, and click Send Email.

If this list is blank, the likely reason is that you need to select To Be Emailed rather than To Be Printed as the Invoice Delivery Status on each invoice. Right now, you can click each sale and change the Invoice Delivery Status; to prevent this from happening in the future, however, go to the Selling Details tab for each customer and select both a default Sales Layout and an Invoice Delivery method.

If you choose to email invoices in batches, rather than individually as you record each sale, be aware that fully paid invoices, credit notes, orders and quotes won't appear in the Print/Email Invoices menu. To get around this problem, click the Advanced Filters button and change the Sales Status to All Sales.

Troubleshooting email problems

When you click Send Email from the Email Invoices menu, MYOB creates an email for each customer, with an invoice attached to each email. Sounds neat, but you may have a few teething problems getting the whole email thing going. Here are a few of the common problems, along with solutions:

- ✔ **Your invoices don't appear in the Outbox or Sent Mail folders of your mail program.** Check that your default email software is correct. Go to your Control Panel, click Internet Options and then click the Programs tab. Make sure that the email program listed is the one you currently use for sending and receiving emails, and then click Apply.

- ✔ **You get an error message saying an email session could not be started.** Microsoft Outlook is the only email software that MYOB officially supports, and only the more recent versions (AccountRight 19.9 or later) are compatible with Outlook 2013. Don't be disheartened — you can configure Outlook to receive and send emails from other email services such as Gmail or Hotmail.

- ✔ **You get an I/O Error.** Try temporarily disabling any firewalls or virus protection programs to see if they are the cause. If so, you may need to add an 'exception' to this program.

- ✔ **You keep getting a really irritating message asking you to click Yes every time you email something.** I have two possible solutions. The first solution is to check your Outlook settings. Go to Microsoft Outlook⇨File⇨Options⇨Trust Center⇨Trust Center Settings⇨Programmatic Access and deselect the option to 'always remind me of suspicious activity'. If changing this setting fails to do the trick, a second solution is to download a nifty bit of software called Click Yes, available from `www.contextmagic.com/ express-clickyes`. The software is free, you can install it in a matter of minutes, and you'll never get that pesky little message again.

- ✔ **Your business logo isn't displaying, or the fonts are looking weird.** I talk about formatting issues with PDF documents in Chapter 12.

If all else fails and you really can't get your email software to talk to MYOB, you can resort to saving your invoice as a PDF by selecting Disk from the Send To menu at the top of the invoice. Save the file to your desktop, open up a new email in your email software, attach the PDF and you're done. This method also works well if you want to send an invoice to a customer but you need to send a longer email than the default message in MYOB allows.

Look in the mirror first

You wouldn't head out for work in the morning without a quick glance in the mirror, would you? So, in the same way, check that your electronic invoices look good by emailing a copy to yourself first (when prompted, temporarily substitute your own email address instead of the customer's email address). That way, you can check the appearance of your invoice when it's in PDF format and tweak anything that's not looking 100 per cent right.

If you have any problems with the format of your invoice — logos not appearing, fields disappearing or the form looking different when it's emailed than when it's printed — skip to Chapter 12, where I go through a few of these problems and include solutions.

Chapter 5

Understanding Bank Feeds and Rules

*P*ut simply, a *bank feed* is where your bank obligingly 'feeds' your MYOB file with a list of transaction details from your bank account. These transaction details appear in MYOB, complete with the date, the amount and, in most cases, the name of the person you were paying or the name of the person who was paying you.

Allocation rules provide bank feeds with the perfect dancing partner. The idea is that you set up rules so that MYOB automatically codes transactions to the correct accounts. So, for example, you can set up a rule so that any time the word 'Telstra' appears on your bank statement, MYOB allocates this withdrawal to Telephone Expense.

The whole deal works a treat, and the combination of bank feeds and bank rules can cut bookkeeping time by up to 75 per cent, depending on the size of the business.

I first started working with bank feeds at the same time as I shifted my own business into the cloud, and I confess that I got a bit muddled about the connection between these two features. The reality is that there is no connection. You can shift your MYOB file into the cloud and choose not to work with bank feeds, just in the same way as you can sign up for bank feeds and work on a local drive on your computer. In other words, you don't need to store your accounts in the cloud in order to take advantage of bank feed features.

A Big Picture View of how Feeds and Rules Work

I find it hard to explain how bank feeds work without providing an example, so with this in mind, Figure 5-1 shares what my bank feed looks like for a few days' worth of credit card transactions. (Judge me if you will!)

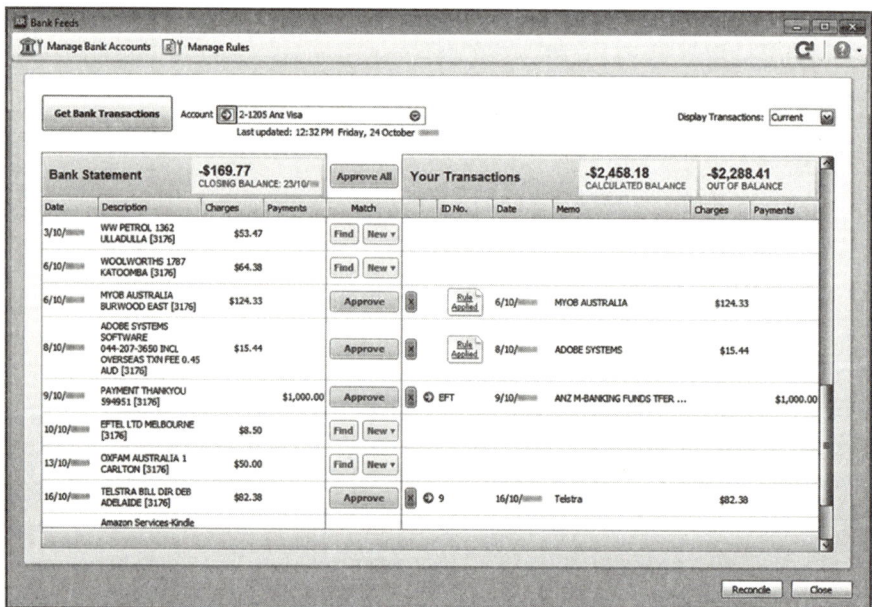

Figure 5-1: A typical bank feed for a credit card.

Can you see how the Bank Feeds window lists all recent transactions on the left and then, on the right, shows how some of these transactions have been matched or allocated automatically? Here's what some of the options mean:

✔ The transactions where the words 'Rule Applied' appear are transactions that MYOB has automatically allocated based on a rule.

✔ The transactions with an arrow next to them are transactions that MYOB has matched to an existing transaction.

✔ The transactions with nothing appearing on the right side are transactions that I've yet to add, create an allocation rule for or identify a matching transaction.

Different businesses tend to use bank feeds in slightly different ways, depending on the size of the business and how they use MYOB. I talk about these different ways of working later in this chapter, under the heading 'Using Bank Feeds to Add and Match Transactions'.

Getting Hooked Up

Given that bank feeds are almost certainly going to save you a whole heap of time, I suggest you apply for this service as quickly as possible. Read on to find out how.

Signing up for a bank feed

Signing up for a bank feed is easy-peasy. Here's what to do:

1. **Check you have a current MYOB subscription.**

   If you want to have bank feeds, you need a current AccountRight subscription. If you purchased your software outright in years gone by, you may feel a bit grumpy about having to pay a monthly fee as well. Fair enough, but you'll probably find that the fee more than pays for itself given the time you save. (Also, the monthly fee doesn't just include bank feeds, but phone support, receipt scanning services, superannuation payment features, tax table updates and a few other things besides.)

2. **Go to the Setup menu and choose Manage Bank Accounts.**

3. **Click Add or Remove a Bank Account.**

   You're transported to the MYOB website and prompted for your login email and password. ***Note:*** You need to use your my.MYOB login, not the login you use to open your company file. (For more on user logins, see Chapter 16.)

4. **Either click Add a Bank Account or Add a Credit Card, and then follow the prompts to complete your banking details.**

   You have to enter your BSB, Account Number and Account Name here. MYOB never asks for your banking passwords.

5. **When prompted to print the BankLink authority form page, go right ahead.**

Don't worry — BankLink may sound like a different company, but MYOB acquired this company a couple of years ago and so you can be assured that your information is safe. (BankLink has been around for years, specialising in bank feeds, and arguably provides the most accurate bank feed service available for any accounting software.)

If you have a problem getting your printer to play along, don't fret. MYOB also emails a copy of this form to you, so you can print this form later if need be.

6. **Sign the form and mail it to MYOB BankLink.**

In order to authorise your bank feed, you need to post a signed form to MYOB BankLink (you'll find the address on the form itself). The only exception to this rule is if you bank with the Commonwealth Bank, in which case you can log into NetBank and follow the prompts to complete your application online.

7. **Click Done.**

The My Products page reappears. The Bank Feeds section is updated with the details of the bank feed you have just applied for.

8. **Repeat this application process for every business bank account or credit card account.**

You can set up bank feeds for as many accounts as you like, and I recommend you set up a bank feed for every account you use for business purposes.

9. **Wait a while. Ta di da.**

Processing your bank feed application takes anywhere from 5 to 14 days. Once approved, MYOB notifies you by email.

(If you're feeling impatient, you can check the progress of your application. From the Banking command centre, click Manage Bank accounts followed by Check/Update Status.)

10. **When you get an email saying your bank feeds are approved, activate your bank feed.**

Not sure how? Read on to the next section to find out.

Are you signing away your life?

I sometimes get asked about how safe the whole bank feeds shenanigans are. Is it okay that MYOB can 'see' your banking transactions? Can MYOB access your bank account? Is your private information secure?

MYOB BankLink has a secure relationship with hundreds of Aussie banks and, in order for MYOB to set up your bank feeds, MYOB BankLink requires your written permission. MYOB BankLink can only access your transaction data in read-only format.

In other words, MYOB BankLink can't do anything to manipulate your bank transaction data and, unlike some other accounting software, you never have to provide your banking logins and passwords in order to activate bank feeds. (And if you do get an email that looks like it's from MYOB asking for this information, it's a hoax.)

So sleep easy. Signing up for bank feeds doesn't mean you're exposing yourself to unnecessary risk.

Activating your bank feed

Once you receive an email notifying you that your bank feed is ready, you can activate your bank feed. Here's how:

1. **Go to the Setup menu and choose Manage Bank Accounts.**

2. **Click Check/Update Status.**

   The Bank Feeds Log In window appears.

3. **Enter your my.myob login details.**

   You get two different levels of online access: You can be an *online file user* or an *online administrator*. In order to activate or update bank feeds, you need to be an online administrator. These online access levels are unrelated to the user roles you set within your company file. (For more about user roles, refer to Chapter 1, and for more about user logins, see Chapter 16.)

   Unlike the regular login to my.myob.com.au, the bank feeds server is case-sensitive. In other words, if you registered your login as patti@gmail.com but you type Patti@gmail.com when you log in to update your bank feeds, MYOB refuses to play.

   In this scenario, log out of your company file and then log back in, ensuring that you enter your login (which is usually your email address) in exactly the same way as you did when you registered as a user with MYOB. (If you're at all unsure, log into my.myob.com.au and go to Manage Users to check this information.)

4. Click OK.

The Manage Bank Accounts window reappears, hopefully showing Bank Feed Ready as the status.

5. Select an account from the list of available accounts in the Associated Account column.

Hopefully you already have an account in your Accounts List that corresponds to the account you've got a bank feed for. If not, create one now, ensuring you select Bank or Credit Card as the Account Type. By now, your Manage Bank Accounts window should look similar to Figure 5-2.

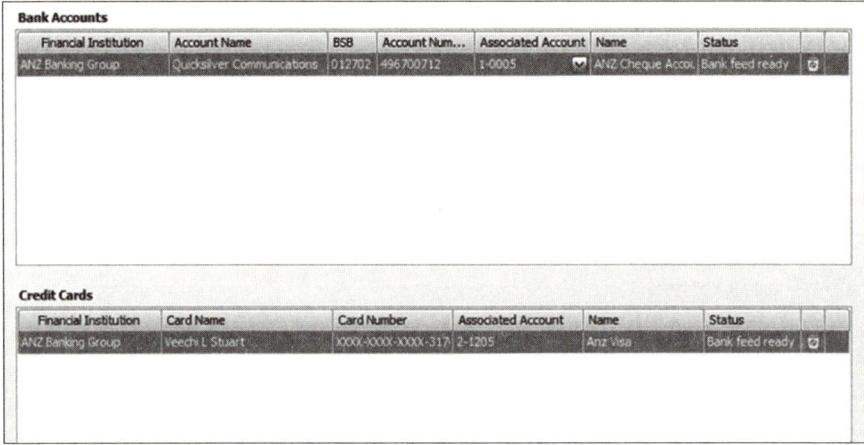

Figure 5-2:
Associating bank feeds with the correct account.

6. Click OK.

Yay. You've now associated this account to your bank feed. You should find yourself at the Bank Feeds window, with the last few days of banking transactions appearing on the screen.

7. Start working through transactions, either adding or matching them one by one.

I talk more about this process later in this chapter, in 'Using Bank Feeds to Add and Match Transactions'.

You only have to associate a bank account the very first time you start using bank feeds. However, you need to click Get Bank Transactions in the top-left of the Bank Feeds window every time you want to update banking transactions.

Dealing with the dim and distant past

If you're new to MYOB, you may well find that you have lots of transactions appearing on your bank statement for the days, weeks or months before your bank feed went live. For example, maybe you opened your business in March, but applied for your bank feed in late April. Your bank feed will only include transaction details from May onwards, leaving you with several weeks' worth of transactions to record.

Don't worry. You can still enter these initial transactions manually. Using your bank statement as a reference, enter each transaction one by one from this statement, keeping the following in mind:

✔ For all withdrawals other than employee pays, go to Spend Money in the Banking command centre. Chapter 6 explains more about the Spend Money feature.

✔ For all employee pays, go to Process Payroll in the Payroll command centre. Chapter 11 explains more about this process.

✔ For all customer payments, assuming you've recorded opening balances for the amounts customers owe you as well as all recent customer invoices, go to Receive Payments in the Banking command centre (Chapter 7 explains more).

✔ For all deposits that aren't related to customer payments, go to Receive Money in the Banking command centre (again, Chapter 7 explains more).

After you catch up to the date where your bank feeds went live, you can change the way you record transactions to take the maximum advantage of the bank feeds feature.

What happens if the bank feeds stop?

Earlier this year I lost my credit card and got the bank to issue a new one. (Alas, only the next day I discovered the missing card, wedged down the side of the sofa.) Unfortunately, I didn't think to notify MYOB of the change and, due to general work-life-children-email overload, I overlooked the imploring emails from MYOB asking me to update my card details. So it wasn't until my bank feeds ceased working that I realised there was a problem. By the time I got the issue sorted, I was left with a gap of a couple of weeks with no bank feed data.

If this kind of thing happens to you, don't worry. Simply figure out which transactions haven't come through on the feed, and enter these transactions manually using Spend Money, Receive Money, Receive Payments or Pay Bills (all of which are explained in Chapters 6 and 7).

Similarly, if your business circumstances change — maybe you feel you can't afford the monthly subscription fee — you can choose to de-subscribe. Assuming you've had an active subscription for at least 12 months, you'll still be able to work on your company file so long as you store the file locally, rather than in the cloud. However, you will have to enter all transactions manually, rather than working from your bank feed.

Using Bank Feeds to Add and Match Transactions

In this section, I assume you've already activated your bank feeds (if not, refer to the preceding section). Whenever you open your company file, start by going to the Banking command centre and clicking Bank Feeds. Click Get Bank Transactions in the top-left, enter your login when prompted, and wait for a moment or two as MYOB downloads recent banking transactions. Magic. With this step complete, you're ready to fulfil your end of the deal.

Understanding the aim of the game

In the same way as the aim of Gin Rummy involves getting rid of all your cards, the aim when working in MYOB is to get rid of all transactions from the Bank Feeds window. At the point when you go to Bank Feeds and no transactions appear, you're winning.

Have a look at Figure 5-3, where I've already worked through some of the transactions. Sharp-eyed readers should be able to spot three different scenarios:

> ✓ **Transactions flagged with a green Approve button.** The Approve button means that *either* MYOB has applied a rule to this transaction

or MYOB has auto-matched this transaction to a transaction that you had already entered.

- ✓ **Transactions flagged with a blue Undo button.** The Undo button means that I've already clicked the Approved button and that the transaction is now marked as reconciled in my bank reconciliation.

- ✓ **Transactions with a choice between clicking Find or New.** In this situation, I have a choice *either* to add a new transaction (and maybe create a rule at the same time) *or* to match this transaction to a transaction I've already entered.

Just because transactions appear in the Bank Feed window doesn't mean they're recorded into MYOB. Transactions that you add by clicking New or by applying a rule aren't recorded in MYOB until the moment you click the Approve button.

When you click Reconcile or Close in the bottom-right of the Bank Feeds window, MYOB removes all approved transactions. When you return to Bank Feeds, these transactions no longer appear.

Figure 5-3:
Once you approve a transaction, the blue Undo button appears.

Bank Statement		-$169.77 CLOSING BALANCE: 23/10/		Approve All	Your Transactions			-$2,316.90 CALCULATED BALANCE	-$2,147.13 OUT OF BALANCE	
Date	Description	Charges	Payments	Match		ID No.	Date	Memo	Charges	Payments
3/10/	SHOEBOXED AUSTRALIA CROWS NEST [3176]	$16.95		Undo	✓ ✪ EFT		3/10/	SHOEBOXED AUSTRALIA CRO...	$16.95	
3/10/	WW PETROL 1362 ULLADULLA [3176]	$37.97		Undo	✓ ✪ EFT		3/10/	WW PETROL 1362 ULLADULLA...	$37.97	
3/10/	WW PETROL 1362 ULLADULLA [3176]	$53.47		Approve	✗ Rule Applied		3/10/	Petrol	$53.47	
6/10/	WOOLWORTHS 1787 KATOOMBA [3176]	$64.38		Find New ▾						
6/10/	MYOB AUSTRALIA BURWOOD EAST [3176]	$124.33		Undo	✓ ✪ EFT		6/10/	MYOB AUSTRALIA BURWOOD...	$124.33	
	ADOBE SYSTEMS									

Matching transactions

Depending on your business, you may not want to work from the bank feed when recording transactions. For example:

- ✓ If you pay employees using MYOB, you record employee pays from the Payroll command centre, not from the Bank Feeds window.

- ✓ If you pay suppliers electronically, and want to create a batch file to import into internet banking, you record supplier payments from the Purchases command centre, not from the Bank Feeds window.

- ✓ If you receive customer payments by cheque or by cash or you issue receipts on the spot, you record customer payments from the Sales command centre, not from the Bank Feeds window.

If you have already entered a transaction, you don't want to add a new transaction from the bank feed. Instead, you want to match this transaction. Mostly, MYOB matches transactions automatically but sometimes, if you have more than one transaction appearing in your bank feed for the same amount, you'll need to match this transaction yourself.

To match a transaction, simply click the Find button. You'll then see a window similar to Figure 5-4. All you have to do next is pick the transaction that matches to the one in your bank feed, and then click Match & Approve.

If you've already recorded a transaction in MYOB, you don't want to add it again from your bank feed. Instead, if MYOB doesn't match this transaction automatically, click the Find button to match it yourself.

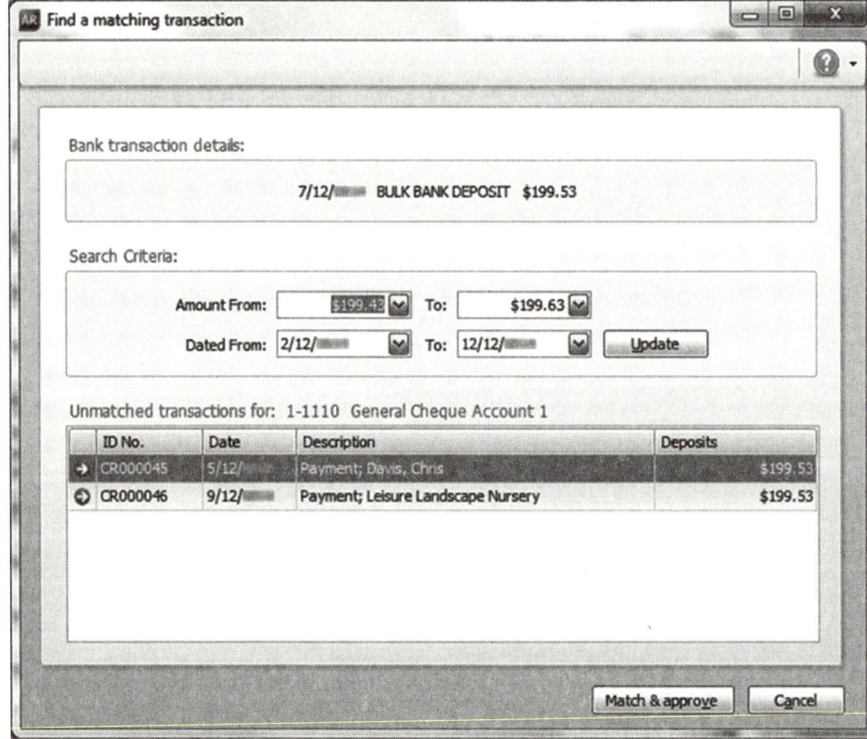

Figure 5-4:
Sometimes
MYOB
needs a
little help
finding a
matching
transaction.

Adding new transactions

I explain in the previous section that if you've already entered a transaction in MYOB, you use the bank feed to match this transaction. However, what about all the transactions on your bank feed that you haven't yet entered into MYOB?

For example, in Figure 5-1, earlier in this chapter, I have four transactions that MYOB hasn't found a match for. One for petrol, one for Woolies, one for a donation to Oxfam and one to Eftel Ltd. To add a transaction, I click the New button. At this point, I have five different options (exactly what wording appears depends on whether I'm dealing with a deposit or a withdrawal):

- ✔ **Spend Money or Receive Money.** I use Spend Money for withdrawals that are one-off expenses or where the expense account varies. For example, the kinds of things I buy at Woolworths (and, therefore, the expense account) vary with each occasion, so I use Spend Money to record this withdrawal. Similarly, I use Receive Money for one-off deposits that don't occur on a regular basis.

- ✔ **Pay Bill or Receive Payment.** Now here's a hint. I hardly ever use Pay Bill or Receive Payment. Why? Chances are, if I receive credit from a supplier or offer credit to a customer, I'm going to have more than one transaction with this person in the years to come. For this reason, I usually create a Bill Rule or an Invoice Rule instead.

- ✔ **Transfer Money.** Although I sometimes use the Transfer Money option to record a transfer of funds from one account to another, I generally prefer to set up a Transaction Rule to record transfers automatically. (See 'Creating rules for funds transfers', later in this chapter, for more details.)

- ✔ **Transaction Rule.** Create Transaction Rules for any withdrawals or deposits that could happen again in the future. For example, I can create a rule that tells MYOB to allocate transactions to Motor Vehicle Expense whenever the word 'petrol' appears in a bank feed. (I talk lots more about creating rules later in this chapter in 'Learning the Rules of the Game'.)

- ✔ **Bill Rule or Invoice Rule.** Create Bill Rules and Invoice Rules for all payments to suppliers or receipts from customers. For example, because I have an account with Eftel and this bill has already been entered as a Purchase, I click Bill Rule to create a rule that tells MYOB that whenever the word 'Eftel' appears on my bank statement, this payment should be matched up against an outstanding bill from this supplier. (For more about creating rules, see 'Learning the Rules of the Game', later in this chapter.)

Every time you add a new transaction, ask yourself if you could create a rule so this transaction could be allocated automatically next time around. Creating rules only takes a few seconds for each one, and saves many hours in the long term.

Balancing your account

Even if you have approved all the transactions from your bank feed, you still need to check your bank account balances. You can do this either by clicking Reconcile Accounts from the Banking command centre, or by clicking the Reconcile button in the bottom-right of the Bank Feeds window.

Once you approve a match in a bank feed, this transaction is automatically ticked off when you go to reconcile the account. If you used to reconcile bank accounts 'the old way' in earlier versions of MYOB software, you'll find that marking off transactions in this way makes the reconciliation process much quicker and simpler. For more about reconciling bank accounts, make your way to Chapter 9.

Dealing with Tricky Situations

Someone wrote me a nice email the other week saying they hardly ever use my book to find out how to do something. (True to the writer's gender, an instruction manual is something to be duly ignored.) Instead, this reader shared, they only refer to this weighty tome when something goes terribly wrong.

With this reader in mind, I'm going to share all the things that can go wrong with adding and matching transactions, along with practical solutions for what to do next.

Transactions that don't match when they should

Earlier in this chapter, I explain that if a transaction doesn't match automatically, you can click the Find button to search for all transactions with that amount. If MYOB fails to find a matching transaction, try expanding the date range in the Find window, which helps match transactions where a wrong date is the cause of the problem. If this doesn't work, ensure that you haven't marked this transaction as being cleared in the Reconcile Accounts.

Sometimes, however, the issue with transactions not matching is more systemic than the occasional error. Here are some common problems, along with suggested solutions:

- ✔ **You receive lots of EFTPOS payments from customers each day and you record these payments individually into MYOB. However, the bank feed only shows a daily total.** The solution is to select Undeposited Funds as the bank account when recording individual payments, and then use the Prepare Bank Deposit feature to transfer funds as a single amount from Undeposited Funds into your bank account. (Chapter 7 explains more about working with Undeposited Funds accounts.)

- ✔ **You use several credit cards associated with a single primary credit card account but only the secondary account appears on the bank feed.** Cancel the bank feed and re-apply, this time ensuring you use the primary credit card number on the application. (Bank feeds can only be associated with a single credit card account.)

- ✔ **You use online banking to pay several different suppliers at once and these payments appear on your bank feed as a single withdrawal.** The solution is to use Prepare Electronic Payments to group payments together. Chapter 8 explains how to work in this way.

Each to their own

I guess it's part of human nature to believe that the way you choose to do things is the best way. However, with MYOB, there is no 'best way' to work.

For example, I have a client who runs a cafe and who lives from day to day in a whirl of activity. Suppliers get paid on a rather ad hoc basis using internet banking, and she never has time to enter bills into MYOB. Bank feeds have transformed the way my client does her books. With the exception of payroll, she uses bank feeds as the starting point to add

all business transactions, and has configured rules so that most transactions are added automatically.

On the other hand, I have a client with a medium-sized manufacturing business who prefers to use MYOB in a more rigorous manner, with purchase orders, supplier bills, electronic payments, payroll and so on. This client uses bank feeds primarily to confirm and match amounts for transactions that have already been recorded.

Getting rid of duplicate transactions

One of the mistakes I often made in the early days of working with bank feeds is that I would add a transaction from my bank feed rather than matching it to an existing transaction that I'd already recorded. This kind of mistake meant that I would end up with two entries in MYOB for the same transaction.

The simplest — and, in my view, much the cleanest — approach to fixing this problem is to delete the duplicate transaction. Go to your Transaction Journal or Bank Register for the date concerned, double-click the transaction you entered manually and select Delete from the Edit menu. (If you receive a warning that this transaction has already been matched to a bank feed, this means you're deleting the wrong one. Click Cancel and instead delete the other transaction out of the matching pair.)

If you find that you've already reconciled the transaction you've entered manually, and you don't want to stuff up your reconciliation, an alternative is to delete the transaction that was matched to the bank feed. If you do this, however, the transaction will re-appear in your Bank Feeds window. To fix this problem, simply right-click on the transaction and select Hide Transaction. This transaction will no longer display unless you select Hidden from the view menu in the top-right corner.

Avoid this problem in the future by always investigating any transactions that show as uncleared in the Reconcile Accounts window. (For more about reconciling accounts, see Chapter 9.)

Dealing with transactions when you don't know where they should go

What should you do if you don't know how to allocate a transaction? The approach I like best is to allocate this kind of transaction to an expense account called 'Suspense' or 'I Don't Know'. Later, you can ask your accountant to review all transactions that have been allocated to this account.

Alternatively, some accountants recommend that when you're in the Bank Feeds window, you right-click transactions you're not sure how to allocate, and then select Hide Transaction. Later, the accountant can go to your Bank Feeds, select Hidden from the Display Transactions menu in the top-right, and review all hidden transactions.

Keep the horse in front of the cart

Do you still occasionally write cheques to suppliers? If so, remember that you don't need to wait for the supplier to present the cheque in order for you to record the payment. Instead, you can record the cheque either using Spend Money or Pay Bills (depending on whether you've recorded the supplier purchase in MYOB, or not). Later, when the cheque appears in your bank feed, you can match it to the transaction you've already created.

I recommend you record cheques as soon as you post them to suppliers. This way,

the balance of your bank account in MYOB more accurately reflects the funds you have available, and your Profit & Loss report stays up to date.

Having said all this, if you are still writing cheques, I recommend you consider shifting entirely to electronic payments (a topic I cover in Chapter 13). Not only are cheques time-consuming and expensive for you, but these days are also usually an irritation for the person who receives them.

The only problem with this method is that if you hide a transaction, it doesn't appear in your Reconcile Accounts window, and you won't be able to properly reconcile your bank account until your accountant has reviewed all hidden transactions. For this reason, allocating tricky transactions to a suspense account is usually a better approach.

Learning the Rules of the Game

As I explain at the beginning of this chapter, the idea of creating rules is to get MYOB to allocate transactions automatically based on the description that appears in the bank feed.

When you go to Bank Feeds you can create Transaction Rules, Bill Rules or Invoice Rules. Use Bill Rules for payments to suppliers where you've already recorded a bill in MYOB; use Invoice Rules for payments from customers where you've already recorded an invoice in MYOB; use Transaction Rules for everything else.

Creating rules for transactions

To add a new transaction based on your bank feed and to create a rule while you're at it, here's what to do:

1. **From the Bank Feeds window, highlight the transaction you want to create a rule for, click New, and then Transaction Rule.**

You end up at a window similar to Figure 5-5, where I'm creating a rule for the payment to Oxfam I made way back in Figure 5-1.

By the way, Transaction Rules are for Spend Money and Receive Money transactions. Invoice Rules are for customer payments; Bill Rules are for supplier payments.

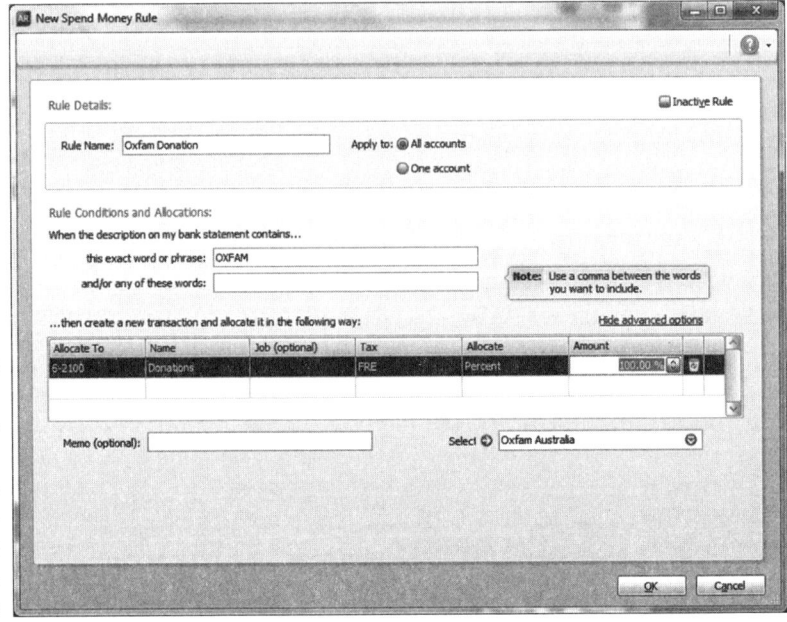

Figure 5-5:
Creating a new transaction rule seems easy, but take care with the detail.

2. **Give the rule a name that's short and sweet.**

   MYOB defaults to using the whole description that was on the bank feed as the Rule Name. However, whatever you choose as the name for a rule ends up doubling as your transaction memo (unless you choose to override the Memo settings in the advanced options). So in my example, although MYOB offers up 'Oxfam Australia 1 Carlton [3176]' as Rule Name (because this was the description from the bank feed), I change the Rule Name to read simply 'Oxfam Donation'.

3. **Choose whether to apply to All Accounts or one account only.**

   Unless you have a good reason not to, always set rules so they run on all accounts. (Otherwise, you have to create a different set of rules for each bank account, which is unnecessarily painful.)

4. **Specify what words or phrase is going to trigger this rule.**

   Incidentally, the text I enter here isn't case-sensitive, so regardless of whether I write 'oxfam', 'Oxfam' or 'OXFAM', the rule will still work.

At the time of writing, MYOB doesn't offer the option to base rules on certain amounts, rather than certain words. So, if you have regular payments of different amounts all going to the same company (maybe you have several different lease payments), the best approach is to set up recurring transactions, as opposed to rules, for each of these payments. See 'Choosing between rules and recurring transactions' later in this chapter for more details.

5. **Click Advanced Options, choose an Allocation Account and check the Tax code is correct.**

   I won't go into all the details about choosing allocation accounts and tax codes at this point — these topics are covered in other chapters. However, the neat thing to note about the Advanced Options is that you can split transactions across two or more accounts.

6. **Select a Card.**

   Still in Advanced Options, enter the name of the person you're paying (or who is paying who) in the Card field.

   Although selecting a card isn't mandatory, remember that unless you select a card, you won't be able to look up all transactions for this supplier in the future. In Figure 5-5, for example, I enter 'Oxfam' as the Card (and, if necessary, I create a supplier card with this name) so that I can generate a report listing of donations made to Oxfam at any point in the future.

7. **Click OK to save your new rule.**

   MYOB not only saves this rule for the future, but also adds a new transaction based on the information you just entered.

8. **Click Approve and, if this rule also applies to other transactions in the Bank Feed window, click the Refresh button.**

   The Refresh button is the green circular arrow in the top-right.

Yay, you've done it! The next step is to see whether you can create rules for customer or supplier payments. Read on, dear friend . . .

Looking at rules for invoices or bills

I was debating with a colleague this week about whether it's worth creating rules for customer and supplier payments. My colleague argued that she doesn't bother, because even when MYOB allocates the payment automatically, she still feels compelled to click the transaction to check whether MYOB has allocated it to the correct invoice or bill. My counter-argument is that even if you do double-check allocations in this way, the rule still makes everything a tad quicker.

Anyway, enough debate. Here's how to create rules for customer or supplier payments:

1. **From the Bank Feeds window, highlight the payment you want to create a rule for.**

2. **Click New followed by Invoice Rule for customer payments, or New followed by Bill Rule for supplier payments.**

3. **Give the rule a name.**

    I find that the supplier or customer name is usually enough here.

4. **Choose whether to apply to All Accounts or one account only.**

    Select All Accounts unless you have a good reason to do otherwise.

5. **Specify what words or phrase is going to trigger this rule into action.**

    With customers, your choice of words very much depends on what that customer chooses to include as the text on their payment. If the customer name appears on the statement, this is usually ideal, as is an account number. Avoid invoice numbers because these change with every payment.

    With suppliers, you control what appears on your bank statement. For this reason, be consistent about what text you enter when making internet payments.

6. **Select the customer or supplier name.**

7. **Click OK to save the rule.**

    You arrive back at the Bank Feeds window.

8. **Click Approve to add this transaction.**

    All done!

Creating rules that make you look really smart

Here are some tips on creating a reliable set of rules that will have everyone singing your praises:

✔ For transactions that tend to be a mixture of taxable and non-taxable amounts, and where the amounts vary (such as any kind of grocery purchase), you can still create a rule. However, in the Advanced Options menu, enter 'Need to Check GST Amounts' as the Memo. This Memo will then appear in the Bank Feeds window and prompt you to check the GST. (You can then edit this Memo once you know the GST is correct.)

✔ Sometimes, you can create a single rule that captures lots of different suppliers. For example, look at Figure 5-6 and how I create a single rule for all the different places where I buy petrol.

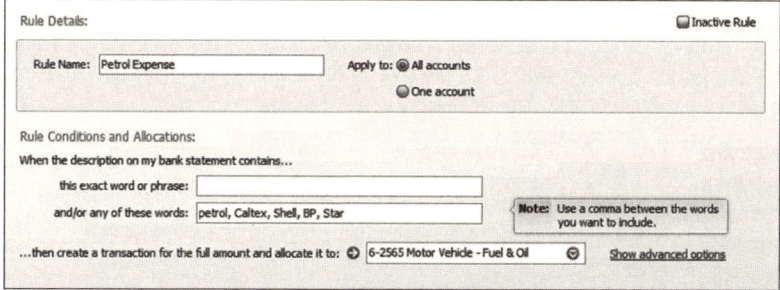

Figure 5-6: You can create a single rule that captures payments to lots of different suppliers.

✔ Go through your list of rules periodically and review how you've set your conditions. If you can see two rules that have the same conditions, either delete one of the rules or vary one of the conditions.

✔ For expenses you regularly split between business and personal (for example, maybe you always allocate 85 per cent of petrol to business and 15 per cent to personal), use the advanced options to create a rule that does this split automatically.

✔ Be vigilant when it comes to spaces. For example, I created a rule for a supplier the other week that just didn't work. It turned out that I'd added a space after the supplier name when listing words in the rule conditions.

✔ Don't get lazy and click Approve without first resting your mouse on the Rule Applied icon. This way, MYOB displays what account the transaction has been allocated to, and you can nip any problems with rules in the bud.

✔ Watch your spelling. (Need I say more?)

Changing transactions when rules apply

What happens if MYOB automatically applies a rule to a transaction but you know the allocation is not quite correct in this instance? For example, maybe you've spent $50 at the petrol station and you can see MYOB has applied a rule to allocate this transaction to Motor Vehicle Expense. However, you are privy to the secret knowledge that actually you only spent $40 on petrol. The remaining $10 was devoured in chocolate.

Although you can't edit a transaction in the first stage when the rule has been applied, you can edit a transaction after you click Approve. So even if you know the transaction isn't quite right, click the Approve button. Then, drill into the transaction by clicking the zoom arrow next to the date.

 At this point, you can confidently change any of the information apart from the total amount. Please don't change the amount. Not only does changing the amount make no sense at all (because you know this amount matches perfectly with your bank statement), but if you do change the amount, MYOB also un-matches the transaction, and many difficulties can unfold.

Keeping Rules Neat as a Pin

I don't know about you, but every spring I'm filled with a somewhat manic wellspring of energy. My husband groans in anticipation as weekend after weekend unfolds in a series of home renovation and spring-cleaning projects.

If you too feel restless, can I suggest you apply any spring-cleaning enthusiasm to your list of rules? Go to Manage Rules from the Bank Feeds window, and review every rule. This section explains just how.

Choosing between rules and recurring transactions

In the past, before bank feeds, I used recurring transactions in two different ways.

- ✔ For transactions that happened on a regular basis, with the same amount each week or month, I created recurring transactions that recorded automatically without me having to do a thing.

- ✔ For transactions that varied in amount but had several allocation accounts, such as BAS payments or daily sales journals, I created recurring transactions that didn't record automatically, and which I edited each time.

Now with bank feeds in the picture, I replace most automatic recurring transactions by creating a Transaction Rule instead. I find the dates end up more accurate this way (because automatic recurring transactions only record when you open your company file, the date can slip off course if you don't open your file every day).

For transactions that vary in amount each time and have complex splits across several accounts, I still use the recurring transactions feature.

Creating rules for funds transfers

On the MYOB forum boards, I've seen several requests asking MYOB for the option to create rules for funds transfers. MYOB have indicated this feature will be considered for a future upgrade and so may even be in place by the time you're reading this. However, if not, I can share with you a really easy workaround.

When you transfer funds with internet banking, the last four digits or so of your account number almost always appear on your bank feed description. All you need to do is to create Transaction Rules that specify that if this number appears in the description, the transaction should be allocated to a specific bank account.

If the description on your bank feed doesn't include the last few digits of your account number (and the descriptions do vary from bank to bank), a neat workaround is to use the supplier payment feature of your internet banking rather than the transfer funds feature. (For example, create a new payee called something like 'Transfer to Savings' and enter your savings account details as the bank account details for this payee.) This way, you can create a transaction rule so that every time the words 'Transfer to Savings' appear in your bank feed, MYOB automatically allocates this transaction to your savings account.

Editing and deleting rules

Keep an eye out for duplicate or conflicting rules, especially those that conflict in the way they treat transactions. For example, imagine I have a lease with ABC Leasing for my car and a lease with ABC Copiers for my photocopier and I create one rule that allocates any transaction with 'ABC' in the description to Photocopy Lease Expense, and another rule that allocates any transaction with 'Leasing' in the description to 'Motor Vehicle Lease Expense'. In this situation, MYOB won't know which rule to select when it sees the words 'ABC Copiers' or 'ABC Leasing' on my statement.

Similarly, imagine I create a rule that says to allocate any transaction that has 'BP' as part of the statement text to Motor Vehicle Fuel expense (I'm thinking of BP petrol stations here). Sounds fine, but this rule can potentially conflict with any other rule that has 'BPAY' as part of the statement text.

I haven't quite figured out what logic MYOB uses when rules conflict with one another in this way, but I have noticed the general result is mayhem and inconsistency!

To review or change rules, go to Manage Rules from the Bank Rules window, double-click the rule you want to edit, make your changes and click OK. To delete a rule, either double-click the wastepaper icon to the right of the rule or right-click the rule and select Delete.

Fixing things when you get a rule wrong

While allocation rules can be a real boon, they can also be a total pain if you get the rule wrong — because, unless you're super sharp-eyed, the mistake gets repeated again and again.

Imagine that somebody else — not you, of course! — has created a rule saying that any transaction with 'Telstra' as part of the description should be allocated to Advertising Expense. You, lucky bunny, are the one left mopping up the mess. Here's what to do:

1. **Find out how long the error has been happening.**

   In my example, I go to Find Transactions (found on the bottom of all command centres), click the Account tab, enter the number for my Advertising Expense account and try to diagnose when the first payment to Telstra appeared in this account.

2. **Reallocate the culprit transactions.**

   You can do this in one of two ways. The simplest approach is to click on each transaction that's wrong and change the allocation code, one by one. However, if you have lots and lots of errors, changing each transaction can be very time-consuming. An alternative approach is to record a journal entry that shifts the total value of the error from one account to another. (Unless you're a trained bookkeeper, you may need to ask your accountant for help with this journal.)

3. **From the Bank Feeds window, click Manage Rules and edit the rule so the mistake doesn't happen again!**

Incidentally, you can usually prevent mistakes in bank rules perpetuating themselves by double-checking how rules are applied. Whenever MYOB applies a rule to a bank feed transaction, rest your mouse (without clicking!) on the Rule Applied icon that appears to the left of the transaction to see a summary of what allocation account MYOB has chosen.

Chapter 6

There Goes Your Cash!

*I*t's funny that I ended up spending so much of my working life ploughing through figures and accounts. I hate finicky details, I get bored by repetitive work and I'm naturally impatient (even eating is often an unbearable distraction from the buzz of life).

Working with accounting software has taught me many lessons over the years. I'm much more careful and precise these days, and on occasions (when no-one is watching) you could even accuse me of being infuriatingly pedantic. Why? Because it's the best way to be when you're dealing with your own money and all those little expenses that nibble away at your bottom line. After all, if I don't get my expenses right I might miss out on valuable tax deductions — the mere suggestion of which makes my Scottish blood run cold.

In this chapter, I explain how to record day-to-day expenses, including how to choose the correct expense account, what tax code to use when, and how to find, change or delete transactions. This chapter also deals with the rather irritating and fiddly topic of petty cash, one of those things in life that takes up a disproportionate amount of time given the small amount of money involved.

Recording Expenses

Regardless of whether you work directly from the Bank Feeds menu or whether you still record transactions manually, you record most day-to-day expenses (other than employee pays or supplier payments) using Spend Money transactions. The main difference when working with bank feeds is that I suggest you set up rules so that you can semi-automate recording most transactions. (For more about bank feeds and allocation rules, refer to Chapter 5.)

Spending money? That's the fun bit

Nervous? Don't be. Take these steps to make sure you do things right:

1. **If you're working with bank feeds, select Spend Money from the New menu next to the transaction you want to add. If you're not working with bank feeds, go to the Banking command centre and choose Spend Money.**

   In Chapter 5, I explain how you may want to create a Transaction Rule rather than recording a Spend Money transaction if you make payments to this person or company on a regular basis.

2. **Ignore the Cheque No. field.**

   Unless you're actually recording an old-fashioned cheque, ignore the Cheque No. Field completely. (If you're working from bank feeds, MYOB populates this field with the word 'EFT', which is just fine; if you're not working from a bank feed, MYOB populates this field with a sequential number, which you can just ignore.)

3. **If you're not working from a bank feed, select your bank account.**

   For cheques that you've already sent or electronic transactions that have already gone out of your bank account, select your business bank account in the Pay from Account drop-down list in the top-left corner (if you only have one business bank account, this account will be selected already).

   If this transaction hasn't actually happened yet, and you want to use MYOB to create an electronic payment batch for you, ready to send off to the bank, click Group with Electronic Payments.

4. **Check that the Tax Inclusive box is selected.**

   See the little box called Tax Inclusive at the top? Click here if you intend to enter amounts including GST (I find this method usually works best).

5. **If you're not working from a bank feed, enter the Date and the Amount.**

If you're feeling cool, calm and collected, take note that you only have to type the part of the date that has changed. For example, if the date says 01/05/15 and you want to change it to 05/05/15, all you have to do is type the number 5 and press the Enter key.

6. **Enter the name of the person you're paying in the Card field and press Enter.**

If you've never recorded a payment for this person before, a list of names appears. Either double-click a name to select it from the list or click New to create a new card. (Chapter 2 explains more about setting up new supplier cards.)

If your transaction relates to a supplier payment, you may get a warning that says you should go to Pay Bills, rather than Spend Money. This message can be perturbing but the answer is simple: If you've already recorded a purchase in the Supplier command centre for this supplier, and this transaction is paying that bill, you need to go to Pay Bills to match this payment against the purchase. If you haven't recorded any purchases for this supplier, click OK to ignore the warning message.

7. **If you've asked to group this transaction as an electronic payment, check the Statement Text.**

The Statement Text shows what will appear on the bank statement of the person or business who receives your payment.

8. **Record a brief but illuminating description in the Memo field.**

Let your literary talents run wild, describing what this payment is all about. Alternatively, if the transaction is self-explanatory (maybe you're paying Telstra and allocating the payment to Telephone Expense), you can simply skip the Memo field or, if you're using bank feeds, accept the default memo that MYOB offers.

9. **Decide which account this expense should go to.**

Everything has a place. You just have to figure out which expense account you want to allocate your payment to. (See also 'Picking the right expense account', next in this chapter.) Press the Tab key to view your Accounts List and then select the relevant account from the list. By now, your payment should look similar to mine, shown in Figure 6-1.

10. **If you want to track cost centres or projects, enter a job or category code in the Job column or Category field.**

If you track expenses by particular jobs, projects or cost centres, record the relevant details in the Job column or Category field (for more details about jobs and categories, see Chapter 17). Otherwise, just cruise on by, pressing the Tab key to progress to the Tax column.

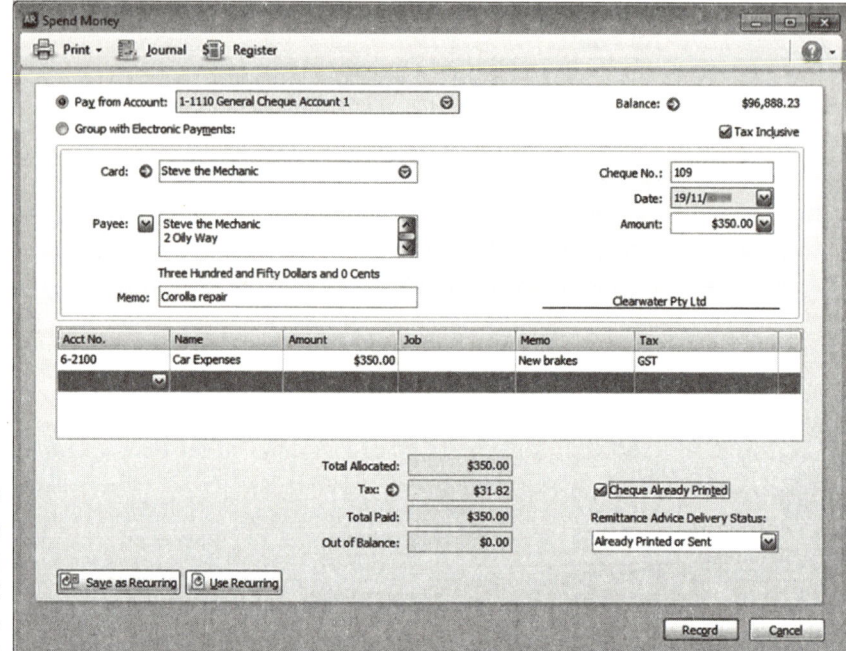

Figure 6-1:
Recording
your first
payment.

11. Double-check the tax code.

Make sure the tax code is correct (see the section 'Choosing the right code', later in this chapter) and that the amount of GST comes up correctly in the Tax total. Most payments either have GST as the tax code (advertising, computer stuff, rent, telephone and so on) or FRE as the tax code (bank charges, donations, government charges and so on).

12. Decide whether you want to email this supplier a remittance advice.

This decision is only relevant if you haven't yet paid this person, and you're going to use MYOB to create an electronic batch file that you then open up in your internet banking. If this is the case, select To Be Emailed as the Remittance Advice Delivery Status.

13. Click Record.

If you want to prepare an electronic payment batch that includes this transaction, proceed to the Prepare Electronic Payments window, which I explore in more detail in Chapter 13.

Picking the right expense account

The real skill of bookkeeping (aside from accuracy) lies in knowing which account to select. Although I can't provide you with hard-and-fast rules about which account you should select in every situation, Table 6-1 provides some pointers on a few of the transactions that are trickiest to allocate.

Table 6-1	Matchmaking Payments and Accounts	
Type of Expense or Payment	*Comments*	*Use This Account*
Bank charges	Regular bank charges go to Bank Fees, and bank charges for merchant facilities (credit cards) go to Merchant Fees. Interest goes to Interest Expense.	Bank Fees Merchant Fees Interest Expense
Coffee, biscuits, tea, toilet rolls	The essentials for happy employees go into an account called Staff Amenities.	Staff Amenities
Government charges	Company return lodgements go to Filing Fees, licence renewals go to Licence Fees and stamp duty on insurance goes to Insurance Expense.	Filing Fees Licence Fees Insurance Expense
Hire purchase/ leases	A hire purchase is a different beastie to a lease. Ask your accountant if you're not sure what you have.	Hire Purchase (liability) Lease Expense
Miscellaneous expenses	Avoid accounts such as Sundry Expense or Miscellaneous Expense. Instead, create a new account or use an existing account which is a close match.	Office Supplies Repairs & Maintenance Staff Amenities
Motor vehicle expenses	If you have more than one vehicle and these vehicles are used for both personal and business, either create separate accounts or job codes for each motor vehicle.	Motor Vehicle Fuel Motor Vehicle Insurance Motor Vehicle Repairs

(continued)

Table 6-1 *(continued)*

Type of Expense or Payment	Comments	Use This Account
New equipment	If new equipment goes over the asset threshold ($1,000 before GST at the time of writing, but do check with your accountant), allocate this purchase to an asset account, not an expense.	Furniture & Fittings (asset) Plant & Equipment (asset) Asset Pool (asset)
Office repairs	If a repair is minor, allocate to Repairs & Maintenance. If a repair counts as an improvement (a new veranda or skylight, for example), it is probably an asset. Ask your accountant if you're not sure.	Repairs & Maintenance Leasehold Improvements (asset) Building Improvements (asset)
Personal spending (sole trader or partnership)	Always be careful to separate personal spending from business spending.	Personal Drawings (equity account)
Personal spending (director or shareholder of a company)	A company director or shareholder can only use company funds for personal purposes if they take these funds in the form of wages or directors' fees or as a debit against a Directors' or Shareholders' Loan account.	Directors'/Shareholders' Loan (liability account) Directors' Fees Wages Expense
Stock purchases	If you track inventory costs and stock levels, allocate new purchases to an account called Inventory. Otherwise, allocate stock purchases to a Purchases account.	Inventory Purchases (cost of sales account)
Subcontractors	Never muddle subbies and employees. Keep subbie payments entirely separate from wages.	Subcontractor Expense
Superannuation	Assuming you're using MYOB's payroll features, allocate super payments to Superannuation Payable.	Superannuation Payable (liability)

Type of Expense or Payment	Comments	Use This Account
Taxes	Every bookkeeper's nightmare! Be careful where you allocate tax payments and remember that the only tax payments that ever get coded as an expense are Fringe Benefits Tax and, in some situations, Land Tax.	Company Tax (liability) Fringe Benefits Tax (expense) GST Collected/Paid (liability) PAYG Payable (liability) Personal Drawings (equity)
Travel	Keep local travel separate from overseas travel (and remember that overseas travel doesn't have any GST on it).	Travel Expense Domestic Travel Expense Overseas
Wages	If you have lots of employees, you may want to consider creating a few wages expense accounts so you can see more detail about wages in your Profit & Loss reports.	Wages Expense

If you're not always sure which account to choose, create a new expense account called 'Suspense' and number this account 6-9999. (Using a suspense account is another way of saying 'I haven't a clue where this should go; maybe someone else knows'.) Allocate transactions to this account whenever you're not sure where they belong and later — perhaps every month or so — ask someone more knowledgeable than yourself (I suggest your accountant) to help you reallocate these transactions to the correct accounts.

Splitting an expense across more than one account

What happens if you want to allocate an expense to more than one account? Simply add another line, splitting the transaction across as many lines as required.

Figure 6-2 shows how to split a single payment across more than one account. In my example, the home office telephone bill is split between Telephone Expense (which I claim as a tax deduction) and Personal Drawings. Lovely.

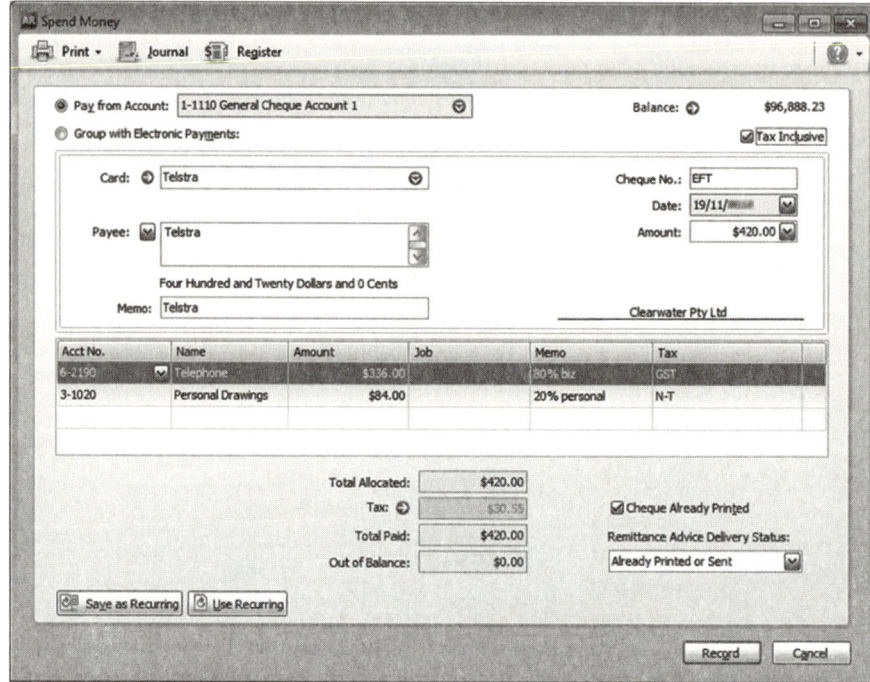

Figure 6-2:
Splitting
expenses
across more
than one
account.

Working with credit cards

Recording credit card transactions is the same as recording any other kind of transactions. However, here are a couple of comments specific to credit cards:

- Bank feeds really come into their own when recording credit card spending. Once you have allocation rules configured, you probably cut the time required to enter transactions by about 90 per cent.

- If you don't have bank feeds enabled, the easiest way to record credit card transactions if from the Bank Register. If your credit card appears in your Accounts List but not as a choice in your Bank Register, go to your Accounts List and ensure you have selected Credit Card as the Account Type.

- If you already have an amount outstanding on the credit card when you create its account, you can record the balance in the Opening Balance field. However, if you do so, make a note of the amount and tell your accountant — the opening balance amount also appears in your special Historical Balancing account, which your accountant can sort out later.

Cards, cards and more cards

You don't have to type a name in the Card field every time you record an expense. It's quite possible to skip straight past this step and either enter a name in the Payee field or leave both the Card and Payee completely blank.

However, I can give you two reasons why it's not a good idea to leave the Card field blank. First, if you set up a Card for someone the first time you pay them, the next time you pay that person you only have to type the first few letters of their name and the rest completes itself — what more could a two-fingered typist wish for? Second, if you enter Card field details for all your payments, later you're able to look things up, sorted by name. For example, if you always enter Telstra in the Card field when paying your telephone bill, you can go to the Find Transactions menu, click the Card tab, enter Telstra as the name and view all payments ever made to Telstra.

If you create a new transaction rule direct from your bank feed, you may think you don't have the option to select Card details. Don't be hoodwinked — click the Advanced Options button to reveal all.

✔ If some of the debits on your credit card statement are for personal purchases (credit cards often end up with a mix of business and private transactions), choose a drawings account or a director's loan account as the allocation account for these purchases.

✔ A credit card is like any other bank account — you need to reconcile your credit card account in the same way as you reconcile your other business bank accounts. (Chapter 9 explains more about reconciling bank accounts.)

To record credit card payments, see 'Transferring money from one account to another', later in this chapter.

Managing Your Bank Accounts

One of the secrets of good bookkeeping is to keep track of every single business bank account. In other words, don't just record transactions for your main business account, but do so for business-related savings accounts, credit card accounts, PayPal accounts, loans and so on.

In the next couple of pages, I explain how to set up multiple bank accounts in MYOB, and how to record the transfer of funds from one account to another.

Dealing with multiple bank accounts

Here's how to add additional bank accounts to MYOB:

1. **Check all your bank accounts are listed in your Accounts List.**

   To view your Accounts List, go to your Accounts command centre and click Accounts List. When you click the Asset tab in your Accounts List you see all your bank accounts listed near the top. (The only exceptions are credit cards and overdrafts, which are listed on the Liability tab.)

2. **If a bank account is missing, work out a suitable number for this account and click New.**

   If you're creating a new bank account at this point, ask yourself where you want the account to appear in the list. Think of a suitable number before you click New.

   If you're going to use this bank account more than any other, give it the lowest number possible. That way, this account appears highest in your Accounts List and comes up automatically whenever you go to Spend Money or Receive Money.

3. **Enter the Account Number and Account Name.**

   Enter the Account Number you just created, press the Tab key with determination, and then type the Account Name — for example, 'Westpac Savings Account'.

4. **Choose the Account Type.**

   This bit is important so listen up. As the Account Type, select either Bank (for asset accounts) or Credit Card (for liability accounts).

5. **Click OK.**

6. **If you subscribe to bank feeds — generally an excellent idea — proceed to the Bank Feeds menu in the Banking command centre and apply for a bank feed for this account.**

   I explain all about applying for bank feeds in Chapter 5.

 If you set up a new bank account in MYOB that is going to be your main trading account, you may also want to edit the linked bank account settings for customer payments, supplier payments and payroll transactions. To do this, go to Setup and check each of the menus under Linked Accounts.

Making electronic payments

Most newcomers to MYOB start out by making payments as they normally would — by cash, cheque, internet transfer or credit card — and then recording these payments in MYOB afterwards, either manually or by adding transactions direct from bank feeds. This method works fine, but if you process lots of supplier or employee payments, I recommend you use MYOB as your starting point instead: Begin by recording the payment in your company file and then send the payment electronically to your bank, ready for transfer.

When I talk about recording your first payment at the beginning of this chapter, I note that if you plan to use MYOB to prepare payments as an electronic batch, you click the Group with Electronic Payments button, rather than selecting a bank account from your list. After that, you progress to the Prepare Electronic Payments window, where you can create a file to send to your bank. What happens next, and much more, is covered in Chapter 13.

Transferring money from one account to another

How you record the transfer of funds from one bank account depends on whether you're using bank feeds or not.

If you use bank feeds, the simplest approach is to set up a transaction rule so that MYOB allocates fund transfers automatically. All you have to do then is review how MYOB has allocated the transfer and click Approve. I explain how to configure a transaction rule for transfers in Chapter 5.

If you're not using bank feeds, go to the Accounts command centre and click Transfer Money. Select the account you're transferring money from, followed by the account that you're transferring money to, enter the amount, a memo if desired, and then click Record.

To check out the balance of your bank accounts, assuming you're up to date with all your recorded transactions, select Account Details from the Business Insights menu in the bottom-right corner.

Understanding GST (You'll Be the Only One)

GST made easy? I may as well be writing a treatise on the inner workings of a guillotine. But I'm not easily discouraged, so here's my very easy to swallow — oops, I mean follow — take on which tax code to choose when, and how to calculate GST backwards. If you're after more nitty-gritty GST details, try Chapter 15.

Choosing the right code

If you're registered for GST, every time you record a transaction in MYOB, you need to complete the Tax column, as follows:

- ✔ If the payment is for goods or services that attract GST, select GST as the tax code.

- ✔ If the payment is for a new piece of equipment or furniture, select CAP as your tax code. (CAP stands for capital acquisitions.) Depending on whether you're eligible for small business entity concessions (ask your accountant if you're not sure), the threshold for capital acquisitions is either $100 (if you're not eligible) or $1,000 (if you are). However, this threshold changes frequently, so do check with your accountant.

- ✔ If the payment is for goods or services that are GST-free (medical supplies, GST-free food and so on), select FRE as your tax code.

- ✔ If the payment is for goods or services that are for your own private use, select N-T as the tax code.

- ✔ If the person you're trading with isn't registered for GST but has an ABN, select FRE as your tax code.

- ✔ If the payment is for goods or services that you'll use to make input taxed sales (perhaps you're a residential landlord and you're paying for plumbing repairs), select INP as your tax code.

Whenever you pay for something and you want to claim a GST credit, make sure you obtain a proper Tax Invoice, complete with the supplier's ABN.

Getting tax codes right, automatically

When you record expenses, does the tax code always come up as N-T, meaning you have to remember to change the code every time? If so, you haven't set up your Accounts List correctly.

Save yourself time by correcting these default codes. Go to your Accounts List, double-click every account one by one, and under the Details tab of each account, edit the Tax Code field.

If you're registered for GST, most income and expense accounts require either GST or FRE as their code (although there are some exceptions, of course). If you need more help figuring out which code to pick, see Chapter 15 or ask your accountant.

Recording mixed transactions

Whenever you buy a mix of things that include GST and things that don't, you'll find that GST ends up not being one-eleventh of the total but something quite different. What do you do?

The trick is to record your payment but split the transaction over two lines. For example, if you pay for insurance and $1,000 attracts GST, but the $250 stamp duty is free, record the transaction's details on two lines. On the first line, select insurance expense as your allocation account, type $1,000 as the Amount and select GST as your tax code. On the next line, select insurance expense as the allocation account again, but this time type $250 as the Amount and select FRE as your tax code.

Depending on the format of the receipt or bill that you're working from, you may find the amounts make more sense if you unclick the Tax Inclusive box at the top of the Spend Money window. You can toggle between viewing amounts inclusive or exclusive of GST simply by clicking and unclicking this box.

Locating and Changing Transactions

So, you've recorded heaps of transactions and now you want to be able to view your work — maybe you want to change a transaction, check whether you've entered something correctly, or even delete a mistake. You can do all these things either by going to your Bank Register or to Find Transactions.

Badgering the Bank Register

Go to the Banking command centre and click Bank Register. (Or, alternatively, click the Register button that appears at the top of your Spend Money window.) A list of all bank account transactions appears (see Figure 6-3 for an example), showing all deposits and withdrawals made over the current month.

If the transaction you're looking for belongs to a previous month, change the dates in the Dated From and To boxes and press the Enter key. Quick as a flash, up come all your transactions listed in date order. Scroll down until you find the transaction you're looking for, and then click the arrow to the left of the transaction to display it.

If you're hunting for a withdrawal that came out of a different bank account, simply change the Account selection in the top-left corner.

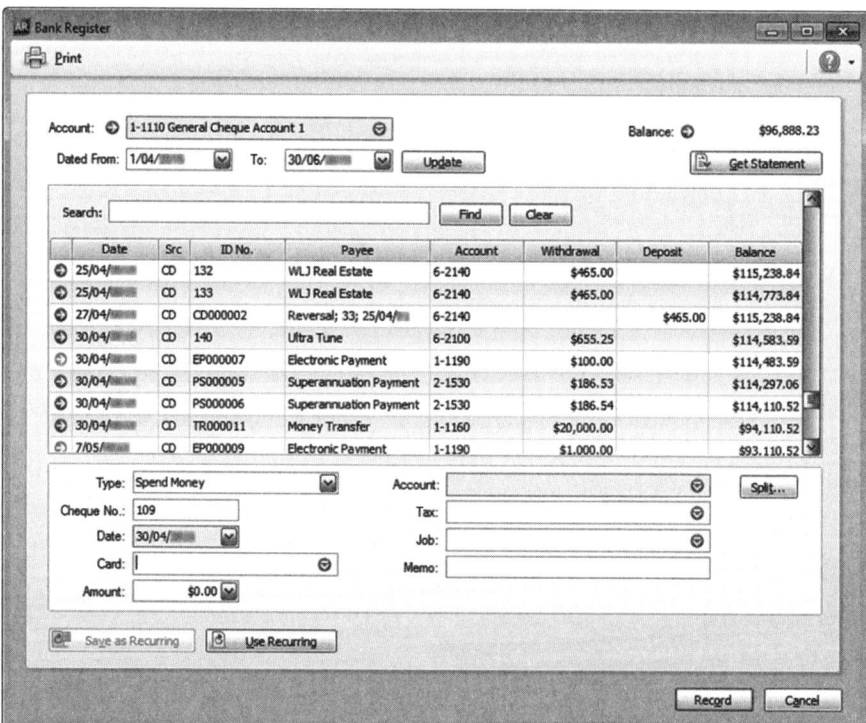

Figure 6-3:
Viewing
transactions
in your Bank
Register.

Flipping out with Find Transactions

Every command centre has a menu at the bottom labelled Find Transactions, with an arrow pointing downwards next to it. When you click this arrow you can select Card from the drop-down menu that appears.

The Find Transactions menu is the best place to find most transactions. Type the name of someone you paid recently in the Card field, and then enter suitable dates in the Dated From and To fields. Press the Tab key and up pops a list of all transactions linked to that person or business for that time period. Double-click any transaction to view the details. (Alternatively, you can click the Account tab from the Find Transactions menu and search by a particular expense or income account.)

When working in Find Transactions (or any similar window in MYOB, such as the Sales or Purchases Register), press Ctrl+Shift+F (that is, hold all three keys down at the same time) to bring up a Search window at the top. Enter whatever text or amount you're looking for, and the list automatically updates to display all transactions that match.

One pitfall when working direct from bank feeds is that MYOB doesn't prompt you to select a Card when creating allocation rules. The result is that MYOB leaves the Card blank and, later on, you're unable to search for transactions according to the name of the person you paid. For this reason, always click Advanced Options and specify a Card when creating rules.

Deleting transactions

You want to delete a Spend Money transaction? Easy:

1. **Find this transaction in your Bank Register or via the Find Transactions menu.**

   Refer to the two preceding sections for help with this.

2. **Double-click the transaction to display it.**

3. **Select Edit⇨Delete Cheque Transaction.**

   The Edit command is right up on the top menu bar. After you select Delete Cheque Transaction, the screen flickers for a second and your payment disappears, never to be seen again.

Sometimes, you can't (or shouldn't) delete a payment. Here's why:

 ✔ If you select the Edit command and you only see the option to Reverse Cheque Transaction, not Delete Cheque Transaction, then you have to reverse this transaction instead. Read the section 'Reversing transactions', later in this chapter, to find out why.

 ✔ If you try to delete a Spend Money transaction and a warning appears telling you that one or more parts of this journal entry have been reconciled, stop dead in your tracks and don't even think of continuing. When you delete a reconciled transaction, you throw your bank reconciliation out of whack — something you'll bitterly regret at a later date. If you really need to get rid of a transaction that has been reconciled (maybe you recorded an amount using Spend Money rather than Pay Bills), your best option is to reverse it. (See 'Reversing transactions'.)

When deleting a transaction, you may also get a warning that changing this transaction may undo the approval and unmatch it. What this message means is that you've already matched this transaction to a bank feed and so, when you delete the transaction, the amount will appear once more in your Bank Feeds menu. No dramas. Because you haven't reconciled this transaction yet, unmatching it is just fine.

Sticky fingers, sticky situations

In this chapter, I explain how to delete transactions. Unlike some accounting software, deleting transactions is something that MYOB permits, so long as your security preferences are configured the right way.

Clients sometimes ask me whether it's safe to allow transactions to be changed or deleted, and in situations where there are a few employees, all working in MYOB, my reply is often ambivalent. On the one hand, you want employees to have the flexibility to fix mistakes but, on the other hand, you probably don't want employees to be able to edit customer invoices after they're sent, or edit the amount of an electronic transaction.

On the whole, I prefer to set security preferences so that transactions can be changed, because this flexibility makes for a less confusing set of books. (People inevitably do make mistakes, and when you can't delete things, you end up with reversals, then reversals of reversals, and so on.) However, if you configure MYOB so employees can edit or delete transactions, you're best to put a few fraud prevention strategies in place.

I could write a whole chapter on fraud prevention, but I can quickly summarise my strategies as follows:

- If possible, don't allow the bookkeeper to handle cash, do the banking or authorise electronic payments.

- Review transaction changes by running the Journal Security Audit report on a regular basis. This report is very powerful and can be filtered to show not only adjustments or changes, but deletions also. You can also filter this report by user name — ideal if you're worried that a particular employee may not be doing the right thing.

- Only the business owner should have access to the Administrator password.

- Define user roles carefully so that employees doing general work in MYOB, such as entering sales, don't have access to other parts of the software.

I talk more about password restrictions and security in Chapter 1.

Changing transactions

Sometimes you may want to change a Spend Money transaction, rather than delete it. Perhaps you allocated an expense to the wrong account or entered the amount as $97 rather than $79. Fortunately, fixing mistakes is easy.

Find the offending transaction in the Bank Register and double-click this transaction to display it. Now, just make your changes and click Record.

If, when you try to change a transaction, a warning pops up (similar to Figure 6-4) telling you that one or more parts of this journal entry have been reconciled, think very carefully. If a transaction has been reconciled, you're safe to change the date, the allocation account (provided this allocation account *isn't* a bank account) or your note in the Memo field, but you're not safe to change the figure in the Amount column. By changing the amount of a reconciled transaction, you ruin your bank reconciliation, which is not a good look.

Figure 6-4:
Take heed of
reconciliation
warnings.

> **Clearwater_Plus_AU.myox - MYOB AccountRight**
>
> **Information**   **MYOB**
>
> One or more parts of this journal entry have been reconciled.
>
> Changing or deleting this entry may affect your next reconciliation.
>
> OK

Similarly, if you see a warning saying that this transaction may undo the approval and unmatch it, be careful what changes you make. You can change the memo, date, allocation accounts and so on with confidence, but you shouldn't need to change the amount (because this transaction originated from a bank feed, the amount is definitely going to be correct).

Reversing transactions

If you set your security preferences so you can't delete or change entries after they're recorded, or if a transaction belongs to a previous financial year that has already been finalised, the only way you can fix incorrect transactions is to reverse them.

The idea of a reversal is that you create a transaction that's exactly the opposite of the incorrect one, so the two entries cancel each other out. You can then have another stab at getting things right by recording the transaction again.

To reverse a Spend Money transaction, first locate the transaction in your Bank Register and double-click to display it. Select Edit⇨Reverse Cheque Transaction from the top menu bar, and then carefully check the date (you're usually best to change the date to the current date, rather than stick with the original date of the transaction). Click Record.

It's a Petty Business

You can find as many different ways to deal with petty cash as there are ways to make pasta sauce. But a few things never change — no matter what type of business you run:

- ✔ Chocolate bars, roses for the beautiful girl at the train station and vet bills are not legitimate petty cash receipts. Get real.

- ✔ When someone takes petty cash from the tin and promises to come back with a receipt, they probably won't.

- ✔ When someone sticks an IOU in the petty cash tin, it means that they'd love to pay you back, but they're just not sure whether it will be this century, or the next.

- ✔ No matter how finicky you are, petty cash will never, ever balance.

In the next couple of sections, I talk about two ways to deal with petty cash. The first method is best for owner-operators paying expenses out of their own pocket. The second method is best for businesses that have employees and need a petty cash tin. Take a look and see which suits you best.

Although I obligingly explain how to deal with petty cash in this chapter, my primary recommendation is to avoid paying for any business expenses using cash. Cash is painful and time-consuming for bookkeepers, especially if you contrast working off a bank feed from a credit card against recording petty cash receipts.

Robbing Peter to pay Paul

If you're a sole operator and you tend to pay for lots of little expenses from your own pocket, record petty cash expenses using this simple method:

1. **Every month or so, go on a mad Mintie hunt for receipts.**

   If you're the business owner reading this book, dig through your pockets, tip out your wallet or look under the seats of your car. If you're a bookkeeper, hassle your employer or client to find every receipt they can lay their hands on.

2. **Clear a patch on your desk and sort the receipts into categories.**

   One pile for stationery, one pile for computer supplies, one pile for postage and so on. (Remember, at this point you only want receipts for business expenses paid for by cash or paid for out of personal accounts that aren't tracked using MYOB; ignore receipts for things paid for by business cheques, EFTPOS or corporate credit cards.)

3. **Use a calculator to add up the total value of each pile, and then write these totals down on the front of an empty envelope.**

   You end up with an envelope that reads something like:

   Total stationery receipts = $15.00

   Total postage receipts = $45.00

   Of course, if you want to type these entries into a simple spreadsheet, that's fine too.

4. **Add up the total value of all petty cash receipts and write this total on the front of the envelope.**

   Alternatively, print your spreadsheet summary and staple this summary to the front of the envelope.

5. **Stuff the receipts into the envelope and close it up.**

6. **Go to the Accounts command centre, click Record Journal Entry, and enter a journal entry that debits each expense and credits Owner's Drawings.**

   I show a typical general journal in Figure 6-5. In this journal, I debit three expense accounts (Office Supplies, Motor Vehicle Expenses and Postage), and credit the Owner's Drawings account.

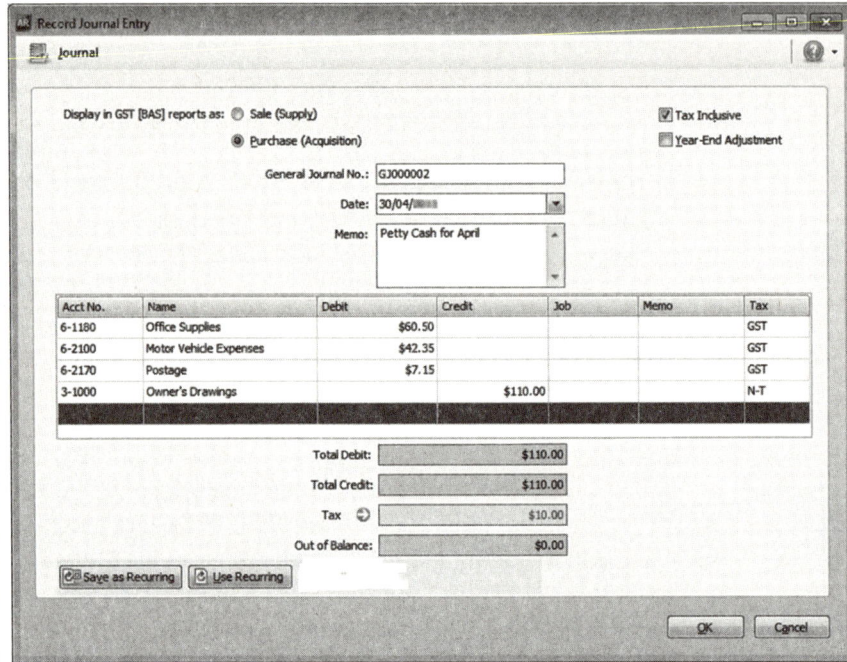

Figure 6-5:
Recording a
journal entry
for petty cash
expenses
paid using
owner's cash.

Lock it up, tie it down

If a business has employees who sometimes pay for business expenses by
cash, you need to set up a decent petty cash system. Here's the whole deal,
from start to finish:

1. **Buy a petty cash box.**

   It's time to liberate your cash from the biscuit tin. Buy a real petty cash
   box with a lock and key. I'm serious.

2. **Appoint a gatekeeper.**

   Put someone in charge of petty cash and make sure no-one else knows
   where the key is kept. This includes you. You're not allowed to raid the
   petty cash tin for Chinese takeaways and meat pies any more. Those
   days are gone.

3. **Start with a float of between $100 and $200.**

   Write a cash cheque (or make an ATM withdrawal) for a round amount
   (about $100) and put the corresponding amount of cash in the tin. When
   you record this withdrawal, allocate the full amount to an asset account

called Petty Cash (there's usually an account there by this name). As the Card, create a new supplier that's simply called Petty Cash.

4. **Every time anyone takes money out of the tin, get a receipt.**

This is the part that requires a huge leap in psychology. Every time someone takes money from petty cash that person has to come back with a receipt. This is pretty radical. It works well if the gatekeeper hassles everyone mercilessly: No receipt, no cash next time.

5. **When petty cash is low, sort out the receipts.**

When petty cash funds dwindle, tip all the receipts out and sort them into piles. Write a breakdown of the receipts on the back of an envelope (for example, $30 postage, $10 cleaning products, $15 chocolate biscuits and so on), and stick the receipts in the envelope. Of course, if you want to list these entries using a simple spreadsheet, that's fine.

6. **Enter the petty cash transactions in Spend Money, splitting these transactions across different allocation accounts.**

Select your Petty Cash account as the Account in the top-left corner. Then look at the back of your envelope or your spreadsheet for the breakdown of receipts (refer to Step 5). Enter each amount, line by line, selecting a different allocation account for each different kind of expense. When you're finished, your Spend Money transaction should look similar to the transaction shown in Figure 6-6.

7. **Write a cash cheque or make an ATM withdrawal to top up the petty cash to the original value of the float.**

It's important to get your head around this part: If you're left with $4.50 in the tin and the original float was $100, write a cash cheque for $95.50. Or, if you're left with $4.50 and the original float was $200, write a cash cheque for $195.50.

8. **Record this cash cheque or ATM withdrawal using Transfer Money (found under the Accounts command centre).**

Select your business bank account as the Transfer Money From account and select your Petty Cash account as the Transfer Money To account. What you're doing at this point is shifting money out of your business account for your petty cash tin.

9. **Check that the balance of your Petty Cash account returns to the original value of the float.**

Imagine I start off with $200 in my Petty Cash account, and then I record expenditure of $110 going out of this account. I then record $110 going back into Petty Cash, transferred from my business account, which brings the balance back to $200.

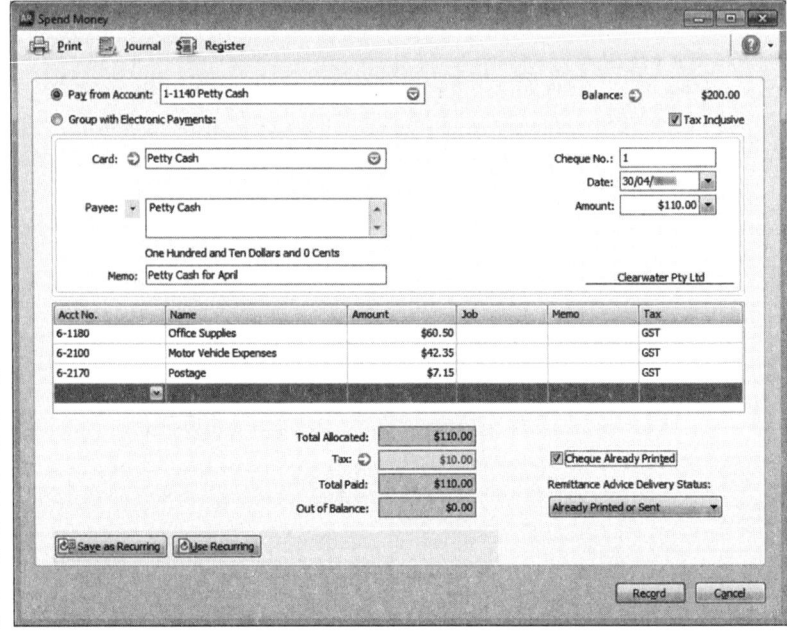

Figure 6-6:
Recording a petty cash transaction when you're running a petty cash tin.

GST — when petty cash gets pettier

If petty cash receipts don't show GST separately, that doesn't mean they're GST-free. A packet of staples for $2.20 includes 20 cents GST. And even if you feel that you've got better things to do than nit-pick tiny details, you still can't afford to lose these valuable input tax credits.

To claim the GST on these petty receipts, even if the tax amount isn't shown separately, click the Tax Inclusive box found in the top-right corner in both the Spend Money and the Record Journal Entry windows. Assuming that the tax code you enter is correct, the GST calculates automatically.

Shortcuts for Regular Payments

If you have an expense that occurs regularly, you can save its details in a special template so that when the expense comes around again, you can record this transaction automatically. This feature makes recording transactions such as leases, rent and direct debits much more efficient.

Paying for set-up expenses from your own pocket

I often get asked how to record business set-up expenses that owners have paid for using their own funds before their businesses got off the ground.

If you're in this camp, talk to your accountant first, because you can't always claim set-up expenses as a tax deduction, especially if the money is spent too far in advance of the business getting established.

However, if your accountant tells you these expenses are claimable, you can record them by going to Record Journal Entry in the Accounts command centre and recording a journal that debits the appropriate expense or asset accounts, and credits your Owner's Drawings account. The petty cash example in Figure 6-5 provides a good example of how this journal might look.

If you're working with bank feeds, I recommend that you don't worry about setting up recurring transactions and instead you work directly from your bank feeds, creating allocation rules to code regular expenses automatically. I prefer to work in this way because your dates end up being more accurate with bank feeds (dates often go awry with recurring transactions that record automatically, especially if you don't log into MYOB every single day). In other words, if you have bank feeds, I suggest you don't worry about recurring transactions and, indeed, I recommend you delete any recurring transactions that you've set up in the past. I only include the information about recurring transactions in this chapter for the people who, for whatever reason, don't have bank feeds enabled.

Setting up a recurring transaction

Whenever you go to record a transaction that you know is going to happen again and again, such as a regular monthly lease payment or rent, follow these steps:

1. **Go to Spend Money and enter this transaction as you would normally do, but instead of clicking Record, click Save as Recurring.**

2. **Give your transaction a name and choose how often it occurs.**

   Create a name for this entry, such as Lease, Hire Purchase or Loan. Select how often the payment occurs in the Frequency box, and then indicate the date that this transaction is going to occur next. For example, if you're just recording a lease payment for 15 July, and you

know that this lease next goes out of your bank account on 15 August, then enter 15 August as the starting date.

3. **Decide whether you want MYOB to record this transaction automatically or prompt you with a reminder.**

   In the Alerts section, you can ask to receive a reminder when this transaction falls due. Reminders are your best bet if the amount of the transaction changes every time. Alternatively, you can choose for MYOB to record this transaction automatically. The automatic method is excellent for recurring debits such as lease payments, fixed bank fees or loan repayments. Figure 6-7 shows how I select the monthly lease payment for my car to record automatically.

4. **Decide whether you want your changes to be saved every time you record this transaction.**

   Think carefully when you reach this option. For example, if you're setting up a recurring transaction for a monthly membership fee that usually increases once a year, selecting the box Save My Changes When I Record This Recurring Transaction tells MYOB to update the template if you ever change the value of the payment. This ensures that future payments automatically come up at the new amount.

5. **Click OK.**

   When you click OK, you're flicked back to the payment you were working on. Don't get confused and think that nothing has happened. It has. All you have to do now is click Record one last time to record your original transaction.

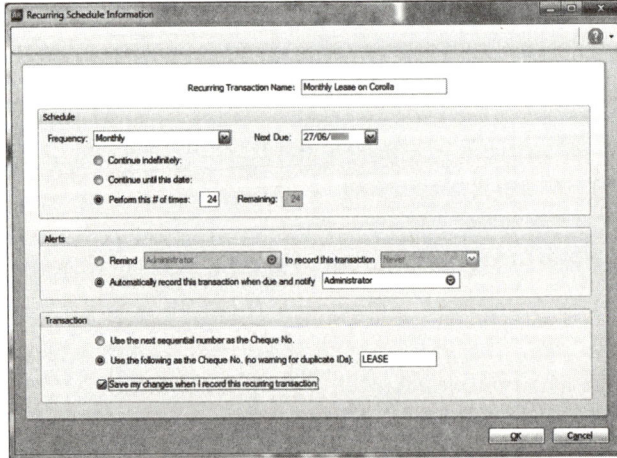

Figure 6-7: You can get MYOB to record regular transactions automatically.

Recording recurring transactions

Next time your recurring transaction is due, you'll discover that either MYOB records the transaction automatically (you'll receive notification that this has happened) or a reminder pops up saying that the payment is due. If you receive a reminder, all you have to do is double-click the reminder, check whether you want to change anything, and then click Record.

Everything sounds pretty simple, I admit, but here are a few possible hiccups you may encounter, along with their solutions:

✔ If you ask for a payment to record automatically, but you don't work on your accounts every day, MYOB only records this transaction when you open your company file. For example, imagine that you have a direct debit that goes out on the first day of every month. However, one month you don't work on your accounts between the end of the previous month and the 14th day of the next month. When you open up your company file on the 14th, MYOB records the transaction, but dates it as the 14th instead of the 1st. The moral of my tale? If you don't work on your accounts every day, don't ask for transactions to record automatically.

✔ If the amount of a recurring payment changes and you can't get MYOB to 'remember' the changed amount, you need to edit the template. Go to Lists and select Recurring Transactions. You can then double-click the transaction to change the details, or click Edit Schedule to change the settings so that MYOB saves your changes when you next record this recurring transaction.

✔ To record a recurring transaction when you haven't asked to receive reminders, or when the Frequency is set to Never, go to Spend Money and click Use Recurring. You can then select the template from the list.

✔ To delete a template, go to Lists, click Recurring Transactions, highlight the template and click Delete. This only deletes the template, and doesn't delete any transactions you recorded in the past using the template.

Chapter 7

Here Comes the Money

*E*ven though I've been running my own business for years, I still feel pretty chirpy when customers pay me. You will too, especially when you find out how easy it is to record customer payments in your accounts.

In this chapter, you discover that there are two ways of recording all the money coming into your business. The first method is in Receive Payments, where you match money received from customers against the invoices they're paying. The second method is in Receive Money, where you record odd bits of income, such as bank interest, money from investors, refunds or income from insurance claims.

This chapter also talks about finding out how much you're owed, sending customer statements and how to squeeze money out of the most reluctant of customers.

Seeing How Much You're Owed

Keeping on top of how much you're owed, and who owes you what, is one of the key ingredients to business success.

Generating a Receivables report

You have two ways of seeing how much your customers owe you — try each one and see which you like the best:

✔ **The Business Insights menu:** Go to the Business Insights menu in the bottom-right corner of any command centre and click the Customer Analysis option. You arrive at a dashboard similar to Figure 7-1. In the top-left corner you see a snapshot of every invoice outstanding, with the oldest invoice listed first. In the bottom-right you see the total owed by each customer, grouped neatly month by month.

✔ **The Reports menu:** If you go to the Sales tab of your Reports menu, you can choose between a few different Receivables reports. The Aged Receivables Summary report shows what you're owed right now, whereas the Receivables Reconciliation Summary shows what customers owed you at a particular point in time in the past (great when reporting for the end of month or financial year). I also like the Aged Receivables Detail report, which lists every single bill owing, not just customer totals.

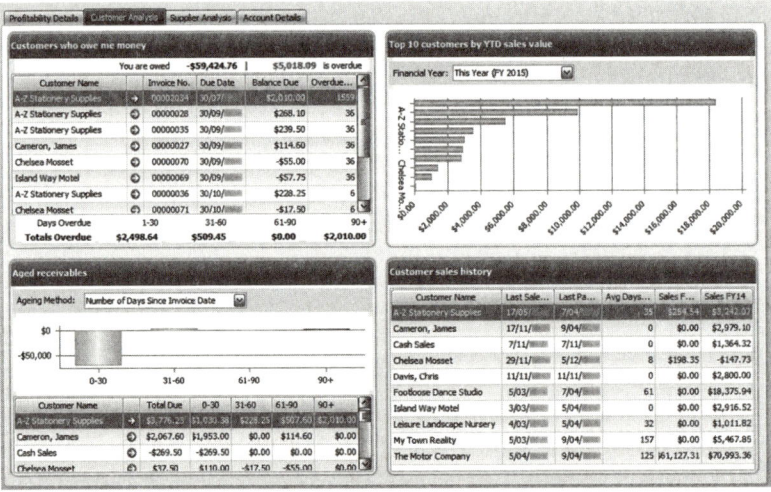

Figure 7-1:
The Business Insights panel is a neat way to see how much customers owe you.

If you find that your Receivables report doesn't include amounts customers owed you before you started using MYOB, you haven't set up customer opening balances yet. For the details on how to get started, turn back to Chapter 3.

Making sense of your Receivables report

Maybe your Receivables report already gives you all the info you need, but just in case it doesn't, check out these tips:

- ✔ **Change the display options:** If you're working with the Business Insights dashboard, remember you can click on any column label to sort by that column. For example, click the Total Due column to show the customer who owes the most at the top of the list, click the Invoice No column to sort by invoice number, or click the Overdue Days column to show the most overdue invoices at the top.

- ✔ **Change your ageing periods:** If you would rather age your receivables based on something other than 30, 60 or 90 days, here's what to do: Head for your Preferences menu, click the Reports & Forms tab, and then choose between Daily Ageing Periods and Monthly Ageing Periods.

- ✔ **Look into the past:** If you want to see how much customers owed you on a date that's already passed (perhaps your accountant wants a Receivables report for a previous month), the regular Aged Receivables report isn't the one for you. Instead, go to Reports and print a Receivables Reconciliation Summary.

- ✔ **Resurrect missing totals:** If your Receivables report doesn't include a total at the bottom, chances are that you are using an older version and have multi-currency switched on in your company file. The solution? Go to the Customise button and select AUD as the currency. You need to display this report one currency at a time in order to view column totals.

Remember that the due date for payment doesn't calculate correctly unless you configure customer terms correctly. To set a default for all customers, go to your Preferences menu, click the Sales tab, and then click Terms in the top-left. Note that *EOM* stands for End of Month. In addition, to set terms for individual customers, go to the Selling Details tab of the customer's card.

Yippee! A Customer Has Paid Up

In the next few pages, I make a couple of assumptions:

- ✔ First, I assume that before you try to record a customer payment, you've already recorded a corresponding sale. (You know, the whole cart-before-the-horse idea. Whoops, I mean horse-before-the-cart.) If you haven't recorded any sales yet, you may want to scoot back to Chapter 4.

✔ Second, I assume that you've already set up customer opening balances, entering historical sales for any amounts that were owing when you first set up your company file. If you haven't set up customer opening balances yet, make your way back to Chapter 3.

Recording customer payments

In this section, I explain how to record customer payments if you don't use bank feeds, or if you receive payments by EFTPOS, cash or cheque. However, if you do use bank feeds and most customers pay by direct deposit into your account, skip ahead to the next section.

With this information in mind, here's how to record a customer payment:

1. **Go to the Sales command centre and select Receive Payments.**

2. **Enter the customer's name in the Customer field, fill in the Date and write the amount in the Amount Received field.**

3. **Decide whether you want to deposit this payment straight into your bank account, or whether you want to use the undeposited funds feature.**

   In the top-left corner of each window, you can choose between depositing customer payments into your choice of bank account or grouping customer payments with undeposited funds. This is a rather momentous decision, so if you're at all unsure, see 'Grouping Customer Payments', later in this chapter.

4. **Select the Payment Method.**

   To add a new Payment Method to this list, type the description in the Payment Method field, press Enter and click New.

5. **Think about which invoice or invoices to allocate this payment to.**

   Your sales preferences may be configured so that MYOB allocates payments automatically, starting from the oldest invoice. However, customers sometimes pay invoices out of sequence so double-check if this payment has been allocated correctly.

   Alternatively, if MYOB hasn't allocated payments automatically, click in the Amount Applied column against the invoices you want to match the payment against.

6. **Check that the Out of Balance amount is $0.00.**

   If a payment matches perfectly against outstanding invoices, the Out of Balance amount should be $0.00. Otherwise, see 'Dealing with underpayments' or 'Sorting out overpayments', later in this chapter.

7. Click Record.

To see a customer payment that's complete and ready to record, check out Figure 7-2.

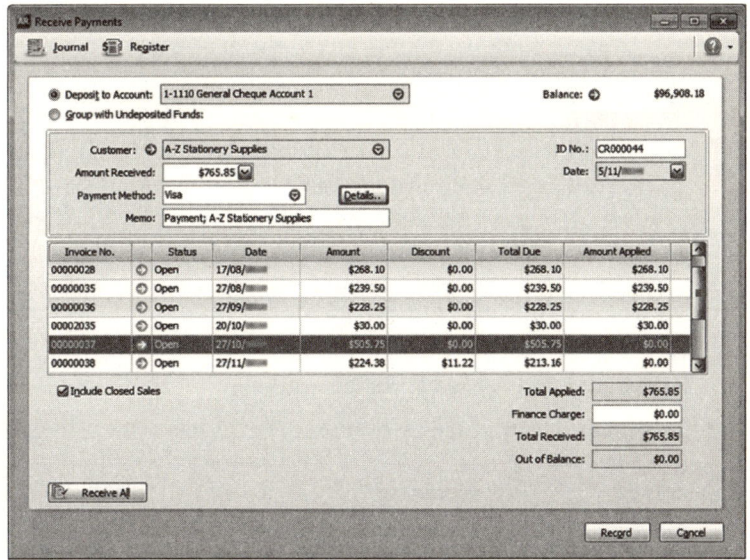

Figure 7-2:
Recording
a customer
payment.

Here are a few extra tips for recording customer payments:

- ✔ Ignore the ID No. field. This is just a number that keeps auditors happy.
- ✔ You can ignore the Memo field too, if you like. Just accept whatever message is offered (in my book, the less typing, the better).
- ✔ To record payments when customers deposit straight into your bank account, click Deposit to Account in the top-left corner and select the correct bank account (don't click Group with Undeposited Funds).
- ✔ If a customer pays all outstanding invoices in one hit (don't you just love that?), cut a few corners by clicking the Receive All button in the bottom left.

Recording direct deposits from a bank feed

In the next section of this chapter, I explain how to record customer payments if you're working from a bank feed *and* customers mostly pay by direct deposit into your bank account. If you receive payments by EFTPOS or cash, refer to the preceding section.

Here's how to record payments from a bank feed:

1. **Working from the Bank Feeds menu, check that the blue Rule Applied icon appears next to the customer payment.**

   As much as possible, I suggest you create an invoice rule for each customer so that MYOB matches payments automatically. The only times I don't bother creating a new invoice rule is if I make a one-off sale to a customer and I'm unlikely to be dealing with them again.

   If you haven't yet created a rule for this customer, click the New button next to any customer payment and then select Invoice Rule. (I explain more about setting up invoice rules in Chapter 5.) Alternatively, you can skip creating a rule by simply selecting Receive Payment from the New menu.

2. **Click the words Possible Invoice Match so that you can view how MYOB has allocated this payment.**

   You're transported to the Receive Payments window, similar to Figure 7-2 a tad earlier in this chapter.

3. **Review which invoice or invoices MYOB has allocated this payment to.**

   If MYOB has allocated a payment to the wrong invoice, click in the Amount Applied column and then press the Delete or Backspace key to set the payment amount against this invoice to $0.00. Then click against the correct invoice, once again in the Amount Applied column.

4. **Click Record.**

   You arrive back at the Bank Feeds window, where you should now see the green Approve button appearing next to the customer payment.

Hot keys for busy people

It gets fiddly moving around with the mouse all the time, especially for stuff that you do often, such as receiving customer payments. That's why MYOB has a whole load of nifty shortcuts called hot keys.

The trick is this. You can hop directly to Receive Payments at any time from anywhere in the program simply by pressing Ctrl+B. This means you hold down the Ctrl key and at the same time you press the letter B.

Try it and see! It's simple and saves precious seconds every time you record a customer payment. Incidentally, I list this hot key, along with lots more, on the *For Dummies* Cheat Sheet for this title, which you can access at `www.dummies.com/cheatsheet/ myobsoftwareau`.

Finding customer payments

Some days have passed since you entered a customer payment and now you want to take another look at it. There may be fifty ways to leave your lover, but only four ways to do this deed:

- ✔ **Bank Register:** Click Bank Register from the Banking command centre. Select the account into which you banked this customer payment and change the date range if necessary (don't forget to select Undeposited Funds if this is the bank account that you normally allocate customer payments to). You should see the customer payment listed in the Deposit column. Double-click to display the details of that payment.

- ✔ **Find Transactions:** Select Find Transactions (which appears along the bottom of every command centre), and then click the Card tab. Enter the customer's name, change the date range if necessary, and you'll see all transactions relating to that customer, sorted by date, similar to Figure 7-3. Double-click any transaction to display the transaction's details.

- ✔ **Payment History:** If you know the invoice number that was paid with the payment that you're looking for, find the invoice from your Sales Register and display it. Then click the History button next to the Applied to Date field in the bottom-right.

- ✔ **Transaction Journal:** Go to the Sales command centre, click Transaction Journal, followed by the Receipts tab. Pick a suitable date range and voilà, a list of all customer payments for that period appears. Scroll down until you find the payment you're looking for, and then click the zoom arrow on the left to display the original payment. Couldn't be easier!

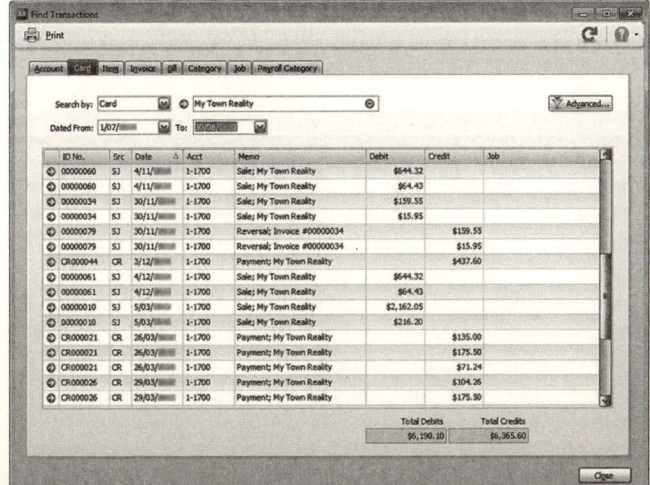

Figure 7-3: Finding a customer payment using the Find Transactions menu.

If you're searching for a particular amount, remember that you can sort by amount when you're in the Find Transactions window. Click the Credit column to see a list of payments, starting with the smallest amount first. Click the Credit column a second time to see this same list of payments, but starting with the largest amount first. You can also type Ctrl+Shift+F to search for any particular amount or string of text.

Grouping Customer Payments

Before you start recording customer payments, take a moment to consider how they appear in your bank account. Try this simple quiz:

1. **When you look at your bank statement, do most deposits on the statement relate to a unique customer payment?**

   Answer 'yes' to this question if your customers tend to pay by electronic transfer to your bank account.

2. **When you look at your bank statement, do most deposits on the statement relate to multiple customer payments?**

   Answer 'yes' to this question if your customers tend to pay by cash, EFTPOS or cheque.

Now, if you answered 'yes' to the first question, you're best to record customer payments direct to your bank account. So, at Step 3 of 'Recording customer payments', covered earlier in this chapter, you select Deposit to Account in the top-left corner, followed by your bank account. You can also skip reading the next few pages of this chapter.

If you answered 'yes' to the second question, you're best to record customer payments using the undeposited funds feature. So, at Step 3 of 'Recording customer payments', covered earlier in this chapter, you select Group with Undeposited Funds in the top-left corner.

Note: If you answered 'yes' to the second question and you're using bank feeds, your bank feed is only going to show daily totals for your banking rather than individual customer payments. The neat thing about working with an Undeposited Funds account (a process I explain in the next couple of pages) is that you can match these daily totals easily.

The idea of an Undeposited Funds account is that you batch cash, cheques and EFTPOS payments together using this account. Later, when you deposit cash or cheques into your bank account, or you close off the EFTPOS machine for the day, you create a bank deposit that transfers the money out of undeposited funds and into your bank account. Hey presto . . . the balance of your undeposited funds account returns to zero, and the deposit of all the customer payments shows up as a single amount in your bank account.

Setting up an undeposited funds account makes sense if you receive more than a couple of customer payments per day, and most customers pay via cash, cheque or EFTPOS. However, if you only receive a couple of customer payments each day or most customers pay electronically, then forget about setting up an undeposited funds account. Instead, simply record all customer payments directly into your bank account, as I do earlier in this chapter in Figure 7-2.

Setting up an account for undeposited funds

If you decide that you want to use an undeposited funds account, your first step is to set up this account properly.

Go to your Setup menu, choose Linked Accounts and then select Accounts & Banking Accounts. Next, make sure that the last account in this list is an asset account called Undeposited Funds (this account always starts with the number 1), then click OK. If you don't already have an account with this name, you'll have to create one in your Accounts List — just remember to select Bank as the Account Type when creating this account.

Now that you've set up your undeposited funds account, all you have to remember is to click the Group with Undeposited Funds button whenever you record a customer payment.

Depositing funds into your bank account

So, you've been to the bank and deposited some cash or even a couple of cheques? Maybe you've also received some EFTPOS payments, a payment by AMEX and a Diners Club payment. Never fear, you can cope! Here's what to do:

1. **Go to the Banking command centre and click Prepare Bank Deposit.**

   I'm assuming that you've already recorded these payments into MYOB using the Receive Payments window, and that when you did so, you selected Group with Undeposited Funds in the top-left corner. Now that you've recorded these payments, you're ready to transfer money out of your undeposited funds account and into your regular bank account.

2. Select which bank account you want to transfer the money into.

See the Deposit to Account box in the top-left corner? Choose the bank account that you're about to deposit funds into.

3. Select a payment method, if you want.

If all your payments are a similar type, you can leave this as All Methods. However, if you receive a mixture of cash, EFTPOS, cheques and so on, you're best to select one payment method at a time (because different kinds of payments show up separately on your bank statement).

4. Enter the date.

You won't see any deposits with dates later than the date you enter here, so don't panic if at first you think some deposits are missing.

5. If you like, write a comment in the Memo field.

I recommend you say something meaningful like 'EFTPOS payments' or 'to be or not to be, that is the question'.

6. Click off the receipts by ticking in the Deposit column.

Go through and click in the Deposit column to select the payments you want to include on this bank deposit. Check out Figure 7-4 to see how a completed bank deposit may look.

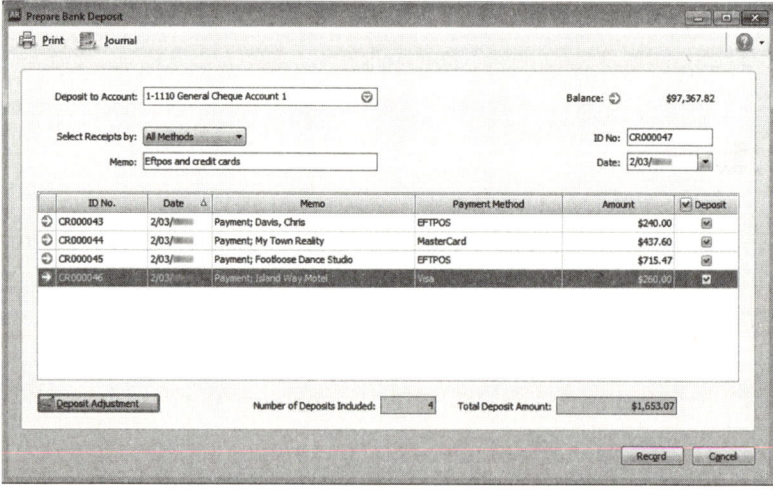

Figure 7-4:
Using the
Prepare
Bank Deposit
window
to group
customer
payments,
ready for
banking.

7. Check that the Total Deposit Amount matches the amount you're actually banking.

If you're banking cash, one of the most common reasons the banking total may be up the spout is if someone (usually the business owner) has got their sticky hands on the cash and spent some before it has been banked. That's okay, so long as you keep track of what's been taken. To get the deposit to balance, click the Deposit Adjustment button and record a transaction for the difference. For example, if the owner has taken some cash, you can select Owner's Drawings as the Expense Account (but do remember that Owner's Drawings is always an equity account, and isn't actually an expense account).

8. **When everything looks sweet as a nut, click Record.**

   When you click Record, MYOB transfers the total from your undeposited funds account into your regular bank account. This amount hopefully then correlates with the deposit on your bank statement (or from your bank feed) for that day.

Deleting undeposited fund transfers

The theory of undeposited funds accounts is all very well, but I find it easy to make mistakes, especially at first. You record a bank deposit and the second after you click Record you think, 'Oh no, I missed one' or '****, I keyed in a payment twice'.

Fixing up bank deposits can be a brain drain, so you need to take it pretty slow:

1. **Go to your Transaction Journal for that date and find the deposit transaction where you transferred the group of customer payments from your undeposited funds account into your bank account.**

   This transaction has the words 'Bank Deposit' in the Memo, as opposed to 'Payment for'.

   If a warning appears stating 'One or more parts of this journal entry have been reconciled', click OK to accept the message, and then pause to consider the importance of your wellbeing. If you delete a deposit that has already been reconciled, you're going to throw your bank reconciliation out of whack. Because of this, only delete this deposit if you plan to enter another deposit for *exactly* the same amount.

2. **If you're sure you want to delete this deposit, go up to the Edit menu and select Delete Bank Deposit Transaction.**

   No turning back now. The deposit is deleted.

3. **Head to Prepare Bank Deposits in the Banking command centre.**

   All the customer payments that were part of the bank deposit you just deleted appear back in this window.

Discover your inner pedant

I know from experience that undeposited funds accounts can become a real pain in the neck if you're not careful about balancing every last itsy-bitsy cent.

The best way to avoid problems is to make sure that the balance of your undeposited funds account always returns to zero after each bank deposit. If a transaction remains at the top of your Prepare Bank Deposit window week after week, this usually indicates a problem.

Take the time to find out why this deposit hasn't been banked. Maybe you recorded a customer payment twice, maybe you've lost a cheque on the way to the bank, maybe the customer paid in cash and you've already spent it. There will be a reason.

If you can't get to the bottom of the mystery, ask your local MYOB Certified Consultant or accountant to help you investigate further.

4. **If you need to, correct whatever it was that went adrift in the first place, and then record the bank deposit again (second time lucky!).**

5. **If the original deposit that you deleted has been reconciled, go immediately to your bank reconciliation and click off this new deposit, and double-check that your bank account still reconciles.**

   Go on, no backsliding now. Follow everything through to its logical end, and the rewards will be many.

If you're anxious about deleting stuff that's already been reconciled — and I'm glad you are — you can go to your Preferences, click the Security tab and temporarily change your preferences so that transactions can't be changed, they must be reversed. You can then reverse, rather than delete, the deposit, thereby maintaining a complete audit trail of your work.

Building Your Survival Kit

What do you reckon you need in order to survive the next few weeks? Maybe a signal mirror, some waterproof matches and some water purification tablets? Oh no, I forgot for a moment. This is *MYOB Software For Dummies*, not *Boy Scouts For Dummies*.

To survive in the harsh world of accounting software, all you need to know is how to fix up mistakes. Your mistakes, your customers' mistakes, your employees' mistakes. And that's what the next few pages are all about.

Changing customer payments

To change a customer payment, first find the payment and double-click to display it. (Refer to 'Finding customer payments', earlier in this chapter, if you're not sure how.) You'll find that you can change the date, ID number or memo, but you can't change the amount, the customer name or the invoices to which this payment is applied. If these details are wrong, your only solution is to delete or reverse the customer payment. Read on to find out more . . .

Deleting customer payments

You may want to delete a customer payment for a few reasons. Maybe you allocated a payment to the wrong customer or entered a payment twice. (MYOB won't let you change the amount or customer name on customer payments; rather, you can only delete a payment and start again.)

Although I explain in these steps how to delete a customer payment, my explanations come with a hefty warning. So read on, but do read carefully:

1. **Find the customer payment and double-click to display it.**

   Refer to 'Finding customer payments', earlier in this chapter, if you're not sure how to locate this customer payment.

2. **Consider your options if any reconciliation warnings appear.**

   If a warning appears saying 'One or more parts of this journal entry have been reconciled', click OK to accept the message, and then click Cancel to close the customer payment. You can't delete this payment; you need to skip to the next section instead. (If you delete a payment that has already been reconciled, you'll throw your bank reconciliation out of balance, which, to put it mildly, is a rather dire and dreadful thing to do. So, don't.)

   You may also get a warning saying that changing this transaction may undo the approval and unmatch it. What this message means is that you've already matched this transaction to a bank feed and so, when you delete the transaction, the amount will appear once more in your Bank Feeds menu. No dramas. If you haven't reconciled this transaction yet, unmatching it is just fine.

3. **Go to the Edit menu and select Delete Payment.**

   In the blink of an eye, MYOB deletes the payment and closes the Customer Payment window. The deed is done.

If, when you go to delete a payment, you don't see an option to Delete Payment under the Edit menu, but instead only see an option to Reverse Payment, then you have three different possible courses of action:

✔ If this customer payment belongs to the current financial year *and* your security preferences are set so that you can normally change transactions in MYOB, the reason you only get an option to reverse this payment is that you've already transferred this payment out of undeposited funds and into a bank account. Your solution is to first delete the undeposited funds transfer that involved this payment (refer to 'Deleting undeposited fund transfers', earlier in this chapter, for more details) and then return to the customer payment and again try to delete it.

✔ If this customer payment belonged to a previous financial year and you've already closed that year, you can't delete the payment. Instead, read on to find out about reversing customer payments (just remember, you need to date this reversal in the current financial year).

✔ If your security preferences are set so you can't edit transactions, read on to find out about reversing customer payments.

Reversing customer payments

Reversing a customer payment is child's play:

1. **Find the customer payment and double-click to display it.**

2. **Go up to the Edit menu and select Reverse Payment.**

   In a flash, a transaction appears that's the exact opposite of the original payment you recorded.

   If you can only see an option to delete this payment, rather than reverse it, go to the Security tab in your Preferences menu and mark the option that specifies transactions can't be charged, they must be reversed.

3. **Double-check the date, changing it if necessary, and then click Record.**

Dealing with underpayments

Depending on the circumstances, I have four different methods of recording payments when a customer underpays:

✔ **Water torture.** Forget that Bill of Human Rights — just kidding!

✔ **Raise a credit note and write off the difference.** If the underpayment is relatively minor and you can't be bothered chasing up the customer for the difference, the easy approach is to raise a credit note. For the full chapter and verse on credit notes, refer to Chapter 4.

✔ **Leave the underpayment sitting on the customer's account.** If you record a customer payment and leave the shortfall as an amount owing on an invoice, this amount shows up on the customer's next statement. Chances are that your customer will make up the shortfall next time they pay you.

✔ **Change the invoice.** Ahem. This method is a bit rough and ready and not what any auditor would recommend. However, if the shortfall is only a couple of cents, you can get away with opening the original invoice and changing the amount.

Sorting out overpayments

If a customer overpays by a few cents, the swiftest solution is to find the sale in your Sales Register, open it and change the Amount column so that it matches what was actually paid.

However, if a customer overpays by anything more than a few cents, don't let temptation lure you in. There's no point in grabbing the loot and running away to deepest, darkest Peru to meet Aunt Lucy. You'll need to come clean and either (a) apply the credit against the customer's account, or (b) send the customer a refund.

Applying overpayments against a customer's account

Here's how to apply overpayments against a customer's account:

1. **Go to Receive Payments as you would to record a normal customer payment.**

2. **Enter the full amount the customer has paid as the Amount Received.**

3. **Decide which invoice you want to apply this overpayment to.**

   You can usually look at the remittance advice the customer has sent you in order to figure out what the customer thinks they're paying.

4. **If the invoice the customer is overpaying has already been paid in full, click the Include Closed Sales box that appears in the bottom-left of the Receive Payments window.**

When you click Include Closed Sales, you see a complete history of all invoices the customer has ever paid, rather than only the invoices that currently have amounts outstanding.

5. **Type the amount the customer has paid against this invoice in the Amount Applied column.**

   For example, if the customer has paid $250 for an invoice that was only $150, you would type $250 in the Amount Applied column against this invoice, similar to how I've done in Figure 7-5.

6. **Click Record, then OK.**

   You see a message warning you that this payment will result in a credit memo. That's fine. Click OK to proceed.

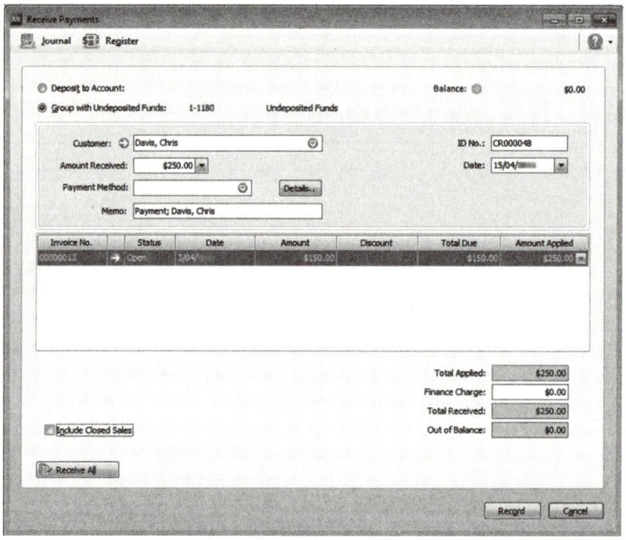

Figure 7-5:
Applying overpayments to a customer's account.

This overpayment now sits as a credit on the customer's account. You can view all customer credits by going to the Sales Register and clicking the Returns & Credits tab. Later on, you can either apply this credit to another invoice (see 'Matchmaking credits with their debits') or you can send the customer a refund. For the lowdown on refunds, read on . . .

Sending a refund

In the next steps, I assume you're sending a refund to a customer because they have a credit on their account. They may have a credit because they've overpaid (in which case, record the overpayment in the way I explain in the steps in the preceding section), or they may have a credit because you've issued them with a credit note (the wonders of which I explain in Chapter 3).

Enough whys and wherefores, here's what you gotta do:

1. **Go to your Sales Register and click the Returns & Credits tab.**

2. **Highlight the credit you want to refund and click Pay Refund.**

   A Settle Returns & Credits window appears, very similar to a Spend Money window, showing the amount of the refund, the cheque number and the date. See Figure 7-6 for an example.

3. **Review the details of this transaction, changing the cheque number, bank account or date, if necessary.**

   I often choose to write a short novella in the Memo field at this point, explaining why this refund is being issued.

4. **Click Record.**

   Now all you have to do is actually pay the customer their refund, whether this is by electronic transfer or by cheque.

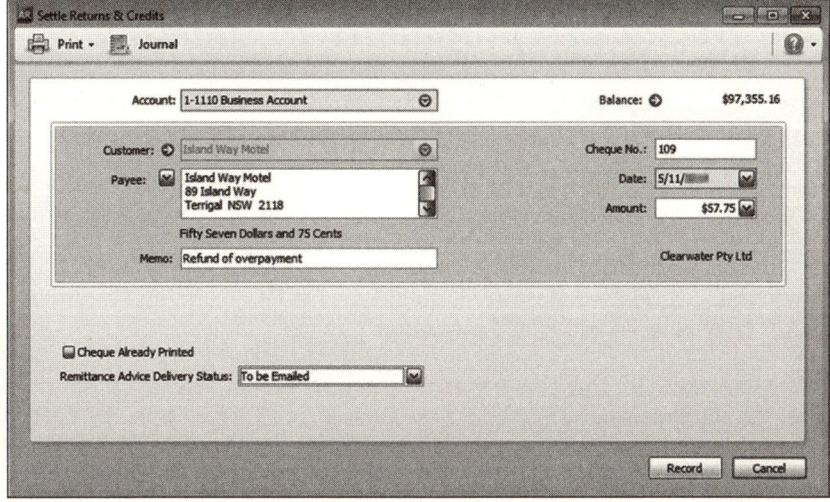

Figure 7-6:
Recording
a customer
refund.

Matchmaking credits with their debits

Often you end up with credits sitting on a customer's account, unallocated and unloved. Not far away, in the same customer's account, are a string of debits, each one looking for a mate. And you, matchmaker extraordinaire, are just the person to put a little bit of spring loving back in the air. Here's how:

1. **Go to the Sales Register and click the Returns & Credits tab.**

2. **Highlight the credit that needs a mate and click Apply to Sale.**

   Up comes the Settle Returns & Credits window, showing all the eligible debits against which this credit could be matched.

3. **Do a quick personality analysis, and then click in the Amount Applied column against the most compatible debit.**

   Polygamy is okay too. So if you want to apply this credit to multiple debits, you can.

4. **Click Record when you're satisfied.**

   Ah, the job of matchmaker brings many rewards.

If you ever come across the situation when you go to apply credits, but MYOB doesn't display any matching debits — even when you're sure debits are in the system — the reason is almost always that the debit has a different category code than the credit. (Chapter 17 talks more about category tracking.) The solution is to edit the category on one or other of the transactions.

Accepting payments in advance

Nothing is much sweeter than a customer who pays in advance. To record their benevolent act in your accounting records, you need to keep your wits about you.

If it's not yet appropriate to record an invoice (you probably only want to do this after the sale is complete), you need to record a sales order instead (refer to Chapter 4 for more detail about raising sales orders). After you've generated the sales order, go to Receive Payments and record the customer payment as you would any other payment.

When recording this payment, the only hiccup may be a warning message that says something like: 'You must specify an account for customer deposits'. In this case, to finish, select a liability account — say, 'Deposits from Customers' (create a new account by this name if you need to).

By the way, when you record a payment against a sales order, MYOB treats this payment as if it's a customer deposit — which it is, really — and allocates the payment to a liability account. Later, when you change the sales order into a real invoice, MYOB automatically transfers the amount of the deposit out of this liability account and into your Trade Debtors account. Miracle stuff really.

Yee Haa! Someone Else Has Given You Money

Sometimes you receive money from sources other than your customers. Perhaps you receive a refund from Optus, the bank pays you some interest or you receive a loan from Great-Aunt Thelma. In these situations, you need to make your way to the Banking command centre and click Receive Money. (Or, if you're using bank feeds, select Receive Money from the New menu.)

You can go straight to Receive Money from anywhere in MYOB by pressing the Ctrl key followed by the letter 'D'.

Recording income that's not from customers

Okay, if you receive money that's not a customer payment (that is, it's got nothing to do with an invoice or a sale), you still want it, right? Here's what to do next:

1. **In the Banking command centre, select Receive Money.**

   Or, if you're using bank feeds, select Receive Money from the New menu.

2. **Fill in the current Date and the Payor.**

   Payor is just a fancy word that stands for the person or company who's giving you this money.

   At this point, pause and ask yourself if the Payor is a customer and, if so, whether you should actually record this payment in Receive Payments, not in Receive Money. (If you record a customer receipt in Receive Money, the payment won't be allocated correctly against the customer's account and their invoices will still appear as outstanding.)

3. **Check the bank account (only relevant if you're not using bank feeds).**

   You have a choice between depositing money received straight into your bank account or grouping money received with undeposited funds. Only select Group with Undeposited Funds if this amount will be combined with other amounts or payments when appearing as a deposit on your bank statement. Otherwise, simply click Deposit to Account and select your business bank account from the list.

4. **Enter the Amount Received and the Payment Method.**

5. **Write a Memo (or accept the one that's offered).**

   The Payor's name automatically appears as the Memo, but I usually prefer to change this Memo and instead add a short description, such as 'Optus refund', 'Bank interest' or 'Massive lottery win' (if only).

6. **Fill in the Account Number or Name and the Tax column.**

   Ask yourself where this income came from and what it's for. (I talk more about choosing allocation accounts and tax codes in the next section.)

   By now, your deposit should look similar to mine, shown in Figure 7-7.

7. **Click Record.**

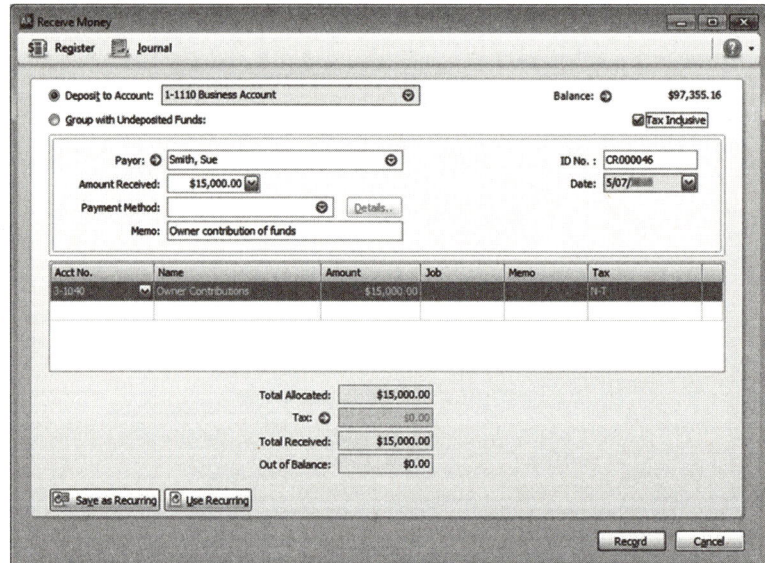

Figure 7-7: Recording bank deposits that aren't related to customer payments.

Figuring out which account to pick

When recording any kind of income that doesn't come from a customer, selecting the correct account can be confusing. But, never fear, Table 7-1 provides a handy reference.

If you still don't have the foggiest where to allocate a deposit, create a new expense account called Suspense Account, number it 6-9999 and use this as your allocation account. (I like the number 6-9999 because it means this account appears at the bottom of your Accounts List.) In the future, whenever you're not sure which allocation account to choose (for any transaction, not just deposits), use the Suspense Account. Every month or so, you can ask your accountant to log in to your company file and review these transactions. Alternatively, if you're not working in the cloud, you can simply print a report of all transactions sitting in this account and ask your accountant to help you work out the correct allocations.

Table 7-1	Matchmaking Receipts and Accounts		
Type of Receipt	*Comments*	*Use This Tax Code*	*Use This Account*
Bank interest or rental income	Note that MYOB has two different kinds of income accounts. Regular income accounts start with the number 4, and other income accounts start with the number 8. I generally prefer to use an '8' account to record interest income or rental income.	ITS (stands for input-taxed sale)	Interest Income or Rental Income
Contribution of owner funds	If you're depositing your own money into your business bank account, select either Owner's Contributions (if you're a sole trader or partnership) or Loan from Directors (if you're a company).	N-T	Owner's Contributions (equity account) or Loan from Directors (liability account)
Proceeds from an insurance claim, including workers comp claims	Create a special income account called Insurance Recovery and use this as your allocation account.	Check the paperwork from the insurance company carefully, as some claims include GST, but others don't	Insurance Recovery (income account)
Receipt of funds as proceeds from a bank loan	For money from bank loans, create a new liability account called Bank Loan. If you have more than one bank loan, include as much of the account number as fits in the Account Name.	N-T	Bank Loan (liability account)

(continued)

Table 7-1 *(continued)*

Type of Receipt	Comments	Use This Tax Code	Use This Account
Supplier refund	As your allocation account, select whatever expense this supplier normally gets allocated to. For example, if Optus sends you a refund, allocate the payment to Telephone Expense. This transaction then credits your Telephone Expense, which is just right.	Whatever tax code you normally select for this supplier	Whichever cost of sales or expense account relates to this supplier
Tax refunds	For Business Activity Statement refunds, split the payment across GST Paid and GST Collected (see Chapter 15 for details). For company tax refunds, allocate to Provision for Company Tax.	N-T	GST Paid, GST Collected, Provision for Company Tax (all liability accounts)

Recording bank interest

If you're working with bank feeds, the easiest way to record a bank deposit is simply to create a transaction rule that automatically allocates any deposit with the word 'INTEREST' to your Interest Income account.

If you're not working with bank feeds, the easiest way to record bank interest is when you're reconciling your bank account. Simply click the Bank Entry button that appears in the bottom of the Reconcile Accounts window and enter the amount of interest received along with the relevant date. Then pick your Income Account (usually Interest Income) and type a brief description as the Memo. You can see how this works in Figure 7-8, where I've recorded the princely sum of $25.20 in interest.

Don't forget to code any interest received with the tax code ITS (*ITS* stands for Input Taxed Sale, just in case you're interested). Interest income is GST-free but you need to report this income separately from other GST-free income on the calculation worksheet for your Business Activity Statement.

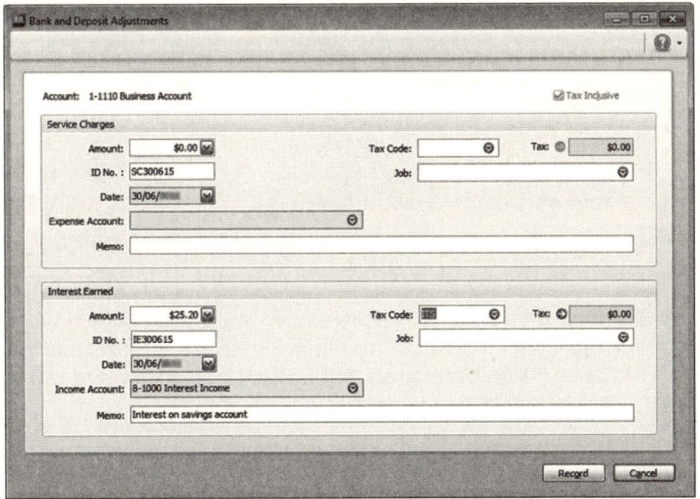

Figure 7-8:
Recording
bank
interest.

Sending Customer Statements

The older an account is, the less likely the customer will pay. So stay on their case and send every customer a statement as soon as their account falls due.

Getting the ball rolling

Here's how to send your customers a statement showing how much they owe:

1. **Go to the Sales command centre and click Print/Email Statements.**

2. **Depending on your preferred poison, either click the To Be Emailed tab or the To Be Printed tab.**

   Not that I'm biased or anything, but spare a thought for the trees.

3. **Select the statement type.**

   You can choose between Invoice statements and Activity statements. I explain the difference between these two types in the next section.

4. **Enter either a Statement Date (for Invoice statements) or From and To dates (for Activity statements).**

   If you choose a Statement Date for Invoice statements, you can tick the option to Only Include Invoices up to Statement Date. This works well if you're already a few days into the month but you want to generate statements that include account activity up to the end of the previous month only.

5. **If you plan to email statements, click the Email Defaults button (top-left corner) and edit the default message. Click OK when you're done.**

   You can change the default email subject and message to suit yourself, maybe mentioning special offers, holiday closures or information about payment terms. Don't forget to include your 'signature' here also — your name and contact details.

6. **Click Advanced Filters and ensure that the Selected Form for Statement is the right template. When you're happy, click OK.**

   By the way, if you haven't customised your statement layout yet, this is your big chance. Select the Plain Paper Statement template, click Customise and do your stuff. (Chapter 12 explains lots more about customising forms.)

7. **Decide who's going to get a love letter this month.**

   Click against all the customers you want to send statements to. If you're going to email these statements, make sure that every customer has a current email address. You can also customise individual customer emails by highlighting their name and changing the Message that appears at the top.

8. **Either click Print or Send Email.**

   If you click Print, your printer should spring into action. If you click Send Email, the statements should be sitting in a batch either in your Outbox or, if you're connected to the internet at the time, in your Sent Items folder.

Choosing your statement type

When you print a customer statement, you can choose between an Activity statement and an Invoice statement.

I usually prefer Invoice statements because they're so straightforward — they simply list all invoices with any amounts outstanding. They don't include any amounts that have already been fully paid.

On the other hand, an Activity statement shows *all* transactions on a customer's account for any specified date range, starting with the opening balance outstanding and then listing every single sale and payment.

For a report that includes all customer transactions, including a running balance, your best bet is the Customer Ledger report, found in the customer section under the Sales tab of your reports menu.

Smartening up your statement

I always know when one of my suppliers has just purchased MYOB but hasn't quite mastered it because their statement is a jumble of fine print, columns that don't line up and boxes with nothing in them. In other words, they haven't customised their statements.

To customise your statement, go to Setup⇨Customise Forms⇨Statements. Select your Statement Layout or Type and click Customise.

Chapter 12 provides lots more information on customising forms.

Chasing Money

Making sales is one thing, but it's another to rake in the cash. The gentle art of extracting money from some customers can be akin to squeezing blood from a stone. In the last few pages in this chapter, I explain how to set credit limits, send reminder letters and keep track of your debt collection activities. Last of all — and most regrettably — I explain how to write off a bad debt.

Set credit limits

Here's how to apply credit limits to customer accounts, as well as how to ensure they're enforced:

1. **Go to your Setup menu, click Preferences and then the Sales tab.**

2. **Click the Terms button in the top-left corner and set a general Credit Limit that applies to all customers.**

3. **Click Close to return to your sales preferences window.**

4. **Set specific credit limits for individual customers.**

    For each customer who has a different credit limit from your default, go to the Selling Details tab of their card and click the Credit Limit & Hold button. Enter the credit limit here.

Show no mercy — cut 'em off

If a customer won't pay, cut 'em off.

To put a customer's account completely on hold (so that nobody else can override credit warnings and no sales can be processed for this customer), go to the Selling Details of this customer's card, click the Credit Limit & Hold button and click Place This Customer on Credit Hold.

When you place a customer on credit hold, nobody can raise an invoice for that customer while the hold is in place. Also, if you go to view that customer's details, the words 'On Credit Hold' appear in red next to their name.

As your business grows, look at your receivable reports every single week. Make sure that the percentage of accounts that are way overdue doesn't increase month after month. Don't wait until it's too late and you're already strapped for cash before you get on the phone and ask your customers to cough up.

One handy little feature in the latest versions of MYOB is the Overdue column that appears in the far-right when you go to view your Cards List. This column provides a quick snapshot of exactly how much is overdue, and you can even click the column label to sort by this column so that the largest amounts appear first.

Keep notes of every promise

One of MYOB's cleverer features is the Contact Log. This is where you record notes about each customer and attach these notes to their cards, so you can look them up whenever you need to. The Contact Log is ideal for keeping track of your debt-collection activities. Perhaps you phone an overdue customer and the receptionist says, 'The accounts clerk only comes in on Wednesdays'. You ring on Wednesday and the receptionist says, 'The accounts clerk took the day off and won't be in again till next Tuesday', and on and on . . .

To create a log entry, go to the Card File command centre and click Cards List. Highlight the customer's name, select New Log Entry and log any phone calls or correspondence in relation to this account. If you want to create a reminder for yourself to follow something up, enter a Recontact Date. When this date comes around, a reminder appears under the Contact Alert tab of your To Do List (alternatively, you can print an Overdue Contacts report, found under the Card tab of your Reports menu).

Know when to cut your losses

You need to be both a fortune-teller and a pragmatist when chasing money; fortune-telling skills to help predict which customers may not pay and pragmatism to accept the fact that some customers, no matter how hard you try, are never going to cough up.

So, in the name of pragmatism, here's how to write off a bad debt:

1. **Click Enter Sales.**

   A blank invoice should appear, ready to go.

2. **Enter the customer's name, click Layout, select Miscellaneous, and then click OK.**

   A Miscellaneous layout is the best kind of layout for any kind of customer account adjustment.

3. **In the Description, write a short story about the bad debt and why you're writing it off. Include the original invoice number.**

4. **As the allocation account, select Bad Debt Expense.**

   If you don't already have an expense account by this name, create one now.

5. **Enter the amount you're writing off as a negative figure and make sure the amount of GST comes up correctly.**

   If GST was included on the original invoice, make sure that GST is on the bad debt also.

6. **Click Record.**

7. **Go to the Returns & Credits tab in your Sales Register and apply this credit to the original debt.**

   Highlight the credit you just created and click Apply to Sale. Apply this credit against the outstanding debt in the same way you would apply a payment, and then click Record.

Customer payment history

Looking for a report that identifies your worst-paying customers? It's called the Customer Payments [Closed Invoices] report and you can find it tucked away on the Sales tab of your Reports menu. This report makes most sense if you choose a time span of at least six months as your date range, so choose your dates carefully.

When you view this report, notice that the Days Until Paid column shows how many days on average it takes each customer to pay. This means that if your credit terms are 30 days from the date of the invoice and the figure in the Days Until Paid column for a certain customer is 43 days, your customer is on average 13 days late with payments.

Chapter 8

Purchases and Supplier Payments

. . . .

In This Chapter

▶ Determining whether you need to read this chapter

▶ Creating and sending purchase orders

▶ Receiving goods and recording supplier bills

▶ Deleting, reversing and changing purchases

▶ Paying up, with blinding efficiency

▶ Troubleshooting odd amounts, credits, unloved debits and more

. . . .

Many people new to running a business take a while to realise how important their suppliers are. Instead, they focus on building relationships with their customers. But the truth of the matter is this: Suppliers are as important as customers, because without suppliers you wouldn't have any goods to sell.

A supplier needs to know what you want, when you want it and where you want it. They need to know when you'll pay them, and how. And guess what? In this chapter, I show you how MYOB helps with all of these things, and more.

(*Note:* If you're using AccountRight Basics, where purchase features aren't available, you probably want to skip this chapter.)

Deciding Whether You Need This in Your Life

Before plunging headlong into this chapter, pause for a moment. Do you actually need to record purchase orders or supplier bills? Maybe not. Probably half of all small businesses using MYOB don't bother recording purchase orders or supplier bills in MYOB at all, and simply record supplier payments using Spend Money.

I can't make this decision for you, but I can explain the upsides and downsides of using the Purchases command centre in MYOB.

The benefits of recording supplier bills and payments in the Purchases command centre, as opposed to simply recording supplier payments using Spend Money, are

✔ You can claim GST on bills that you've received, but haven't paid for yet (this only applies if you report for GST on an accruals basis). For more details, see the sidebar 'Claiming GST on unpaid supplier bills'.

✔ At the click of a button, you can see exactly how much you owe suppliers.

✔ You can see what bills you have to pay when, and plan your cash flow better.

✔ Your monthly Profit & Loss reports are more accurate, because expenses show up in the month to which they belong, rather than in the month that you pay them.

✔ When payment is due to suppliers, processing payments is quick, easy and efficient.

The downsides of recording supplier bills and payments in the Purchases command centre, as opposed to simply recording supplier payments using Spend Money, are

✔ Every supplier bill involves two entries instead of one. That's because you first record the supplier's bill using Enter Purchases and then you record the payment in Pay Bills, instead of recording the purchase and payment as one transaction in Spend Money.

✔ Getting your head around supplier bills and payments can be hard, especially if you're new to MYOB.

Creating Purchase Orders

Want to know how to create purchase orders to send to suppliers? The next couple of pages in this chapter explain just how.

Claiming GST on unpaid supplier bills

When you first register for GST, you have to choose whether to report for GST on a cash or an accruals basis. If you choose to report for GST on an accruals basis, you need to account for GST on all outstanding supplier bills, not just the ones you've already paid.

This means that if you want to produce a report that claims all the GST credits due on supplier bills (both the ones you've paid and the ones you haven't yet paid), you need to record these bills in your accounts. To do this, you use the Purchases command centre.

Most of my retail clients fall into this category. Because they own shops, almost all their sales are cash, but the stock they purchase is almost always on account. (That's why it's good for them to report on an accruals basis.) To claim all the GST credits as soon as possible, they record all supplier bills as Purchases in their accounts.

Clear as mud? For more on this fascinating topic, make your way to Chapter 15.

Ordering up big time

Here's how you create a purchase order:

1. **In the Purchases command centre, choose Enter Purchases.**

   Easy peasy.

2. **Fill in the supplier name and press Tab.**

   If this is the first time you're using this supplier, click New to add this supplier's name and address to your list.

3. **Select ORDER as the Purchase Type in the top-left corner.**

   On your screen the colour of the Purchases window changes to a rather sickly beige colour.

4. **Click the Layout button (found at the top) and select Item as your purchase layout.**

   You should now see an Order column and a Received column. (At this point, you can only enter figures in the Order column.)

   You can set default layouts for each of your suppliers, so that MYOB automatically comes up with the correct layout as soon as you enter the supplier name. To do this, go to the Buying Details tab of the supplier's card and select the Purchase Layout.

5. Accept the Purchase No. and check the date.

Unless you have a different kind of system, go with whatever purchase order number comes up (the number automatically increases by one with every new purchase).

6. Enter quantities in the Order column and item codes in the Item Number column.

If you're ordering an item that you haven't set up in your Items List already, add it now. (For more details about items, go to Chapter 10.)

To enter a purchase order for something that's not a stock item — maybe you're sending a purchase order through to a supplier for a new computer system or some stationery — create a new item called Stationery Supplies, Computer Equipment, Cleaning Supplies or whatever, making sure to link the item to an expense account that makes sense.

7. Check the item Description and Price and change them if necessary.

If this is the first time you're purchasing this item, complete the Price column. If you've purchased the item before, either the last price or the standard cost comes up, depending on how you set up your inventory preferences.

8. Fill in any other necessary information.

All other fields on this purchase are entirely optional. For example, you can add comments, shipping information or a Promised Date for delivery. Leave the Journal Memo as is (the default memo usually works just fine).

9. Click the Send To button followed by Email, or simply click Print.

Figure 8-1 shows a finished purchase order, which includes columns for quantity, description, price, discount and so on. You may be interested to note that, in my example, the business is ordering silk, thread and lace for making handmade lingerie — beats talking about widgets and water filters, if you ask me.

For more about emailing and printing purchase orders, see 'Sending purchase orders', later in this chapter.

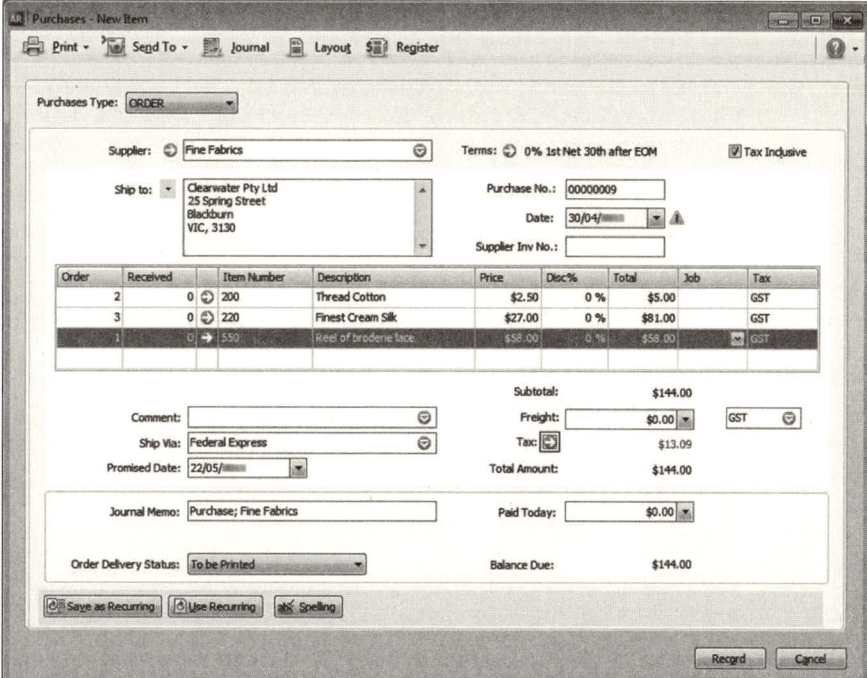

Figure 8-1: A typical Item purchase order looks something like this.

Short of time? Order automatically

Do you often receive orders for stuff that you don't hold in stock? Then save yourself time by generating purchase orders automatically.

To do this, create a sales order (not a sales invoice) for the product or goods the customer wants, but before recording this sales order, click the little button at the bottom labelled Create PO. This creates a new purchase order with exactly the same details on it as your sales order.

Assuming you've set up primary suppliers for all your items and every item on the sales order has the same supplier, the purchase order comes complete with the supplier name. Smart stuff. However, if you get a customer order that requires ordering goods from more than one supplier, the supplier name on the purchase order comes up blank. You then have to edit the purchase order, creating a separate purchase order for each additional supplier.

I find that automatic purchase orders work a treat for many Web-based businesses, such as eBay-trading companies or virtual shopfronts.

Giving your purchase order a makeover

To customise your purchase order, go to your Setup menu and select Customise Forms⇨Purchase Orders. Select your Purchase Layout and the template that you want to use as your base. Then click Customise.

I talk lots about the basic techniques for designing forms in Chapter 12, but here are a few points that apply specifically to purchase orders:

- ✔ You can customise your purchase order to show prices either as tax exclusive or tax inclusive. By this I mean you can include the GST in the price of each item, or you can leave the GST out and show it as a lump sum at the bottom. Choose the method that suits you best.

- ✔ When customising your purchase order, click the Fields button to see a list of all available fields, including many fields that don't appear automatically on standard purchase orders but that you may find useful.

- ✔ The standard purchase order shows the supplier's item number, not your item number. (This may seem confusing, but makes perfect sense to your suppliers.) If you find your purchase order shows no item numbers at all, chances are you haven't entered supplier item numbers in the Buying Details tab for each item. Your solution? Either add supplier item numbers to each item or customise your purchase order to show your item numbers, rather than your suppliers'.

Sending purchase orders

To email a purchase order, first display the purchase, and then click the Send To button (found at the top, next to the Print button). Check the supplier's email address, change the message if you need to, pick the Selected Form and click Send. (You can change the default message that appears — go to Print/Email Purchase Orders from the Purchases command centre and click Email Defaults. Alternatively, if you only want to personalise one or two emails, simply highlight the email you want to change and alter the message, as I've done in Figure 8-2.)

The first time you want to email a purchase order from MYOB, send a test email to yourself first (simply enter your own email address instead of the supplier's email address when emailing a purchase order).

Alternatively, to print a purchase order, simply click the Print button (found at the top left of the purchase order) just before you record the order.

To fax a purchase order, first display the purchase, click the Send To button, choose Fax and click Send. Wait a second or two and your fax software should jump to attention, ready to do its stuff.

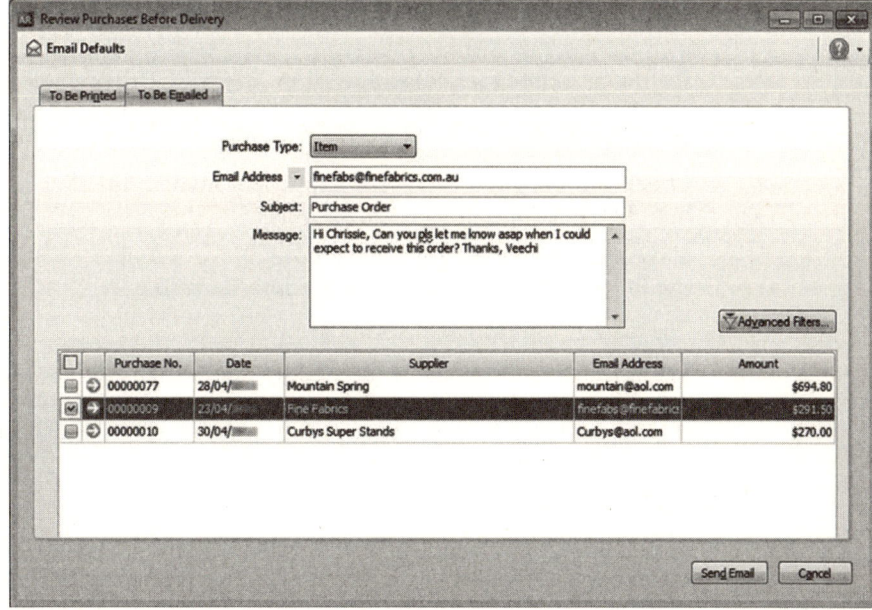

Figure 8-2:
You can
edit the
standard
message
when
emailing
purchase
orders to
suppliers.

Recording Supplier Bills

In this section, I explain how to record supplier bills for both items and services. I also explain how to deal with backorders, check supplier ABNs and ensure you pick the correct tax codes.

Receiving a bill (items only)

I explain here how to record a supplier bill for inventory items. For all other supplier bills, see the following section.

Follow this process for recording a bill for inventory items:

1. **In the Purchases command centre, choose Enter Purchases.**

2. **Enter the supplier's name and press Tab. If relevant, select your original order or item receipt from the list.**

   If you already recorded a purchase order for these goods, you see a list of outstanding orders or item receipts for this supplier. Highlight the original order and select Use Purchase. Alternatively, if you haven't yet recorded a purchase order for these goods, you may need to click the Layout button and select Item as the layout.

3. Either click the Bill button or select BILL in the top-left corner.

If you already recorded a purchase order or receipt for these goods, click the Bill button to switch from a yellow Purchase Order window to a cool sky-blue Bill window. Otherwise, go to the top-left corner of the purchase and select BILL.

4. Check the date and enter the supplier's invoice number in the Supplier Inv No. field.

Make sure the Date matches the date on the supplier's invoice and put the invoice number in the Supplier Inv No. field.

5. Check that the payment terms are correct.

Payment terms may seem like a fiddly detail at this point, but a moment spent getting this info right helps heaps later on. To change the terms, click the arrow to the left of the supplier's name and then click the Buying Details tab.

6. Check that all quantities are correct.

I find MYOB quite counterintuitive when it comes to recording quantities, so read this carefully. Imagine you ordered ten units of something and you only receive eight units and you don't want to backorder the two missing units. You'll find you can't change the number of units in the Received column — you have to change the number of units in the Billed column first, which then changes the number in the Received column.

Alternatively, if you want to put the missing units on backorder, enter **8** in the Billed column followed by **2** in the Backorder column. This quantity will stay as an Order in your Purchases Register until the whole order is filled.

7. Check all prices and descriptions.

Make sure all the quantities and prices are correct and that the Total Amount on this transaction matches the total on your supplier bill. If you're having trouble matching up the Tax amounts, you can click or unclick the Tax Inclusive button in the top right so that you're viewing prices using the same format as your supplier's invoice (some suppliers show prices exclusive of GST; others show prices inclusive of GST).

8. Click Record.

You may get a message saying this supplier has no ABN on file. See 'Checking supplier ABNs', later in this chapter, for more about this topic.

To guard against entering a supplier bill twice (and, therefore, accidentally paying the supplier twice), go to the Purchases tab in your Preferences menu and click the option to Warn for Duplicate Supplier Invoice Numbers on Recorded Purchases.

Receiving goods when you still have no bill

In the unlikely event that you receive goods without a bill (sometimes suppliers only send delivery dockets with shipments and the bills arrive separately), you can receive goods without finalising the supplier invoice.

Highlight the purchase order in your Purchases Register and then click the Receive Items button. (If you're prompted to select a liability account for item receipts the first time you do this, simply select a liability account called something like 'Items Received No Bill Yet'.) Then all you have to do is enter quantities in the Receive column, and click Record.

However, the simplest approach when receiving goods is to cut to the chase and record a supplier bill.

Recording bills for services, not items

Of course, most businesses receive lots of different kinds of bills, not just ones for inventory items. In fact, your business may not buy and sell inventory at all and you may never need to record an Item purchase. So, what do you do if you get a bill for something like advertising, consultancy fees, electricity or telephone?

The answer is that you record a Service purchase. These kinds of purchases are super-easy to record, so here I just give you a quick run-down on what's important:

1. **In the Purchases command centre, choose Enter Purchases.**

2. **Enter the supplier's name and press Tab.**

   If you don't already have this supplier in your card file, click New when prompted and complete all the supplier's details.

3. **Click the Layout button and select Service as the layout.**

4. **Check the Date matches the date on the supplier's invoice and enter the supplier's invoice number in the Supplier Inv No. field.**

5. **Complete the Description field, if desired.**

   For purchases such as electricity or telephone bills, you don't really need a description so you can leave this space blank, as I do in Figure 8-3. If you want a description for this purchase to appear on your transaction reports, use the Journal Memo field, rather than the Description field.

6. **Check that the payment terms are correct.**

7. **Select the expense type in the Account No. column, enter the Amount and then, if you want, enter Job details.**

In the Account No. column, you select the relevant type of expense. For example, select Telephone Expense as the account for a telephone bill, or Travel Expense for your family holiday in New Caledonia (just kidding). Also, if you want to allocate this purchase to a particular project, job or cost centre, complete the Job column.

If you want the expense account to appear automatically every time you record a bill from this supplier, click the arrow to the left of the supplier's name (at the top of the purchase) and then click the Buying Details tab of the supplier's card. Enter the default account in the Expense Account field.

8. **Check the Total Amount is correct and click Record.**

By now, your service purchase order should look similar to mine (see Figure 8-3).

Figure 8-3:
A typical service purchase.

Enter bills the smart way

If you receive lots of supplier bills by email, you may want to experiment with MYOB's supplier invoice service. At the time of writing, this service is only in the testing stage, but apparently the service is going to be ready 'any day now'. Here's how the service is going to work:

1. A supplier emails you an invoice.

2. You forward this invoice directly to an email address at MYOB (the address will probably be something like `bills@accountright.myob.com.au`).

3. When you next log in to your file, you'll see this bill appear in your 'in-tray' (which will be a new icon in AccountRight).

4. Next you'll go to your in-tray and click Create New Bill. MYOB will use optical character recognition (OCR) to enter this purchase into MYOB, reading and automatically completing as many of the fields on the bill as possible. All you will need to do is check the details that MYOB has entered, and add any additional details as required.

Sounds good? If the feature already exists by the time you read this chapter, I suggest you give it a go!

Calculating GST correctly

GST is actually fairly easy to get right, but here are some pointers in case you're new to the whole deal:

- **Buying goods or services for your own private use.** Pick N-T as your tax code.

- **Changing the way GST displays.** Sometimes a supplier provides an invoice or receipt that is tax inclusive (that is, you've been charged GST, but the invoice doesn't show how much). If this happens, all you have to do is select the Tax Inclusive box at the top of the purchase window. Then, simply enter the tax-inclusive amount in the Amount column of the purchase. Press the Enter key and voilà! The GST calculates correctly.

- **Coding transactions when you're not registered for GST.** In this situation, enter N-T as the tax code on every line, regardless of whether your suppliers charge GST, or not. (You may want to change the default tax codes in your Accounts List so that this N-T tax code comes up automatically, every time.)

- **Dealing with rounding problems.** Occasionally MYOB calculates the amount of GST on a purchase slightly differently to your supplier and the GST total differs by a cent or two. Don't tear your hair out wondering why this is (although I can tell you now that it's due to the way different software packages deal with rounding cents up and down). Instead, be pragmatic and ignore the difference. After all, two cents doesn't mean much in the grand scheme of things.

✔ **Purchasing new equipment or tools.** Select CAP as your tax code (CAP stands for Capital Acquisitions). Depending on whether or not you're eligible for small business entity concessions (ask your accountant if you're not sure), the threshold for capital acquisitions is either $100 (if you're not eligible) or $1,000 (if you are).

✔ **Trading with someone who isn't registered for GST.** Select FRE as your tax code.

Checking supplier ABNs

In theory, whenever you receive a Tax Invoice, especially if this is the first time you've dealt with a particular supplier, you're meant to double-check that the ABN is valid and that the supplier is registered for GST. In the past, the only way to do this was to visit the Australian Business Register website and check each ABN manually.

In the latest versions of MYOB, however, MYOB automatically checks the supplier ABN every time you add a new supplier card. If the ABN is good, a green icon appears next to the ABN field; if the ABN has expired or is invalid, a brown icon appears. You can also rest your mouse on the icon to see more details about a company's ABN status, including whether or not this supplier is registered for GST.

Note: You need to have both an active subscription to MYOB as well as an internet connection in order to use this service.

If a supplier fails to supply you with a valid ABN and their invoice is for more than $75, you are obliged to withhold 48.5 per cent tax from the supplier's payment and report this payment separately on your Business Activity Statement. Personally, I find such shenanigans are usually more trouble than they're worth, and prefer to deal only with suppliers who have a legitimate ABN.

Getting Everything Just Right

If you're at all like me, you sometimes make mistakes. In fact, if you're anything like me, you often make mistakes. Fortunately, you can cover your tracks so that no-one need ever know a thing.

If a purchase belongs to a previous period *and* you've already completed your Business Activity Statement for that period, *and* you report for GST on an accruals basis, don't delete the purchase or make any changes that affect the amount of GST. Instead, change your security preferences so that you can reverse the purchase, and then date the reversal with the current date. (I talk more about reversals in the section 'Reversing everything', later in this chapter.)

Deleting purchases — zap, they're gone!

You've recorded a purchase and now you want to delete it. Doing so is easy:

1. **Locate your purchase in the Transaction Journal or in your Purchases Register, and then double-click to display it.**

   For more information on locating purchase orders, skip to 'Looking up purchases and payments', later in this chapter.

2. **From the top menu bar, choose Edit⇨Delete Purchase.**

   See Figure 8-4.

   Your purchase has now gone to live in the land of odd socks and ballpoint pens, never to be seen again.

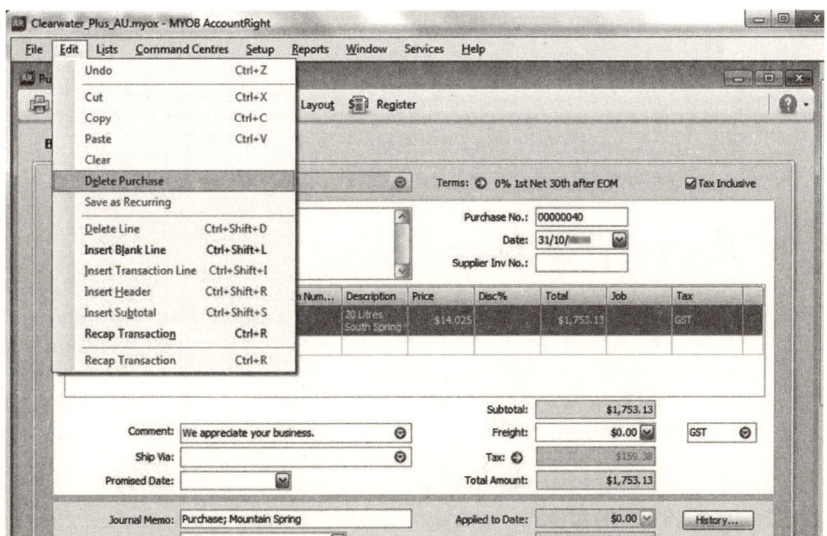

Figure 8-4: Deleting a purchase.

Entering credit notes

Entering a credit note is the same as entering a purchase; the only difference is what's normally positive becomes negative. In other words, to credit items, use negative figures in the Ship column; to credit a service, use negative figures in the Amount column.

If it's helpful to you, enter a brief description about why the credit note has been issued in the Journal Memo field.

After you have created the credit note, you need to match it against the bill that it's crediting. For more details, see 'Matching credits with their debits', later in this chapter.

Sometimes, when you try to put a credit note through for inventory items, you get the message 'The purchase of this item would value your inventory at less than $0.00'. The solution to this particular problem is a bit long to fit into this book, but don't despair. Visit www.myob.com.au/support and search for support note 9168 for a nifty help document on this subject.

Changing your mind

Sometimes you may want to change a purchase, instead of deleting it. Perhaps you want to fix up a quantity or price or perhaps you selected the wrong tax code. This is no problem.

Find your purchase in the Transaction Journal or Purchases Register (refer to 'Looking up purchases and payments', later in this chapter), and double-click the purchase to display it. Make any necessary changes and click Record.

Reversing everything

If you've set your preferences so that you can't delete or change entries after they're recorded, or if a purchase belongs to the previous financial year, the only way you can change or delete purchases is to reverse them. (This is obvious when you display a purchase and then go to the Edit menu — you don't see a Delete Purchase option and instead see Reverse Purchase.)

The idea of a reversal is that you create a transaction that's exactly the opposite of the incorrect one, so the two entries cancel each other out. (Think of it as two wrongs making a right.) You can then enter the purchase again, hopefully getting it right this time.

To reverse a purchase, first find it in the Transaction Journal or Purchases Register (see 'Looking up purchases and payments', later in this chapter), and then double-click to display it. From the top menu bar, choose Edit⇨Reverse Purchase. Check all the details on the reversal carefully, making sure the reversal has the correct date (you're usually best to enter the current date rather than the date of the original purchase), and then click Record Reversal.

Paying the Piper

Shakespeare wrote, 'He who dies pays all debts'. I really hope you don't have to resort to anything this drastic in order to do the right thing by your suppliers. Here's the clean-living, happy-go-lucky method with no blood or guts involved.

Facing the music (How much do you owe?)

You have two ways of seeing how much you owe suppliers. Like tall men versus short, blond versus dark, there's no saying that any single way is better than another. You just have to try each one and see which you like the best:

- ✔ **The Business Insights menu:** Go to the Business Insights menu (also called the Analysis menu in earlier versions) in the bottom-right corner of any command centre and click the Supplier Analysis or Payables option. You arrive at a dashboard similar to Figure 8-5. In the top-left corner you see a snapshot of every bill outstanding, with the oldest bill listed first. In the bottom-left you see the total owed to each supplier, grouped neatly month by month.

- ✔ **The Reports menu:** If you go to the Purchases tab of your Reports menu, you can choose between a few different Payables reports. The Aged Payables Summary report shows what you owe right now, whereas the Payables Reconciliation Summary shows what you owed suppliers at a particular point in time in the past (great when reporting for the end of month or financial year). I also like the Aged Payables Detail report, which lists every single bill owing, not just supplier totals.

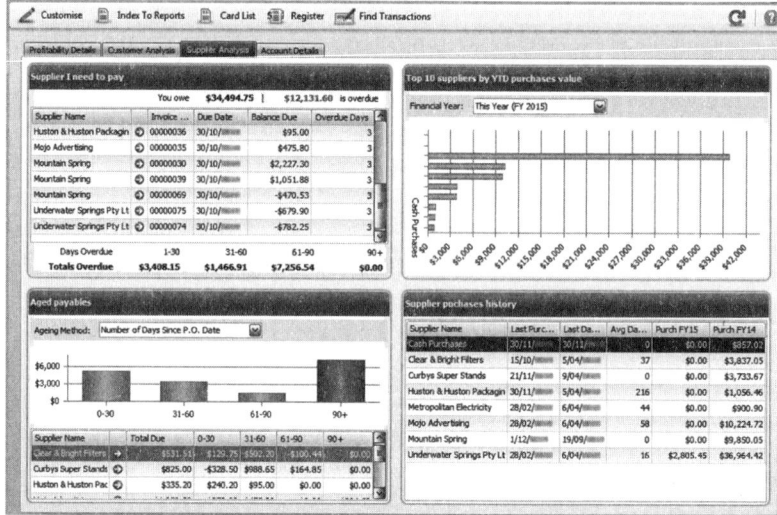

Figure 8-5:
Seeing
how much
you owe.

Of course, the due date for payment doesn't calculate correctly unless you configure supplier terms correctly. Keep the following in mind:

✔ To set a default for all suppliers, go to your Preferences menu, click the Purchase tab, and then click Terms in the top-left. Note that *EOM* stands for End of Month.

✔ To set terms for individual suppliers, go to the Buying Details of the supplier's card.

Tweaking your reports

Maybe your Payables report already gives you all the info you need, but just in case it doesn't, read on for a few tips:

✔ **Changing display options:** When you go to Supplier Analysis from the Business Insights menu, remember you can click any column label to sort by that column. For example, click the Total Due column to show the supplier that you owe the most to listed at the top, or click the Invoice No. column to sort by invoice number.

✔ **Displaying bills according to how overdue they are:** With any payables report, you can toggle between displaying bills according to how many days have passed since the invoice date or, alternatively, how many days overdue each bill is, based on the due date for payment. You can also choose to display the Due Date next to each bill on the more detailed reports. Neither method is right nor wrong — try both and see what works best for the business.

✔ **Troubleshooting missing totals:** If your Payables report doesn't include a total at the bottom, chances are you have an older version with multi-currency switched on in your company file. The solution? Go to the Customise button and select 'AUD' as the currency. You need to display this report one currency at a time in order to view column totals.

✔ **Understanding months versus days:** If your report lists accounts in 30-day periods (0–30, 31–60, 61–90 and so on), don't be fooled into thinking these days correspond to months, because most months don't have exactly 30 days. To group accounts month by month (which is usually the best way to work), go to Setup, click Preferences and then open the Reports & Forms tab. Under the Ageing option, select Monthly Ageing Periods.

✔ **Viewing Payables for a date that has already passed.** The Payables Reconciliation Summary allows you to pick a date from a previous week, month or year.

At the end of each month, generate a Payables Reconciliation Summary report and match the totals on this report against your suppliers' statements. This simple act of checking that you have the same figures that your suppliers do means you can be confident when making supplier payments.

Recording supplier payments

You can square up with your suppliers in two different ways. Go with the method you like best:

✔ Pay suppliers electronically, by cash, credit card or even by cheque, and then record the payments in your MYOB company file.

✔ Use MYOB as the starting point for paying your suppliers. Record the payment in your company file first, and then generate a payments file to import into your banking software. Chapter 13 explains more about electronic banking.

Regardless of whether you're recording supplier payments before or after the financial transaction has taken place, the way you record a supplier payment is much the same. Here's how it works:

1. **Go to the Purchases command centre and select Pay Bills.**

2. **Enter the supplier's name in the Supplier field.**

3. **Select your bank account.**

In the top-left corner, where it says Pay from Account, select the correct bank or credit card account — if you only have one business bank account, this selection is probably correct already. If you haven't made this payment yet, and you want to create an electronic transaction using MYOB, don't select a bank account. Instead, click Group with Electronic Payments.

4. Leave the Memo as is, and fill in the Cheque No. and Date.

Rather than make extra work for yourself, it's usually best to leave the Memo field as is. The cheque number comes up automatically and, rather bizarrely, still appears even if you've selected to process this transaction electronically. You can change the Cheque No. if need be, but if this is an electronic payment, simply ignore the Cheque No. field altogether.

5. For electronic payments, check the Statement Text.

The Statement Text shows what will appear on the bank statement for the supplier. You may want to include your customer number or the invoice number(s), whatever is most practical. In Figure 8-6, I list my customer account number.

To change the default Statement Text that appears, click the blue arrow to the left of the supplier name and go to the Payment Details tab.

6. Fill in the Amount field.

You can either enter the amount you intend to pay or you can click the Pay All button to automatically calculate how much the total would be if you were to pay all outstanding bills for this supplier at once.

7. Click against the bills that you're paying in the Amount Applied column.

Depending on your settings in Preferences, you may need to click in the Amount Applied column to apply your payment against the outstanding bills. By now, your payment should look similar to mine shown in Figure 8-6.

If you only see purchase order numbers as the reference on the left side, rather than supplier invoice numbers, you need to change your preferences. Go to Preferences, click the Purchases tab, and select Show Supplier Invoice Number in Supplier Payments.

8. If you intend to email this supplier a remittance advice, select To Be Emailed as the Remittance Advice Delivery Status.

9. Click Record.

If you've already paid this supplier and all you're doing right now is recording the transaction in MYOB, you're home and hosed. However, if you're recording an electronic payment, go to the Prepare Electronic Payments window and continue to process this payment from there.

Don't forget that you can sort any of the columns when making a supplier payment. So, for example, if you're applying a supplier payment against a particular invoice number and you can't see that invoice number easily, simply click the Supplier Inv No. label at the top of the column to sort by that number.

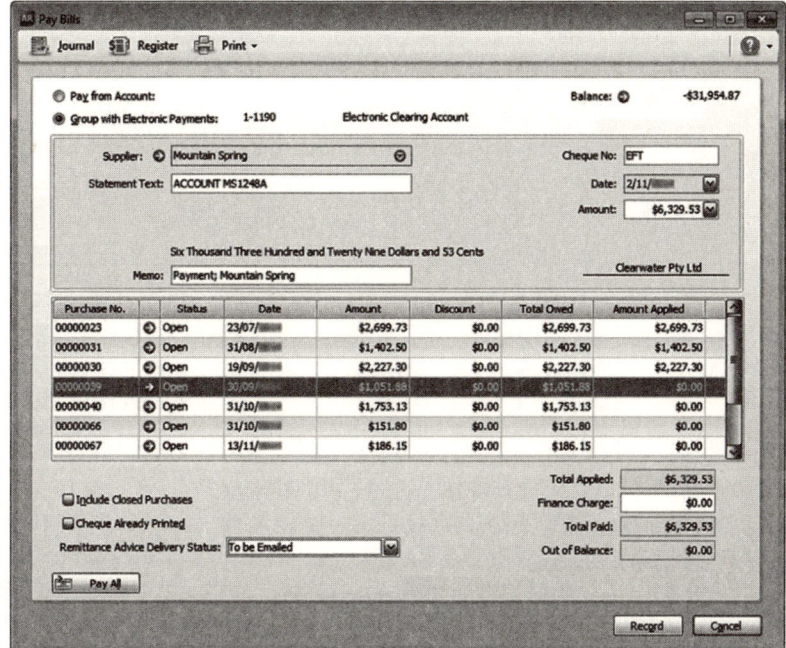

Figure 8-6: Recording a supplier payment.

Looking up purchases and payments

How do you look up information about suppliers, purchase orders, payments or bills? Try these ways:

✔ **Search through the Purchases Register.** Click All Purchases to view purchases and orders, click Orders to view purchase orders only, or click Open Bills to view unpaid purchases. On each of these tabs, you can choose between searching by All Suppliers or by one Supplier. Figure 8-7 shows a typical Purchases Register.

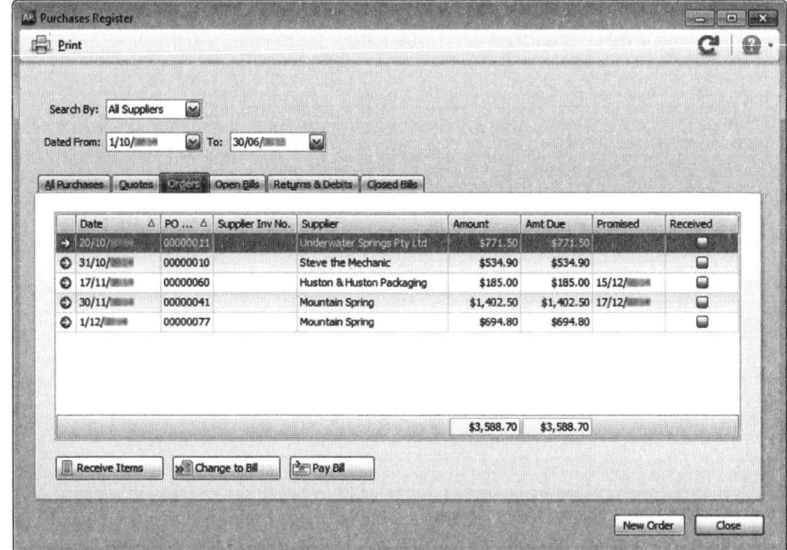

Figure 8-7:
Looking up
supplier
orders
in the
Purchases
Register.

✔ **Search by supplier name.** Sophisticated and rather stylish, the Find Transactions menu is my favourite way to view all financial transactions for a particular supplier. Go to the Find Transactions menu (at the bottom of any command centre) and click the Card tab. Enter the supplier's name and, if necessary, change the dates. You should see a list of all bills and payments (but not orders or item receipts) relating to that supplier.

✔ **Search by item.** If you want to look up purchases relating to a particular item, go to your Inventory command centre and click Items Register. Search by the item in question to view all purchases, sales and inventory transfers.

✔ **Search through the Transaction Journal.** If all else fails, try your Transaction Journal. The Purchases tab shows all supplier purchases, and the Disbursements Tab shows all supplier payments.

No luck finding what you're looking for? Try typing Ctrl+Shift+F (that is, holding all three keys down at the same time) when in any of the enquiry or transaction windows to search for a particular amount or string of text.

Taking the short road home

When it comes to paying suppliers, anything that saves me time and money makes me happy. Here are my favourite shortcuts:

✔ Hide your mouse. (Sit on it if necessary — I know some habits die hard.) Instead, move around by using the Tab key.

✔ Change your settings in Preferences so that you automatically apply payments against outstanding purchases, starting with the oldest one first. Go to Setup and click Preferences and then click the Purchases tab. Select the box Apply Supplier Payments Automatically to Oldest Bill First.

✔ Take the time to set up payment terms for each supplier (found on the Buying Details tab in each supplier's card). That way, you can rely on your To Do List to prompt you when bills fall due.

✔ Pay suppliers by electronic transfer. (I talk more about electronic transactions in Chapter 13.) Electronic payments save more time than you could ever imagine.

✔ Many utility companies, such as telecommunications or electricity providers, provide the option to debit your account automatically when a bill falls due. Why not pay the bill this way? (Hey, let them do the work, rather than you.)

✔ Don't pay your bills. This is really quick. (Just kidding.)

Sending remittance advices

After you record a supplier payment or payments, you're ready to send the supplier a remittance advice.

Here are the dance steps for this particular polka:

1. **From the Purchases command centre, click Print/Email Remittance Advice, followed by the To Be Emailed tab.**

   If no supplier payments appear in this list, click the To Be Printed tab instead. Click the payment you want to email an advice for, and select To Be Emailed as the Remittance Advice Delivery Status. Or, to resend a remittance that you've emailed or printed before, click Advanced Filters and unclick Unprinted or Unsent Remittance Advices Only.

   Under Advanced Filters, you can also select individual supplier names or a date range.

2. **Click against all payments that need a remittance advice, checking as you go that every supplier has a current email address.**

3. **Ask yourself whether you're content with the standard Message.**

   If not, click the Email Defaults button and do your stuff. Or to edit the message for one supplier only, highlight that supplier's name and edit the Message at the top.

4. Click Send Email.

Make your way to your mail program and double-check that the emails have gone through okay. If you're connected to the internet all the time, the emails should have already shuffled over to your Sent Items folder. If you're not currently online, the emails will be sitting in your Outbox, ready to send.

Sometimes the message field in MYOB doesn't provide enough room for me to say what I want to the supplier — maybe I want to apologise for a late payment or query a particular amount. In this situation, I replace the supplier's email address with my own. This way, I receive the email in my Inbox. I then click Forward, enter the supplier's email address, edit the email as required, and click Send.

You can see what a standard remittance looks like in Figure 8-8. You're probably fine with this format, but if you do want to customise the layout, simply go to your Setup menu, select Customise Forms, and then select Remittance Advices.

Printing remittance advices is almost exactly the same as emailing remittance advices. Go to Print/Email Remittance Advice and click the To Be Printed tab. Click against the payments that need a remittance advice, or to change the settings, click Advanced Filters. Here, you can select particular supplier names, choose a date range or cheque number range. With your selections complete, click Print.

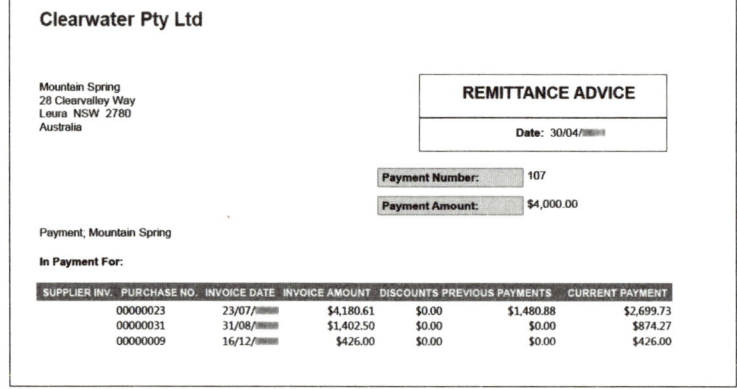

Figure 8-8:
Emailing a
remittance
advice
is quick
and easy.

Keeping Things in Tune

Using the Purchases command centre is like keeping a car on the road — doing so requires a certain amount of maintenance. Odd amounts crop up that you can't delete, credits appear that won't go away or accounts show up as owing when you know they're not. Here's the practical mechanic's guide to a six-month service and tune.

Recording overpayments

Don't feel too bad; everyone accidentally overpays a supplier sooner or later. Here's how to record the payment so you can keep track of how much you've overpaid, ready to either claim a refund or apply this credit against a future account:

1. **Go to Pay Bills as if to record the payment as normal and enter the full amount that you paid in the Amount field.**

2. **Type the amount that you paid, including the overpayment, in the Amount Applied column.**

   For example, if you paid $600 when you should have paid $420, type $600 in the Amount Applied column next to this bill (you can see how this would look in Figure 8-9). Alternatively, if you've double-paid a bill, and this bill isn't showing up as owing, click Include Closed Purchases. Then type the amount of your overpayment against the bill that you've already paid.

   You get a warning saying that applying the payment in this way will result in a credit invoice.

3. **Click OK to record this credit.**

   This credit is now sitting in your Purchases Register under the Returns & Debits tab. At this point, you can either apply the credit against another supplier bill, or you can wait until you receive a refund.

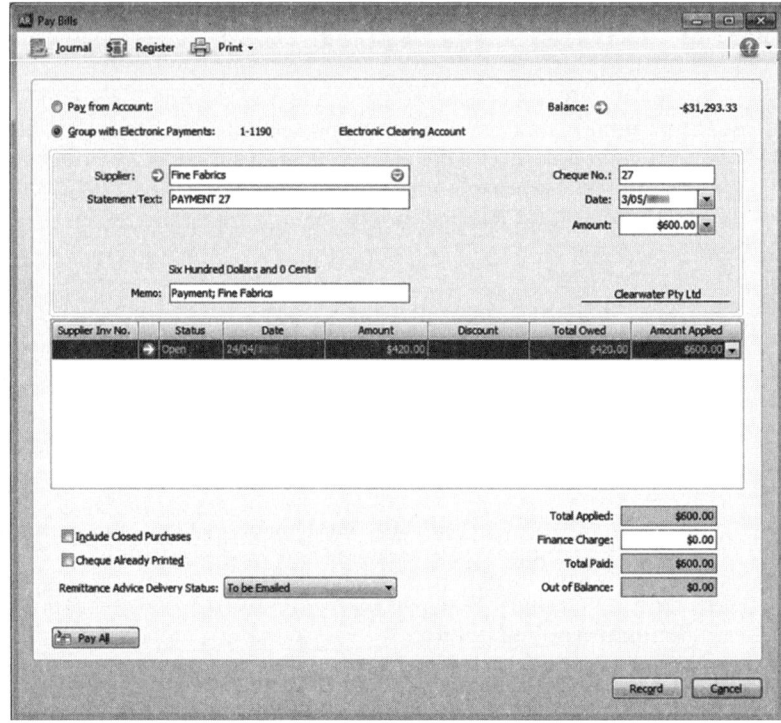

Figure 8-9:
Dealing with
supplier
over-
payments.

Recording part-payments or discounts

Sometimes, you may have a good reason not to pay a supplier's bill in full. Maybe you're making a part-payment only at this point, or maybe you're taking an early-payment discount.

To pay only part of a bill now, go to Pay Bills as normal, click against the bill you want to part-pay and enter the amount you want to pay in the Amount Applied column. Easy.

To apply a discount against a bill, enter the amount of the discount that you're taking in the Discount column. (If you've set up your supplier payment terms correctly, this Discount amount should calculate automatically.)

Fixing up supplier payments

Have you made a mistake with a supplier payment? Although you can change the date or the cheque number of a supplier payment, you *can't* change the amount or how you've allocated the payment. Instead, you need to delete or reverse this payment and then have another stab at getting it right.

To delete or reverse a supplier payment, follow my lead:

1. **Go to Find Transactions and click the Card tab.**

   To delete a payment, you first need to find it. The Find Transactions menu (which appears on the bottom of every command centre) is your best bet.

2. **Enter the supplier's name as well as an approximate date range.**

3. **Double-click the supplier payment you want to change.**

   At this point, you may encounter the message, 'One or more parts of this journal entry have been reconciled'. Don't go any further. Click OK and then Cancel. (If you delete the payment, you'll throw your bank reconciliation out of balance, which is not a good idea.)

4. **From the top menu bar, choose Edit⇨Delete Payment or Edit⇨Reverse Payment.**

   Go to the Edit command on the top menu bar. Whether you can see Delete Payment or Reverse Payment at this point depends on how you set your preferences. Either method is okay. However, if this is a payment you made electronically, you'll need to make your way to Chapter 13 for more details about reversing transactions that are part of a batch.

5. **If you chose Reverse Payment, check the reversal transaction, changing the date if necessary.**

   If you're reversing a payment that belonged to a previous quarter, and you've already completed a Business Activity Statement for that quarter, you're best to date the reversal with today's date, not the date of the original transaction.

Zapping bills you know you've paid

If your Payables report says you owe a supplier money and you're positive that you've paid the account, you almost certainly used Spend Money when recording the payment, instead of Pay Bills. Just like putting diesel in an unleaded fuel car, this upsets the works.

To fix this problem, simply remove the outstanding purchase, either by deleting or reversing it, depending on your Preference settings. (I explain deletions and reversals in more detail earlier in this chapter, in the section 'Getting Everything Just Right'.)

Occasionally, when you try to delete a purchase you get a message saying you can't, either because the purchase belongs to a previous financial year or because payments have already been applied. In this case, create a credit purchase for the amount outstanding, and date this credit in the current financial year. See 'Getting rid of odd amounts'.

Matching credits with their debits

Sometimes you get an amount showing up twice for a particular supplier on your Payables report — the first time as a positive amount, the next time as a minus amount. The total amount due is zero, but the Payables report keeps listing both amounts. To fix this problem, head for your Purchases Register and click the Returns & Debits tab, where a list of all outstanding credit purchases appears. Highlight the offending credit and click Apply to Purchase. Click in the Amount Applied column and then hit Record. Problem fixed.

Getting rid of odd amounts

No matter how meticulous you are, odd amounts inevitably creep into your supplier accounts. Here are a few maintenance tricks:

✔ For most credits, go to Purchases and create a new purchase, entering a minus quantity in the Received column for an Item purchase, or a minus figure in the Amount column for a Service purchase.

✔ To get rid of odd little amounts (perhaps five cents is outstanding on an account), go to Purchases and select Miscellaneous as your purchase format. Create a credit purchase for this amount and then apply it in the Returns & Debits tab of your Purchases Register.

✔ To spring-clean your credits, go to the Returns & Debits tab in your Purchases Register and look at every credit listed. Wherever possible, apply these credits to outstanding purchases.

Reporting for taxable payments

If your business earns income from building and construction and you pay subcontractors then you will most likely have to report for taxable payments. For more info, head to my website at www.veechicurtis.com.au, and look for the ebook on this topic in the Online Bookshop.

Chapter 9

Reconcile Yourself

. . . .

In This Chapter

▶ Understanding what bank reconciliations are all about

▶ Preparing to do your first reconciliation

▶ Doing the deed — reconciling your bank account

▶ Digging your way out of tricky situations

▶ Tackling a bank account that doesn't balance

▶ Saving bank reconciliation reports

. . . .

*Y*ou have to reconcile yourself to a lot in this life. When you go for a picnic, it always rains. When your computer crashes, it's the one time you didn't back up. When you drop a piece of toast, it lands jam-side down.

Another fact of life that you have to reconcile yourself to is this: If you're going to use MYOB, you have to reconcile your bank account. The good news is that reconciling accounts is actually quite easy, and can even be fun, in a nerdy kind of way.

In this chapter, I explain how to go about this process. I explain how one of the benefits of using bank feeds is that reconciling accounts is about ten times easier than if you're not using feeds — but, regardless, I show you how to reconcile either way. I also share my guerrilla tactics for getting bank accounts to balance, no matter how harsh your enemy or how difficult your situation. I end with some points on generating a reconciliation report.

What Reconciling is All About

Reconciling a bank account means comparing the balance of your bank account in your MYOB company file against the balance for the same date on your bank statement. For example, if your bank statement or bank balance according to internet banking says you have $5,000 in the bank and you double-check that the balance of your bank account in MYOB says the same thing, you can say that your account is reconciled.

Reconciling bank accounts isn't an activity for bookkeepers who have nothing more exciting in their life to do. Instead, reconciling accounts is often the only way to pick up mistakes, such as a payment entered as $900 instead of $90, a deposit entered twice, or a missing bank charge.

Most businesses have lots of bank accounts — from savings accounts and term deposits, to credit cards and loans. Although you don't have to reconcile all these accounts, if you don't your accountant probably will. An easy way to determine your priorities is to divide your accounts into three categories:

✔ **Accounts you have to reconcile:** As a bare minimum, always reconcile your business bank account. Unless you do this, you can't rely on any of your financial reports.

✔ **Accounts to reconcile if you have time:** It's a good idea to reconcile all credit card, savings and PayPal accounts, as well as your business bank account.

✔ **Accounts to reconcile if you're feeling conscientious:** Ideally, reconcile all your loan accounts as well. Loan accounts can be tricky, because you have to split up interest and principal on each loan repayment.

Getting Ready to Reconcile

The first time you reconcile your bank account is the hardest because you have to allow for any uncleared payments or deposits that existed before you started using MYOB. Although this process can be tricky, don't worry. In the following sections, I guide you safely through the whole kit and caboodle.

Listing uncleared transactions

The first time you reconcile your bank account, you need to draw up a list of all uncleared payments and deposits as at the date you started using MYOB. *Note:* You may not have any uncleared transactions at your start date. That's fine — simply skip this step.

By *uncleared payments*, I mean any cheques you posted to suppliers before your start date, but haven't yet cleared through your bank account. By *uncleared deposits*, I mean any money received before your start date, but which you haven't banked, or which hasn't cleared. (For example, maybe you received an EFTPOS payment on 30 June that didn't appear on your bank statement until 1 July, or maybe a customer has sent you a cheque but you haven't banked it yet.)

My list of uncleared payments and deposits in Figure 9-1 shows two uncleared payments plus one uncleared deposit. The total value of uncleared transactions is minus $900.

Figure 9-1:
A list of
uncleared
transactions
at your
start date.

Uncleared cheques	
Cheque 950 (Fastway couriers)	-200.00
Cheque 951 (Superannuation)	-1900.00
Uncleared deposits	
Credit card payments	1200.00
Total Value Uncleared Transactions	-900.00

Recording bank opening balances

After listing uncleared transactions (refer to preceding section), the next step is to record the opening balance of your bank account. Here's my neat 1-2-3 approach:

1. **In your Accounts List, create a new bank account called Uncleared Transactions.**

   Make sure this account sits immediately below your regular bank account in your Accounts List. (You only need to create this account if you had uncleared transactions at your start date. Refer to the preceding section if you're not sure.)

2. **Go to Setup, then Balances, followed by Account Opening Balances. Enter the opening balance from your bank statement as the opening balance for your bank account.**

   Find your bank statement, circle the balance on this statement as of your start date, and enter this amount as the opening balance for your bank account. You can see how my opening balances look in Figure 9-2 (the opening balance on my bank statement was $3,650 in credit).

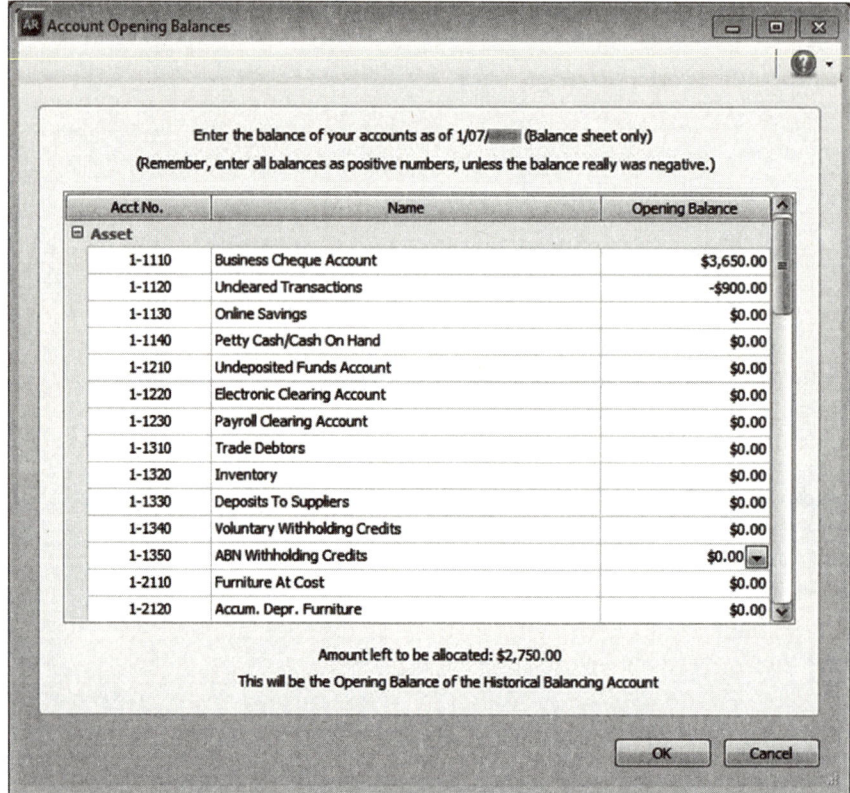

Figure 9-2:
Entering
opening
bank
account
balances.

3. **Enter the combined balance of uncleared transactions as the opening balance of your Uncleared Transactions account.**

Using the example in Figure 9-1, the combined balance of uncleared transactions is minus $900.

All done? With opening balances for your bank account entered, you're ready to reconcile your bank account.

Reconciling Your Bank Account

The method for reconciling your bank account depends on whether you're using bank feeds or not. I explain both methods in the following sections.

Reconciling if you're not using bank feeds

This section explains how to reconcile your bank account manually if you're not using bank feeds. This section is also relevant if you ended up with a few weeks or even months between starting to use MYOB and enabling bank feeds.

I assume here that you've already set up your opening balances (if not, return to 'Recording bank opening balances', earlier in this chapter), that you've already entered a few transactions, and that you have your bank statement close to hand. Here goes:

1. **In the Banking command centre, select Reconcile Accounts.**

2. **Press Tab, select your bank account, and then click Use Account.**

   When you press Tab a list of accounts appears. Pick your bank account from the list — it's near the top.

3. **Check your Calculated Statement Balance.**

   Assuming you haven't yet marked off any transactions, the Calculated Statement Balance should equal the opening balance on your bank statement.

   No? If this is the first time you've ever reconciled this account, return to 'Recording bank opening balances', earlier in this chapter, and make sure you recorded your opening balance correctly. Alternatively, if this bank account has already been reconciled in the past, skip ahead to 'Identifying your starting point' for more tips on starting off at the right point.

4. **Enter the date you're reconciling up to in the Bank Statement Date field.**

   Enter the date that your bank statement goes up to. In the example shown in Figure 9-3, I'm reconciling my statement up to July 6.

   If you're reconciling manually for the gap of time before your bank feeds went live, ensure you only reconcile up to the date when your bank feeds began, even if your bank statement goes beyond this date

5. **Click off your payments and deposits, one by one.**

   Work down your bank statement and, one by one, find each transaction and click against it. The result should look similar to Figure 9-3.

   When uncleared cheques or deposits that belong to the period before your start date eventually appear on your bank statement, go to Transfer Money in the Accounts command centre and transfer funds between your Uncleared Transactions account and your regular bank account.

6. If you see any mistakes, fix them up right here and now.

Perhaps you entered a payment as $800 instead of $80, or a deposit as $78 instead of $87. To fix a mistake, click the arrow next to the transaction, change any details that you need to, and then click Record. Alternatively, if MYOB doesn't let you make the change that you need to, see 'Dealing with transactions that can't be changed', later in this chapter.

7. After half a page or so, enter the running balance from your statement in the Closing Statement Balance field, and then press Tab.

When you first work on reconciling, don't try to do a whole page at a time. Instead, work in small, bite-sized chunks of a third, or half of a page. When you complete a stage, look at the running balance on your bank statement and enter this amount in the Closing Statement Balance in the top-right, and then press Tab. In Figure 9-3, my Closing Statement Balance is $6,808.27.

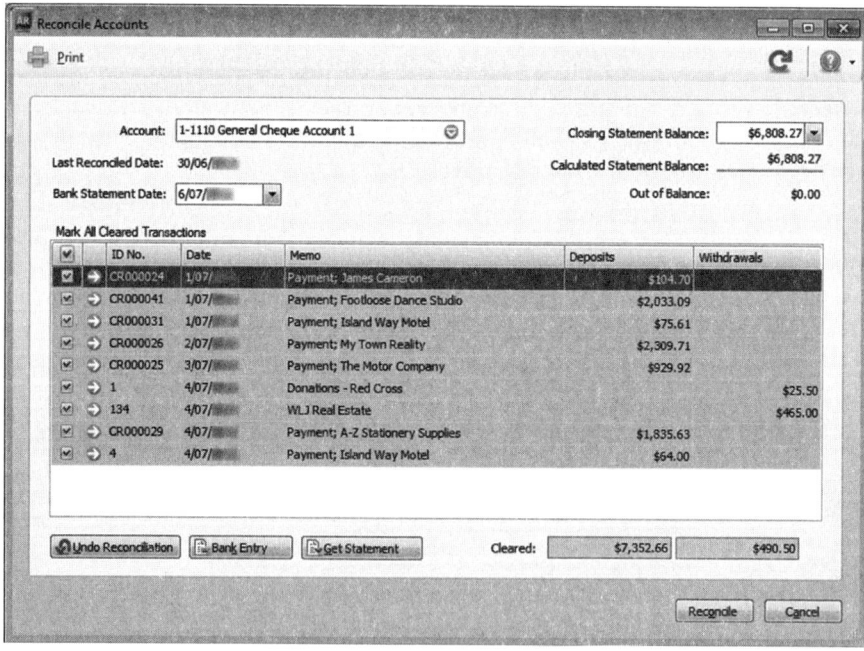

Figure 9-3: Reconciling your bank account is easiest if you do bite-sized chunks at a time.

8. Cross your fingers and check that the Out of Balance amount is zero.

If the Out of Balance amount is zero, give yourself a pat on the back. If your bank account doesn't balance, don't be discouraged. Work through these instructions one more time, checking each step as you go, and you should be able to find where you went wrong.

Still no luck? Skip ahead to the section 'When Your Bank Account Just Won't Balance', later in this chapter.

9. **Click Reconcile and then Reconcile again.**

   Yippee! You receive a message saying 'Your account reconciles'. It's a good feeling, isn't it? All you have to do now is click Reconcile to continue or click Print Report to generate a summary report of everything you've done.

Reconciling if you're using bank feeds

Although the concept of reconciling a bank account if you're using bank feeds is essentially the same as if you're not using bank feeds, the process itself is a little different. Follow these instructions to see what I mean:

1. **In the Banking command centre, click Bank Feeds.**

2. **Work through the transactions adding, approving or matching each one as you normally would.**

   For more about recording transactions direct from a bank feed, refer to Chapter 5.

3. **If you're not sure how to allocate a particular transaction, record it anyway, selecting a Suspense account if necessary.**

   For transactions where you're not sure what to do, select either Spend Money (for withdrawals) or Receive Money (for deposits) from the New menu, and allocate this transaction to an expense account called Suspense. (If you haven't already got an account by this name, create one now, and give this account the number of 6-9999.)

4. **If you know the bank feed is essentially correct, but it doesn't match against a transaction you've already entered because of merchant fees or payments being batched together, consider hiding this transaction.**

   As a way of working, hiding transactions is never a long-term solution, but can make sense if you have a whole heap of transactions you've processed in the wrong way. See 'Ditching transactions that won't go away', later in this chapter, for more details.

5. **When you have added, approved or matched every single transaction in your bank feed up to a certain date, click Reconcile in the bottom-right.**

   You can see that I'm ready to reconcile up to 30 December in Figure 9-4 and, because I've approved every single transaction in the Bank Feeds window, the Out of Balance amount appears as $0.00 (a promising sign for the reconciliation process!).

When you click Reconcile, you arrive at the Reconcile window.
All transactions that you've approved from your bank feed are marked
as reconciled.

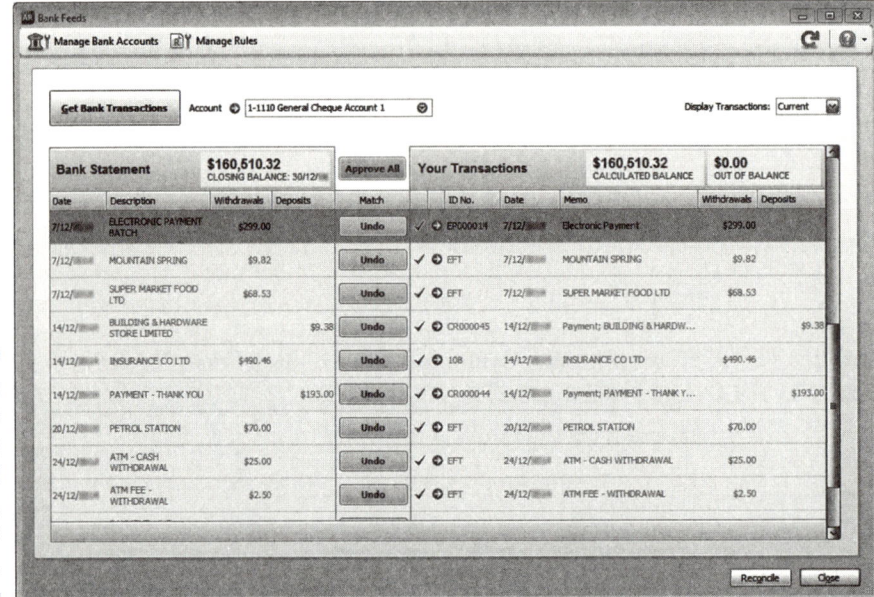

Figure 9-4:
With every
transaction
approved
or matched,
you're ready
to reconcile.

6. **Check the date you're reconciling up to in the Bank Statement
   Date field.**

   If you've worked through every transaction in your Bank Feeds window,
   this date will automatically be the last date from your bank feed, and
   almost certainly correct. However, if you've chosen to reconcile a
   smaller date range, enter the date up to which you're reconciling in the
   Bank Statement Date field.

   If you change the date, don't enter a date beyond the period for which
   you've approved transactions in your bank feed. Why? If you reconcile
   a transaction in the Reconcile Accounts window *before* you've matched
   it in the Bank Feeds window, when you later return to your bank feeds,
   MYOB won't be able to match the transaction.

7. **Check the closing balance from your bank statement in the Closing
   Statement Balance field, and then press Tab.**

   Look at the closing balance on your bank statement for the date up
   until which you're reconciling and enter this amount in the Closing

Statement Balance in the top-right (if you're reconciling right up to the current date, this balance comes up automatically). For example, earlier in this chapter in Figure 9-3, the Closing Statement Balance is $6,808.27.

8. **Check that the Out of Balance amount equals $0.00.**

   In the perfect world, your Out of Balance amount should be $0.00. If not, skip ahead to 'Troubleshooting Tricks', next in this chapter.

9. **Click Reconcile and then Reconcile again.**

   Yippee! You receive a message saying 'Your account reconciles'. It's a good feeling, isn't it? All you have to do now is click Reconcile to continue or click Print Report to generate a summary report of everything you've done.

10. **Review any transactions that remain in the Reconcile Accounts window.**

If everything is on track, you should have no transactions showing when you return to the Reconcile Accounts window, with the only possible exceptions being uncleared cheques that suppliers haven't banked yet, or EFTPOS receipts that haven't yet appeared in your bank account. If you do have any other transactions showing here, go to 'Ditching transactions that won't go away', later in this chapter.

Troubleshooting Tricks

In this section, I explain how to deal with some of the trickier aspects of bank reconciliations, such as figuring out where you left off, entering missing transactions and fixing up mistakes.

Time for a little housework

In this chapter, I suggest using an account called Uncleared Transactions to store the opening balance of all the uncleared payments and deposits as at your start date. I also suggest that when these transactions eventually clear through your bank account, you allocate them to your Uncleared Transactions account. In the perfect world (and who is to say that it isn't?), what happens is that the balance of

your Uncleared Transaction account eventually returns to zero.

After the balance of Uncleared Transactions does return to zero, you can use the Combine Accounts feature to get rid of this account from your Accounts List. I explain more about combining accounts in Chapter 2.

The bigger, the better

Reconciling accounts is much quicker and easier if you make the Reconcile Accounts window as big as possible on your screen, so that you can see lots of transactions at one time.

If you're using a PC, maximise the window by clicking on the square sitting at the top right of the Reconcile Accounts window (between the hyphen and the cross). If you're using a Mac, drag the corners out as far as you can.

Identifying your starting point

Unless you're working with bank feeds, the first step in reconciling a bank account is always to figure out where you finished working the last time.

Go to Reconcile Accounts as normal, select your bank account in the Account field and enter the current date in the Bank Statement Date field. But before you do anything else, write down the amount sitting in the Calculated Statement Balance field, and note down the date in the Last Reconciled Date field. This provides a good indication of where you got up to in your last reconciliation.

Rummage through your bank statements for this period, scanning the running balance column. Sooner or later (hopefully sooner), you find the amount you just wrote down when you looked at the Calculated Statement Balance. Yippee! You've found it. This is the spot you need to start from.

Note the following:

- ✔ I assume here that you've reconciled your bank account at least once before. If not, go back to the beginning of this chapter and start reading from 'Reconciling Your Bank Account'.

- ✔ You can avoid losing your 'reconciling' place in future by using a highlighter pen on your bank statement to mark the spot you got to.

- ✔ If you already have transactions marked as reconciled, you may need to 'untick' these transactions in order to find your starting point.

If you find that the Calculated Statement Balance displayed in Reconcile Accounts when you open up your reconciliation doesn't match the ending balance on your bank statement from the last time you reconciled *and* you haven't marked any transactions as cleared yet, then you're in trouble. Skip ahead in this chapter to the section 'Undoing the previous reconciliation'.

Locating transactions that disappear

You're absolutely, totally, 100 per cent positive that you recorded a particular transaction (perhaps only a few minutes before). Yet when you go to Reconcile Accounts, the darned thing won't show up on the screen. Where's it gone?

Don your detective hat and try the following:

- ✔ **Ensure you enter a date in the Bank Statement Date field.** Unless you enter a date here, you won't see any transactions at all.

- ✔ **Change the Bank Statement Date to a date way in the future.** Whenever you reconcile an account, you only see transactions that have a date on or before the Bank Statement Date. By temporarily changing the date to sometime in the future (for example, 12/12/2099), you can pick up on transactions that you have entered with the wrong date.

- ✔ **Check which bank account the transaction went to.** Perhaps you accidentally sent the missing transaction to a different bank account. Go to your Find Transactions menu, click the Card tab and enter the name of whomever you made the payment to, or received the deposit from. When you find the transaction, double-click to display it and check you selected the correct bank account in the top-left corner.

Sweeping stuff under the carpet

My high school daughter used to do admin work for my business, and some years ago I decided to teach her how to reconcile my business bank account. I was in the middle of showing her how the process worked when the phone went, and I had to dash off to see a client. I was gone most of the morning.

When I returned, she was lying happily in the hammock listening to Jack Johnson. 'How did you go?' I asked. 'Fine,' she answered, 'I reconciled the last six months of your bank statements without a problem; it really doesn't seem that hard.' I approached my shiny silver iMac with a sense of trepidation that was soon justified. 'What's this entry?' I asked. 'And this one?' I highlighted a whole bunch of transactions simply labelled

'Miscellaneous', some of which were for thousands of dollars.

'Well,' replied Isla. 'When I couldn't get the statement to balance, I calculated the difference, entered a transaction for that amount, marked the statement as reconciled, and then kept going. Seemed logical to me.'

I tried to explain to Isla that inventing transactions to patch up bank reconciliations is like posting prawn shells inside the curtain rods at your ex-lover's apartment. The problem simply festers and gets worse as time passes. After all, the idea of reconciling accounts is to find your mistakes and fix 'em up. 'What if the whole relationship was a mistake?' she asked. 'You're not getting the point,' I answered. 'Never mind,' she replied, and rolled over in the hammock.

Entering missing transactions on the fly

If you're in the middle of reconciling and realise you've forgotten to enter a transaction, you don't need to close Reconcile Accounts. All you have to do is go to Command Centres on the top menu bar and select the function you need. Go ahead and record your missing entry. When you're finished, click Cancel and you arrive back at Reconcile Accounts.

Alternatively, if you come across bank charges, interest payments or direct debits, your other option is simply to click the Bank Entry button at the bottom of the Reconcile Accounts window. Here you can record bank charges or interest earned, similar to Figure 9-5.

Figure 9-5:
Recording
bank
charges
or interest
earned.

> **Bank and Deposit Adjustments**
>
> Account: 1-1110 General Cheque Account 1   ☑ Tax Inclusive
>
> **Service Charges**
> Amount: $6.50   Tax Code: FRE   Tax: $0.00
> ID No. : SC301214   Job:
> Date: 31/05/
> Expense Account: 6-1130 Bank Charges
> Memo: Transaction fee
>
> **Interest Earned**
> Amount: $0.00   Tax Code: Tax: $0.00
> ID No. : IE301214   Job:
> Date: 30/12/
> Income Account:
> Memo:
>
> Record   Cancel

If you're using bank feeds, you should never have a situation where a transaction appears on your bank statement but not on your bank feed. (Possible exceptions are if your subscription lapses and your bank feeds are interrupted, or rare situations where the bank feed itself is wrong.) So, if a transaction appears to be missing from the Reconcile Accounts window, return to your Bank Feeds window first and double-check that this transaction isn't showing.

Hot keys to stop you sweating

I find that when I'm reconciling bank accounts, I often want to hop to somewhere else in the program without having to quit from where I am.

This is where shortcut keys are so useful. Press Ctrl+H (if you're using a PC) or Cmd+H (if you're using a Macintosh) and you arrive in an instant at Spend Money. Record your payment, press Escape or click Close, and you're back at your bank reconciliation.

Do the same with deposits. Press Ctrl+D (if you're using a PC) or Cmd+D (if you're using a Macintosh). In the blink of an eye, you arrive at Receive Money.

If you're using Windows, you can even cycle though all the windows you have open without having to close them. To do this, while holding down the Ctrl button with one finger, press Tab again and again and watch as you cycle through the open windows.

Dealing with transactions that can't be changed

I mention earlier in this chapter that when you discover a mistake, all you have to do is click on the arrow that appears on the left of the transaction. This displays the original transaction and, from here, you can usually fix up your mistake. However, for some kinds of transactions, such as employee pays, supplier payments and customer payments, you can only change the date and reference number, not the amount.

For supplier or customer payments, if the mistake is simply that you entered the amount incorrectly, it's probably okay to delete the transaction and then enter it again, but correctly this time. (Double-check your records first, however, and make sure that the mistake was definitely at your end, and not a mistake made by your bank.)

For employee pays, it may be okay to delete the pay and re-enter it, but only if you haven't yet parted with the cash, nor issued a pay slip yet. (I don't recommend you attempt to change amounts by deleting and re-entering employee pays, because you need to maintain a full audit trail for all payroll transactions. If necessary, you can reverse the pay and then re-enter a transaction instead. Chapter 11 explains how.)

Ditching transactions that won't go away

At risk of this chapter ending up as a litany of everything that can go wrong, I'm now going to talk about two more tricky situations: Unmatched transactions that stick around in your bank feeds, and uncleared transactions that remain in your bank reconciliation window.

Table 9-1 explores the different reasons these problems occur. You can see that the suggested solution in several instances is to hide the transaction from the bank feed. To do this, simply right-click the transaction from within the Bank Feeds window and select Hide Transaction.

Table 9-1	Dealing with Uncleared and Unmatched Transactions		
Problem	*Cause of Problem*	*Short-Term Solution*	*Long-Term Solution*
You have an unmatched transaction in your bank feed, but you can see from your transaction registers that this transaction is already entered and reconciled. When you click Find from the Bank Feed, MYOB finds no transaction it can match to.	You have gone to Reconcile Accounts direct from the Banking command centre (rather than clicking Reconcile from the bottom of the Bank Feeds window) and have marked a transaction as cleared before it has been matched in the bank feed.	Hide the transaction in your bank feed.	Always work through your bank feed first before reconciling accounts and always click Reconcile from the Bank Feed window.
When you click Find, you can't find a match for a banking deposit, yet you can see that the payments belonging to this deposit have already been recorded.	You recorded individual payments as going into your bank account, but the bank statement shows a daily total.	Hide this transaction in your bank feed and then reconcile the individual payments in your bank reconciliation.	Use an Undeposited Funds account when processing customer payments. (Chapter 7 explains how Undeposited Funds accounts work.)

Problem	Cause of Problem	Short-Term Solution	Long-Term Solution
A transaction shows twice in your bank feed but only once on your bank statement.	The bank feed itself is wrong.	Hide this transaction in your bank feed.	Problems with bank feeds are very rare but if this issue occurs again, contact MYOB Technical Support.
You have an old transaction showing as uncleared in your Reconcile Accounts window, even though you've already reconciled for that period.	When you look through your transaction registers, you can see you've entered this transaction twice.	Delete the duplicate.	If you haven't done so already, consider subscribing to bank feeds to reduce the likelihood of data-entry errors.
A cheque you've sent to a supplier shows as uncleared.	The supplier hasn't banked it yet.	Wait a while.	If several months pass, you can reverse the cheque, dating the reversal with the current date.

When Your Bank Account Just Won't Balance

It would be embarrassing if I owned up to the number of times I've had trouble reconciling a bank account. But the upside of this is that my troublesome times have taught me a few tricks. And I'm really happy to share them with you.

Tricks to try before you kick the cat

When your bank account doesn't balance, stay calm and try the following:

✔ **Look for a missing line.** Have you missed something on your bank statement that should have been ticked in the Reconcile Accounts window? Look at every line on the statement and check that a tick appears next to the corresponding entry.

✔ **Count the ticks.** Have you ticked something in the Reconcile Accounts window that isn't on your bank statement? If your eyes are going crooked looking from the statement to the screen and back to the statement again, try counting the number of ticks in your Reconcile Accounts window and then the number of lines on your bank statement. They should be the same!

✔ **Call on your hidden powers.** How much are you out by? Does this amount ring a bell?

Tricks to try before you kick the computer

If you've tried the suggestions so far with no success, take a walk around the block and think about something totally different for a while. Then try the following:

✔ **Watch for overdrafts that go into credit.** If your bank account is an overdraft but you're actually in credit, you need to enter the Closing Statement Balance as a minus amount. (This seems weird, but it's true.)

✔ **Make sure you're in the right spot.** Did you start off from the right spot in your bank statement? It's easy to accidentally skip a page or part of a page. (Refer to 'Identifying your starting point' earlier in this chapter.)

✔ **Compare the magic totals.** Somewhere on your bank statement you can usually find a summary of total debits and total credits. This corresponds to the bottom of the Reconcile Accounts window, where you see totals for Deposits and Withdrawals. Try comparing these totals with your bank statement's totals to see whether the problem lies with deposits or withdrawals (or both!).

✔ **Do the number nine trick.** If your Out of Balance amount is a multiple of nine, look to see if you put in two numbers back to front — for example, you entered 43 instead of 34, or 685 instead of 658. (It's a curious thing, but if you turn a number back to front and subtract your result from the original number, the difference is always exactly divisible by nine.)

✔ **Divide by two.** Try dividing your Out of Balance amount by two, and look for a transaction for this amount. In other words, if your Out of Balance amount is $90, look for a transaction equalling $45. This trick helps locate transactions that have been entered the wrong way round (a debit instead of a credit, a payment instead of a deposit and so on).

Tricks to try before you kick the bucket

You've tried all of the preceding suggestions and your account reconciliation still doesn't balance. Don't abandon ship yet, there's still hope. Here's my last-resort approach, which (almost) always works:

1. **Untick all transactions to take you right back to the beginning.**

   Edit the Bank Statement Date so that it's several months into the future, and then remove the ticks from every transaction on your reconciliation. I know this may undo some of your work, but it's time for radical action.

2. **Check that your opening balance was right.**

   I talk a lot about checking your opening balance earlier in this chapter, in the section 'Identifying your starting point'. If you don't start off from the right spot, you're never going to get anything to balance. Go back and check this one more time.

   If you find that your opening balance is wrong, skip ahead to 'Undoing the previous reconciliation'.

3. **Start marking off the transactions again, but only do a few at a time.**

   When you're sure you're starting from the right spot, start marking off the transactions one by one, as you did before. But this time, only do a few at a time (perhaps five or ten at the most), working your way down to the next balance on your bank statement. (Bank statements usually have a closing balance for the end of each day.)

   Don't try to reconcile a whole page at a time, because this makes it so much harder to pinpoint your problem.

4. **When you get to the next balance on your bank statement, enter this amount in the Closing Statement Balance field, and then press Tab.**

   Enter the next balance on your statement in the Closing Statement Balance field, close your eyes and cross your fingers. When you press Tab you should find that your Out of Balance amount is now zero. (The trick to this method is that by doing small bits at a time, you narrow down the problem, making it really easy to spot.) Yippee!

5. **Click Reconcile and then Reconcile again. Continue till you're done.**

   You're returned to your Reconcile Accounts window. Now, continue in the same way, working down your bank statement section by section, until your final balance reconciles.

Undoing the previous reconciliation

One of the stickiest situations is when the Calculated Statement Balance displayed in Reconcile Accounts when you first open up your reconciliation doesn't match the ending balance on your bank statement from the last time you reconciled.

What this usually means is that you've inadvertently edited or deleted a transaction that had already been reconciled. For example, you've already reconciled up to October but, in a fit of creativity, you decided to change a transaction belonging to September that had already been reconciled. In doing so, you made your beginning balance very sick indeed.

If your beginning balance is definitely wrong, your next course of action is to undo the previous reconciliation, as follows:

1. **Do a backup.**

   No ifs, no buts. What you're about to do is a bit drastic, after all. Remember to note down where you save this backup, just in case you need to do a restore.

2. **Go to Reconcile Accounts as normal, entering the bank account number, date and so on.**

3. **Click Undo Reconciliation.**

   You see a reminder suggesting you back up, similar to Figure 9-6. That's okay, 'cos you already have.

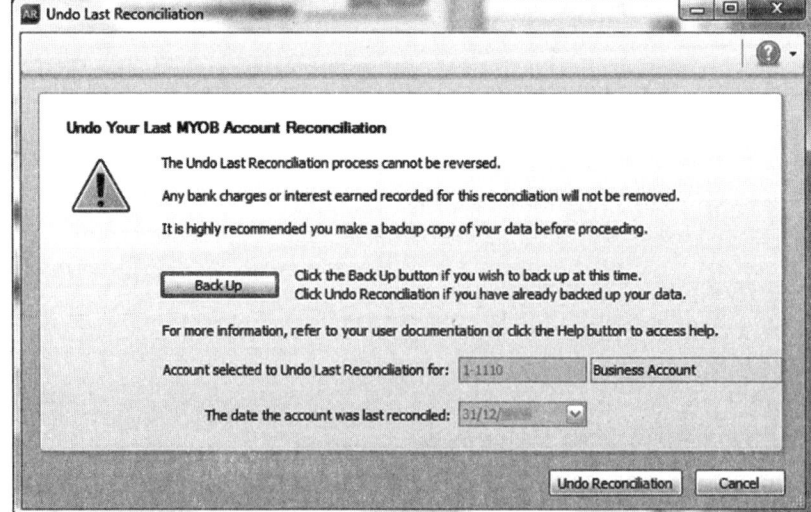

Figure 9-6: Backing up before you undo a previous reconciliation.

4. **Click Undo Reconciliation one more time, and then click OK.**

   Hopefully, you see a message saying that the process has been successful and, when you click OK to this message, you return to your Reconcile Accounts window. All transactions marked as cleared during your last reconciliation will now appear again.

5. **Compare the new Calculated Statement Balance with your bank statement as at the Last Reconciled Date.**

   If the Calculated Statement Balance matches up with your bank statement for that date, you're cooking with gas. All that remains to be done now is to redo your bank reconciliations up to the current date.

   If the Calculated Statement Balance *doesn't* match up with your bank statement for that date, don't sweat. Repeat the Undo Reconciliation process again and again until they do.

6. **Assuming you've now found the problem, consider whether you want to restore your backup or continue with your current company file.**

   Sometimes the cause of a bank reconciliation being out of balance can be many months back. For example, it could be June now but you end up having to undo reconciliations all the way back to February. You realise that the cause of your problems is that you inadvertently deleted a February transaction that had already been reconciled.

   In this situation, you're best to note down the details of the offending transaction and then restore the backup that you made before undoing your reconciliation. You can then fix the problem transaction, check that your bank account reconciles and continue. (Don't forget to rename your backup file, because this will now become your current file.)

   Now that you've done it, do you get a sense of how radical the Undo Reconciliation command is? For this reason, always make a backup of your file before executing this command.

Keeping Good Records

Whenever you reconcile your bank account, you have the option of generating a reconciliation report. Should you or shouldn't you? Here's my take on it:

- ✔ If you don't use bank feeds and only reconcile your bank account every month or so, I recommend you print a Reconciliation Report every time you reconcile your bank account. Staple this report to the bank statement and file away in a folder.

✔ If you reconcile every few days or so — which is much more likely if you're working from bank feeds — I suggest you save your bank reconciliation report as a PDF in a folder called Bank Reconciliations.

✔ Even if you don't choose to print a Reconciliation Report every time, at the very least always print a Reconciliation Report when you reconcile up to 30 June (or whatever the last day of your financial year is). Your accountant won't be happy if you don't.

✔ To save your Bank Reconciliation report as a PDF, click Print at the end of the reconciliation when prompted. This takes you to the Print Preview window. From here, click the drop-down arrow in the top-left and select PDF from the Send menu.

Finally, if you forget to save a Bank Reconciliation report, you can go back and recreate this report days or even weeks later (although remember that this report will show transactions as they stand at that date, and won't reflect any transactions you've edited or deleted since the reconciliation date). To reprint a Bank Reconciliation report, go to Reports, click the Banking tab, and click Reconciliation Report. Select the bank account and then filter by the List of Recorded Statement Dates.

Part III
Moving On

Five Tips for Perfect Payroll

- **Ask for help:** If you've never worked with payroll before, get your accountant or an MYOB Certified Consultant to help set up your employees and check your first couple of pay runs.

- **Use the timesheets feature:** The timesheets feature provides the ideal way to calculate pays for casuals, especially if you employ lots of casuals and hours vary every day.

- **Get wise with super:** Understand who you have to pay, how much and how often. Use MYOB's super payment features to pay superannuation and, ideally, slot money away in a business savings account every week so you always have the funds to pay PAYG tax and super on time.

- **Look after employees:** Know how to check minimum hourly rates for employees, and get familiar with statutory pay conditions and the NES (National Employment Standards).

- **Take your time:** Paying employees can be fiddly and surprisingly time-consuming. Take the time to double-check figures, get employee tax rates right, and review calculations for tricky things such as holiday leave and personal leave.

Visit www.dummies.com/extras/myobsoftwareau for a free article about generating end-of-year employee payment summaries using MYOB.

In this part ...

- Master the black art of items, unit costs and inventory control.

- Calculate employee pays correctly, including tax, superannuation, holiday pay and much more besides.

- Project a professional image and get your business forms looking good.

- Pay employees and suppliers electronically, direct from MYOB.

Chapter 10

Managing Items

I call this chapter 'Managing Items' as opposed to 'Managing Inventory' because lots of businesses that use the Items List in MYOB don't have any inventory at all, and instead use the Items List to bill customers for services, listing each service as a separate item. On the other hand, many other businesses make full use of items in MYOB for managing everything to do with inventory, including pricing, stock levels, reporting and much more.

Here, I share the essentials for working with your Items List, including how to create new items, price items and group items. I also delve into the intricacies of managing inventory, explaining how to do stock counts (pretty easy), inventory adjustments (not so easy) and record opening inventory balances (pretty tricky, in the scheme of things).

But don't be anxious. Your persistence and patience, combined with my dazzling brilliance (a quality only exceeded by my modesty), are enough to master this topic in nothing flat.

Placing Your Bet on the Right Horse

Different products in the MYOB family offer different degrees of sophistication in their inventory features.

Keep the following points in mind before you cross the MYOB finish line:

- MYOB Essentials offers item names and descriptions only, so that you can use items for sales, but you can't keep track of inventory levels or generate purchase orders.

- AccountRight Standard and AccountRight Plus offer full inventory management, with purchase ordering, stock-level management, solid reporting and auto-build features. The latest versions of all products in the AccountRight range also allow for up to six pricing levels on each item, with prices linking back to the specific Price Level you select in each customer's card.

- The 'classic' versions of AccountRight Premier Enterprise also allow you to set your preferences so that inventory can go into negative quantities, as well as manage inventory in multiple locations. You can define locations in any way that you choose (from separate aisles in a warehouse to separate buildings in different countries), process sales from any location and move items between locations. These extended inventory features aren't available yet in the new generation of AccountRight Premier, but are scheduled for release by late 2015.

Adding Items to Your Items List

Regardless of what kind of business you're running, creating a new item in your Items List is an easy song to sing.

Creating a new item

So you're ready to create your first item? Follow my lyrical song sheet:

1. **Select Items from the Lists menu, and then click the New button.**

   Alternatively, click Items List from the Inventory command centre.

2. **Enter an Item Number for this item, and then press the Tab or Enter key.**

   The Item Number doesn't have to be a number. In fact, using letters instead of (or as well as) numbers often makes more sense. For example, a penguin fridge magnet could have FM-Penguin as its number, or a small black T-shirt could be TS-SmBl. Above all, be consistent with item numbers — follow a pattern from one inventory item to the next.

3. Enter a Name for the item.

Enter a brief description as the Name for this item, such as 'Fridge Magnet, Penguin Design'. You're limited to 30 characters, so be concise. (Too limited? See the following section for information on how to get around this nutty 30-character constraint.)

4. Click the buy, sell or inventory boxes for the item.

If you buy this item for resale, and you want to track how many you have in stock at any one time, click all three boxes. If you don't buy this item for resale and you're not sure which boxes to tick, check out the section 'Specifying whether you buy, sell or stock items', later in this chapter.

5. Select the income, cost of sales and asset accounts, where prompted.

When you click the boxes labelled I Buy, I Sell and I Inventory, you're prompted to complete the corresponding income, cost of sales and asset accounts, as shown in Figure 10-1. This feature is MYOB's way of saying, 'You've told me that you sell this item, now tell me what kind of income account this sale should go to' or 'You've told me that you buy this item, what's the cost of sales account?'

For example, in Figure 10-1, I specify that sales of Thai silk fabric should go to Fabrics Sales, and that the Cost of Sales account is Fabric Cost of Goods Sold. (I talk more about selecting these accounts in the section 'Telling things where to go', later in this chapter.)

6. Click the Selling Details tab and enter the price and tax code.

For items that you sell, you can decide whether your Base Selling Price includes GST or not. If this price includes GST, click the box Prices are Tax Inclusive.

On the Selling Details tab of every item, note that you can choose to calculate GST on the Actual Selling Price, or calculate GST on the Base Selling Price. Be careful here, because in order for GST to calculate correctly, you must always select to calculate GST on the Actual Selling Price.

7. Click OK to record your new item's profile, and select the buying tax code if prompted.

You may be prompted for a Tax Code When Bought. Usually, the tax code is either FRE or GST.

8. Click OK again.

Your new item is now added to your Items List. If you like, you can add even more information to your new item by editing this item and clicking the Item Details or Buying Details tabs. I talk about these settings later in this chapter.

If you're setting up a whole load of new items, and you already have these items in a list elsewhere on your computer (maybe in a spreadsheet or document file), you're best to *import* this list, rather than type it from scratch. To import data, select Import/Export Assistant from the File menu and follow the prompts from there. After all, the less time spent typing, the more time you have to relax.

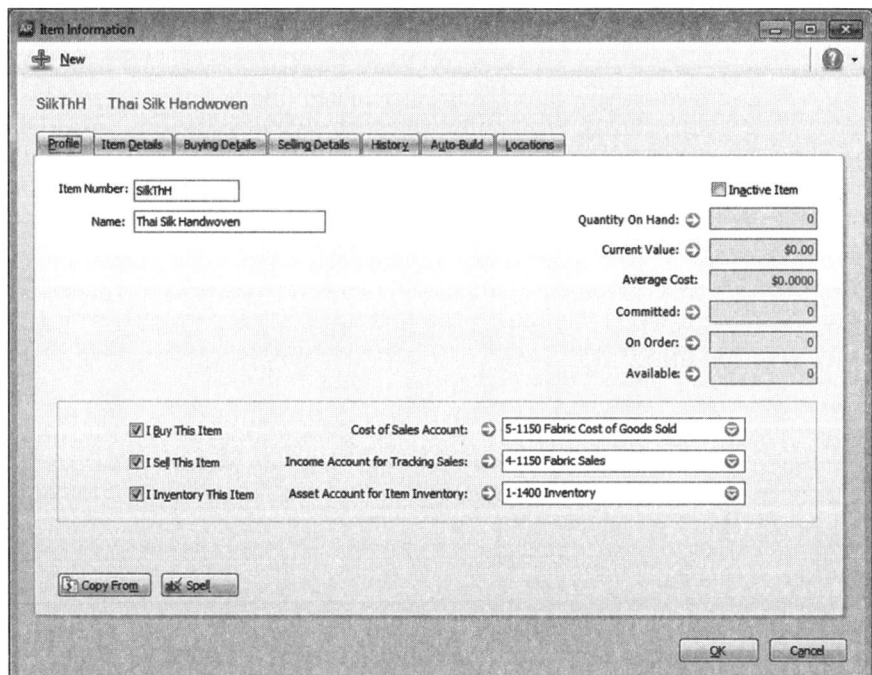

Figure 10-1: Creating a new item.

Adding extra descriptions

The Item Number and Name fields don't provide much room to move, but don't let this cramp your style. Tucked away in the Item Details tab of any item is an extra Description field.

I find this extra description comes in handy in many different kinds of situations. For example, I know of a book publisher who uses the Item Number field for the book's code, the Name field for the book's title, and the Description field for the ISBN. Another client of mine sells large kit sheds, and uses the additional Description field to provide a long description of everything included in the kit, and this description appears on every invoice.

Below the Description field is an option to Use Item Description on Sales and Purchases. Click here to show the item's Description rather than the item's Name when recording sales and purchases.

To display both the Item Name and the Description on your final invoice — as well as the Item Number — you need to customise your invoice layout, selecting to display both the Item Description and the Description/Backordered Label fields. However, you can't tweak the invoice entry screen itself (where you create the actual invoice) to display both fields. Instead you have to choose one or the other.

Specifying whether you buy, sell or stock items

Those three little innocent boxes I Buy This Item, I Sell This Item and I Inventory This Item can cause such confusion. Which boxes you tick depends on the kind of business you operate. Here goes . . .

When you buy something and then sell it

If you buy items for resale, whether they're clothes or medicines, books or shoes, tick all three boxes: I Buy This Item, I Sell This Item and I Inventory This Item.

When you just sell something

If you sell things that you don't buy, the only box you have to tick is I Sell This Item (leave the other boxes unticked). 'Hang on,' I hear you cry. 'How is it possible to sell something you've never bought?'

Believe me, it is possible. Here are some examples:

- ✔ Lots of my clients sell their time. They create an item called Labour and price it with their hourly rate.

- ✔ I've set up MYOB for heaps of associations and clubs that charge membership fees. They set up annual subscriptions in their Items List, creating different items with different prices for each membership type.

- ✔ Backpacker hostels, guesthouses and caravan parks often create items for Nightly Rates, Weekend Rates, Linen Hire and so on, similar to the example shown in Figure 10-2.

> ✔ My local computer shop offers photocopying services and internet access.
> It sets up items for copy charges per page or internet access per hour.

By the way, I talk more about setting up items for services at the beginning of Chapter 4.

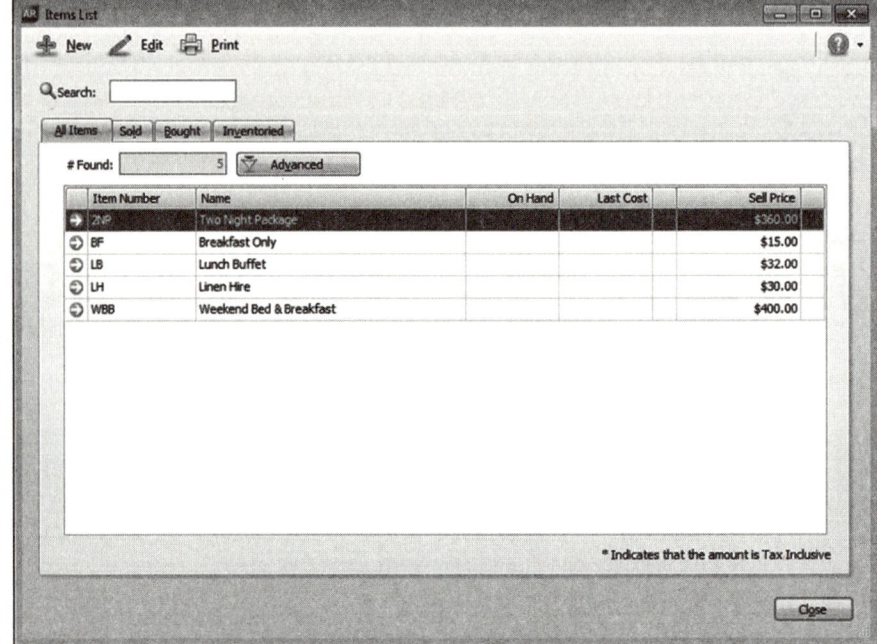

Figure 10-2:
An Items
List can
include
services you
provide, not
just items
you buy for
resale.

When you make something with your own fair hands

If you buy separate items and then join them together to make something else (maybe you buy vegetable oil, perfume essences and bottles, and then combine these products to make massage oil), then tick all three boxes: I Buy This Item, I Sell This Item and I Inventory This Item.

When you buy something but don't sell it

Sometimes you only want something in your Items List so that you can produce purchase orders. Lots of things fall into this category — for example, office stationery, packaging for sending out goods, or miscellaneous manufacturing supplies, such as rags, oil or gas.

For these types of items, only tick the box I Buy This Item.

Copy and paste

Do you stock a lot of similar items? Perhaps you sell a range of hats that are all the same except for their colour, or a range of pots that only differ by size.

If you do, give your weary fingers a typing holiday and make friends with the Copy From command. In the Inventory command centre, click New, type an Item Number, press Tab and then click Copy From. Select a similar item from the list and, before you can say knife, all the details from this item copy across to the new one you're creating. All you have to do now is fix up any information that's different.

If you already have your Items List in a spreadsheet format, an alternative way to populate your Items List is to export data straight out of Excel and then import this data into MYOB. Doing so can save hours, maybe even days of work. To import data, select Import/Export Assistant from the File menu and follow the prompts from there.

Telling things where to go

Whenever you create a new item, you have to select corresponding income, cost of sales and inventory accounts. Be careful when selecting these accounts, though, because your choice ultimately affects both your Profit & Loss and Balance Sheet reports.

Income accounts

If you click I Sell This Item when you create a new item, you're prompted to select an income account. Plunge in and select whatever income account best relates to this item.

For example, a client of mine does Web design and his Items List includes lots of different items for the services the business provides. Every item in his Items List links to one of three income accounts: Web Design Income, Hosting Income or Domain Name Sales.

Creating several income accounts in your Accounts List usually works well so that you can track your different revenue sources (refer to Chapter 2). By linking items back to these different accounts, you can see at a glance from your Profit & Loss report how much revenue each kind of item (or service) generates.

Cost of sales and expense accounts

If you click I Buy This Item when you create a new item, you need to select a cost of sales or expense account.

For items that you keep in stock, the simplest method is to have a single cost of sales account called Cost of Goods Sold. A more complex approach is to create several cost of goods sold accounts, with each one corresponding to an equivalent income account. (Either method is okay; ask your accountant if you're not sure.)

For non-inventory items, the account you choose depends on what the item is. For example, an item called Office Supplies probably hooks up to an expense account like Office Expenses. An item for purchasing manufacturing supplies probably hooks up to a cost of sales account, such as Factory Consumables (as shown in Figure 10-3). Alternatively, you may prefer to create an item called Consumables and use this item when generating purchase orders for factory consumables, simply overriding the description each time.

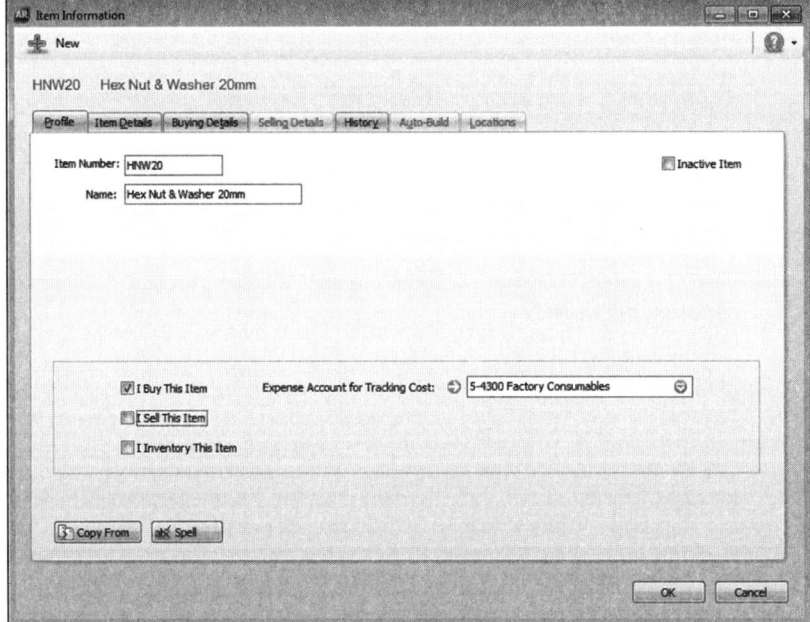

Figure 10-3: You can set up items for things you order from suppliers, even if you don't resell them.

Inventory accounts

If you click I Inventory This Item when you create a new item, you're prompted to select an inventory account.

TECHNICAL STUFF

What happens behind the scenes?

Lots of people say that one neat thing about MYOB is that you don't have to get to grips with those dreaded debits and credits. True enough, but what if you have a masochistic streak, and you want to know what happens behind the scenes?

Here's a tip, just for you. Go and create an item purchase, an item sale, an item receipt and maybe an item adjustment too. For each transaction, just before you click Record, hop up to the Edit menu and select Recap Transaction. With an eagerness to satisfy your thirst for knowledge, MYOB obligingly displays the debits and credits behind each transaction, showing what goes where.

TIP

Don't get tied up creating lots of different inventory accounts. You only need one inventory account to keep track of the stock you have on hand. Surprisingly enough, this account is called Inventory and you find it sitting in the Assets section of your Accounts List.

Recording opening stock counts

After you have set up numbers, descriptions and selling prices for all your items, you're ready to record how many units you have on hand for each item, as well as the cost of each item. (Obviously, you only need to do this for items where you want to track the quantity you have on hand.)

I explain this process in detail in Chapter 3, which covers everything you need to know about opening balances.

Taking Things an Extra Step

In many situations, you'll find that adding an item code, description, price and quantity is enough information. However, MYOB does provide room for a whole heap of additional info, such as supplier details and item categories, as well as the capacity to manufacture new items using specified quantities of other items. I talk about all these features in the next couple of pages.

Setting up supplier details

If you buy certain items from the same supplier each time, I suggest you record the supplier's details in the item's record. (***Note***: With the exception of the Tax Code When Bought field, everything on the Buying Details tab is optional. If you can't be bothered entering any of these details right now, that's just fine.)

Here's how you set up supplier details:

1. **Open your Items List, select the item you want and click Edit.**

2. **Click the Buying Details tab.**

3. **If you want to, enter a Standard Cost for this item.**

   Many manufacturers and importers find standard costs are a handy reference. If you're not sure whether you want to run with standard costs for inventory items, see the sidebar 'When cost price isn't quite what it seems', later in this chapter.

   If you're one of those observant nerdy types, you may notice that you can't enter a Last Purchase Price under Buying Details, just as you can't enter the Average Cost in the Item Profile. Don't worry — the Last Purchase Price updates itself the first time you buy the item, as does the Average Cost.

4. **Enter your Minimum Level for Restocking Alert (this option appears only if you select that you inventory this item).**

   Think about how low you're prepared to let the stock fall before you buy more. For example, if you know that you always want to keep at least 10 units in stock, enter **10** as the Minimum Level.

5. **Enter the supplier's name in Primary Supplier for Reorders.**

   Enter the usual supplier for this item. It doesn't matter if you occasionally buy this item from someone else.

6. **Enter your supplier's code for this item in the Supplier Item Number field.**

   Sometimes this info is useful, sometimes it isn't. If you think your suppliers like to see their own item codes on purchase orders, enter their codes in this spot. Otherwise, don't bother; it's only another time-consuming job.

7. **Enter the quantity you normally order as the Default Reorder Quantity.**

   If you normally order 20 of these items at a time, enter **20** as your Default Reorder Quantity. This means that when your stock falls below minimum levels, you can use your To Do List to automatically create a purchase order for this quantity.

For example, say your minimum stock level for something is 10 units and you normally order the item in lots of 20. If your stock level falls to 8, a purchase order for 20 units, not for 2, appears.

8. **Check your details, and then click OK.**

   Your screen should look similar to the one shown in Figure 10-4. Go ahead; click OK if you feel ecstatically happy with your work.

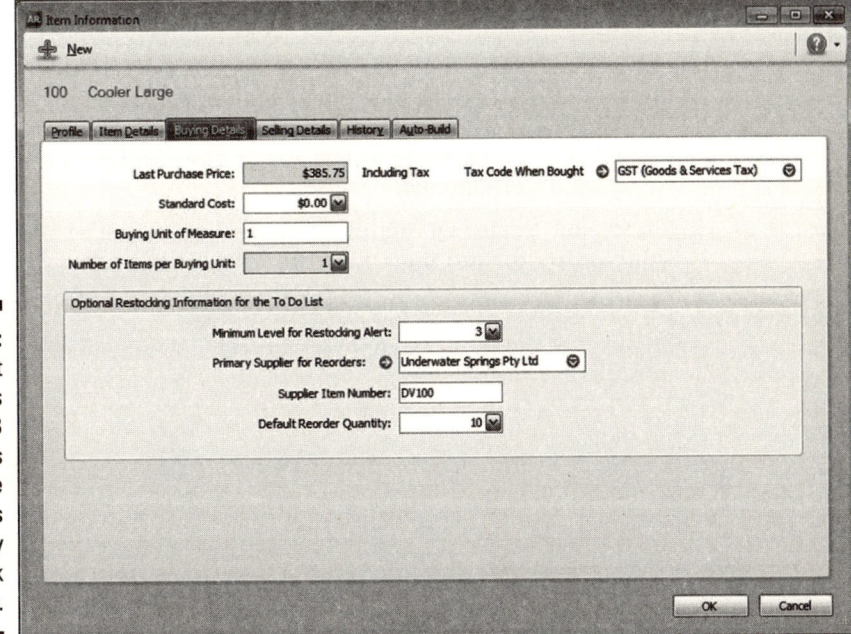

Figure 10-4:
You can set re-order levels so that MYOB generates purchase orders automatically when stock runs low.

Getting items organised

Sometimes you need to record more information about items, maybe organising them into groups, detailing colour or size, or recording additional buying information. This is where custom lists work a treat.

In your Items List, every item has three Custom List fields, shown on the Item Details tab. Here's how to customise these lists so they work for you:

1. **From the top menu bar, choose Lists⇨Custom Lists & Field Names and then select Items.**

2. **Enter descriptions for your item groups or categories and click OK.**

   Your choice of description will vary, depending on the kind of products you sell. For example, if you sell clothing and you want to categorise items according to colour and size, you might enter Colour and Size as the names of Custom Lists #1 and #2. Or, if you sell CDs, you could enter Artist and Distribution Method as the names of Custom Lists #1 and #2.

3. **Back at the top menu bar, choose Lists⇨Custom Lists, and then select Items.**

   Spot the subtle difference between this step and Step 1? This time you navigate to the Custom Lists menu, not the Custom Lists & Field Names menu.

4. **Add new entries for each Custom List and click OK.**

   For example, if the description for your Custom List #1 is Colour, you might add entries for Blue, Red and Yellow. If the description is Distribution Method, you might add entries for Account Sales, Sale or Return and Consignment.

5. **Go to your Items List, highlight an item you want to add custom information to, and then click the Item Details tab.**

6. **Select the appropriate custom list info.**

   Figure 10-5 shows an example of a finished item, complete with custom information.

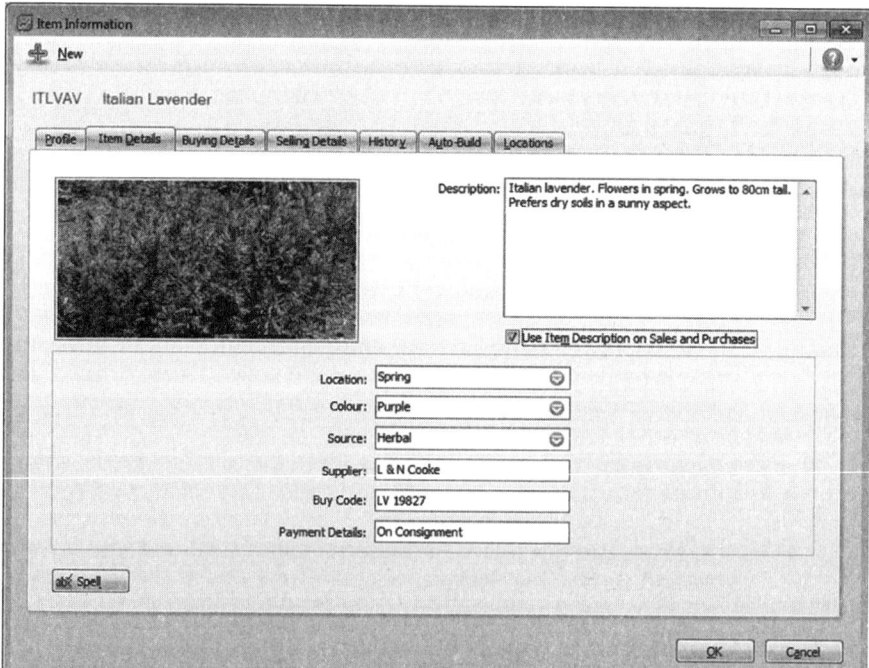

Figure 10-5:
Organising items using custom lists and fields.

Creating new items from other items

In the same way the proverbial magician combines a handkerchief with a ping-pong ball to create a rabbit, so too can you combine a couple of items to create something quite new.

Start by heading to your Items List and creating a new item that's the 'finished' item, such as a delicious, authentic Italian lasagne. In the item profile, make sure you have a tick against I Inventory This Item and then click the Auto-Build tab.

Next, click the Edit List button and select the ingredients (or components) that make up this item. In Figure 10-6, you can see that I select tomatoes, parmesan, eggplant and so on. A more prosaic example could be for a dining suite, with one table and six chairs.

To create a finished item, click Auto-Build Items (this command sits in the Inventory command centre). Locate whatever it is you want to 'build', specify the quantity and click Build Items. Voilà. The quantity of the finished dish increases, the quantity of all the ingredients decreases. My mouth waters at the very thought.

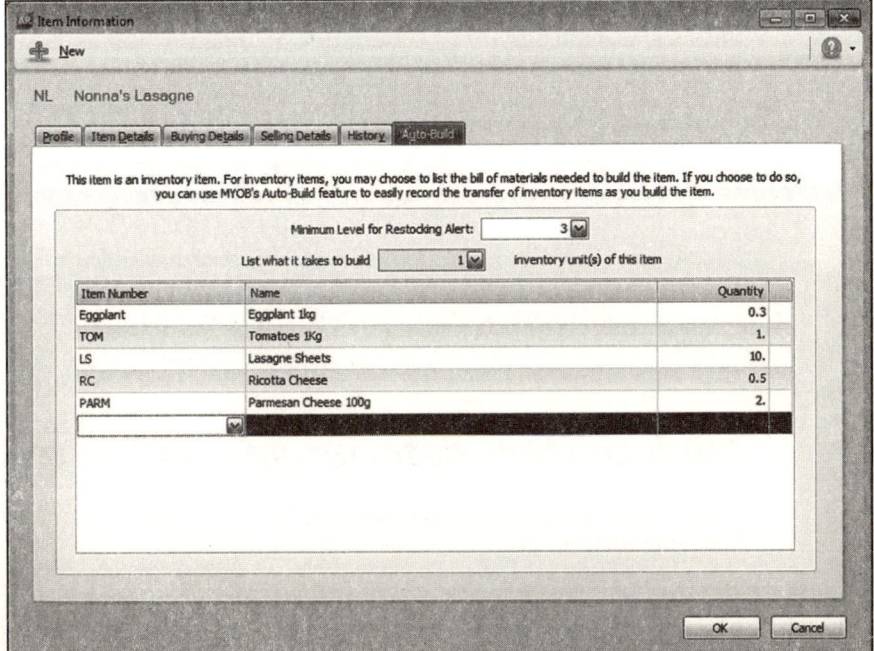

Figure 10-6:
The time-honoured recipe for Nonna's lasagne.

Add-on products and where they fit

I'm going to whisper something now so listen up. Whatever praises the evangelists may sing about MYOB, the inventory features are still pretty limited. Flexible methods of inventory costing, detailed job costing, bills of materials, and accurate calculation of landed costs are all tricky to manage using MYOB. (Sure, you can find workarounds, but often making a silk purse out a sow's ear takes too much time.)

The good news is that lots of developers out there have come up with add-ons that dovetail well with MYOB, and help you manage inventory, job costing, serial number tracking and lots more. I've personally used Ostendo

for a couple of clients with great success. My clients were chuffed to hold onto MYOB for all their financial reporting, payroll and so on, but use Ostendo to do the tricky job of costing and inventory management. I've heard other consultants sing the praises of Datapel Warehouse Management System as well.

For a list of a whole heap of products that hook up with MYOB, including Ostendo and Datapel, visit the MYOB Add-Ons page at www.veechicurtis.com.au. One tip, however: Remember to check that the add-on is compatible with the version of MYOB you're using.

If you regularly invoice customers for a certain combo of items, you can use this Auto-Build feature to bunch these items together and speed your billing process. To display the detail of each item on your invoices, use the additional Description field on the Item Details tab of the finished item.

Giving Your Items List the Once-Over

Regardless of whether your Items List is short or long, it needs a certain amount of tender loving care. In the next few sections, I provide the ultimate set of care instructions, explaining not only how to find items, but also how to delete items, change items and view item transactions.

Finding item descriptions and details

Before you plunge into the haystack in search of that needle, try the following hunting tips:

✔ **Search on a string of text:** The easiest way to find an item is to go to your Items List and type any of the letters or numbers of the Item Number or Item Name in the Search field. For example, if I type the

word *black* in the Search field, MYOB only displays items that have this
word in their Number or Name.

✔ **Try an Advanced search:** Click the Advanced button that appears at
the top of your Items List to search by Description, Primary Supplier or
Supplier Item Number.

✔ **Sort your Items List in a way that makes sense to you:** An alternative
approach is to click any of the column labels to sort by that category.
For example, if I click at the top of the Name column (actually clicking
the label 'Name' itself), then I can sort by that column.

✔ **Create a custom printout:** If you're one of those people who prefer
printed lists (old habits die hard), then go to Reports, click Inventory
and print your Items List Summary report.

If you have a huge Items List, looking for stuff gets much easier if you
organise items into groups. Refer to 'Getting items organised', earlier in this
chapter, to find out more.

Viewing item transactions

MYOB offers a couple of different ways to look up item transactions. Try the
following and see what suits you best:

✔ **Cruise the Items Register:** To find transactions relating to a particular
item (including stock counts and adjustments), go to your Items
Register and choose to Search By Item. Select the item in question,
enter a date range, and the Items Register displays every sale,
purchase and inventory adjustment for that item, as shown in
Figure 10-7. You can then double-click on any transaction to view it
in all its glory.

✔ **Click next to the Quantity when viewing an item:** This takes you
straight to the Items Register for a particular item.

✔ **Go to the Find Transactions menu:** If you only want to view
financial transactions for a particular item — without being confused
by inventory counts and other adjustments — go to your Find
Transactions menu and click the Item tab. Enter the item code,
followed by a suitable date range, and a list appears, showing
all sales and purchases for this item. (This is probably my least
favourite method, because I can't see a running stock count for
the item.)

Viewing by name, not by number

Did you know you can sort your Items List either by name or by number? To select items by name, go to Setup➪Preferences and then click the Windows tab. Click the option Select Items by Item Name, Not Item Number.

Whenever you're creating an invoice or a purchase order, or you're searching through your Items List, type the first letters of the item name and, hey presto, there you have it.

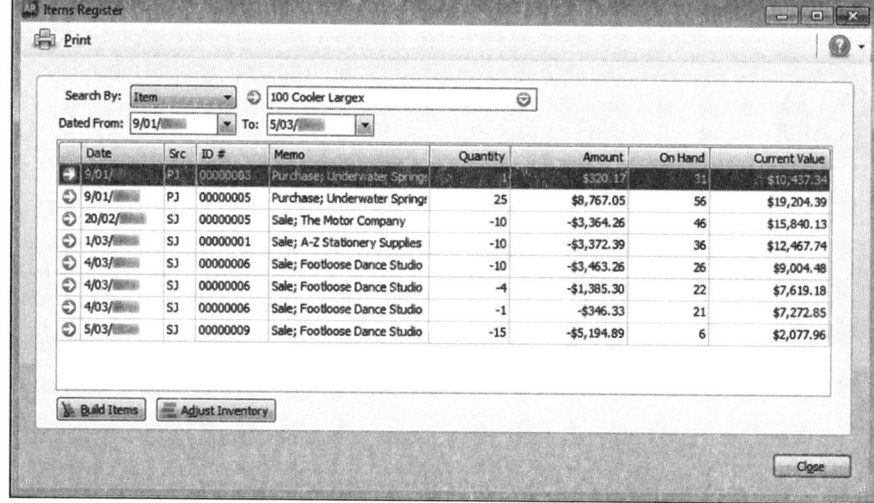

Figure 10-7:
The Items Register displays every sale, purchase and inventory transaction.

Changing items

Most item changes are easy as pie. All you have to do is locate the item in your Items List, double-click, and make your changes. (If you change the Item Number, you get a warning that sales or purchases may be affected by this change. That's okay — MYOB is simply saying that the Item Number is going to change on these transactions too. Have confidence and click OK to do the deed.)

The only change that sometimes proves difficult is if you want to change the I Buy, I Sell or I Inventory selections. For example, if you have an item that already has purchases or sales on file, and you want to unclick I Inventory This Item, then you'll get a message saying you can't.

Don't feel thwarted. If you can't change an item in the way that you want to, make that item inactive by clicking the Inactive Item button in the top-right corner of the Item Information window, and then type the letter **z** in front of the Item Number so that the item gets banished to the bottom of your list. Then create an all-singing, all-dancing new item that's just the way you want it.

Deleting items

To delete an item, look for it in your Items List and double-click on it. Go to the Edit menu on the top menu bar and choose Delete Inventory Item.

No luck? If you already have invoices or purchases for this item in your company file, a warning appears stating you can't delete this item. If this happens to you, your best bet is to type the letter **z** in front of the Item Number, forcing this item to the bottom of your list, and also make this item inactive. (Inactive items don't display if you look up items when recording sales or purchase transactions.) To make an item inactive, click the Inactive Item button in the top-right of the Item Information window. Later, you can choose to hide or display inactive items in your Items List by toggling the Show Inactive button at the top.

Are you wondering why it's not possible to combine items in the same way as you can combine customer cards or accounts? I am too — one for the MYOB wishlist, I reckon!

Managing Inventory

If your business buys and sells items, chances are that managing your inventory well is a cornerstone to your business success. In the next couple of pages, I look at the issues of pricing and reporting for inventory.

Pricing to sell

Whether it's a market price, standard price, retail price, wholesale price, discount price, list price, fee for a service, fare, quoted price, flat charge or some other exotic beast, the time has come to price your goods.

So, in order of complexity, I explain how to price a single item, how to price a few items and how to price a whole lot of items at once. I also explain how to set up special pricing deals for those customers you love the best. Here goes:

✔ **Pricing one item at a time.** Do you want to change the price on something? If so, double-click on the item in your Items List, select the Selling Details tab, change the Base Selling Price and click OK. That's all there is to it. (Remember to check whether the Tax Inclusive button is ticked, or not. If this button is ticked, you must include GST in your selling price.)

✔ **Pricing a few items at a time.** Go to the Inventory command centre and click Set Item Prices. A list appears showing item numbers and names, average cost and current price. Scroll down to find the items you want to change and fix up the price in the Current Price column. If you want to check out the last price you paid for this item, select Last Cost as the Calculation Basis at the top.

✔ **Pricing lots of items in one hit.** If you find that the Set Item Prices menu doesn't really work for you — updating prices this way can get a bit cumbersome if you have hundreds of items because it's so easy to lose your place — then an alternative is to export your Items List out of your company file and load it into a spreadsheet, such as Excel. You then fix up the prices in Excel, save the spreadsheet as a text file, and import this text file back into your MYOB company file. If you think this task sounds a bit scary — and it is a little daunting the first time — get an MYOB Certified Consultant to help you.

✔ **Offering discounts to specific customers.** Go to the Selling Details tab on the customer's card and enter their particular sweetheart deal in the Volume Discount % field.

✔ **Setting up pricing breaks.** If the discount you offer varies according to the quantity customers purchase, you can set up a pricing matrix under the Selling Details tab of each item. You also have to change the Item Price Level in the Selling Details tab for these customers. You can see how this works in Figure 10-8.

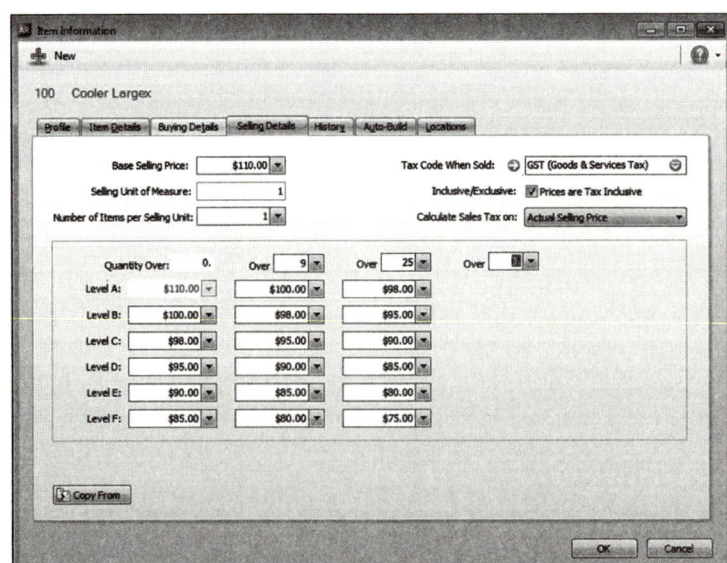

Figure 10-8:
Price matrix features mean you can structure selling prices in complex ways.

Reporting for what's on hand

The kinds of reports you'll need for inventory are going to vary depending on the nature of your business. However, start by going to your Reports menu, clicking the Inventory tab, and checking out the following:

- ✔ **Items List Summary report.** The best report for viewing the total value, based on average cost, of your inventory. This report lists the quantity and total value of each item on hand, as well as a grand total of stock value at the bottom of the report.

- ✔ **Inventory Value Reconciliation report.** If you want to view a valuation report for a prior date (maybe it's mid-July but you want to generate a stock valuation for the end of June), this report is your best bet.

- ✔ **Analyse Inventory report.** This stock availability report analyses not just the quantity you have on hand, but also the quantity you have on order from suppliers and on order from customers. You can check out this report in Figure 10-9.

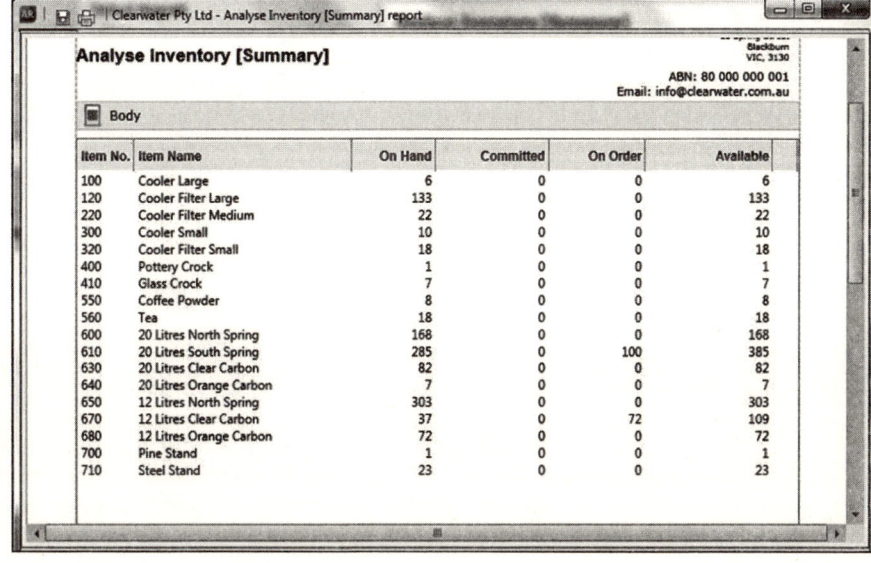

Figure 10-9: The Analyse Inventory report is handy for looking at stock availability.

Analyse Inventory [Summary]

Blackburn
VIC, 3130
ABN: 80 000 000 001
Email: info@clearwater.com.au

Body

Item No.	Item Name	On Hand	Committed	On Order	Available
100	Cooler Large	6	0	0	6
120	Cooler Filter Large	133	0	0	133
220	Cooler Filter Medium	22	0	0	22
300	Cooler Small	10	0	0	10
320	Cooler Filter Small	18	0	0	18
400	Pottery Crock	1	0	0	1
410	Glass Crock	7	0	0	7
550	Coffee Powder	8	0	0	8
560	Tea	18	0	0	18
600	20 Litres North Spring	168	0	0	168
610	20 Litres South Spring	285	0	100	385
630	20 Litres Clear Carbon	82	0	0	82
640	20 Litres Orange Carbon	7	0	0	7
650	12 Litres North Spring	303	0	0	303
670	12 Litres Clear Carbon	37	0	72	109
680	12 Litres Orange Carbon	72	0	0	72
700	Pine Stand	1	0	0	1
710	Steel Stand	23	0	0	23

If you can't find an inventory report that provides the exact information you're looking for, Chapter 14 offers some creative approaches for customising standard reports, and also explains how to send reports to Excel. Alternatively, if you would like to get a custom report to meet very specific requirements, I recommend a company called SmartReports (www.smartreports.com.au), which specialises in custom reporting that links with MYOB.

When cost price isn't quite what it seems

In the Set Item Prices menu and many of the item pricing reports, MYOB refers to Average Cost, Last Cost and Standard Cost. If you're going to make bags of profit and live in the manner to which you'd like to become accustomed, you're going to have to nail what these different costs represent.

Average Cost divides the total cost paid for an item by the quantity on hand. Average Cost doesn't include GST, early payment discounts or freight.

Last Cost is whatever you entered in the Price column on the most recent purchase of this item. Last Cost doesn't include supplier discounts, early payment discounts or freight. Last Cost may or may not include GST, depending on whether you entered this Price as tax-inclusive or tax-exclusive. (Because of all these variables, I find Last Cost isn't a very reliable indicator of how much something truly costs me to buy.)

Standard Cost is a figure you can enter yourself, and isn't something that the system calculates automatically. Some businesses use standard costs as a benchmark price to refer to, especially if their actual purchase price varies from week to week. Other businesses choose to record standard costs that include both materials and labour, so they can generate custom reports that allow for the cost of manufacturing. (You can set your preferences so that standard cost comes up whenever you generate a purchase. To do this, go to Preferences, click the Inventory tab and click Use Standard Cost as the Default Price on Purchase Orders and Bills.)

The moral of my technical tale? When calculating how much an item costs you, and what price you think you need to sell it at, remember to factor *everything* into account, including freight, GST, supplier discounts, early payment discounts and currency exchange variations.

Fixing Things Up When Stuff Goes Wrong

Put together, computers and humans open up endless possibilities for disaster. Therefore, it's not surprising that sometimes your inventory costs or counts go completely out of whack. However, you can make inventory adjustments to fix things up.

Adjusting the quantity of an item

What do you do if you know you have three stuffed bears on the shelf but your Items List says you have four? Or, perhaps you can see that you've completely sold out of lemonade but your Items List says you have 50 crates left?

Follow these steps:

1. **In the Inventory command centre, choose Count Inventory.**

2. **Enter the quantity you have on hand in the Counted column and click Adjust Inventory.**

   As you enter your quantities, the difference between the On Hand column and the Counted column calculates automatically. Feel free to adjust more than one item at a time.

3. **Select your Default Adjustment Account and click Continue.**

   Your best bet is to choose a cost of sales account called Stock Adjustments. (If you don't have an account by this name, create one now.) Alternatively, if you know the reason your stock was out of balance, you may want to select a different account. For example, if you gave away stock to use as samples, you may want to select an expense account called 'Samples Given'.

4. **In the Adjust Inventory window, check the Date and type an explanation in the Memo.**

   Look at Figure 10-10 to see an example Inventory Adjustment. Note that although you can fit a whole essay in the Memo field, only the first seven words or so appear on reports.

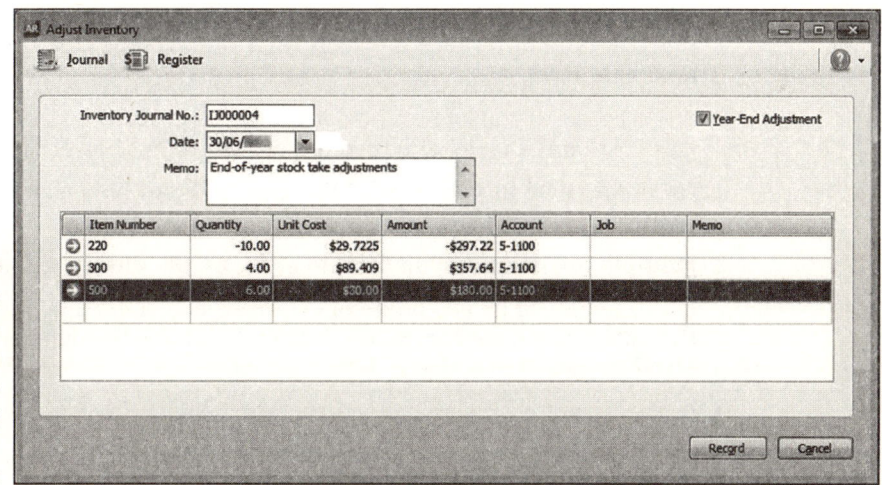

Figure 10-10: Changing item quantities using Adjust Inventory.

5. **Check that you're happy with the journal and click Record.**

   Check that the Quantity and Amount columns make sense before you click the Record button. And, unless you want to adjust the Average Cost for this item (something I explain in more detail next in this chapter), leave the Unit Cost column untouched, accepting whatever figure MYOB comes up with.

Can you see how I've ticked the Year-End Adjustment button in the top-right corner? Stocktake adjustments often happen at year-end, and you may not want these adjustments to distort your financial reports for June.

Adjusting the cost of an item

Oscar Wilde once said that experience is the name that people give to their mistakes. I think he had some insight into how easy it is to really mess things up, especially when you're first working with inventory.

There's no quick explanation for why, one day, you look up the average cost on an item and it's completely out the window. You know that a box of CDs doesn't cost $1,500 or that a new laptop costs more than $50, but suddenly your Items List says that this is the case. Don't con yourself into thinking MYOB has made a mistake — the cause is always human error, somewhere!

One way to fix unit costs is to go to your Items Register, select the item in question and double-check the cost price for every purchase for that item. Hopefully, you can see where the mistake is and fix it.

An alternative approach that's more practical if you have lots of purchases to look through is simply to fix the average cost so that it's correct. Here's how:

1. **Calculate the difference between what the average cost should be and what it is.**

   For example, if you know a box of blank CDs costs $5 to buy, but the unit cost comes up as $15, then the difference per box of CDs is $10.

2. **Go to this item in your Items List and check out how many of this item you have in stock.**

3. **Multiply the quantity you have in stock by the difference in unit cost.**

   For example, if I had 20 boxes of CDs in stock, I'd multiply $10 (that's the difference in cost price per unit) by 20 (that's the number of units I have on hand) to arrive at $200.

4. **In the Inventory command centre, select Adjust Inventory.**

5. **Enter the date and write a clear, concise note in the Memo.**

   Use the Memo field to explain why you're adjusting inventory value. Then, if someone asks you months later why you did this, you're able to justify your actions.

6. **Enter zero in the Quantity column and your dollar difference in the Amount column.**

   Figure 10-11 shows how your inventory adjustment should look. The dollar difference should be the amount you calculated in Step 3.

You can ignore the Unit Cost column. In this case, because I'm reducing the value of an item, I enter the adjustment in the Amount column as a negative figure.

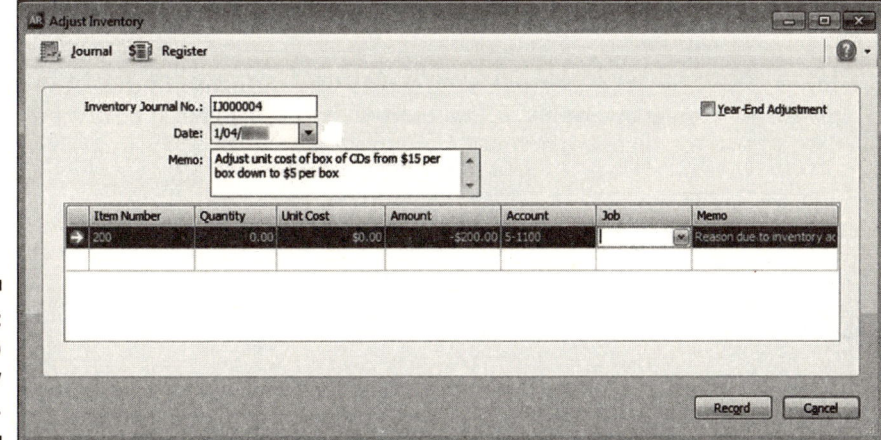

Figure 10-11:
Fixing up inventory costs.

7. **Select an expense account for this adjustment.**

   Either select the cost of sales account that this item or these items normally go to, or select your Stock Adjustments account, if you have one.

   When working with any inventory adjustment, never select Inventory as your expense account or adjustment account. This throws your reports out of whack and turns your accountant into a dribbling, moaning, nervous wreck.

8. **Click Record.**

   Phew! It's over and done with. Don't forget to go straight to the Item Profile for the item you just adjusted and check that the Average Cost is now correct.

Finding solutions when MYOB doesn't let you do an adjustment

You may encounter a couple of situations when MYOB doesn't let you record an inventory adjustment:

✔ **You get a message saying that this item has 'outstanding receive items'.** What this message means is that you have an item receipt outstanding for which you haven't yet recorded a supplier bill. Time to become a detective: Go to the Orders tab in your Purchases Register and look for orders that have a tick in the Received column. Drill down into each of these orders until you find an order that includes the item you wanted to adjust. What next? If you have already received the supplier invoice for this receipt, record it now. Otherwise, you have no choice but to wait until you receive this invoice before processing your inventory adjustment.

✔ **You get a message saying that 'The purchase of this item would value your inventory at less than \$0.00'.** The solution to this problem is a tad convoluted, but if you visit www.myob.com.au/support and search for support note 9168, you can view a nifty help document on this subject.

Standing Up and Counting Down

I've done oodles and oodles of stocktakes over the years. The one I remember best was years ago in a huge warehouse when the stocktake took about ten hours, with eight staff counting all day. Then the manager and I stayed up till 2 am, typing the counts into the computer one by one.

Things seemed fine until two days later when the computer crashed. Stay calm, I declared, we can restore the information from our backup. This we did, restoring the data from the day just before the stocktake. Never mind, I said, we'll just type in the stock counts from the stocktake sheets one more time.

This is where the trouble hit. We looked high and low, far and wide, but the stocktake sheets had disappeared forever — through the shredder, I suspect. And so we did the stocktake all over again. What a way to spend a weekend!

Getting ready for D-Day

Before you start your stocktake, make your way to Reports, click the Inventory tab and print an Inventory Count Sheet.

As you do your stocktake, keep an eye open for any item counts that look odd, or where they're significantly different from what you should have — you can see how much you should have by referring to the On Hand column.

Doing the grand reckoning

On the face of it, entering stock counts is pretty simple. Go to Count Inventory in the Inventory command centre, enter your counts from your count sheet in the Counted column and record your adjustment.

Here are a few tips to make sure things go swimmingly:

- ✔ **Avoid confusion.** Before starting your stocktake, make sure you finalise all pending sales, and enter supplier bills for all goods that have already been received in the warehouse. Print a report showing stock on hand at this point in time, and then begin your stocktake. If possible, avoid recording any sales or receiving goods until the stocktake is complete.

- ✔ **Be clear about what you need to count.** Make sure you allow for goods in transit, goods on consignment, goods in delivery vans or in other locations.

- ✔ **Take bite-sized chunks.** Only enter counts for 10 or 20 items at a time. It's easier to see what you're doing this way, and if you (or your computer) do something silly, you won't lose too much work in one hit.

- ✔ **Think carefully about where you allocate the difference.** When prompted for a Default Expense Account, allocate the difference to a special cost of sales account called Stocktake Adjustments.

- ✔ **Never select Inventory as your Default Expense Account.** If you do, you'll cause your inventory control account to go out of balance.

- ✔ **Get the date right.** If you do a stocktake on 30 June, date the journal 30 June. (Even if you enter the stock counts a week later, this has to be the date — otherwise, nothing makes sense in your financial reports.)

- ✔ **Double-check at the end.** When you're done, generate an Inventory Value Reconciliation report for the stocktake date and compare the final counts with your handwritten stock count sheets. This way you can spot if you've made a blunder.

- ✔ **Make sure your inventory account balances.** Skip to Chapter 18 to find out how.

- ✔ **Keep records in a safe place.** In the final wash-up, staple your original Inventory Count pages and your final Inventory Value Reconciliation report together.

Balancing Your Inventory

In the perfect world, the total cost value of items in your Items List needs to balance with the value of your Inventory Asset account in your Balance Sheet. For example, if you only had two items in stock — a marble fountain that cost $700 and a concrete fountain that cost $300 — then not only should the total value of your Items Value Reconciliation report be $1,000, but the balance of your Inventory asset account should also be the same ($1,000).

To find out more about making sure your inventory balances — as well as what to do if it doesn't — skip ahead to Chapter 18.

Chapter 11

Saving Money on Payday

· ·

In This Chapter

▶ Setting up payroll for your business

▶ Getting your wages categories organised

▶ Paying up, in style

▶ Calculating leave entitlements

▶ Setting up super, reporting for super and paying your dues

▶ Deducting tax from employee pays

▶ Saying farewell to an employee

▶ Getting ready for the new payroll year

· ·

Setting up payroll and keeping track of employee pays and entitlements is probably the most technical aspect of working with MYOB. As well as understanding how to process transactions, you need to have some insight into employee awards, pay rates, how superannuation is calculated and more.

In this chapter, I try to strike a happy balance between explaining the software features and sharing my knowledge about working with payroll. Reading this chapter may not be the most enthralling way to spend a sunny afternoon, I admit, but my noble aim is to minimise your pain and maximise your gain.

If you have employees and you're using a version of MYOB software that doesn't include payroll features — such as AccountRight Basics or AccountRight Standard — then I suggest you upgrade. MYOB's payroll features not only save heaps of time, but also ensure you get on top of the trickier aspects of superannuation, PAYG tax and leave entitlements.

Getting a Head Start

If you're just starting up a new MYOB company file and you've yet to set up any employees, the first step is to work through the Payroll section of the Easy Setup interview, which I explain in the next couple of pages. On the other hand, if the payroll setup is complete (maybe you're in a new role as a bookkeeper, but MYOB is already up and running), skip ahead to 'Paying Up' a little later in this chapter.

Surviving the easy setup interview

The Easy Setup Assistant provides the easiest way to configure payroll. To access this menu, go to Setup on the top menu bar, select Easy Setup Assistant, and then click the Payroll button.

I could write a whole chapter about each stage of the Easy Setup Assistant interview, but I know you don't need me to explain every teensy bit. Instead, I'm going to give you a few tricks to make things easier and point out a couple of traps that you don't want to fall into, as follows:

✔ **Get the year right.** The Payroll Year menu asks you to select your Current Payroll Year. Your Current Payroll Year is the year that it will be when you next complete your end-of-financial-year payment summaries. (For example, if it's July 2015 now, it will be June 2016 by the time you're due to complete payment summaries.)

✔ **Get the working hours right.** The Payroll Information menu asks about the number of hours in a Full Work Week (as a self-employed business person, I'd be most reluctant to answer this question about myself). Look up your award if you're not sure about how many hours this is — the National Employment Standards stipulate that 38 hours is the maximum number of hours in a regular week, but some awards specify fewer hours. If you have multiple awards within your business, check the award or agreement that relates to the majority of your employees.

✔ **Review your linked accounts.** The Linked Accounts menu asks you which accounts you want to use to pay your employees. Usually, you select a Cash Drawer or Undeposited Funds account for Cash Payments, your regular business bank account for Cheque Payments, and your Electronic Clearing Account for Electronic Payments. As the Account for Employer Expenses, select Superannuation Expense.

✔ **Ignore entitlements for the moment.** If you're not a payroll expert and you're just getting started, don't worry about setting up leave entitlements right now. You can return to these later.

✔ **Drill down behind the scenes.** The Employee Cards menu involves setting up employee contact details, pay rates, superannuation details and more. To view these details, remember to click both the Payroll Details and the Payment Details tab for each employee. Skip to the next section to find out more.

Setting up employee details

All employees have their own card in the Card File. The idea is that you list an employee's name, address and phone number in the Profile window (this is the first screen you come to when creating a new card) and then you complete the employee's payroll information by clicking the Payroll Details tab.

Figure 11-1 shows a typical Payroll Details view. At the top you list personal details, such as Date of Birth, Gender and Start Date. Then you click the menus on the left to enter more details. Click Wages to record pay rates and pay frequencies, Superannuation to enter fund details, Entitlements to select annual or personal leave info, and Taxes to select the appropriate tax scale.

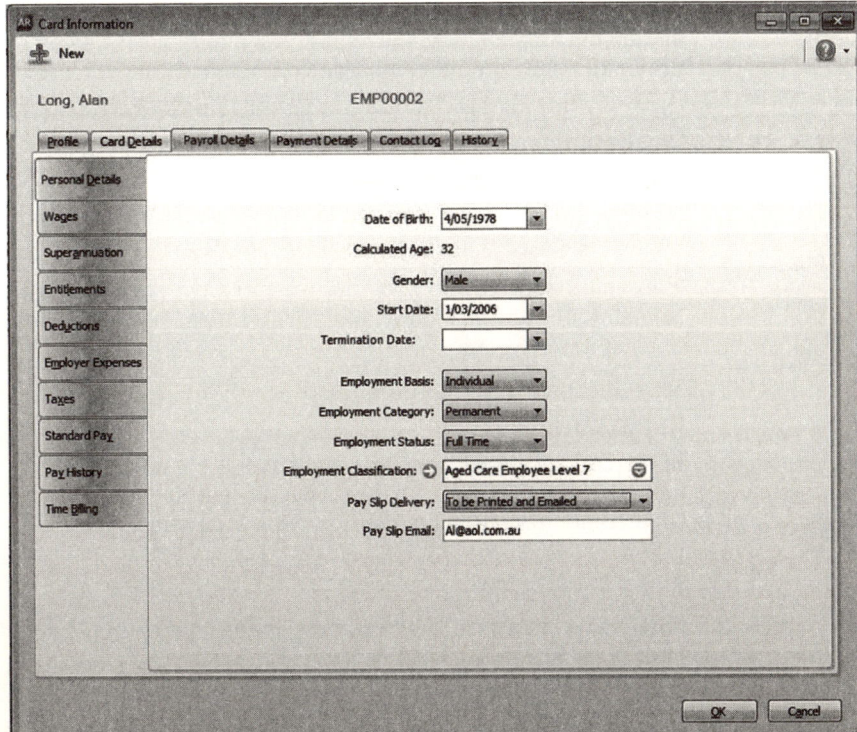

Figure 11-1: Storing an employee's payroll information on the Payroll Details tab.

So are you ready to set up your employees' details? Then here goes:

1. **From the Card File command centre, select Cards List, click the Employee tab, and then New.**

   This instruction applies if you want to enter a new employee. However, if you're setting up payroll for the first time, you can reach this spot in the Easy Setup Assistant by selecting Payroll, followed by Employee Cards, followed by New.

2. **Fill in the name, address, email address and so on.**

   A full address is particularly important because this info is vital at the end of the payroll year. You don't want to find an employee has long since resigned and you never completed this info.

3. **Ignore the Card Details tab.**

   Alternatively, you can use this area to insert a photo or add extra info if necessary.

4. **Click the Payroll Details tab and complete all Personal Details.**

   You're required to enter a Date of Birth (often surprising), Gender (usually obvious) and a Start Date. Unless the employee is a subcontractor, select Individual as the Employment Basis. You also need to enter an Employment Classification to show what award or agreement this employee is employed under, and select whether you prefer to print or email employee pay advices.

5. **Click the Wages side menu and choose either Salary or Hourly as the Pay Basis.**

   Choose Hourly if the employee's hours vary from week to week, the employee receives any kind of loadings, penalties or overtime, or if the employee's award limits the daily hours of work.

   If an employee's award provides for the payment of overtime, you need to maintain records of start and finish times, and keep these records for at least seven years.

6. **Stay in the Wages side menu and check the Pay Frequency and Hours in Weekly Pay Period.**

   Be careful with these settings, because one wrong click now can mean big trouble later. When setting up employee payroll, you need to become intimately acquainted with each employee's award — if you haven't already done so, visit the Fair Work Commission at www.fwa.gov.au and download the relevant award(s).

7. **Still in the Wages side menu, choose an expense type for this employee for your Profit & Loss.**

   Choose a Wages Expense Account that reflects the type of work the employee does. If you employ office staff, factory staff and management, I recommend you create different expense accounts for each category of staff.

8. **Complete the Wages side menu by selecting all wages categories that apply to this employee.**

   You're feeling daunted? Don't be. Instead, ask yourself which wages categories apply to this employee. For casuals, you only need to select Base Hourly, but for permanent employees, you also need to select Holiday Pay and Personal/Carer's Leave, as well as any other regular payments. Figure 11-2 shows an example.

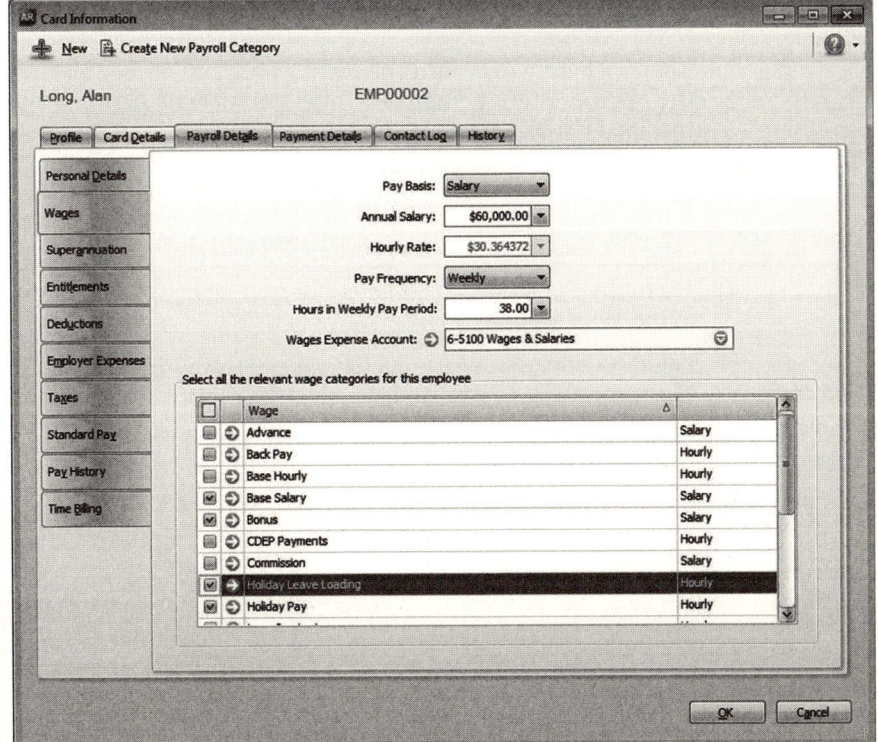

Figure 11-2: Completing wages information for an employee.

9. **Click the Superannuation side menu and set up superannuation details for this employee.**

   Unless the employee isn't eligible for super (and beware, almost every employee is!), you need to fill in the Superannuation Fund and Employee Membership No. fields. If you don't have this info yet, make a note to get it as soon as you can. Then, from the list of superannuation categories, select the category that applies to this employee. Unless the employee has something unusual, such as additional superannuation or salary sacrifice, your best bet is simply to click against the Superannuation Guarantee category.

10. **Click the Entitlements side menu and figure out what you're going to do about leave entitlements.**

    Yep, I know I'm being vague here. However, check out 'Taking a Siesta' later on in this chapter — this section covers annual leave and personal leave in detail — before you proceed. Then, when you've figured out what you want to do, go to the Entitlements side menu on the Payroll Details tab for this new employee and click off the appropriate categories.

11. **Click the Taxes side menu and set up the employee's tax info, and record any rebates.**

    This is where you record the employee's Tax File Number and select the appropriate Tax Table. For most full-time or part-time employees, the Tax Free Threshold setting works fine, but for employees for whom this is a second job, select No Tax Free Threshold as the Tax Scale (check with your accountant if you're not sure about tax scales). Also, if the employee is entitled to any offsets or rebates, put the amount they're owed for the whole year in Total Rebates.

12. **Go to the Standard Pay side menu and make a stab at completing the employee's standard pay.**

    I'm chickening out of explaining everything about standard pays here. Make your way to the following section to get the whole picture.

13. **Click the Payment Details tab and fill in the employee's banking details.**

    Take your pick for the Payment Method: Cash, Cheque or Electronic.

    If you intend to generate a batch file from MYOB to import into your internet banking (a topic I explain in more detail in Chapter 13), select Electronic as the Payment Method. However, if you plan to log onto internet banking and pay each employee individually (which is the method most people use when first getting started), select Cheque as your Payment Method. Sounds weird, but by selecting Cheque as the Payment Method, MYOB shows each employee pay as a separate debit on your bank statement, rather than batching all employee pays together as a single sum.

14. **Heave a huge sigh of relief and click OK, and then OK again.**

    You get a real sense of achievement the first time you set up a new employee, don't you? Well done.

Setting up standard pays

The idea behind a standard pay is you can set up a default for each employee's regular pay, specifying how many hours an employee works each week, what allowances they receive, whether the employees contribute additional superannuation and so on. These details then flow through to the Process Payroll window, ready to record each employee's pay automatically.

Of course, you can still edit an employee's pay before you record it (for example, to record holiday pay), but the default makes a good starting point. To view an employee's standard pay, go to the employee's card, click the Payroll Details tab and head for the Standard Pay side menu. What you should see is every element of the employee's pay, with amounts against each payroll category that applies, as shown in Figure 11-3.

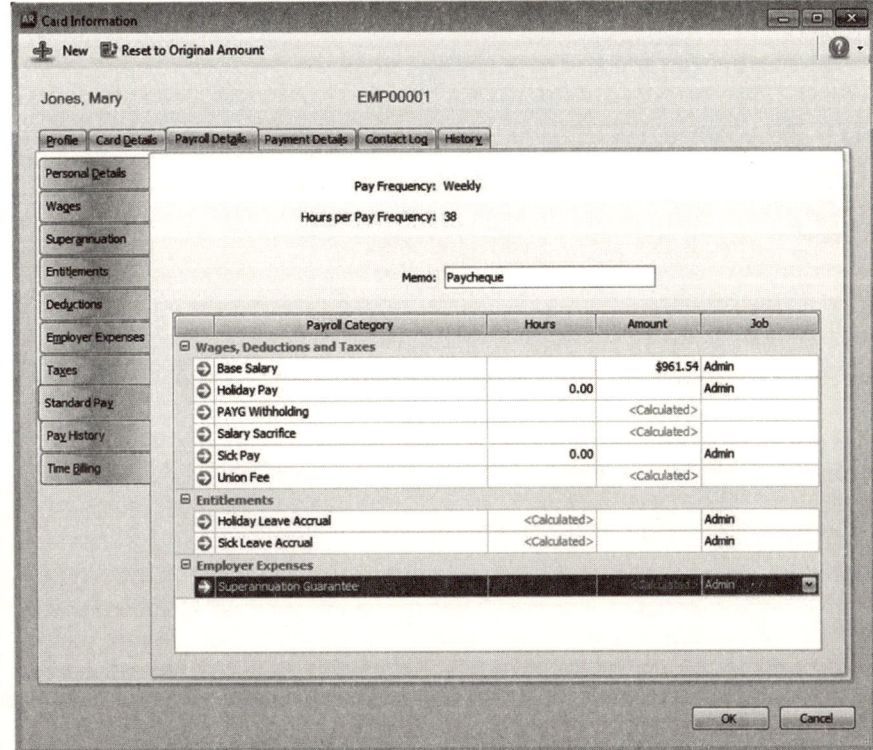

Figure 11-3: Standard pays are the easiest way to ensure each employee's pay calculates correctly every pay period.

Here are some tips about applying standard pays to your employees:

- ✔ **Missing payroll categories:** If a payroll category doesn't show up in the employee's standard pay, it's because you haven't specified that the employee is eligible for this category. Return to the relevant side menu (wages, entitlements, super or whatever), select the payroll category, and then return to the standard pay.

- ✔ **If you intend to use the timesheets feature, set the number of hours in the standard pay to zero:** Otherwise, MYOB will add the standard pay hours onto the timesheet hours, potentially doubling the hours on an employee's pay.

- ✔ **Part-timers:** If the Hours Per Pay Frequency doesn't come up right in an employee's standard pay, you need to go to the Wages side menu of that employee's card and change the number of Hours in Weekly Pay Period.

- ✔ **Casuals:** If you employ casuals whose hours vary every week, get wise and change the number of hours in the Hours column of their standard pay to zero hours. That way you don't risk accidentally paying a casual for hours that they didn't work.

If you're not sure whether your standard pays are all set up correctly, the proof of the pudding is this: If you find yourself making the same change to an employee's pay every pay period (for example, changing the amount of an allowance or deduction), this means that the employee's standard pay info isn't right and you need to fix it.

Setting Up Wages Categories

Wage categories cover everything you pay to your employees — salaries, holiday pay, personal leave, allowances, penalty loadings, bonuses and so on. What you need to do is allocate a separate wages category for every type of payment you give an employee.

Your Payroll Categories List comes well stocked with lots of wages categories. These categories fit the bill for most businesses, but you may need to add one from time to time. Here's what to do:

1. **Select Payroll Categories, click the Wages tab and then click New.**

2. **Give the new category a name and select whether it's Salary or Hourly.**

   You can name the category anything you like, such as Overtime, Leave Loading or Allowance. For fixed amount allowances employees receive each pay, pick Salary as the Type of Wages. For additional payments based on the number of hours worked (such as overtime or penalty rates), choose Hourly.

3. **If you choose Hourly, select how you want to calculate the rate.**

    You can choose between multiplying the regular rate by a number (for example, enter **2** in the field for double-time), or choose a Fixed Hourly Rate.

4. **If you want these wages to be reported separately, click Optional Account.**

    Selecting an Optional Account enables you to report payroll categories separately on your Profit & Loss report. For example, instead of including motor vehicle allowances as part of ordinary wage expenses, you can click the Optional Account button in the Motor Vehicle Allowance payroll category, selecting Motor Vehicle Allowance as the account in the Override Account box. Motor Vehicle Allowance then appears as a separate line in your Profit & Loss report. (I recommend you select Optional Accounts for both allowances and reimbursements, so you can report on these categories separately.)

5. **If the new category is exempt from PAYG, click Exempt.**

    Sadly, there's not much left in life that's exempt from tax other than direct reimbursements. If you're sure a wage category is exempt from PAYG, click the Exempt button, click against PAYG Withholding, and then click OK.

6. **Save your incredibly fantastic work by clicking OK again.**

    You've done it!

Paying Up

Once you complete reviewing your payroll categories, as I explain earlier in this chapter, you're ready to record your first employee pay.

Doing your first pay run

In this section, I explain how to record an employee pay with the assumption that you've already added up the total hours the employee is due to be paid. However, if you prefer to enter daily start and finish times in MYOB so that MYOB can calculate hours for you, skip ahead to the next section. With the timesheets complete, you can then return to this section and process pays.

Ready to go? Here's how to record your first pay run:

1. **From the Payroll command centre, click Process Payroll.**

2. **Decide whether you want to pay all employees in the one hit, or pay one employee only.**

   Usually, it's best to process all pays as a single batch. The only reason you would pay one employee separately is if you were processing a pay adjustment or termination pay.

3. **Select the Pay Frequency, pick your dates and click Next.**

   The Pay Frequency refers to whatever you chose as the Pay Frequency in each employee's card. You have to do pays as separate batches (weekly, fortnightly, monthly and so on). For example, even if payday falls due on the same day for both your weekly and fortnightly employees, you do two separate batches.

   With dates, be careful to get them right. The Payment Date is usually one day after the Pay Period End date. Also, if you use timesheets, you need to be scrupulous that your pay period start and finish dates match exactly with the timesheet start and finish dates.

   Also, don't worry if pay periods straddle the end of financial year. For example, if a pay period goes from 26 June to 3 July, that's fine.

4. **Make sure that all employees you want to pay are on this list and that employees who have left or resigned aren't on this list.**

   The Employee Pays window (shown in Figure 11-4) shows a summary of all the employees in this pay run.

   If an employee is missing from this list, it's probably because you set up the employee's Pay Frequency incorrectly (for example, selecting Monthly instead of Weekly). To change this, go to the employee's card and open the Payroll Details tab. On the other hand, if an employee who has long since departed shows up in the list, fix this error by going to that employee's card and making it inactive. (Click the Profile tab for this employee, followed by the Inactive Card checkbox in the top-right corner.)

   If an employee is casual and didn't work this pay period, remove the tick from against this person's name.

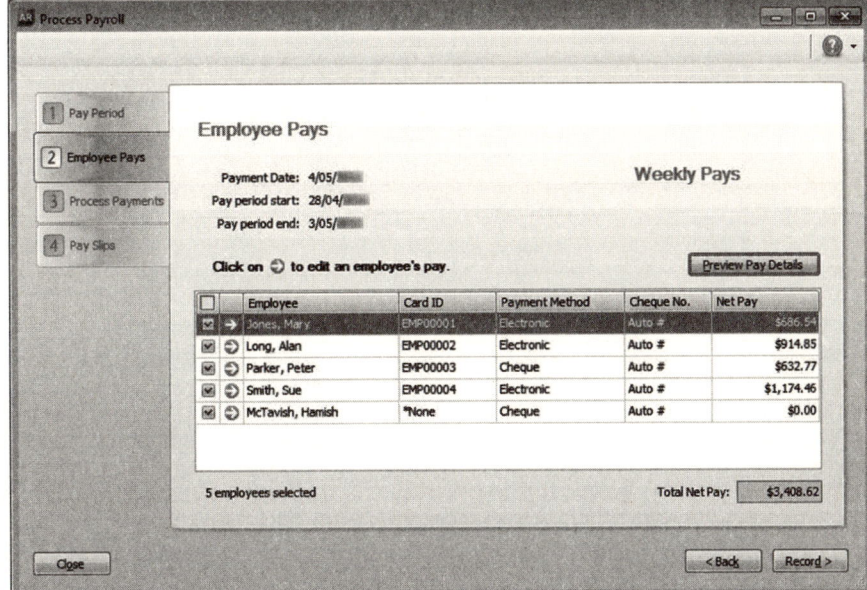

Figure 11-4:
The
Employee
Pays
window.

5. Edit the pays for any employees whose standard pay was different from normal.

If any employees have variations to their standard pay for this period (perhaps they did some overtime, went on leave or had a sickie), zoom in on their pay and fix up this information.

Figure 11-5 shows an individual employee's pay. The first section of each pay shows wages, where you can change the hours; for example, adding overtime hours, inserting hours next to Holiday Pay and reducing the number of hours next to Base Hourly, or adding reimbursements.

The second and third sections of an employee's pay shows entitlements and superannuation. If you've set up these payroll categories properly, both sections should calculate automatically.

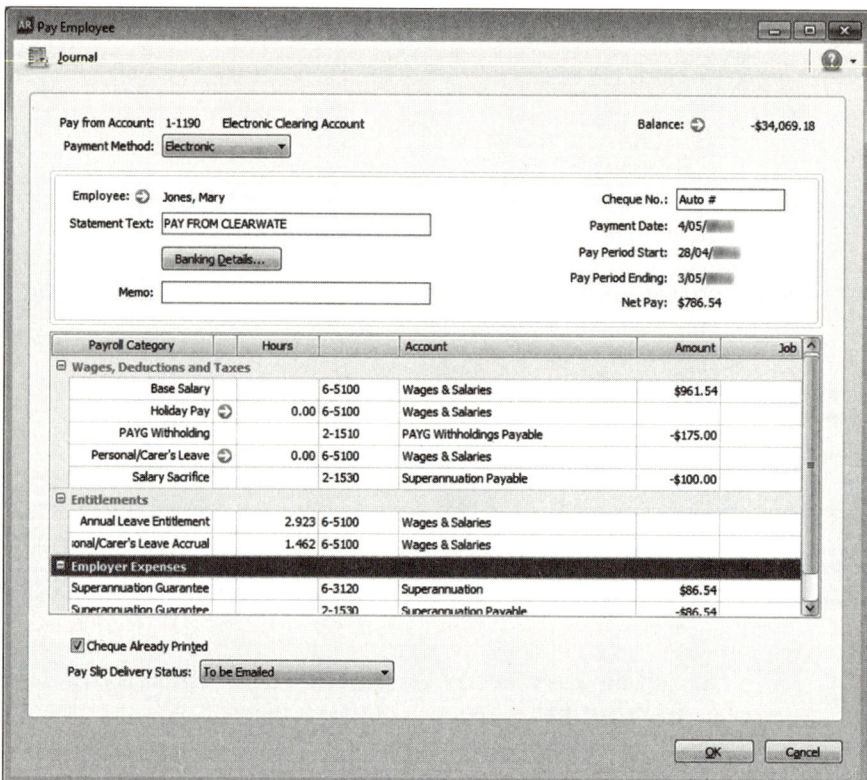

Figure 11-5:
An
individual
employee
pay.

6. When you're happy that all the pays are correct, click the Preview Pay Details button.

The Payroll Verification report appears, summarising pay details for each employee. I like to have a squiz at this report before I finalise the pays, and you may even want to save a copy of this report as a PDF to keep as a record.

7. Click Record.

Clicking Record means that you process a pay transaction for each selected employee. No going back now!

8. Depending on which payment method (or methods) apply, click Print Paycheques, Prepare Electronic Payments or Spend Money to process the payment batch. Then click Next.

Eek! I wish I could make this sound less technical. But here's the rub:

- If you pay employees one-by-one using internet banking, ignore all three of these options and simply click Next.

- If you pay employees electronically, creating an 'aba' batch file in MYOB and then importing this file into your internet banking, click Prepare Electronic Payments.

- If you pay in cash, click Spend Money.

For more detail about electronic payments, make your way to Chapter 13.

9. **Print or email your pay advices.**

Employee names appear either under the To Be Printed tab or the To Be Emailed tab, depending on what you selected as each employee's Pay Slip Delivery method. To change the delivery method for an employee on an ongoing basis, go to the Personal Details side menu in the employee's Payroll Details. To change the delivery method for an employee whose pay you have already recorded, click the pay transaction itself and change the Pay Slip Delivery Status.

Assuming that access to your emails is password-protected, I recommend emailing pay slips rather than printing them. Email is quicker and less vulnerable to nosey-parker types, especially in an office environment where printers are shared.

10. **Click Close.**

Working with timesheets

So far I've explained how to record pays in batches, using the information that you set up in the standard pay for each employee. However, if you have lots of casuals, or the start and finish times for your employees vary every week, an easier approach is to record employees' times into a timesheet and then carry the information from the timesheets across into payroll.

To check out the timesheet feature, click Enter Timesheet in the Payroll command centre and, for each employee, create a new timesheet using the employee's name and inserting how many hours worked. Figure 11-6 shows an example timesheet. (If this is the first time you're viewing the Timesheet menu, you're also prompted to click the Preference called 'I use Timesheets for Payroll'.)

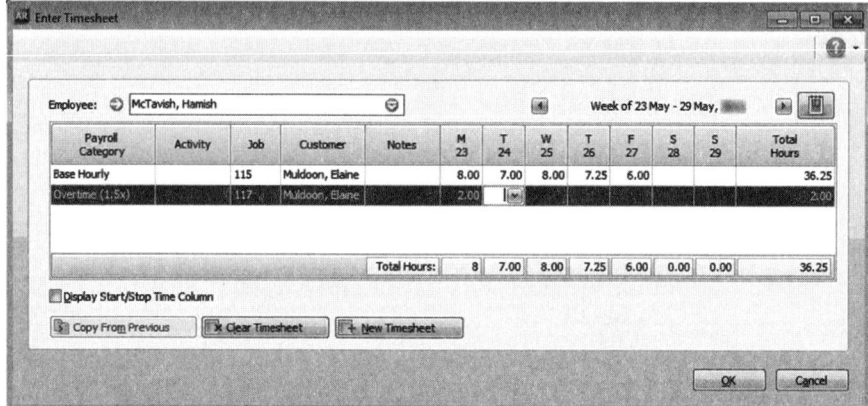

Figure 11-6:
Timesheets work well if you employ lots of casuals.

You'll probably find that you can follow your nose to make timesheets work, but here are some tips that may help out:

✔ Timesheets are sensitive beasts when it comes to dates. For example, if you've recorded a timesheet for the dates 01/07/15 to 07/07/15 but you enter 02/07/15 to 07/07/15 when selecting the pay period in Process Pays, then the hours for that first day won't carry across to the employee's pay.

✔ For most employees, you can save time with future pays by clicking the Copy From Previous button on the bottom left of the Enter Timesheet window. That way all the payroll categories come up automatically and all you have to do is change the number of hours against each category.

✔ If the pay week starts on the wrong day (for example, a Monday rather than a Tuesday), you need to go to Setup⇨Preferences, click the System tab, and then select the day your pay week starts.

✔ Always press Tab or Enter after entering figures in the hours columns. (If you just type the figure in the column and click OK, your changes don't go through.)

✔ Remember to enter hours as decimals. For example, if an employee works 8 hours and 15 minutes, this actually means the employee worked eight and a quarter hours. You should key this in as 8.25 hours, not 8.15 hours. (Maybe now you'll regret all those times when you went surfin' instead of going to maths class . . .)

✔ Some awards stipulate that you have to keep written records of employees' start and finish times. If this is the case, make sure your employees complete a timesheet every week, and file these sheets with your other payroll records. (The timesheet feature in MYOB also includes a Start/Stop column where you can record this info, but if the start and stop times are already tracked elsewhere, there's not much point in re-keying this data.)

Producing pay slips

The easiest way to generate pay slips is to click Print or Email Pay Slips when you're at the end of the payroll process cycle. Seems simple? Read on for more twists in the tale:

✔ To reprint pay slips for a previous pay cycle, head for the Payroll Advice report, found on the Payroll tab in your Reports menu.

✔ Make sure that the details of each employee's award shows on each pay slip (this is a legal requirement from Fair Work Australia). To do this, complete the Employment Classification field (found on the Personal Details tab) in each employee's record.

✔ To customise the format of your pay slips, go to Setup⇨Customise Forms⇨Pay Slips. Click Customise and do your stuff. To print future pay slips using this new layout, make sure you select this customised form in the Advanced Filters from the Review Pay Slips Before Delivery window.

✔ To email pay slips direct to employees, click Print/Email Pay Slips from the Payroll command centre.

Keeping everything sweet

If you're having problems getting an employee's pay to calculate correctly, try these tricks:

✔ **Check the tax.** If the tax doesn't come up right, check the tax scale you selected for the employee in the Taxes side menu, found on the Payroll Details tab of the employee's card. (If you're not sure what the tax should be, www.paycalculator.com.au is the spot to go.)

✔ **Check the Pay Basis.** If the pay is coming up as a ridiculous amount of, say, a few cents per week, chances are you've entered an hourly rate but set the Pay Basis as Salary in the employee's card. No matter how radical Australia's industrial relations reform, you won't get away with paying anyone 35 cents per week.

✔ **Make sure the standard pay is set up correctly.** Regular payments such as allowances and deductions should come up automatically — if they don't, go to the employee's card and change the employee's standard pay.

✔ **Check super is calculating correctly.** Make sure that the Superannuation Guarantee category appears on every pay (even if the amount next to this category is zero). The only reason for this category not to appear is if you forget to select superannuation in the employee's setup — a big mistake! However, don't worry if super comes up as zero in the first or second pay period of the month. That's because MYOB (with true brilliance) doesn't calculate super until employees hit the $450 monthly threshold.

✔ **Make sure the working week is the right number of hours.** Always make sure the total hours come up correctly. You don't want a 40-hour week to show up on each employee's pay if the standard working week according to the employee's award is actually 38 hours.

Deleting or adjusting pays

Employee pays differ from most other transactions in MYOB in that after you record a pay transaction, you can't change any amounts or the payment date (the only info you can change is the pay period dates).

So what do you do if you make a mistake? If you haven't paid the employee yet, nor handed over a pay slip, your best bet is to delete the pay completely and start again:

1. **Go to the Payroll command centre and choose Transaction Journal.**

2. **Scroll up or down to find the offending pay and then click the zoom arrow on the left to display it.**

3. **On the top menu bar, choose Edit⇨Delete Transaction.**

   If the only option here is to reverse the transaction, rather than delete the transaction, this means you've already recorded an electronic payment batch that includes this pay. If you haven't uploaded this electronic payment batch to your bank yet, the best approach is to find the electronic payment and delete it. Then return to the pay transaction and try again to delete it.

Never delete a pay transaction if you've already paid an employee and supplied a pay slip. This pay slip is a legal record and, even if incorrect, shows how you calculated the employee's pay. Your only solution in this scenario is to process a pay adjustment. You can make an adjustment in one of two ways:

✔ The easiest way to adjust a pay is to incorporate the adjustment into the next pay period. For example, if you underpaid someone by

> two hours one week, simply add these two hours onto their pay the next week.
>
> ✔ Alternatively, if the adjustment relates to the pay category rather than the pay amount — maybe you processed a pay as 38 regular hours, rather than 38 holiday hours — you can record an additional pay for that pay period. For example, you would enter 38 hours against Holiday Pay and minus 38 hours against the Base Hourly Pay. The final result would be a nil value pay, but your leave totals would now be correct.

Taking a Siesta

I reckon that tracking employee leave is the trickiest part of managing payroll. Not only do you need to understand how leave is calculated, but you also need to be very familiar with each employee's award and employment conditions.

I cover the basics of employee entitlements in the next few sections, but for a detailed document explaining all facets of managing entitlements, visit www.veechicurtis.com.au and follow the eBooks link in the Online Store.

Setting up annual leave

Wondering what I'm meaning by the term *annual leave*? I'm talking holiday pay here, using the jargon that government departments prefer. Whether you're talking annual leave or holiday pay, six or half a dozen, property developers or white pointers, makes no difference to me.

First things first: Before you can be sure that annual leave calculates properly, you need to set up your entitlement categories correctly. Here's how:

1. **Choose Payroll Categories, click the Entitlements tab and double-click the Annual Leave Entitlement category.**

2. **If you have employees on hourly rates, check that the entitlement is calculated on a percentage basis.**

   If your employees work on an hourly rate, click against Equals 7.6923 Percent of Gross Hours, as shown in Figure 11-7. (This sounds like a weird figure, but it translates into 20 days of holiday per year. This is the standard amount of annual leave most employees receive. Of course, if employees receive more than 20 days' leave per year, adjust this percentage accordingly.)

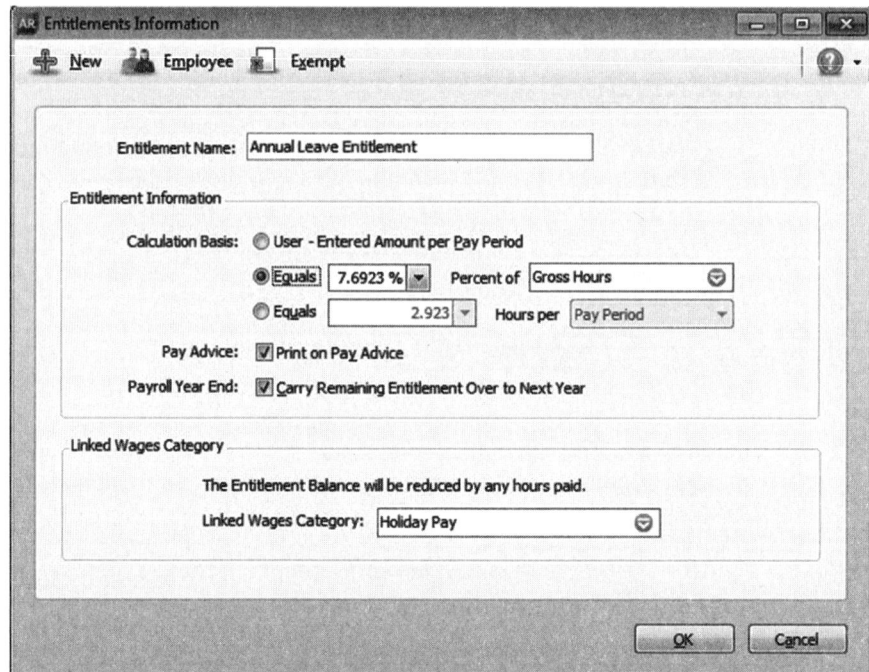

3. **If you have salaried employees, create a new entitlement called Annual Leave Entitlement Salaried.**

   If you have both hourly and salaried employees on your payroll, you're going to need two Annual Leave Entitlement categories. Change the name of the Annual Leave Entitlement category so it's called Annual Leave Entitlement Hourly and call the new category Annual Leave Entitlement Salaried.

4. **For salaried employees, calculate how many hours entitlement they receive each pay period and then edit the Annual Leave Entitlement Salaried category so that it calculates this number of hours per pay period.**

   Here's an example. Suppose a salaried employee is due four weeks per year. If the employee works a 38-hour week, that's 4 multiplied by 38, which equals 152 hours per year. If the employee gets paid fortnightly, you divide 152 by 26 (there are 26 fortnights in a year). This gives you the number of hours annual leave a salaried person accrues each fortnight — 5.846 hours per Pay Period. (Ah, don't you just love maths?)

5. **For each annual leave category, click the checkboxes Print on Pay Advice and Carry Remaining Entitlement Over to Next Year.**

   I find it works best if you print how much annual leave employees are due on their pay advices. Certainly, you need to click Carry Remaining Entitlement Over to Next Year — otherwise, annual leave returns to zero when you hit 30 June.

6. **Make sure the Linked Wages Category is Holiday Pay.**

   The Linked Wages Category for each annual leave entitlement category should be Holiday Pay, as shown in Figure 11-7. If it's not, change it now.

7. **For each annual leave entitlement category, click the Employee button, select which employees receive that kind of entitlement, and then click OK.**

   To select employees, click in the column against their names.

8. **For employees on hourly rates, click Exempt to select any wages categories that are exempt from accruing holiday pay.**

   If you accrue leave on a percentage basis, be careful that employees don't build up leave on miscellaneous payments, such as allowances, bonuses, annual leave loading, overtime or reimbursements.

9. **Click OK to record and save your changes.**

10. **Click Close to return to the Payroll command centre.**

Preparing for the plague

Setting up *personal/carer's leave* (the new approved term for sick leave, because you can now take time off to look after your nearest and dearest) is exactly the same as setting up annual leave. So, I won't bore you to death by explaining basically the same stuff again, but instead point out some salient things that relate only to personal/carer's leave:

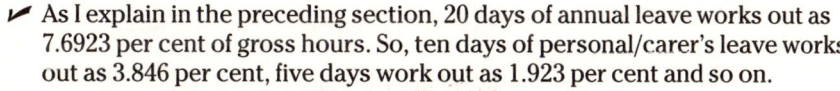

- As I explain in the preceding section, 20 days of annual leave works out as 7.6923 per cent of gross hours. So, ten days of personal/carer's leave works out as 3.846 per cent, five days work out as 1.923 per cent and so on.

- I don't normally select the box Print on Pay Advice. I reckon that if employees aren't told how much personal leave they're due on every pay slip, this is probably a good thing.

- You link Personal/Carer's Leave Accrual to Personal Leave.

Catching up on what's already owed

In order for leave entitlements to calculate correctly, you first need to record how much annual and personal leave your employees were due at the point you start using MYOB payroll. Here's how it's done:

1. **Calculate how much leave you owe each employee.**

   Always remember to express entitlements in hours (and never in dollars or days). For example, if an employee works a 38-hour week, this converts to 7.6 hours per day. If this employee has two days' leave owing, this converts to 15.2 hours leave.

2. **Go to Process Payroll and click Next.**

3. **Zoom in on the first employee's pay and set all amounts to zero.**

   I'm talking dollar amounts and any amounts sitting against leave accruals here.

4. **Enter the number of hours that you owe this employee against each leave accrual category.**

   For example, if you owe this employee 38 hours in annual leave, enter 38 against the Annual Leave Entitlement category, as I do in Figure 11-8.

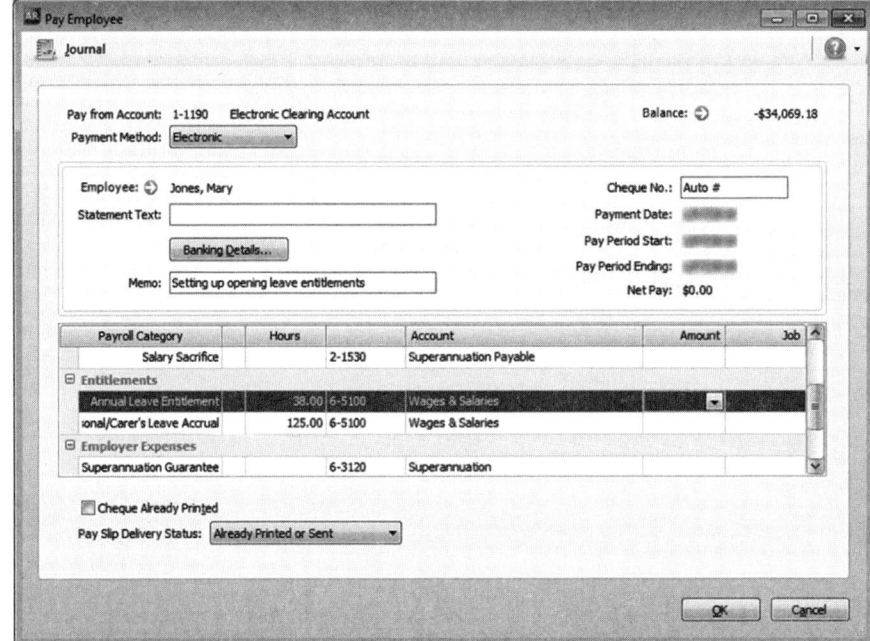

Figure 11-8:
Recording opening employee entitlements.

5. **Click OK, and then OK again.**

   MYOB asks if you want to void this paycheque. You do, so go right ahead.

6. **Repeat this process for all employees.**

7. **Click Preview Pay Details and print a copy of your Payroll Verification report.**

   I'm not normally one for printing reports, but this report is vital because it provides a record of how many hours you entered in leave for each employee.

8. **Click Record and then Next to finalise these transactions.**

Paying annual leave or personal leave

So what do you do when an employee takes some annual leave or personal leave? Take your time, go slow, and follow these instructions:

1. **Check that the employee has enough hours built up in leave.**

   Not sure? The Entitlements Balance Summary report is the quick way to see how much an employee has accrued in leave.

2. **Go to Process Pays as normal and proceed to the Employee Pays window.**

   If an employee receives annual leave in advance — for example, you're processing a single payment for one week's regular pay plus two weeks' holiday pay — click Process Individual Employee, rather than Process all Employees Paid. Click Pay Leave in Advance and enter the number of weeks of leave you're paying in advance.

3. **Double-click on the employee taking leave, and enter the number of hours' leave this employee has taken.**

   Enter annual leave against Holiday Pay, and personal leave against Personal/Carer's Leave.

4. **Click the arrow that appears next to Holiday Pay or Personal/Carer's Leave and record all the details about the leave taken.**

   Include the dates that leave was taken, the total number of hours paid, and any other notes about this leave, such as whether the employee supplied a medical certificate.

5. **If this employee is eligible for leave loading, enter the number of hours' of leave taken against Holiday Leave Loading.**

   Figure 11-9 provides an elegant example.

6. Complete your pay run in the normal way.

You're done, you clever thing!

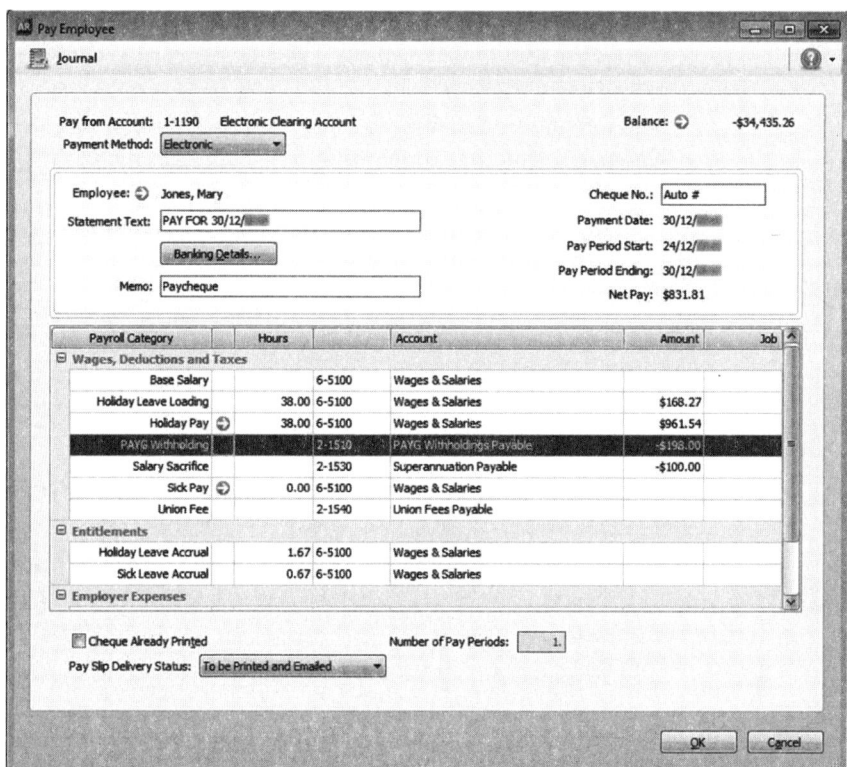

Figure 11-9: Processing holiday pays.

Keeping things to yourself

Payroll information is sensitive. There's no better way to create friction between employees than have them compare wages with one another, especially in family businesses (where the children of the employers so often end up with a sweetheart deal). However, not only is payroll information sensitive, but some employee information is actually also protected by the Privacy Act. In particular, you're obliged to keep employee tax file numbers secure.

The only sure way to do this is to password-protect the whole of your company file and then define user roles so that you restrict access to the payroll section of your file. I explain how to set up user roles and passwords in Chapter 1.

Fixing up leave when it's up the spout

So, you know for sure that an employee is owed three weeks' annual leave, but the employee's pay slip shows a ridiculous number of hours' entitlements, which has no bearing on reality. How do you fix things up? Here's how:

1. **Calculate the difference between how many hours of leave the employee is really owed, compared to what shows up in the employee's payroll records.**

   For example, if you know the employee is owed 120 hours' leave but the payroll record shows 30 hours, then the difference is 90 hours.

2. **Go to Process Payroll, select Process Individual Employee and click Next.**

   'Process Individual Employee' sounds rather Orwellian, don't you think?

3. **Double-click this employee's pay and set all amounts to zero, including any hours showing up in leave accrual categories.**

4. **In the leave accrual category that you're trying to fix, enter the number of hours that the employee's record is out by.**

   You can make this amount positive or negative, depending on whether you need to increase or decrease the employee's entitlement.

5. **Click Record and then OK to continue.**

   You see a message asking if you want to record a nil pay. Click Yes to continue.

6. **Return to Entitlements in the Payroll Details tab for this employee and check that the number of hours shown in the Total column is now correct.**

   As part of double-checking your work, call up an Entitlements Balance Detail report (found in your Reports menu), where you can view a complete history of each employee's leave accruals and leave taken.

7. **Communicate! Yes, you can do it . . .**

   You may not be the bouncy bubbly communicative type, but you can't make sweeping changes to the leave showing on an employee's pay slip without letting this person know what you're doing.

Planning for Super

Superannuation is a big deal, not just in terms of how much money is involved, but also because of the onus on businesses to get super payments right. The superannuation audits I've experienced are sombre indeed and auditors aren't shy about delivering hefty fines for the slightest transgression.

Even the date when you have to pay superannuation is crucial. Super payments are due within 28 days after the end of each quarter (that's 28 July, 28 October, 28 January and 28 April). Also, if your super payments don't reach employees' funds by 30 June, you can't claim them as a tax deduction for that year. And if those payments don't reach the funds by 28 July, you may never be able to claim them as a tax deduction. You will also be fined.

So the moral of the tale is this: Be diligent, set up superannuation in MYOB correctly and pay up frequently.

Setting up your super categories

In order to be certain that superannuation works correctly, you should double-check your settings. Here's how:

1. **Choose Payroll Categories, click the Superannuation tab and double-click the Superannuation Guarantee category.**

2. **Check that the Linked Expense Account is an account called Superannuation Expense.**

   If it isn't, select Superannuation Expense as your Linked Expense account (this account starts with the number 6). If you don't see this account in your list, head over to your Accounts List and create one now.

3. **Check the Linked Payable Account is an account called Superannuation Payable.**

   This bit is important to get right, so be careful. The default that appears here is an account called Payroll Accruals Payable. I hate this, because you end up with the same liability account for both PAYG tax and superannuation. If you haven't done so already, go to your Accounts List and change the name of Payroll Accruals Payable to PAYG Tax Payable, and then create a new account called Superannuation Payable.

   Back in your super payroll category, pick Superannuation Payable as your Linked Payable Account.

4. **Check that the Contribution Type shows up as Superannuation Guarantee (expense).**

5. **Click Print on Pay Advice.**

   When you click here, the amount of superannuation shows on employee pay slips. (I recommend you do this, because it's the law.)

6. **Enter the current percentage in the Calculation Basis field.**

   Enter the current super percentage as a Percent of Gross Wages. At the time of writing, the minimum percentage is 9.5 per cent, but this rate is subject to change, so do double-check with your accountant or the ATO.

7. **Make sure the limit is set to No Limit and that the minimum wages threshold is $450.**

   If an employee earns less than $450 a month, you usually don't have to pay super, and MYOB automatically takes the $450 threshold into account when calculating super. However, some awards have a lower threshold than this, so you may want to double-check the fine print of the relevant award before proceeding.

8. **Click Exempt button at the top of your screen to mark off any wages categories that are exempt from super.**

   Make sure that you mark off all the wages categories that are exempt from superannuation, such as bonuses or overtime. Take a look at the next section to find out more.

9. **Check your work and click OK.**

   Check your screen against Figure 11-10 to make sure everything looks fine.

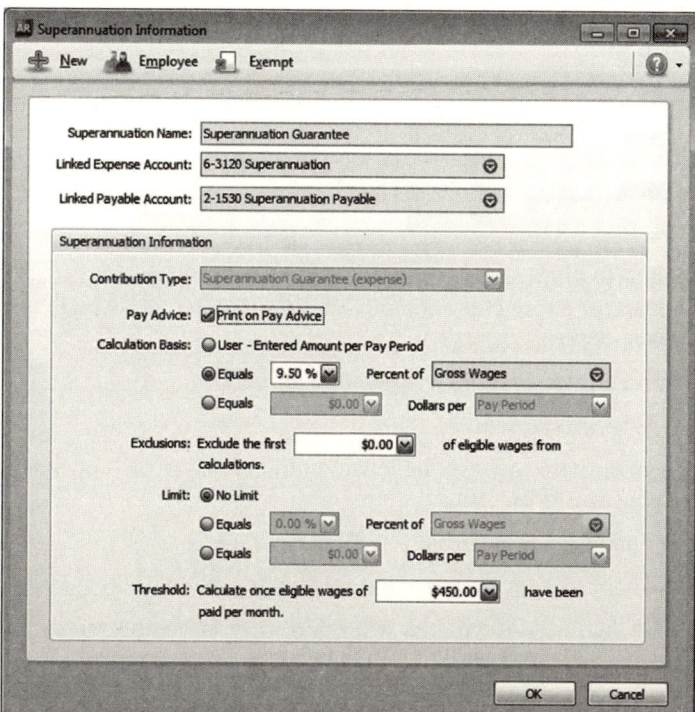

Figure 11-10:
Setting up super-annuation.

Ensuring you don't pay too much super

Maybe it's my Scottish blood, but I hate paying more than I have to.
I especially hate seeing my clients do the same — I'm astounded how often
I come across clients who pay too much super on behalf of their employees.

The trick is to remember this: Superannuation is only due on what is termed
ordinary time earnings (OTE). If you like, you can contact the Australian
Taxation Office for a detailed document explaining what OTE is all about.
However, this government's fine example of English double-speak might be
more understandable were it written in pig-Latin, and so in the interests of
your blood pressure, I summarise the main points in this section.

In most cases (with the exception of a few obscure awards), wages
categories that you do need to pay superannuation on include

- ✔ Allowances (other than reimbursement of expenses)
- ✔ Bonuses and commissions
- ✔ Casual loadings and shift loadings
- ✔ Directors' fees
- ✔ Holiday pay, personal leave or long service leave
- ✔ Payments in lieu of notice (for example, if you offer an employee $1,000 just so they will leave now, rather than later)

Now here's the good news. In most cases, wages that you don't need to pay
superannuation on include

- ✔ Annual leave loading
- ✔ Benefits subject to fringe benefits tax
- ✔ Expense allowances that employees are likely to fully spend in the course of producing income (for example, motor vehicle allowances for salespeople)
- ✔ Maternity or paternity leave payments
- ✔ Overtime payments
- ✔ Payments for any annual leave, personal leave or long service leave owing at termination
- ✔ Redundancy payments
- ✔ Reimbursement of expenses such as travel costs
- ✔ Workers comp payments where no work is being performed

To make sure that you're not paying super when you don't have to:

1. **Go to your Payroll Categories list.**

2. **Click the Superannuation tab and double-click your Superannuation Guarantee category.**

3. **Click the Exempt button and ensure that all wages categories that don't attract super are marked.**

Dealing with RESC

You need to report for some kinds of employee superannuation separately, as follows:

✔ Super that you deduct from an employee's pay under a salary sacrifice arrangement.

✔ Any super over the minimum (9.5 per cent at the time of writing) that you pay to the employee as part of an employment offer. (If a business or organisation offers all employees more than this minimum, and the employee isn't able to influence this decision, then the amount over the minimum doesn't count.)

These two kinds of additional employee super are called *Reportable Super Contributions (RESC)*, and you have to report all RESC super separately on your employee payment summaries.

The good news? If, like 98 per cent of employers, you simply pay your employees the legal minimum of super, you don't have to do anything. You don't need to change any MYOB settings, and you don't need to report employee super on your next batch of payment summaries. Yippee. Alternatively, if any employees have a salary sacrifice arrangement, or you pay any employees at a rate that's higher than the minimum, you may have to report the additional amount of this payment separately. For a detailed document explaining all facets of managing employee superannuation, visit www.veechicurtis.com.au and follow the eBooks link in the Online Store.

Reporting for Super

As I write this, the legislation governing the reporting and paying of super is in a state of flux, with changes slated for 1 July 2015 for businesses with 20 employees or more, or 1 July 2016 for businesses with fewer than 20 employees.

The crux of this legislation (which goes under the dubious title of *SuperStream*) is that you will no longer be able to pay super to individual funds, but instead you will have to pay a single sum for the total of all employees' super to a *clearing house*. (In this instance, a clearing house means an organisation that's registered to process super on behalf of others.) The clearing house will then pay the super to your employees' funds.

Sounds a pain, but the good news is that MYOB has set itself up to be a clearing house, and so you can pay your superannuation contributions direct to MYOB, who will then forward these contributions to your employees' funds. So long as you have a current MYOB subscription, you won't be charged for this service.

Reporting on how much super you owe

To see how much super you owe, the best report to choose is the Superannuation Accrual by Fund Summary report, found under the Payroll tab of your Reports menu. This report groups employees according to the fund, and lists each employee's name, their membership number, the amount of super owing and the fund total. Perfect.

Generating a Superannuation Accrual report only shows the amount of super you owe for the date range you select, and doesn't report for any superannuation owing before that point in time. For example, maybe it's October and you're reporting for September's superannuation. However, how can you double-check that you don't owe any super for July, August or even earlier?

To be sure you capture every cent of super owing, go to Pay Liabilities in the Payroll command centre, select Superannuation as the Liability Type, and enter the last 12 months as the date range. So, for example, if I want to double-check that I've paid everyone's super up until the end of August 2015, I select 01/09/14 to 31/08/15 as my date range.

If any amounts for previous months show here, chances are that you've missed these payments and this amount of superannuation is still outstanding.

Paying super using MYOB as your clearing house

As I mention in the intro to this section, in order to comply with the government's SuperStream legislation (which is pending at the time of writing but may be in force by the time you read this), you can no longer pay employee superannuation directly to employee funds, but must instead use a clearing house. If you subscribe to a current version of MYOB — and in this section I assume that you do — I suggest you take advantage of MYOB's clearing house service to pay employee super.

Here's how the whole concept works:

1. **You sign up to MYOB's superannuation service.**

   To initiate the sign-up process, click Pay Superannuation in the Payroll command centre and follow the prompts from there. *Note:* As part of this process, you provide your banking details to MYOB and the authority for MYOB to debit your account. (Read on, and you find out why.)

2. **Using MYOB, you look up how much super you owe to each employee and record a payment for the month or quarter.**

   To do this, you go to Pay Superannuation in the Payroll command centre, enter your date range, and mark off whose super you want to pay (usually everyone's, unless you have a good reason otherwise).

3. **You authorise and process the payment.**

   To authorise a payment, you enter your login and password for my.myob.com.au and then, when prompted, request a code to be sent to your mobile.

4. **MYOB sends an SMS authorisation code to your mobile.**

   This extra level of security is because MYOB is about to debit your bank account for the superannuation payments you selected. (MYOB can't just take money out of bank accounts willy-nilly without these kinds of protocols in place.)

5. **You enter the code when prompted into MYOB.**

   At this point, you get an encouraging message saying that MYOB has authorised the payment and it's being processed.

6. **Enjoy the sunshine and have a snooze.**

   MYOB takes care of the rest, forwarding employee's super contributions to individual funds, along with the necessary details such as the employee membership numbers.

   Payment processing normally takes a couple of days, but you can monitor the status of your contributions at any time by going to Manage Payments in the Payroll command centre.

Paying super using a different clearing house or no clearing house at all

In this section, I assume that you've chosen not to use MYOB's superannuation clearing service (refer to the previous section for more details). Maybe the legislation hasn't come in yet, maybe you still have an older version of MYOB, maybe you don't have a current software subscription, or maybe you've chosen to use a different clearing house service, such as the Small Business Superannuation Clearing House.

Regardless of the reason for going your own way, here's how to proceed:

1. **Go to the Payroll command centre and click Pay Liabilities.**

   I haven't gone bananas — I do mean click Pay Liabilities and not Pay Superannuation. (The Pay Superannuation feature is only relevant if you choose to use MYOB's super clearing house service.)

2. **Enter the payment details in the same way you do for a regular Spend Money transaction.**

   Use your animal instincts. Complete the Cheque No., Payment Date, Supplier (the name of the superannuation fund) and Memo fields.

3. **Select Superannuation as your Liability Type.**

4. **Select the date range.**

   Pick your date range carefully. For example, if you're in October 2015 and you're paying superannuation for the first quarter, the date range needs to be 01/07/15 to 30/09/15. You should be able to see all superannuation amounts that were due for that date range, grouped by fund.

5. **Select all employees you're going to pay.**

   If you're not using a clearing house service — maybe the new legislation isn't in place by the time you're reading this — you need to record a separate transaction for each fund, so click against employee names for one fund at a time.

   If you're using a clearing house service that isn't MYOB, such as the Small Business Superannuation Clearing House, click off every employee. You only need to process a single payment.

   Your transaction should look something like mine, shown in Figure 11-11.

6. Click Record and then, if necessary, repeat this process for each fund.

After you click Record and return to the Pay Liabilities window, entering the date range once more, the employees who have been paid disappear. You can then repeat the process for each fund until no more names appear. (***Note:*** If you're using a clearing house service, you don't need to do this step.)

You can be confident that you have recorded super payments for all employees if, when you go to Pay Liabilities and enter the relevant date range with Superannuation as the Liability Type, no employees are listed. If an employee's name still shows up, this almost certainly means you've missed recording a payment for that employee.

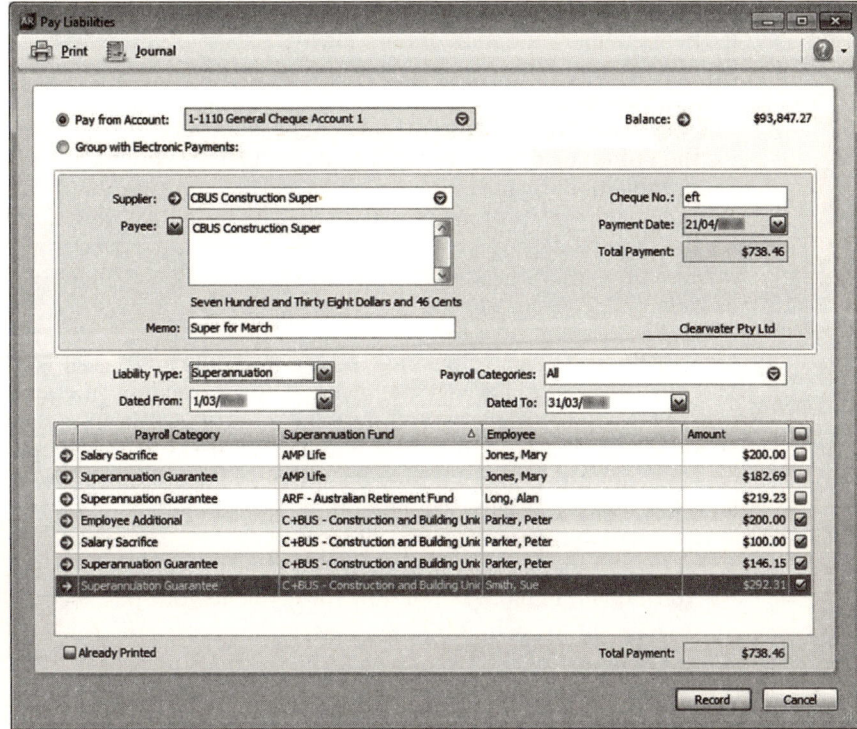

Figure 11-11: Recording your super-annuation payment using the Pay Liabilities window.

Small Business Super Clearing House

If you don't want to use MYOB's clearing house service — maybe you have an older version of the software or you don't want to pay a monthly subscription fee — a good alternative is the Small Business Superannuation Clearing House (www.humanservices.gov.au).

This government-run service operates in the same way as any other clearing house (you make a single payment to the Clearing House, and they manage the individual payments to each fund). The service is free, but only available for businesses with 19 employees or fewer.

Getting super to balance

In theory, superannuation should always balance. However, because I'm a bit of a fusspot, I like to make sure it really does.

The quick and dirty way to do this check is to display your Balance Sheet for the month or quarter you just paid and look at the balance of your Superannuation Payable account. This balance represents the amount you actually paid. For example, if you paid $2,010 superannuation in October for the months July, August and September, you can expect the balance of Superannuation Payable in your September Balance Sheet to be $2,010 as well.

If super doesn't seem to balance, return to Pay Liabilities (if you don't use MYOB's clearing house service) or Pay Superannuation (if you do). This time, as the date range, enter **1 July** for Dated From and the date up to which you've just paid as your Dated To. See if any old super payments for previous months pop up. If they do, chances are you missed these payments and that's why your superannuation isn't balancing.

If you do all this and you still can't get super to balance, skip to Chapter 18, where I explain in more detail how to reconcile your payroll liabilities.

Withholding PAYG Tax

Managing PAYG Tax (in other words, the tax you deduct from employee pays) involves two things. First, you need to be confident that you're deducting the right amount of tax each week. Second, you need to report for how much tax you deduct each month or each quarter, and make a payment to the Tax Office.

Checking your tax tables

Tax tables don't have anything to do with tax executives sitting in a flash boardroom. Rather, tax tables are special formulas for calculating Pay As You Go (otherwise known as Pay All You've Got) on employee wages. Tax tables tend to change slightly in July of each year due to changes in marginal tax rates or adjustments to the Medicare levy or other levies. (If you're unsure whether or not your tax tables are current, go to your Company Data Auditor and look at the Payroll Tax Tables Date.)

If you have a current MYOB subscription, you'll automatically receive tax table updates or product upgrades every time tax tables change. Alternatively, if you don't have a current subscription, your only solution is to manually check the tax calculations on each employee's pay every week, and then edit the tax amount on each pay.

Paying as you go

As you approach the 28th day of each month or each quarter, you need to get ready to pay your PAYG tax (this is part of your Business Activity Statement, if you're registered for GST). Here's what to do to see how much you have to pay:

1. **Go to Reports, click Payroll and highlight the Payroll Activity [Summary] report.**

2. **Specify which month or quarter you want figures for.**

3. **Click Display.**

   For a shining example of what this report looks like, see Figure 11-12.

4. **Look at the total of the Taxes column to see how much tax you need to pay.**

Figure 11-12:
A Payroll
Activity
[Summary]
report.

Payroll Register [Summary]

ABN: 80 000 000 001
Email: info@clearwater.com.au

Employee		Wages	Deductions	Taxes	Net Pay	Expenses
Jones, Mary		$4,807.70	$500.00	$1,000.00	$3,307.70	$432.69
Long, Alan		$3,461.55	$0.00	$936.00	$2,525.55	$311.54
Parker, Peter		$2,307.69	$0.00	$513.00	$1,794.69	$207.69
Smith, Sue		$4,615.38	$0.00	$1,488.00	$3,127.38	$415.38
	Total:	$15,192.32	$500.00	$3,937.00	$10,755.32	$1,367.30

Recording tax payments

To record payment of PAYG tax, go to the Payroll command centre and click Pay Liabilities. You should see a window that looks very similar to the regular Spend Money window. Now follow these steps:

1. **Enter the payment details as you would a regular Spend Money transaction.**

   I usually enter Australian Taxation Office as the Supplier name.

2. **Decide whether you're paying this transaction from your regular business account or from your Payroll Clearing Account.**

   If you're paying PAYG tax as part of your Business Activity Statement, don't select your bank account in the top-left corner. Instead, select your Payroll Clearing Account. (I explain more about recording Business Activity Statement payments in Chapter 15.)

3. **Select Taxes as your Liability Type.**

4. **Pick the date range carefully.**

   A single total for all PAYG tax owing for that period should come up.

5. **Tick this total and then click Record to complete the transaction.**

   To double-check that your PAYG tax account balances, skip to Chapter 18, where I talk more about reconciling payroll liabilities.

Biting the Bullet

Were they pushed or did they jump?

Recording a termination pay is similar to recording any other kind of pay, except that you may need assistance calculating how much annual leave the employee is due on termination, and how much tax to deduct. (Remember that you don't usually pay out unused personal/carer's leave at termination; rather, you only pay out unused annual leave. Also, super isn't usually paid on unused leave.)

When you've recorded an employee's final pay, go to the Personal Details tab of the employee's card and record a Termination Date. This sets all the leave accruals to zero.

Although you can't completely remove an employee from your company file, you can hide ex-employees from your drop-down lists. To do so, click Cards List, double-click on the employee's name and then click the little box in the corner called Inactive Card. Making employees inactive also prevents their names appearing when you go to process payroll.

Starting a New Payroll Year

Most people don't even realise they have to start a new payroll year until, one day in early July, they go to process pays and they see the rather cheerless message that you can only enter pays for the current payroll year.

The solution seems easy: Simply start a new payroll year. But wait! You need to do four things first:

1. **Make sure wages balance for the year just completed.**

   Generate a Profit & Loss report and check that total Wages Expense on this report matches with total Wages according to your Payroll Activity [Summary] report for the year. If they don't match, run these two reports for each month of the year until you can identify where differences arise.

2. **Balance PAYG tax and superannuation.**

   I explain how to balance PAYG tax and superannuation in Chapter 18 in the section about reconciling payroll liabilities.

3. **Generate a payment summary for each employee.**

   For more information on this, see my online article 'Producing Payment Summaries', available at www.dummies.com/extras/myobsoftwareau.

4. **Back up.**

   Back up as you normally would, saving your company file onto a CD, removable hard drive, flash drive or onto a cloud location. However, when naming your backup file, don't accept the name that MYOB offers. Instead, type your own file name, something like **EOY Payroll 2015**. (For more about backup procedures, refer to Chapter 16.)

   After you've made one backup, make an extra backup just in case. Name both backups clearly and store in a safe place, with at least one backup set off-site or in the cloud. Note that end-of-payroll-year backups need to be kept in a safe place for a minimum of seven years.

All done? The final step of starting a new payroll year in your company file is so easy, it's almost surprising. Go to File⇨Close a Year⇨Close a Payroll Year. You see a warning saying after you complete this process, you can't edit any pay transactions for that year. So, if you really did balance payroll for the previous year and made two sets of backups, go ahead and click Continue. With a brief flicker on the screen and a couple of seconds' delay, the process is complete.

Chapter 12

Looking Good with Forms

· ·

In This Chapter

▶ Figuring out what the fuss is all about

▶ Upgrading form customisations from previous versions

▶ Understanding the theory and learning the lingo

▶ Deciding what you want to show and what you want to hide, all without a weight-loss program

▶ Dressing up, looking good

▶ Looking over your work before the whole world sees it

· ·

*W*hen you're a small business owner, your personal identity and the image that you want your business to portray are often intertwined. You're in business because you love what you do so, in turn, you're passionate about your business.

I reckon any correspondence you send from your business, in particular invoices to customers, provide a chance for you to project your image, and create a sense of enthusiasm for your business and what you do. Whether your business is involved in looking after children or caring for the elderly, cooking up great food or saving water in the cities, your invoices provide a brilliant opportunity to project your image — even your brand, if you've got one — to the world.

With MYOB, customising forms is not only pretty easy, but also kinda fun. Forget about searching for numbers and totals, balancing your tax or sweating over your inventory. Instead, this is the activity where your creativity can blossom. In this chapter, I take you through everything you need to know to get your forms looking just how you want them to.

Understanding What Forms are All About

For every key activity in your business, MYOB has a corresponding form, with different forms for invoices, mailing labels, purchase orders, pay slips, customer statements and supplier remittances. You can personalise each of these forms in almost any manner you like, and you can even choose to have multiple versions of each form. For example, you may have one sales invoice layout for off-the-street cash customers, and another invoice layout for regular account customers.

Figuring out why good-looking forms are smart

So it's ten o'clock at night, and maybe you're reading this chapter at home, tucked up on your sofa with a mug of hot chocolate. As your eyes skim the beginning of this chapter about customising forms, you may think to yourself, why bother? Put simply, here's why:

✔ **You get to look better than your competition**. Ever noticed how the larger a business is, the more daggy its invoices and statements? Many large businesses have accounting software that is about as flexible as my 75-year-old mother. (Am I talking temperament here, or hamstrings? You'll have to guess.) With MYOB, you can take advantage of this competitive edge and beat 'em hands down.

✔ **You can add important info**. Got a disclaimer you want to appear on your sales invoices? Customise your forms so this shows automatically.

✔ **You can (hopefully) get paid earlier**. By spelling out your payment terms, maybe making the Due Date appear in a larger font or in a bright colour, you might actually hurry along payment.

✔ **You can attract attention**. You can format your invoice to be in any colour scheme you like. So if you're an accountant struggling to break away from society's stereotypes, feel free to start sending out invoices formatted in flamingo pink and custard yellow.

Now you see it . . .

Whenever I customise sales invoices or other forms for clients, I suggest they start by drawing a sketch of what their perfect sales invoice would look like. Where does the logo appear? How should the company name be formatted? What do they want customers to see?

Sometimes my clients come up with pretty idiosyncratic requirements, such as wanting to include drop-off delivery details on purchase orders or print Medicare numbers on sales receipts. MYOB doesn't provide any of these fields as standard, but I explain to my clients that what they can do is recycle a field that's not being used for anything else.

Figures 12-1 and 12-2 show how a firewood company applies this method, adapting a regular sales template to become a delivery docket. In Figure 12-1, you see the data-entry screen where the Salesperson field is used for the driver's name, the Comments field provides special delivery instructions and the Promised Date field is the Delivery Date. Figure 12-2 shows the final result — a practical delivery docket that fits the bill exactly.

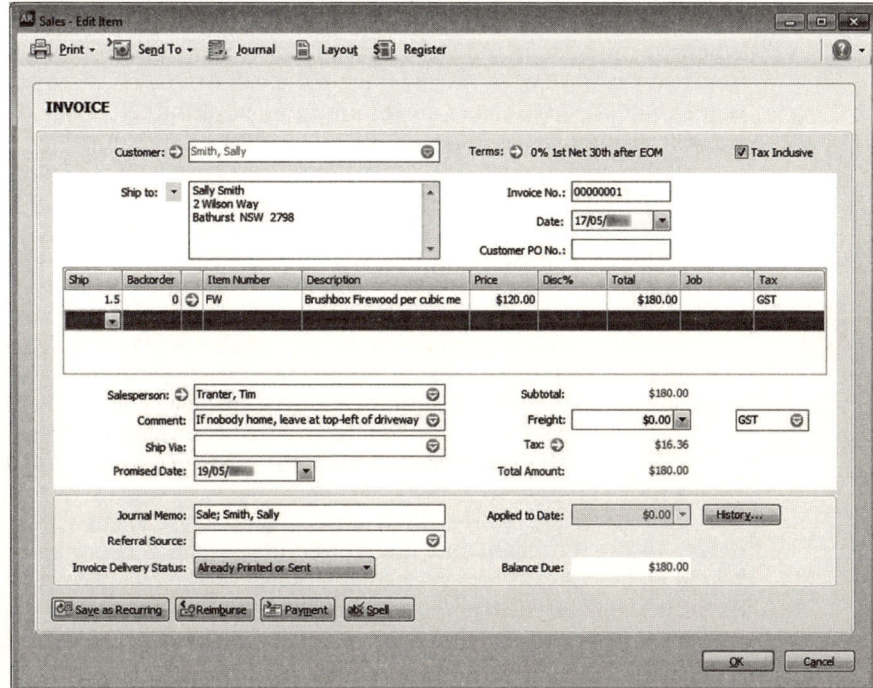

Figure 12-1:
Want to make a silk purse from a sow's ear? Anything is possible.

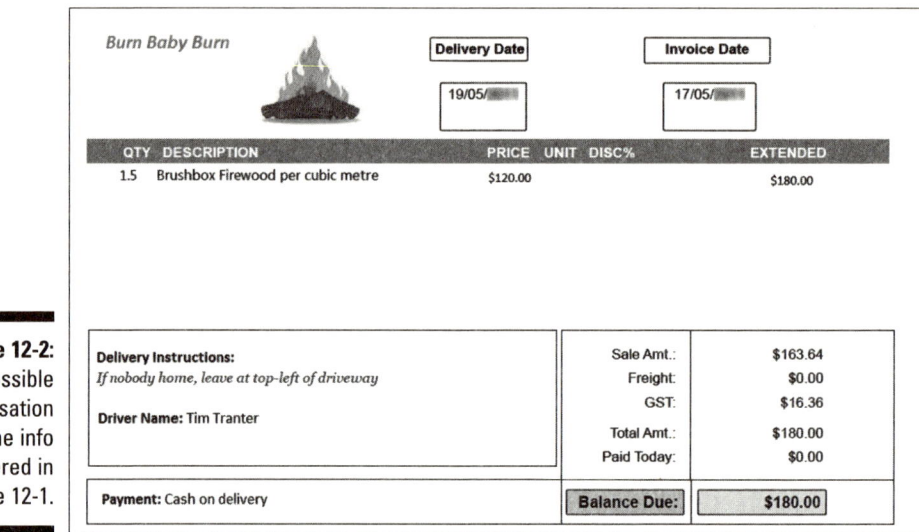

Figure 12-2:
A possible
customisation
for the info
entered in
Figure 12-1.

. . . and now you don't

When you've been in the software game as long as I have, you sometimes forget to explain the obvious. I once got a call from a client so frustrated that I could almost see the steam pouring out of the telephone. Her gripe? However carefully she followed the instructions for customising a purchase order, whenever she went to enter a new purchase in MYOB, the screen looked just the same.

When replying to my client, I explained Newton's first law of nerd-formatting: Although you can customise a form to print in any way you fancy, you're powerless to change the actual data-entry screens. The Enter Sales or Enter Purchases window always look the same, regardless of how you customise customer invoices or supplier purchase orders. For example, my client was trying to show supplier item numbers on her purchase orders. I clarified that although she can *print* this field on her orders, when she goes to enter a new order, she still only sees her own item number in the data-entry screen.

The same principle applies if you choose to 'recycle' fields. Imagine you decide to use the Comments field to record special delivery instructions as I do in Figure 12-1. Although I can customise my invoice to print a comment about the delivery instructions as I do in Figure 12-2, my sales data-entry screen will always label this field as being the Comment, regardless of the final printed result.

Migrating Forms from Old to New

Have you recently upgraded to the latest version of MYOB AccountRight and you're swearing and cussing 'cos all your customised forms have disappeared? Don't worry, you can retrieve most of your previous customisations and upgrade these to the latest format.

 To upgrade your previous customisations, go to your File menu, select Migrate Custom Forms and click Browse. Now for the tricky bit: navigate to the folder where your old forms used to live. Usually, these forms live in a folder called Forms, which lives inside your previous MYOB program folder. For example, before upgrading, my old forms lived in the Forms folder inside the Premier19 folder on my C: drive.

Click OK to select this folder and you'll see a list of all the forms (both customised and default) from the previous version. Either select the forms you want to upgrade, or click the checkbox at the top of the list to upgrade all forms in one hit. Click Migrate and wait a few seconds. Scroll up and down this list to check if your mission was successful. Most forms come across just fine, with a green tick against their name, but occasionally you get a big red cross next to a form's name indicating that the upgrade was unsuccessful. In this scenario, you have no choice but to re-customise that form from scratch.

 After you migrate forms into the latest version of MYOB AccountRight, these forms no longer sit separate to your company file, but now form an integral part of the data. In practical terms this means that if you move your company file from one computer to another, the forms automatically move too.

Laying Down the Theory

In this section, I explain how to start customising forms from scratch. I also explain some key terms used in relation to forms design.

Customising a sale, just like that

I tend to zone out if someone tries to give me too much theory without some practical stuff. So I'm going to leap into the thick of it and get you to start customising your first sales invoice. (After you get the hang of how a sales invoice works, you can apply the same principles to any other form.)

Here's how you customise a sales invoice:

1. **Go to Setup⇨Customise Forms⇨Invoices.**

2. **Select your preferred Sale Layout.**

   As I explain in Chapter 4, invoices come in different layouts, such as Service, Professional and Item. Pick the layout you use when billing customers.

3. **As the Form to Customise, choose between Plain Jane and Pre-Printed.**

   Unless you already have pre-printed stationery (something that largely died out with the dinosaurs), I suggest you select Plain Paper as your layout.

4. **Click Customise.**

   You're away! You arrive at the rather odd customising window ready for you to do your stuff.

5. **Have fun.**

   I'm not going to be too specific here, because in the rest of this chapter I rave on about tweaking colours, columns, text, tables and much more. But feel free to experiment — move text around, change font sizes, add images. If you want to close without saving your changes, select Exit from the drop-down menu in the top-left.

Getting into the lingo

Did you know that if you order tuna at a restaurant in Mexico you're more likely to receive an edible cactus dish than you are a tuna salad? Which is why, when dealing with new and foreign things, it pays to learn the language. For example:

✔ **Text field:** A *text field* provides a space where you can include any text that you like. A text field can be a label, such as 'Date', 'Amount' or 'Invoice Number', or a long and wordy disclaimer. See where it shows the word Date in bold in Figure 12-3? This is an example of a text field.

✔ **Data field:** A *data field* displays data that you've already recorded. For example, the data field 'Date' prints the actual date of the transaction, and the data field 'Amount' prints the actual amount of the transaction. In Figure 12-3, an example data field is where the word [Date] appears with square brackets around the word.

✔ **Table:** New to the latest versions of MYOB AccountRight is the concept of tables. A table is basically chunks of information that relate to one another, so that if you move or resize one part of the table, the rest of the rows or columns go with. For example, in Figure 12-3, the Qty, Item No., Description, Price and Code columns are all tied together in the form as a table.

✔ **Picture:** A *picture* isn't necessarily a picture, but can be an image of any kind, including logos, photos or illustrations. Most businesses use the Picture command to insert logos.

✔ **Watermark:** A watermark can be a logo or text that appears in very light print as if behind the text of the form itself. For example, Figure 12-3 has the words 'CONFIDENTIAL' right across the centre of the form.

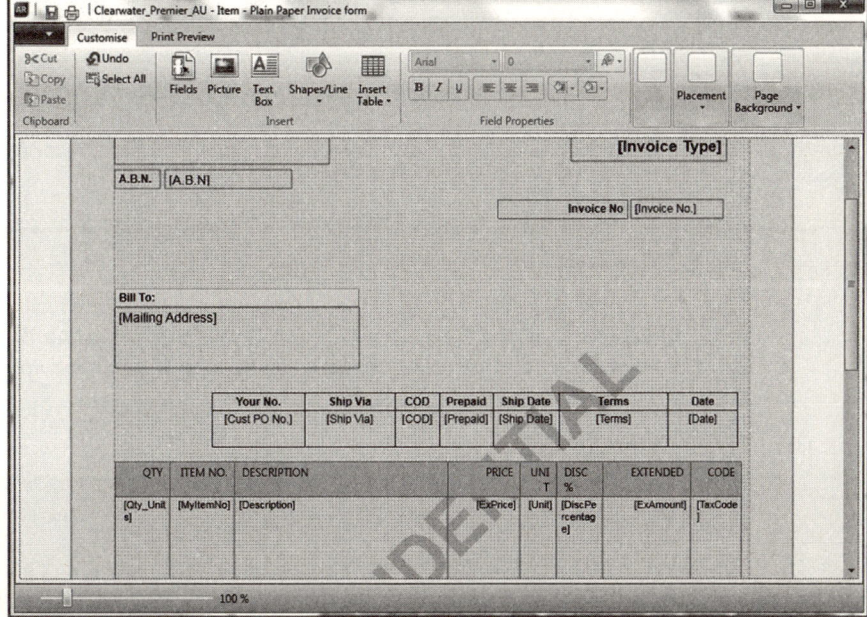

Figure 12-3:
Try to understand the difference between text fields, data fields and tables.

Saving when the day is done

When you finish customising a form, you need to save your changes. Here's how:

✔ To save as you go along, click the floppy disk icon in the top-left corner (next to the purple AccountRight icon) and then click Save.

Finders keepers, losers weepers

With the latest versions of MYOB AccountRight, whenever you create a customised form, this form becomes part of your company file itself. (This contrasts with previous versions, where customised forms would exist as documents that were separate from the company file, living in a separate folder on your computer.)

The upside of this new way of working is that if you move your company file from one computer to another, your customised forms automatically move too. However, the downside is that you can't readily share your customised forms between different company files.

There is a solution. To share a customised form between company files, first open the company file where you created this custom form. Go to the Setup menu and select Export

Customised Forms. Follow the prompts to save this form in a folder where you can find it again, such as My Documents or your desktop. Then open up the company file where you want to be able to use this custom form, go to the Setup menu but this time select Import Customised Forms. Navigate to where you saved your customised form and click Import.

(With older versions, every company file on a particular computer can view all customised forms, regardless of which company file the form was created in. If you shift computers, you need to copy and paste all the files from the Forms folder, which lives within the MYOB program folder, from one computer to another.)

There you have it. The spirit of sharing and caring lives on.

✔ To save a form under a different name — maybe you want to create multiple versions of a form — go to the drop-down menu in the top-left corner and select Save As, enter a new Name and click Save.

✔ To undo the changes you just made, but keep the form open, click the Undo button.

✔ To quit without saving, go to the drop-down menu in the top-left corner and select Exit.

When recording a new name for a form, pause for a moment. This is the name by which you (or anyone else working with your company file) will identify this form in the future. A name such as 'Item Invoice Template for Cash Customers' is going to be much more meaningful than 'INCPSIPR-2', which is the kind of default name MYOB typically offers.

Choosing What Info to Display

I have the same piece of advice when designing forms in MYOB as I do for wedding speeches: Remember that less is more. So in the same way as the groom is ill-advised to reminisce about the day his bride-to-be turned up at his door with a massive cold sore on her face (I actually heard this anecdote during one particularly excruciating wedding speech), I recommend you keep your forms short and sweet, and as free of unwanted information as possible.

Getting rid of the dead wood

One of the hassles about MYOB's standard forms is the way they include everything you might ever need and a heap more besides. It's a bit like going on holidays with the kitchen sink and 150 rubber plants. I bet if you look carefully, you find superfluous information: Salesperson details, shipping information, tax breakdowns or whatever.

When you spot something you don't need, get rid of it. To do this, click the field to highlight it and then press the Delete button on your keyboard.

Adding new fields and extra columns

When my forms have evolved somewhat, I often end up wanting to undelete something I deleted earlier. Or I decide that I want to make use of a field that doesn't normally print, such as a job column or a memo.

To add a new field, go to your forms toolbar and click the Fields button. A list of available fields appears (similar to my example shown in Figure 12-4), covering everything from additional addresses to customer ABNs and due dates. Select the field or fields you want to add, and then click OK.

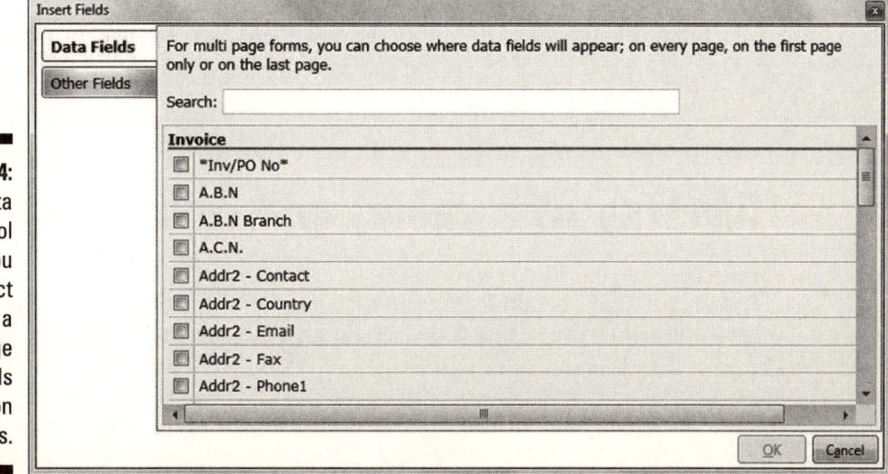

Figure 12-4: The data field tool allows you to select from a whole range of fields for use on forms.

When adding a new field, you can also choose whether this field appears on every page, at the start of the form or at the end of the form. An example of a field that appears on every page of an Item invoice is the Item Number field; an example of a field that only appears at the end of the form is the Total field. If a field only appears at the start of a form you see a little orange 'A' in the corner; if a field only appears at the end of a form you see a little blue 'Z' in the corner. All extremely cute, but if your invoices never go longer than a page, you don't have to worry about this level of finesse.

Inserting text with a personal touch

If you want to insert text into a form — maybe you want to stick a standard disclaimer at the bottom of each invoice or add your phone number to the top of customer statements — here's what to do (I'm assuming you're already in the Customise Forms window at this point):

1. **Click the Text Box button on your forms toolbar.**

2. **Click on the form that you're customising, roughly in the spot where you want the text to appear.**

3. **Drag out the bottom-right corner of the text field until it looks roughly the right size.**

4. **Type the text you want to show on your form.**

   Double-click the text field and then type in the Text box.

5. **Adjust the font, size and colour of your new text.**

   Highlight your text and click the bold, italic or underline buttons or select the font style and font size in the same way as you do in Word, Excel or similar programs.

6. **Drag the Text box to wherever you want it to appear in your form.**

   Splat! (Do it again if this makes you feel good, or if you want to move the Text box some more.)

Working with tables and connecting data

The concept of *tables* is new to the latest versions of MYOB AccountRight. The idea is that certain forms (invoices and purchase orders in particular) have some info that's tied together. So if you move one column, you end up moving other columns, or if you make one column taller, you make all columns in the table taller.

You can see an example of an invoice table earlier in this chapter in Figure 12-3, where columns for the Qty, Item No., Description and so on appear as a group together.

To add a new table to a form, go to the Insert Table button on the forms toolbar. Sometimes you have a choice between more than one table. For example, on an invoice you can choose between an Invoice Table (which includes fields for description, quantity and so on) and a GST Summary Table (which simply summarises amounts for each tax code).

To change what columns appear in a table, highlight the table with a single click of your mouse and then go to the Table Layout button on the forms toolbar and select Show/Hide Columns. To add a column to the table, highlight the column on the left pane and click Show; to remove a column, highlight the column on the right pane and click Hide.

You can also choose to add Row Shading, so that every alternate line on your invoice has a light grey shade behind it (very handy if most of your invoices have many line items). Simply select Show Row Shading from the Table Layout menu.

To edit the headers that appear at the top of your table (for example, to change 'ITEM NO' to 'Item Number') select Edit Column Headers from the Table Layout menu.

Share the love

One of the things I love about customising forms is that the possibilities are endless. Clubs adapt invoices to become annual subscription reminders, colleges adapt invoices to become course enrolment forms and factories change purchase orders into production run lists. The only limit is your imagination.

One neat trick here is that you can customise forms more than once. With one standard invoice and one company file, you can create lots of different forms for different situations. For example, I have a standard item invoice template for book sales made on credit, and another for book sales that I make on my website shopping cart.

To create multiple versions of a form, simply click File then Save As from within the Forms Customisation window and differentiate each version using a different filename.

Dressing Up for a Night on the Town

I once read in the *Sydney Morning Herald* (the font of all antipodean wisdom, after all) that the average Aussie woman spends a whopping 24 minutes a day on personal grooming (and that doesn't even include showering, ironing and getting dressed).

Whatever gender you may be, I suggest you sacrifice just one of these 24-minute time slots and instead use this time to get your form looking as beautiful as possible.

Making things bigger or smaller

You want to make a field bigger or smaller? No cosmetic surgery required. Grab your furry friend and click once on the field so that a box appears around it. Magic! Now click on the bottom-right corner of this box, holding down your mouse button and dragging the corner downwards and to the right to make the box bigger, or upwards and to the left to make it smaller.

By the way, making a field bigger or smaller doesn't make what prints out bigger or smaller. To do that, you need to adjust the size of the font. Read on to find out more . . .

Fiddling with fonts

Fonts are like clothing. If you like to dress up a little and add that extra spark, I suggest you start by changing the fonts on your forms. Out with Times New Roman, in with Tahoma.

To change a font, all you have to do is click any field and select your font and font size from the Font menu at the top, just as you would with Microsoft Word or most other programs. Be careful, however: If you choose a font larger than the one you previously had, it may well be too tall or too wide to fit into the field. If this happens to you, enlarge the field by dragging out the bottom corner with your mouse.

To change a font on several fields at once, hold down the Ctrl key with one finger and then use your mouse to click on each field you want to change. Alternatively, click on a blank area of the form then drag your mouse over the fields you want to change to highlight them. Then make your changes.

Adding colours willy-nilly

Henry Ford may have said '. . . any colour — so long as it's black',
but you have to endure no such constraints. Try it and see! The four
options are:

- ✔ **Change the colour of text:** Click the icon with the artist's palette and
  select whatever colour takes your fancy.

- ✔ **Change the colour of the background behind text:** Click the left icon
  with the paint pot.

- ✔ **Change the colour of the border around text:** Click the right icon with
  the paint pot.

- ✔ **Change the background colour of the whole page:** Go to the Page
  Colour menu on the right of your forms toolbar. (Hint: If you want a
  background colour for the whole page, you're best to pick a really pale
  colour.)

I used to shy away from using too much colour on my forms, because it
got expensive with printer ink. These days, however, I email 99 per cent of
invoices and purchase orders, and so I have no qualms about adding a bit of
colour.

Inserting logos or images

The single biggest improvement you can make to your form is to add a
company logo. Here's how:

1. **Locate the file for your logo and check the file type.**

   Acceptable file types are bmp, gif, jpg, png or tif. If by chance your logo
   is in a different format, you may need to scan the logo and resave.

2. **Check that the file size is no bigger than 200 kilobytes or so.**

   Images with large file sizes may not display correctly when you add
   them to your form. Not only that, large images increase the file size
   when you create PDFs, which in turn can create problems when
   emailing invoices to customers or remittance advices to suppliers.

   To decrease the file size of an image, you may have to lower the
   resolution, reduce the image size or greyscale the image.

3. **Click the Picture icon, navigate to the folder where you stored the
   image, highlight your image file, and then click Open.**

4. Drag and drop the image to where you want it to appear on the form.

5. Adjust the size of the image.

Drag the bottom corner upwards to make the graphic smaller or drag the bottom corner downwards to make it bigger.

6. If you like, turn the image on an angle.

See the anchor head (the pin with the green circle) in the middle at the top? Grab this anchor point and move your mouse up or down to rotate the image.

7. Print and then email this form to test that your logo comes out properly in both.

For more on this topic, skip ahead to 'Previewing Your Handiwork'.

Moving stuff around

To move a field to a different spot, grab your mouse and position it over the item you want to move. Click once so that a box appears around the item, and then drag the item to its new spot and let go of the mouse button. To move more than one field at a time, hold down the Shift key and click each field you want to move, and then drag these fields as a group.

Sometimes, the field you try to move (or edit) gets stuck behind another field, and you only seem able to select the field that sits on top of it. This often happens when you add boxes or lines to forms.

To select a hard-to-get-to field, click once on the field you don't want to edit. Then, go to your forms toolbar and select Send to Back from the Arrange menu. Hey presto! The field you want to edit will now be on top.

Going for that boxed-in look

Want to portray an image of someone who is super-organised? Try adding boxes and lines to your invoices and purchase orders to make them look lean and mean.

Here's how to add boxes or lines around your text:

1. Click the Shapes/Line button.

You can select between a rectangle, a rounded rectangle or an ellipse (oval) shape.

2. **Position your mouse roughly where you want the top left corner of the box to be.**

3. **Click and hold the mouse button down and drag the corner of the box downwards and to the right.**

4. **Let go and hey presto!**

   You have a box on your form. Figure 12-5 shows how rounded rectangles add that bit of pizzazz.

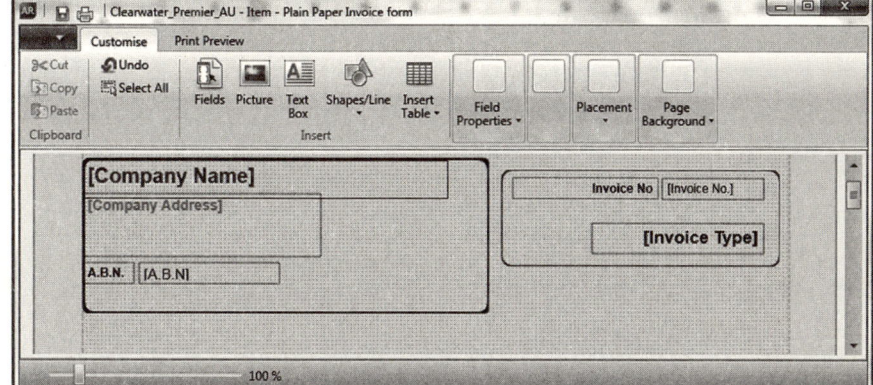

Figure 12-5:
Try adding
rounded
rectangles
for a touch
of class.

Now for some nips and tucks . . .

✔ **Move the box again.** Grab your mouse again and position it over the box. Click once, holding the mouse button down and adjust the position of the box.

✔ **Add a line to your form.** Click the Shapes/Line button and position your mouse roughly where you want one end of the line to be. Click and hold the mouse button down and drag the line downwards (for a vertical line) or sideways (for a horizontal line). Let go and the line magically appears.

✔ **Adjust the thickness of boxes or lines.** Highlight the line or shape and then click the right paint pot icon, selecting Border Width from the drop-down menu. Size 0.25 is the thinnest; Size 6 is the thickest.

Sometimes, the best way to add a box to your form is to add a border instead. For example, instead of drawing a rectangle around your shipping address, you can simply click the Shipping Address field and add a border. To change the formatting of a border, click the right paint pot icon and change the colour and the weight as the mood takes you (or, alternatively, click No Colour to remove the border altogether).

Lining everything up

After you get the basics of your form design in place, you're ready to do the finishing touches. One important detail is to ensure that everything on your form lines up perfectly. (Remember, you're talking to someone for whom the idea of torture is to watch someone fold a road map the wrong way.) Keep the following in mind:

- ✔ **To line stuff up on a reference grid:** Go to the Grid Options button and click Display Grid on Screen. To force fields to line up to the grid, click Snap to Grid and 0.1 or 0.25 centimetres as the spacing.

- ✔ **To line stuff up on the left margin:** Hold down the Shift key, select the fields you want to fix up, and then choose Align Left from the Arrange menu.

- ✔ **To change the justification of a field:** Things ain't ever going to look top notch if the text in some of the fields you're trying to line up is centred but other text is aligned to the left or right. Fix this by clicking the justification icons (the ones with the horizontal lines).

Previewing Your Handiwork

To finalise your customised form, I suggest you print a sample or two to preview your changes. I often find that what looks good on the screen can look like a dog's breakfast when printed out. Then, after you're happy with the printed version of your form, email it to yourself and check the PDF version. (Sometimes what comes out fine in print looks different on the PDF.)

Creating your very own test bunny

To get a true picture of what your final form will look like, your best approach is to record a dummy transaction — such as a sale or a purchase order — and then print it out. When creating this dummy transaction, ensure that you have lots of lines of information, the customer or supplier address details are complete and every field that you ever plan to use has some info in it.

You may end up printing the form for this dummy transaction several times before you arrive at the result you want, tweaking your customisation each time. Just try to block out images of those native forests being woodchipped.

Ironing out the bugs with emailed forms

So you've customised your forms and they're looking pretty crash hot in their printed form. However, when you email invoices to unsuspecting customers, or purchase orders to expectant suppliers, the PDF attachments may end up looking kinda weird.

Here are some of the problems you may come across, along with my oh-so-helpful solutions:

- ✔ **Some fields don't come through on the emailed version, even though they print okay**. The cause of this problem is that sometimes in the process of creating a PDF file the font gets too big for its boots and can't fit into the field. The solution? Go to customise the form, identify the culprit field, and either make the font smaller or the field size larger.

- ✔ **The logo won't print.** Easy. You need to install QuickTime, which you can find as a free download on www.apple.com.au. Remember to uninstall any earlier versions of QuickTime first.

- ✔ **Things won't print, but there's no rhyme or reason to it and none of the other solutions work**. Software can be so cruel sometimes. If your form was created in an earlier version of MYOB and won't play fair, a practical approach is to ditch this form and customise a new one from scratch.

Before emailing an invoice to a customer, or a purchase order to a supplier, double-check the electronic version of this form looks okay also. The best way to do this is to email a version to yourself. For example, go to Print/Email Invoices, select an invoice that's ready to be emailed, and temporarily change the customer's email address so that it's your own. Alternatively, click the Send To button when you're in a sale or purchase and click Disk to save this form as a PDF file on your desktop.

Get the form template right, every time

Forms are fickle things. One of the cries of complaint I often hear is 'Why does the form layout always default to the wrong one, so that I have to change it every time I print?'

The answer is quite simple. In order to change the default, you have to go to the Print menu for that form (such as Print/Email Invoices, Print/Email Statements or whatever) and click the Advanced Filters button. Choose the customised form layout that you want as your default from the Selected Form menu and then click OK.

That's all you have to do, but remember that your default form choices are user-specific. What this means is that your choice of default form won't carry across if anyone else logs into the company file. In other words, every employee has to log in with their own user ID and set up their own form defaults.

If you use different form customisations for particular customers, you may also want to change the default Printed Form setting under the Selling Details tab of each customer's card.

Chapter 13

Making Electronic Payments

*O*ne of the easiest ways to save money in your business is to move away from paying suppliers and employees by cheque or cash, and move towards electronic payments.

MYOB offers a couple of different ways in which to manage electronic payments. In this chapter, I explain these different approaches, and discuss the pros and cons of each one. What works best for you is going to depend on which version of MYOB you're using and how many electronic payments you make each week.

What I can say — with both aplomb and an authoritative edge to my already rather bossy voice — is that if you want to save time and become blindingly efficient, get all those dog-eared cheque books that are lying around the office and chuck 'em in an archive box. Don't write a cheque ever again.

Paying Electronically in Three Different Ways

You can pay people electronically in three different ways:

✔ **Recording electronic payments using a batch payment file, generated in MYOB:** With this method, you record the payment in your MYOB company file, create a batch payment file, open this batch file using your bank's internet banking service and then send your payment to suppliers and employees. Banks often refer to this file as a *direct entry batch file*.

Although most Aussie banks let you import batch files as part of their regular internet banking service, at the time of writing, ANZ and Westpac only offer this service if you subscribe to business transaction banking services.

✔ **Recording transactions both in internet banking and in MYOB:** With this method, you record the payment using internet banking, paying one employee or supplier at a time. Later on, you rekey this transaction into your MYOB company file. Alternatively, you record transactions first in your MYOB company file, and then open up your internet banking and rekey the payment details there.

✔ **Using M-Powered Payments:** With this method, you pay suppliers and employees electronically direct from your MYOB company file, without using your bank as an intermediary. *Note:* M-Powered Payments are only available for the earlier 'classic' versions of MYOB. However, MYOB is planning to replace this service with a new electronic payments service late in 2015 and, by the time you read this chapter, this new service may be available. I suspect the name of M-Powered Payments itself will change, but the service itself will be much the same.

Obviously, the first and the third methods are heaps more efficient than the second method, because you only enter data once, not twice. In this chapter, I explain how to make electronic payments using either one of the first and third methods.

What I don't talk about in this chapter is the second method, where you type the details first in MYOB and then again in internet banking (or vice versa). Why not? First, because I already explain how to record supplier payments in Chapter 8 and employee pays in Chapter 11. Second, if all you're doing next is logging onto internet banking and rekeying the details of each payment, this book isn't going to help (the idea of writing a how-to guide explaining how to use internet banking for each of Australia's banks makes my blood run cold).

Getting Ready for Electronic Payments

Okay, so I'm assuming that you want to use MYOB to streamline your electronic payments, first recording payments in MYOB and, second, sending these payments to your bank, either by exporting a batch payments file or using M-Powered Payments. All good so far? Then now's the time to get started.

Setting up employee and supplier details

In order to pay suppliers and employees electronically (no matter which method you use), you first need to enter their bank account details in your MYOB company file, as follows:

1. **Go to Cards List in the Card File command centre.**

   (I thought you'd like to start off with something easy.)

2. **Double-click on the name of the person or company you plan to pay electronically and click the card's Payment Details tab.**

3. **If you're paying an employee, specify how many accounts you want to split the pay between.**

   For example, some employees like to split their pay across a couple of accounts, maybe paying $200 against a mortgage, $100 into a savings account and the balance into a cheque account.

4. **Complete the account details.**

   Complete the BSB Number, Bank Account Number and Bank Account Name, as shown in Figure 13-1. (The BSB Number is a special six-digit code that represents the bank's name and branch.)

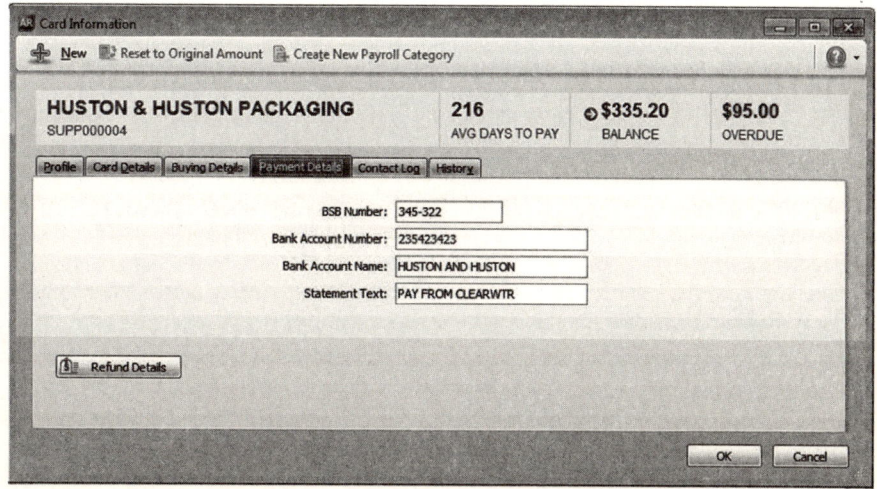

Figure 13-1: Entering banking details for a supplier.

5. Complete the Statement Text for suppliers, but leave the Statement Text for employees blank.

For suppliers, detail what you want the suppliers to see on their statements when you pay them, such as your customer account number. Alternatively, if you usually pay a particular supplier only one or two invoices at a time, leave the default Statement Text blank. That way, when you pay that supplier later on, you can enter specific invoice numbers in the Statement Text field.

For employees, simply leave the Statement Text blank. That way, the default message on their statements appears as 'PAY for', followed by the pay period (for example, PAY for 25/10/15), which is about as clear a message as you can get.

6. Double-check the banking details, and then click OK.

I know I may strike you as Fixated, Insecure, Neurotic and Emotional (otherwise known as FINE), but be ultra-careful when recording banking details. Even if you only enter one teensy-weensy figure incorrectly, your bank happily transfers money to the wrong bank account! Random acts of kindness are one thing, but donating funds to completely unknown individuals is pretty extreme.

Guard yourself against online fraud

The most common way employees do the dirty is by substituting a supplier's banking details with their own. (Although banks ask for an account name, the only thing the bank matches when making a transfer is the account number and branch.)

If you're a business owner — rather than a bookkeeper — remember that even if you authorise all the electronic payments your bookkeeper prepares for you, you certainly won't have time to check the bank account details for every person or company listed on every payment. In other words, the account name on a payment may be that of a known supplier, but the banking details could have been changed.

To combat this potential vulnerability, I suggest you spot-check account details on a regular basis (and ever-so-casually let your bookkeeper know you do so). Depending on what version of MYOB you use, you can also implement password restrictions so that only you can access the Payment Details tab for employees and suppliers. (Refer to Chapter 1 for more about passwords and security.)

Hooking up your bank account

Head to your Accounts List and double-click on the name of the bank account from which you want to make electronic payments. Click the Banking tab and complete your banking details, bearing in mind the following:

✔ The BSB Number is a special six-digit code that stands for your bank and branch. This number is listed just before your account number on any bank statement or cheque book.

✔ If you want the option to pay by regular electronic payments (not just by M-Powered Payments), click I Create Bank Files [ABA] for This Account.

✔ The Bank Code is a three-letter code that stands for your bank (NAB, CBA, WBC and so on).

✔ Your Direct Entry User ID (this field only appears if you select the option to create bank files for this account) is a special code that your bank gives you when you register for internet banking. If you don't yet know your code, phone the bank, explain you want to import direct-entry files for paying suppliers or employees, and ask them what the code should be.

✔ You only need to tick Include a Self-Balancing Transaction if your bank requires a self-balancing transaction (most banks do) for each electronic payment you lodge.

To see how the Banking tab for my business bank account looks, check out Figure 13-2. (Please feel free to credit this account at any time.)

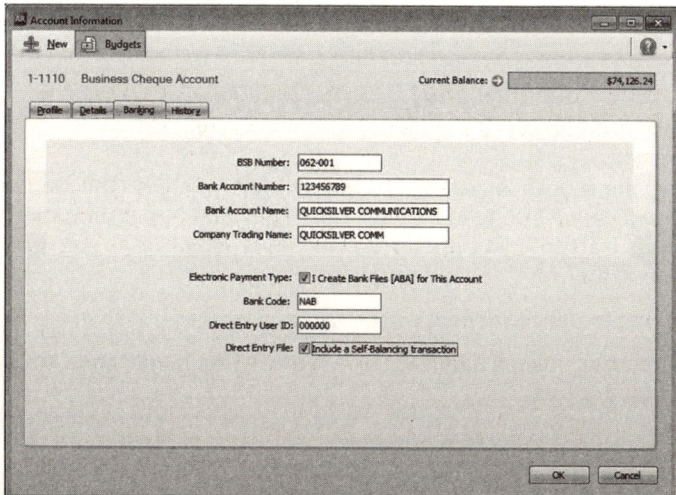

Figure 13-2:
Completed bank account details.

M-Powering yourself — ready or not?

Throughout this chapter, I make the distinction between M-Powered Payments (making electronic payments directly from your MYOB company file) and regular electronic payments (made by sending a payment batch from your MYOB company file into your internet banking).

Although using M-Powered Payments is more efficient and usually more cost-effective than making regular electronic payments, I do have some valid reasons for covering both options. First, M-Powered Payments isn't available for all versions of MYOB software; second, M-Powered Payments isn't available at all banks; third, you still need to ensure that working with M-Powered Payments is cost-effective for your business. Finally, the application process takes some time, so you may want to use regular electronic payments while you're waiting for your M-Powered application to go through.

Understanding when M-Powered Payments isn't an option

Although the M-Powered Payments option is a wonderful thing, not everyone can access the service:

- At the time of writing, M-Powered Payments isn't available for any of the current versions of AccountRight, nor for any AccountEdge (Macintosh) products. *Note:* This situation may have changed by the time you're reading this chapter, but bear in mind that the name of the M-Powered Payments service is set to change.

- At the time of writing, the only banks that have a direct facility with MYOB software are ANZ, the Commonwealth Bank and Westpac. However, you may be able to get around this by arranging a *TNA* (Transaction Negotiation Authority) — contact MYOB support for more information.

Costs (and hidden savings) of M-Powered Payments

The current M-Powered Payments fees are as follows:

- $10 per month access fee to M-Powered services (the fee covers all services, including M-Powered Invoices and Superannuation). This fee is waived if you are an MYOB Cover client or an AccountRight subscriber.

- 30 cents per electronic payment.

- 25 cents per remittance advice sent by fax. Remittance advices sent by email are free.

So how do the total costs work out? MYOB charge 30 cents per transaction, which is similar to what most of the big banks currently charge per transaction. You also pay an additional bank fee per payment batch to your bank, which is likely to be another 25 to 35 cents or so. In other words, your transaction fees with M-Powered Payments aren't going to differ much from what you pay if you use regular electronic payments.

The cost savings come into play if you put a value on your time. With M-Powered Payments, you don't have to create a payment batch, open up your internet banking, log on, import a batch, verify the batch and then complete the transaction. Instead, the process of paying your employees or suppliers all happens within MYOB.

Applying for M-Powered Payments

Click the M-Powered Services icon that appears in the bottom-right corner of any command centre and follow the prompts to apply online. The application form is rather daunting, but don't be deterred. I'm convinced the process is easier than climbing Mount Everest (not that I've ever tried the latter).

Approving your application can take as long as six weeks, depending on how well you dance the paperwork polka and also on whether your bank has a direct facility with MYOB or you need to apply for a TNA. When your application is approved, you'll be asked to go to the M-Powered Service Centre and activate your service. This complete, you're ready to go.

Making Your First Electronic Payment

So you're ready to record your first electronic payment using MYOB? You can process this payment either via internet banking or via M-Powered Payments. This section explains both methods and how they work.

Recording supplier payments

Creating an electronic payments file ready to send to the bank is easy. Here's how it's done:

1. **Go to record a supplier payment in the normal way**.

    Record your supplier payments the same way you normally do, either in Spend Money or Pay Bills, depending on your preference (refer to Chapters 6 and 8 for more details). Complete the date and the transaction details as per any other transaction, but ignore the Cheque No. field. ('Cos guess what? This payment isn't a cheque.)

2. **Still in the supplier payment, click the Group with Electronic Payments button**.

   You find this button in the top-left corner of the Spend Money or Pay Bills windows. When you click this button, you group this electronic payment in a batch with any other electronic payments you make that day. Figure 13-3 shows how this works.

3. **Check the words in the Statement Text field**.

   If I'm only paying one or two invoices, I usually write the invoice numbers as the Statement Text. Otherwise, I write my company name. That way, my supplier can identify where the payment is coming from.

   To see if this supplier's banking details are complete, click the arrow to the left of the supplier name and go to the Payment Details tab on the supplier's card. Update the supplier's details if necessary, and then click OK to return to the payment screen.

4. **Leave the Memo as is, unless there's something particularly unusual about this payment**.

5. **Record your payment as normal and repeat this process for anybody else you plan to pay electronically that day**.

   After you record your first electronic payment, record any other payments that you want to make electronically so that you can combine all your payments in the one batch.

Figure 13-3:
Select
Group with
Electronic
Payments to
indicate that
you intend
to pay a
supplier
elec-
tronically.

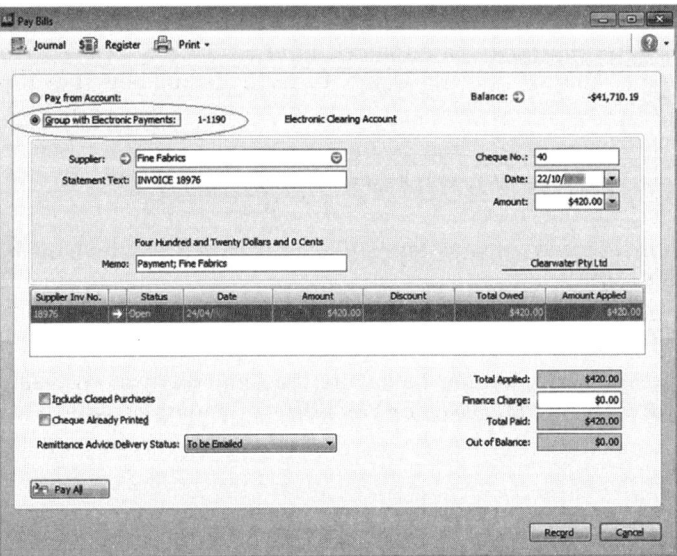

You're now ready to process all electronic payments. To find out what to do next, see the section 'Marking payments for processing'.

Recording employee payments

Before you attempt to pay employees electronically, first go to each employee's card, select Electronic as the Payment Method and complete all the employee's banking info. (Refer to the section 'Setting up employee and supplier details', earlier in this chapter, for more details.)

With your setup complete, recording employee payments is easy-peasy. Simply record pays in the normal way, as described in Chapter 11, until you reach the Process Payments window. At this point, click the Prepare Electronic Payments button. This takes you to the Prepare Electronic Payments window, from where you can make your selections to send electronic payments to the bank. Read on to find out more ...

Marking payments for processing

If you record a supplier or employee payment and select Electronic as the Payment Method, that payment goes into a batch with all other payments that you mark for electronic processing. When you're ready to process these payments, this is what you do:

1. **Click the Prepare Electronic Payments button**.

   If you're paying suppliers, go to Prepare Electronic Payments from either the Banking or the Purchases command centre. If you're paying employees, you arrive at Prepare Electronic Payments in the third step of the payroll process.

When a supplier only accepts BPAY

You can't use regular electronic payments or M-Powered Payments to pay suppliers that only accept BPAY, such as Telstra or AGL. Your only option is to record the payment in MYOB using Pay Bills or Spend Money, and then open up your internet banking and record the payment there.

However, what I do with my BPAY suppliers is set them up so that they debit my bank account automatically on the day payment is due. I've also created a bank rule for each one, so that when the debit appears on my bank statements, MYOB allocates the payment automatically.

2. **Look at what comes up and consider whether it's reasonable**.

If no transactions appear, or you can't see all the transactions that you know should be there, choose or tweak the selection using the Select Payment By menu. I find the easiest and quickest method is to select All Payment Types here.

If you find that a whole swag of transactions appear, dating back to the Dark Ages, it's probably because you've been using MYOB for a while and other transactions were allocated to your Electronic Clearing account in the past. For details of how to extricate yourself from this particular pickle, see the sidebar 'When old payments clog up the works', later in this chapter.

3. **In the Pay From Account box select which bank account to make the payment from**.

This is usually your business bank account or something similar.

4. **Review the message in the Bank Statement Text field**.

The Bank Statement Text shows what's going to appear on your bank statement — not your suppliers' or employees' statements.

5. **Check the Bank Processing Date**.

As the Bank Processing Date, choose the date that you want these payments to go out of your bank account. If you're creating this file after-hours, choose the next day as your date — otherwise, your bank may get nasty and reject the file. You can even choose to process payments to be made at a future date — great if you're going away on hols — as long as the date isn't more than 45 days into the future.

6. **Select the payments you want to process**.

Select all payments you want to process in this batch by clicking in the far right column, as shown in Figure 13-4.

What happens next depends on which method of electronic payments you intend to use. If you want to generate a batch payment file that you can open in your internet banking, go to the next section in this chapter. If you plan to use M-Powered Payments, skip ahead to 'Transmitting an M-Powered Payments file', later in this chapter.

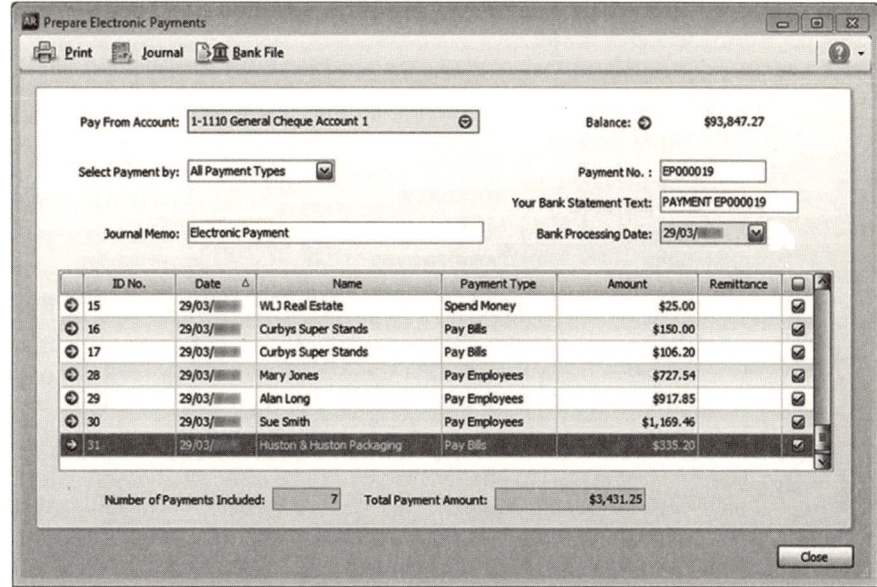

Figure 13-4:
Marking
payments
for
electronic
processing.

Creating and sending a batch payment file

In this section I assume you want to create a batch payment file ready to open in your internet banking. (If you're wondering what I'm raving on about, refer to 'Paying Electronically in Three Different Ways' at the beginning of this chapter.)

Here's how you create and send a batch payment file:

1. **In the Prepare Electronic Payments window, ensure you've marked all payments you want to process, and then click Record.**

   For help at this step, refer to the previous section.

2. **Click the Bank File button, and then click OK.**

   You find the Bank File button tucked away in the top-left corner.

3. **Navigate to a folder that's relevant to what you're doing (create a new folder called Bank Files if you like) and click Save.**

   I also like to change the file name so that it includes the date, but then I'm the kind of irritating pedant who can drive anyone to distraction.

4. **Fire up internet banking and navigate to the multiple funds transfer menu.**

   Different banks have different names for this feature. Look for terms like multiple funds transfer, file import, direct entry file import, payment batch import or something similar.

5. **Open your electronic payment batch file.**

   If you're not sure how to do this step, contact your bank and ask for help — let your bank earn those hefty fees.

6. **Check your payments and send them off into the wild unknown.**

   When you open your electronic payments file, you should see each payment listed one by one, complete with banking details. Check these payments one last time and then send the file. The deed is done!

Here's a frugal way to ensure that your first attempt at electronic payments isn't a disaster: On your first go, pick three suppliers or employees and pay them (electronically) ten cents each. If the payment works, they'll go wild with gratitude. If the thing is a flop, you haven't lost much. I reckon this test-run is much better than waiting till crunch time, such as payday, and having to deal with 15 irate staff if the whole thing stuffs up.

Transmitting an M-Powered Payments file

If you're using M-Powered Payments, the next step after marking payments for processing (covered in 'Marking payments for processing', earlier in this chapter) is to finalise the payment batch, and then transmit this payment to your bank, as follows:

1. **Go to the Prepare Electronic Payments window, ensure you've marked all payments you want to process, and then click Record.**

   If you need help at this point, refer to 'Marking payments for processing', a tad earlier in this chapter.

2. **Select either Authorise Now or Authorise Later.**

   If you're ready to go ahead with this payment, click Authorise Now. If you need to get a second authorisation password, or maybe you're not quite ready to do the deed right now, click Authorise Later.

3. **Click the M-Powered Services Centre button that appears at the bottom-right of every command centre.**

4. **Click Send/Receive.**

   All electronic payments with To Be Sent as their status fly off into the ether, fattening other people's accounts (usually the next day).

When old payments clog up the works

Sometimes when you first try to prepare electronic payments, you find that a whole bunch of transactions appear, dating months or even years back. Don't sweat. You can get rid of these old transactions by heading to your Accounts List and creating a new Electronic Payments account (make sure you select Bank as the Account Type). Then go to your Linked Accounts menu (found under Setup) and click Accounts & Banking Accounts. Select this new account as your Bank Account for Electronic Payments.

5. **Read the Transmission Summary and click OK**.

Assuming your payment instructions go through successfully (and they should do if you're currently online!), a Transmission Summary appears. Check that all your payments were processed successfully.

Letting Suppliers Know You've Paid Them

So you've benevolently sent money electronically to all your suppliers! Now you need to inform them of your good work.

Go to Print/Email Remittance Advices in either the Banking or the Purchases command centre. Click the To Be Emailed tab, and then select the payments that you want to email an advice for, as I do in Figure 13-5. The first time around, check that supplier email addresses are up to date (if not, type them in on the fly). You may also want to change the message (click the Email Defaults button).

Click Send Email and MYOB automatically emails individual, rather handsome, remittance advices to each of your suppliers. (Although if you want to customise your remittances, you can: Go to the Setup menu, and click Customise Forms.) Life doesn't get much better than this.

If you find that no payments appear under the To Be Emailed tab, click the To Be Printed tab instead. Zoom in on the payment that you want to email a remittance advice for, and select To Be Emailed as the Remittance Advice Delivery Status.

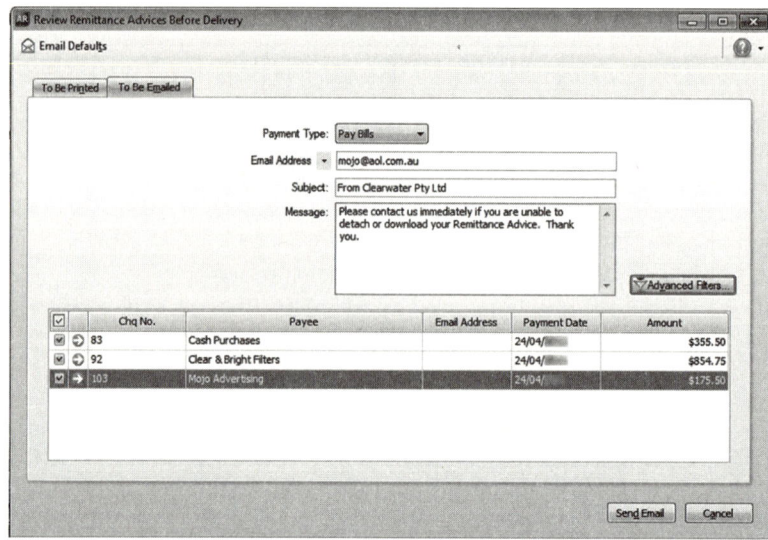

Figure 13-5:
It's easy
to email
remittance
advices
to your
suppliers.

Reversing a Payment When Something Goes Wrong

Rejected payments are surprisingly common, usually caused by getting an account number wrong or trying to process payments when you don't have enough money in your account. Here's how to deal with a rejected electronic payment:

1. **Go to your Bank Register and display the payment batch that includes the rejected payment.**

   You may have a whole heap of transactions in this batch, or you may just have the one payment.

2. **Identify the rejected transaction in this batch and double-click it.**

   In other words, double-click the individual transaction that was rejected, not the whole payment batch itself.

3. **Go up to the Edit menu, select Reverse Payment, and click Record.**

   Quick as a flash, MYOB records a reversal transaction for the rejected payment and returns you to the Prepare Electronic Payments window.

4. **Close the Prepare Electronic Payments window, and then click Prepare Electronic Payments once more.**

   Sounds daft, but trust me!

5. **Click against the reversal you just recorded, and then click OK when prompted**.

   You'll see this reversal appearing as a negative amount. When you click this reversal, a rather daunting warning message appears, saying that continuing may result in bank reconciliation problems. Don't worry, click OK to continue.

6. **Click the Bank File button in the top-left**.

   A warning message tells you that this transaction will be recorded, but no bank file created. Click OK.

7. **Check everything has worked out by going to your Bank Register and viewing both the original transaction and the reversal**.

   The rejected transaction should appear as a deposit in your account (just as it will on your bank statement). All good.

8. **Start the dance again from the top, this time getting everything right**.

   Process the payment once again, but this time be sure to double-check the account details.

The mysterious electronic clearing account

Whenever you record an electronic payment, you click the button in the top-left corner called Group with Electronic Payments. By working in this way, this payment doesn't come out of your business bank account but instead comes out of a special electronic clearing account.

When you're ready to process these payments, you go to Prepare Electronic Payments. After they're processed, the combined total of these electronic payments comes out of your business bank account and goes into your electronic clearing account. The balance of your electronic clearing account (which doesn't exist in reality and is just a mythical creation) always starts with zero and returns to zero.

The moral of the story? If you see that the balance of your electronic clearing account isn't zero (assuming you've processed all electronic payments at that point), you have a problem. Try to figure out when it went out of balance.

One of the easiest ways to troubleshoot clearing accounts is to go to Reconcile Accounts, select the clearing account in question, and click off all the withdrawals and deposits, making sure that the New Statement Balance is $0.00 every time you click the Reconcile button. After you match all possible transactions, the transaction or transactions that remain should be the ones that are causing the problem.

Part IV
Pulling It All Together

Five Reasons You Should Consider Working in the Cloud

- **You can access your data from wherever and whenever.** No matter whether you're out on the road selling to customers or stuck on a train, working in the cloud means that you can always access your accounts, wherever you are (so long as you have an internet connection, of course).

- **Your accounting data is arguably way more secure in the cloud than it is on the hard drive in your office.** If your backup systems tend to be a little scrappy, storing data in the cloud is a perfect solution. MYOB invests far more in data security than you ever will on your own.

- **Working with your company accountant can be a whole heap easier.** Instead of having to make a copy of your company file and sending this to your accountant, you simply set up your accountant as a separate user and invite them to come join the fun. Your accountant can log in and view your data at any time — you can even both log in at the same time and view the same transactions, sorting through queries using your live data.

- **More than one person can work on the accounts at one time.** The cloud makes it easy for more than one person to work in your company file at one time, meaning that you can be reviewing reports while somebody else raises invoices, and someone else records payroll transactions.

- **You can use your smartphone or tablet to view data, raise invoices and receive customer payments.** When your company file is in the cloud, you can take advantage of apps such as MYOB OnTheGo, which allows you to raise invoices from your smartphone or tablet, or MYOB PayDirect, which enables you to receive EFTPOS or credit card payments while you're away from the office.

Visit www.dummies.com/extras/myobsoftwareau for a free article and more tips about pulling everything together in MYOB.

In this part ...

- ✔ Knock up reports that give you all the information you need, and look good besides.

- ✔ Get your head around GST and find out how to complete your first Business Activity Statement (oh, joy of joys).

- ✔ Think through the pros and cons of working in the cloud, and figure out what's going to work best for you.

- ✔ Protect yourself from the forces of evil — discover how to back up and protect your data.

- ✔ Understand Profit & Loss and Balance Sheet reports, and analyse where you're making (or losing!) money in your business.

- ✔ Give your company file a 'health check' so that you can keep everything in tiptop shape.

Chapter 14

Reporting for Business

. . . .

In This Chapter

▶ Discovering five ways to get exactly what you want (only five?)

▶ Separating the (reporting) wheat from the chaff

▶ Making a splash with quirky fonts, wild colours, shapes and more

▶ Sending reports out into the world

▶ Finding solutions when MYOB doesn't give you everything you need (sigh!)

. . . .

*B*eneath its cool, calm exterior, your MYOB company file is a seething mass of information. Click a couple of buttons to reveal a squillion standard reports, all of which can be customised in different ways by changing report selections, adding columns, formatting headings, changing fonts and much more besides.

If you only recently upgraded to the latest version of MYOB AccountRight, you'll find that the reporting features have had a major renovation. Don't stress too much, though. Just like a home renovation, everything may look really different but the essentials remain the same: A sofa is still a sofa, the kitchen is still chaos, and the fridge remains chillingly bare (if you have teenagers, that is).

In this chapter, I explain how to use AccountRight's report designer to generate and customise reports that provide the information you need and look good into the bargain.

Five Ways to Cook up a Storm

Before leaping straight into a chapter that focuses on how to create reports in MYOB, I'm going to stress that reports are only one way of retrieving information. In fact, you have five different ways to look up info in MYOB, all of which are perfectly valid:

✔ **The Find Transactions menu:** This menu is my personal favourite when looking up transactions for a particular customer or supplier. The Find Transactions menu appears at the bottom of every command centre; click Account to search by account, click Card to search for transactions relating to a particular customer or supplier, or click Invoice to search by invoice number. Try a few searches yourself in your company file and see what you can find.

✔ **Cards:** I like to go to my Cards List (found in the Card File command centre) when looking up individual customer or supplier details, or if I want to sort customer details in particular ways (maybe according to postcode or amount owed).

✔ **The Business Insights dashboard:** Ideal for that management overview, I use the Business Insights dashboard (found in the bottom-right of all command centres) for a quick synopsis of the health of a business. I find that bookkeepers tend to ignore many of the Business Insight reports, but managers — especially after I show them how these reports work — love to generate reports from here. Check out the Customer Analysis and the Supplier Analysis tab for your business, and you'll see what I mean.

✔ **The Sales Register, Purchases Register and Bank Register:** I find the Sales and Purchases Registers to be the best spot to investigate quotes, orders or credit notes, and to get a quick synopsis of the history of a particular customer or supplier. The Bank Register is a neat way to view withdrawals and deposits for any chosen bank account. You find the Sales Register in the Sales command centre, the Purchases Register in the Purchases command centre, and the Banking Register in the Banking command centre.

✔ **The Reports menu:** 'At last,' I hear you groan, 'She's getting to the point!' Yes, the Reports menu is where you go for all other kinds of enquiries or analysis. And guess what? This menu is what the rest of this chapter is all about.

Generating Reports

To view the list of standard reports in MYOB, either select Reports from the top menu bar or go to the Reports menu that appears on the bottom of each command centre. When you arrive at the Reports window, tabs for each of the report categories appear on the left, similar to Figure 14-1.

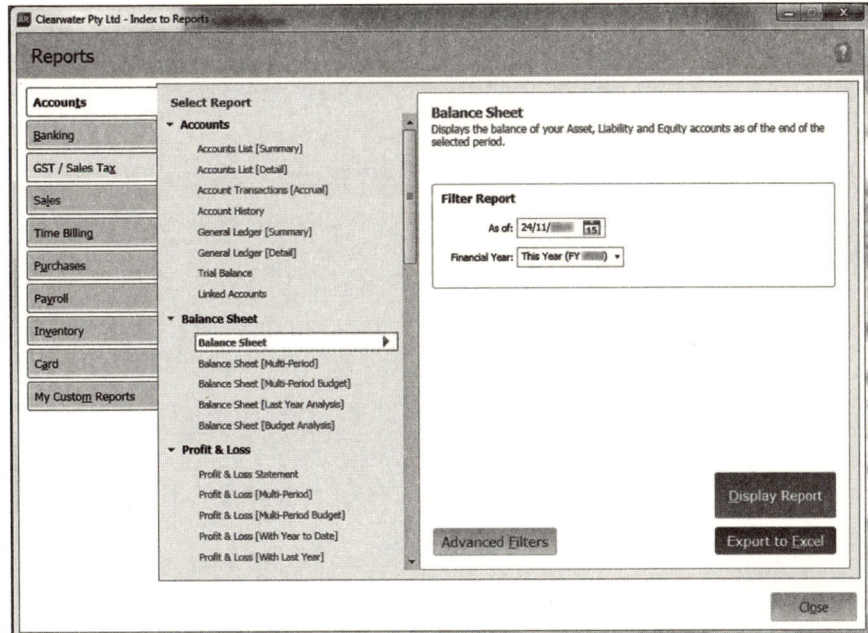

Figure 14-1:
The Index
to Reports
window.

Click Display Report to see the default format for whatever report you've chosen, usually with the current month as the date range. Now you're ready to transform this report into a document that gives your business the specific information it needs.

Adding or removing report columns

Ready to customise your first report? Grab your dancing partner (that's MYOB, in case you're wondering) and swing into action:

1. **Go to the Sales tab and click the Sales [Customer Detail] report.**

   I'm assuming that you've already gone to Reports⇨Index to Reports.

   If you don't have any customer sales in your company file, you may want to open the Clearwater sample company file and experiment using this data. (I explain how to open the sample company file in Chapter 1.)

2. **Make sure the date range is something relevant and click Display Report.**

3. **Click the Insert/Modify tab.**

   See the three tabs along the top, labelled Filters, Print Preview and Insert/Modify? The last little bunny is the one you want.

4. **Click the Show/Hide button.**

5. **Select which columns you want to display.**

   On the left pane, select the columns you want to include and click Show. On the right pane, select the columns you want to exclude and click Hide.

   If the information you're looking for isn't displayed (maybe you want to include the Comment field on a Sales Summary report, but this isn't an option), your best bet is look at what's available on the other standard reports.

6. **Click OK.**

   Looking good? Now you're ready to see if you want to narrow down this report data, filtering by customer, amount, date or category. Read on to find out more.

Narrowing down the data

All standard reports in MYOB come with the maximum amount of information. For example, a sales report is going to list sales to all customers, including all items sold and all salespeople. But what if you want to narrow down this report to only list some customers, certain items or particular salespeople? You do this by applying *report filters*.

Opening a sales report provides an excellent way to see exactly what I'm talking about:

1. **Go to the Sales tab of your Reports menu and select the Sales [Customer Detail] report.**

2. **Select a date range that you know contains some sales and click Display Report.**

3. **Click the Filters tab.**

4. **From the Customers menu, click the drop-down arrow and select the customers you want to include in this report.**

5. **Change the Sales Status to All Sales.**

   All Sales includes quotes and orders, whereas All Invoices displays actual sales only.

6. **Click the Additional Filters button and decide whether you want to restrict the information on this report in any other way.**

   For example, I could choose to only display amounts over $1,500, or sales made by specific salespeople or sales sent by a particular courier.

Don't hesitate to apply more than one filter at a time. Each additional filter further narrows the information displayed in the report.

7. **Admire your handiwork.**

These filters are pretty powerful, aren't they? I just picked a standard sales report to give you a sense of how you can manipulate information in MYOB, but obviously every report has a different set of filters. The only way you can be sure to get the reports that your business needs is to get in there and experiment.

Sorting info in different ways

The sorting feature is new to the latest versions of MYOB AccountRight and is one of those little things that really adds flexibility to the information you can generate. To sort data in almost any way you like, simply go to the Filters tab and click the Sort button.

Take a look at Figure 14-2, for example. With this Sales Customer Detail report, I can sort by Card Name, Status, Date and ID No. Alternatively, I can click Add Sort Level to sort by the Amount, listing the highest value sales first.

Figure 14-2:
The Sort feature gives you more ways to display information on your reports.

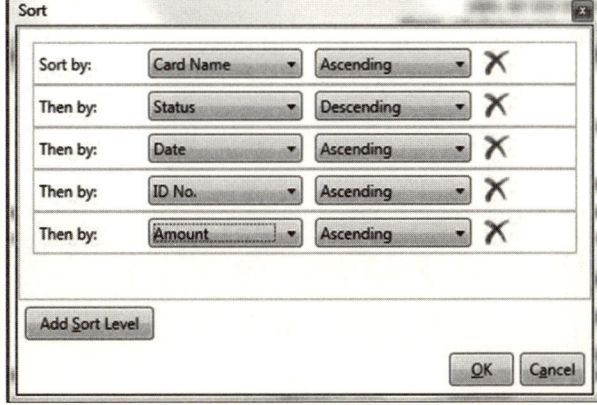

Of course, you may still hit limitations with the Sort feature. For example, if I'm working with a customer sales report and I want to sort the whole report according to item codes, rather than customer name, I can't. This particular report always sorts first by customer, and the Sort feature only lets me control how I sort the data within each individual customer's transactions. In this kind of situation, my best bet is either to experiment with item reports (which do sort first according to item codes) or to send my report into Excel. See 'Getting Excel to fill the gaps', later in this chapter, for more information on using this workaround.

Adding the finishing touches

When working with reports in MYOB, you just have to get in there and experiment, while being on the lookout for extra options that vary from report to report. For this reason, I always suggest you review your settings on the Filters tab before finalising a report.

For example, if you generate a Profit & Loss report, the settings under the Filters tab include the option to include zero balances, or to round figures to the nearest dollar. Similarly, with a Purchases Detail report, you can choose whether to show totals for each item, or simply show totals for each supplier.

Formatting Reports

So far in this chapter I've focused on how to get exactly the information you want on a report by inserting or deleting columns, applying report filters or sorting data in different ways.

The next step is to get your report to look beautiful, formatting report headers and applying enough colour to put the average Wiggles concert in the shade.

Before you plunge into formatting a report, take note of one thing: The moment you close a report, MYOB loses all your settings. The only way to retain these settings for the future is to save your work as a custom report — for help doing so, see 'Saving reports for next time around', later in this chapter.

Changing and adding headers

Every report in MYOB has a header section that shows basic stuff such as your company name and address, and report name. To choose which of these items to include, go to the Insert/Modify tab of the report and click the Fields button.

A new feature in the latest versions of MYOB AccountRight (for which no previous versions have an equivalent) is the ability to insert text boxes in this header section. To use this feature, go to the Insert/Modify tab, click the Text Box button and drag out the shape of a box where you want the text to appear. Double-click inside this box to enter the text itself.

One of the limitations of MYOB is that you can't change the name of a report. For example, one of my clients, a non-profit organisation, likes to rename its Profit & Loss report so that it says Income and Expenditure report instead. With the latest versions of MYOB AccountRight, I figured out a neat little workaround: I go to the Fields button and deselect the option to print the report name. I then add a text box in the spot where I want the report header to appear. Easy.

Designing your colosseum

After I decide what columns I want to display on a report (refer to 'Adding or removing report columns', earlier in this chapter), I often like to shift these columns around and, if necessary, resize them.

To widen or narrow a column, rest your mouse on the line that appears between that column label and the next, and drag to the right or to the left.

To change the order in which columns appear — for example, maybe you want to display the Date column before the Invoice number column — go to the Insert/Modify tab at the top of the reports toolbar and click the Order button. Highlight the column you want to move and click the Up or Down arrow.

Bringing out the artist within

Have you always fancied yourself as an artist? To format any of the text in the Header part of a report, first display the report and go to the Insert/Modify tab. Next, click to highlight any text or data field and try the following:

To Change	Do This
Font	Select the font and font size from the Font menu
Colour of text	Click the icon with the artist's palette
Colour behind the text	Click the paint pot icon
Row shading	Select Show Row Shading
Report's background colour	Go to the Page Colour menu (which may appear under the Page Background menu, depending on the width of your display)

If you hold down the Control key and then click on the fields you want to format, you can highlight — and therefore change — more than one field at a time.

Note: At the time of writing, MYOB have not reinstated the ability to edit the font choice or font size for the text in the body of a report (rather bizarrely, this feature was available in older versions, but not in current versions).

I recommend steering clear of using colour in most reports (bank reconciliations, stock listings and so on), because colour cartridges are so expensive and environmentally unfriendly. I reserve the use of colour for important reports that I plan to distribute to others, such as Profit & Loss or sales reports, or for reports that I plan to save as PDF files only.

Adding logos, shapes and lines

Here's how to add boxes or lines in the header of your report:

1. **On the Insert/Modify tab, click the Shapes/Lines button.**

2. **Position your mouse pointer roughly where you want the top left corner of the box or line to sit.**

3. **Click and hold the mouse button down and drag the corner of the box downwards and to the right (for a box) or simply to the right (for a line).**

4. **Let go and hey presto!**

   To adjust the thickness of boxes or lines, highlight the line or shape and click the paint pot icon, selecting Weight from the drop-down menu.

You can also add your company logo to this header area:

1. **Click the Picture icon, navigate to the folder where the company logo lives, and click Open.**

   Your logo can't be any bigger than 200 KB or MYOB will refuse to play.

2. **To move the logo around, click the image and drag your mouse up or down, right or left.**

   Looking good? I hope so.

For your eyes only — the watermark

Afternoon shadows cast across the room. She hesitates as she pulls a slim folder from her briefcase, before gazing up at her interrogator with steel-grey eyes. The folder falls open as she places it on the desk, revealing a document with TOP SECRET stamped across it in large letters.

This document sounds intriguing, doesn't it? You too can put stamps on your reports,

using the new watermark feature. Go to the Watermark menu and select the 'stamp' you want to emblazon across your report. (The Watermark menu may be hidden underneath the Page Background menu, depending on your screen width.) Alternatively, click Custom Watermark to enter your own choice of text.

Printing and Saving Reports

So your report is looking as perfect as that first summer mango? Now you're ready to send this report into the big, bad world:

✔ **To print your report:** Click the tiny little print icon on the top menu bar. Very subtle.

✔ **To save your report as a PDF:** Click the File menu (that's the blue drop-arrow in the top left) followed by Export, followed by PDF. Think up a name for your PDF file, navigate to a folder where you want to store this report and click Save.

✔ **To send your report to Excel:** Click the File menu, followed by Export, followed by Excel. Excel opens up automatically, displaying your report in all its finery.

✔ **To email your report:** Click the File menu followed by Send, followed by PDF, Excel or XPS (depending on which format you want the email attachment to be in). Enter the name and email address of the person you want to send this report to, along with a short message. (Alternatively, if you want to email your report to more than one person or you want to format your email message, save the report first as a PDF file. Then go to your mail software and create your email, attaching this PDF file to that message.)

Getting stuff to fit on one page

Sometimes when you print a report, not everything fits on the page and the stuff on the far right of the report simply 'falls off', never to be seen again. To resolve this situation, try the following tactics:

✓ **Change the orientation.** Go to the Print Preview tab and change the direction the report prints on the paper by selecting Landscape from the Orientation menu.

✓ **Narrow some columns (where possible).** First click the Insert/Modify tab. Next, rest your mouse on the separator after each column label and drag your mouse to the left.

✓ **Trim unnecessary data.** Remove any columns you don't need. Refer to 'Adding or removing report columns', earlier in this chapter.

✓ **Tweak the margins.** Go to the Print Preview tab and try selecting 'Narrow' from the Margin menu.

Saving reports for next time around

One thing that gets irritating is the way report settings only last for the current session — you close the report and the report returns to its default settings. The solution to this problem is to create a custom report. Here's how:

1. **Create the report of your dreams.**

   Refer to the first half of this chapter for info on how to customise and format your report. Never mind if the final report is tall, dark and handsome or if it's small, fair and intelligent (like yours truly, although the intelligent bit is always up for debate). You can tweak the final look later.

2. **Before closing the report, go the File menu (the blue drop-arrow in the top left) and click Save As.**

3. **Give your new report a name and description.**

   Make the Report Name short and sweet and the Description something meaningful (to remind you later why you created the report in the first place). You can see how I do this in Figure 14-3.

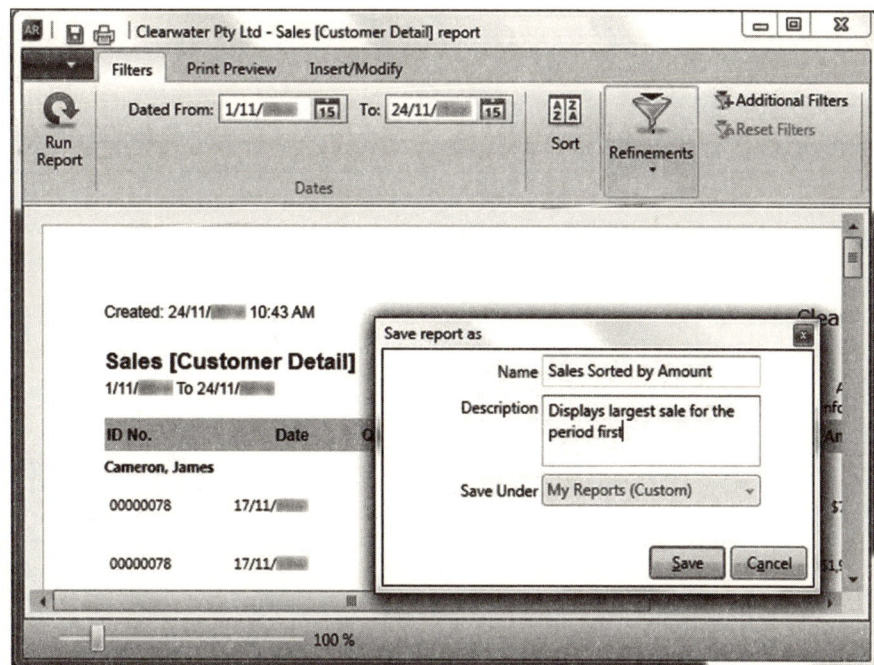

Figure 14-3:
Saving
custom
reports.

4. **Click Save.**

5. **Back on the main reports menu, click the tab labelled My Custom Reports and ponder your brilliance.**

   A list of all your custom reports appears, including the report just created. Select this report, click Display and note that all your custom settings have been saved. What more could one wish for?

Chuck that printer out the window

In my work as a consultant, I can't fail to notice how much time people waste printing, collating, filing and storing reports that nobody ever reads. Wherever possible, I suggest that you save your reports as PDF files instead.

For example, I don't print Bank Reconciliation reports anymore but instead save these reports as PDF files, storing them in a folder that I back up regularly.

Creating Custom Reports When MYOB Doesn't Fit the Bill

You can bend the rules with MYOB's standard reports to arrive at some pretty creative results: I've done everything from generating livestock reports to creating run sheets for couriers. However, sooner or later you may come across a situation where MYOB's standard reports can't deliver the goods.

You have two choices. Your first choice is to send information to Excel and manipulate this data from there. Your second choice is to get a developer to create a custom report just for you.

Getting Excel to fill the gaps

If you have a report that almost does everything you want, but not quite (and isn't that often the case?), the solution is to send the report out of MYOB into Excel. When the report is in Excel, you can change headings, cut and paste columns, convert figures into graphs and much, much more.

To get a report from MYOB into Excel, go to the File menu (the blue drop-arrow in the top left) and select Export, followed by the Excel button. In Figure 14-4, you can see what happens when I send a Profit & Loss report to Excel in this manner. The report isn't so beautifully formatted, I admit, but is still a perfectly useable document.

Here are a few tips to ensure everything goes smoothly when sending reports to Excel:

- ✔ In order to send a report to Excel, you don't need to open Excel first. MYOB automatically tells Excel what to do and, unbelievably enough, Excel follows suit.

- ✔ The totals that appear at the bottom of columns in Excel are simply text that has come across from MYOB — in other words, these totals aren't formulas that automatically total the figures that appear above. If you plan to edit a report and manipulate figures, you need to replace these totals with formula.

- ✔ If you use an older version of Excel, you may encounter the problem that totals don't update automatically, even though the formulas are fine. You can fix this in Excel by navigating to Tools⇨Options and clicking the Calculation tab (or in Excel 2007, going to Options and clicking the Formula menu). Ensure that all calculations are set to Automatic, not Manual.

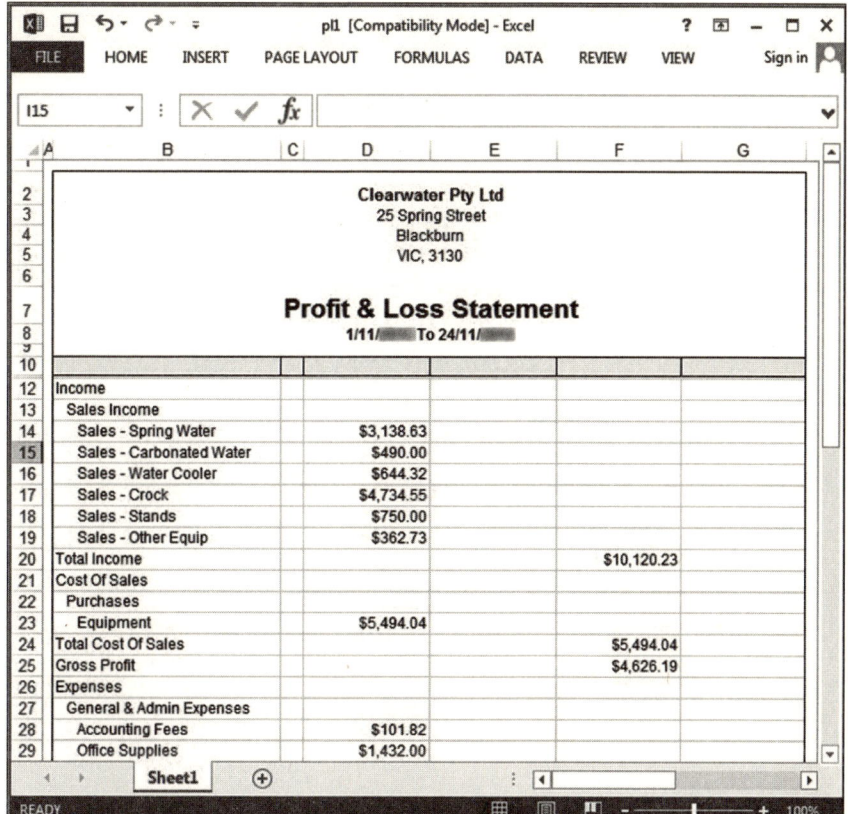

Figure 14-4:
You can
send any
MYOB
report to
Excel.

Paying for a custom report, just for you

Sometimes, customising standard reports or sending standard reports to Excel isn't enough. You need a report that gets a bit of information from one place, a bit of information from another place, multiplies one column by another and so on.

Happily, you have plenty of reporting solutions available:

✔ **Get a report custom-written.** If you don't have any programming experience, or you're only looking for one or two custom reports, the best approach is to get the report written for you. SmartReports (www.smartreports.com.au) is a company that specialises in creating custom reports that integrate with your MYOB company data. This company also has a list of custom reports that you can buy off the shelf, including many sought-after reports not standard to MYOB.

✔ **Purchase a reporting tool.** Lots of companies offer add-on reporting solutions, but some of the more established contenders include Calxa (specialising in budgets and cashflow), Fathom (specialising in KPIs and benchmarking), BI for MYOB (a suite of additional reports linking to Excel) and Interactive Reporting (a web-based analysis tool).

✔ **Visit the add-ons page at MYOB.** Go to the add-ons page at MYOB (visit `www.myob.com.au/addons`) for an ever-increasing list of developers who can create custom reports and add-ons that integrate with MYOB.

If you haven't upgraded to the latest version of MYOB AccountRight yet, I suggest you do so before investing in any kind of custom reporting. The structure of the latest versions of MYOB AccountRight is totally different to earlier versions, and any custom reports that work with earlier versions need to be rewritten when you upgrade.

Chapter 15

The Gist of GST

*T*hey don't it call it the Gouge and Screw Tax for nothing. If it moves, tax it. If it makes a noise, tax it. If it's cash, tax it extra, just for revenge. (Unless it's a life essential, of course.)

I'm not cynical, just bewildered by the confusion that this tax has brought and by how so incredibly human it is to create this complex labyrinth of rules. Why coffee beans are GST-free but takeaway coffee is taxable, or why medical supplies are GST-free but contraceptives aren't, defeats me.

But I'm not here to lecture you about the politics of GST. Instead, I'm here to explain how MYOB makes this complicated tax really quite simple and how you can make the paperwork as painless as possible.

Understanding Where Everything Fits

To pave the way, here are a few definitions about GST:

✓ **Taxable supplies:** Taxable supplies are any goods or services that attract GST. Examples include computers, consultancy fees, electrical goods and clothes.

✓ **GST-free supplies:** GST-free supplies are goods or services that are GST-free. Examples include fresh food, many medical services and products, many educational courses, childcare, exports and a range of religious supplies.

✔ **Input-taxed supplies:** Input-taxed supplies are supplies that don't have GST added to the final selling price. Examples include bank charges and residential rents. If your business sells an input-taxed supply (maybe you're a landlord of residential property), you can't claim input tax credits for the GST you pay on your supplies.

Setting Up Your Tax Codes

I recommend you give your Tax Code List a good spring clean, checking that your Tax Codes are set up correctly and adding codes where necessary.

Looking for speed? Three's all you need

When you first create your MYOB company file, you find that your Tax Code List comes with codes for all types of businesses and includes everything from Wine Equalisation Tax to Luxury Car Tax. But the good news is that, 95 per cent of the time, most businesses need only three codes. Here's how to check that they're set up correctly:

1. **From the top menu bar, choose Lists➪Tax Codes.**

   Your Tax Code List pops up.

2. **Make sure that the Rate for GST is 10% and that this code is linked to GST Collected and GST Paid.**

   Double-click on your main GST code, the one called GST — wonders never cease! Check that the Rate is 10 per cent, and that the linked accounts are liability accounts called GST Collected and GST Paid, as shown in Figure 15-1, and then click OK.

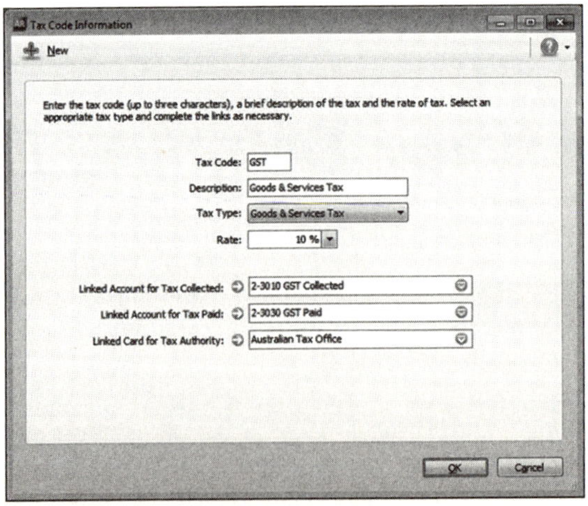

Figure 15-1: Your run-of-the-mill GST code info.

3. **Make sure that the Rate for FRE is 0% and that this code is linked to GST Collected and GST Paid.**

   Double-click on your GST-free code, the one called FRE in your list. Similar to your main GST code, make sure the linked accounts are GST Collected and GST Paid (the only difference is that the Rate is 0 per cent, not 10 per cent), and then click OK.

4. **Make sure that the rate for CAP is 10% and that this code is linked to GST Collected and GST Paid.**

   The CAP code stands for *capital acquisitions*, meaning capital purchases such as new equipment, new furniture and new motor vehicles. (You have to show capital acquisitions separately on your Business Activity Statement so this code is important.)

   Double-click your capital acquisitions code and check that the Rate is 10 per cent, and that the linked accounts are GST Collected and GST Paid (see Figure 15-2 for an example), and then click OK.

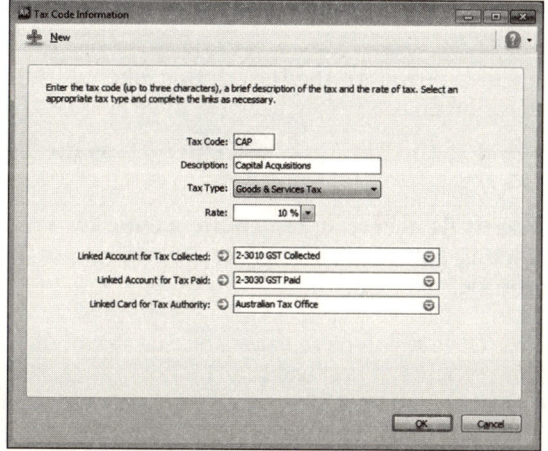

Figure 15-2:
Checking your tax code for capital acquisitions.

5. **Consider whether your business needs any additional Tax Codes.**

   After you have checked the setup for these three essential Tax Codes, browse through the following sections of this chapter to see whether your business needs any additional codes.

Dealing with input-taxed sales or purchases

Do you own a house that brings in rental income, or do the books for an organisation that's involved in fundraising activities?

If you earn income from financial services, residential rentals or charity fundraising activities, you need an additional Tax Code called ITS (standing for input-taxed sale). If you have expenses that relate to input-taxed income (such as expenses on your residential investment property, or expenses relating to fundraising activities), you need an additional Tax Code called INP (standing for input-taxed purchase).

Here's how to create these codes, from go to whoa:

1. **From the top menu bar, choose Lists⇨Tax Codes.**

2. **Click New.**

3. **Enter ITS (standing for Input-Taxed Sale) as the Tax Code and then type a Description.**

   Enter something meaningful for the Description, such as Interest Income or Rental Property Income.

4. **Select Input Taxed as the Tax Type and enter 0% as the Rate, and then click OK.**

5. **Repeat this process (if necessary) to create a code for input-taxed purchases, selecting INP as the code (not ITS) and Input Taxed Purchases as the Description.**

You only need the INP code if you have expenses that relate directly to input-taxed sales. For example, if you use the ITS Tax Code for residential rental income, you need to use the INP code to track all expenses relating to the property.

Exporting goods to foreign lands

If you export goods overseas, you need an additional Tax Code called EXP (which stands for export sales).

In this scenario, go to Lists⇨Tax Codes and create a new Tax Code called EXP. This code is set up exactly the same way as your FRE Tax Code, with a 0 per cent rate. As the Description, enter something like Export Sales.

Creating a query code when you don't have a clue

Sometimes you may not be sure whether or not an expense has GST on it. Although it's pretty tempting just to pick any old code and ignore the problem, you're best to use a special query code called QUE instead.

Using this code means you can still record the transaction and continue working on your accounts. Later on, you can print a report listing all transactions allocated to the QUE code and investigate these transactions further, or, if you're working in the cloud, ask your accountant to log into your company file and allocate these transactions correctly.

Here's how to create this code:

1. **From the top menu bar, choose Lists⇨Tax Codes.**

2. **Click New.**

3. **Enter QUE as the Tax Code and Don't Know in the Description area.**

4. **Select Goods & Services Tax as the Tax Type and enter 0% as the Rate.**

   I suggest you enter 0% as the Rate, because under-claiming GST is better than over-claiming. You can always make an adjustment if this query ends up having GST on it.

5. **Link this account to GST Collected and GST Paid.**

   Simply select these accounts from the drop-down lists next to the fields Linked Account for Tax Collected and Linked Account for Tax Paid.

6. **Click OK to save your Tax Code.**

Getting rid of excess fat

Figure 15-3 shows an example of a lean, clean Tax Code List, with a total of only five Tax Codes. Chances are that if your business makes no input-taxed sales and doesn't export goods overseas, you'll only need five Tax Codes too.

If you spot a code in your Tax Code List that you're sure you don't need, I suggest you delete it. To do this, double-click on the Tax Code, go up to the Edit menu and select Delete Tax Code.

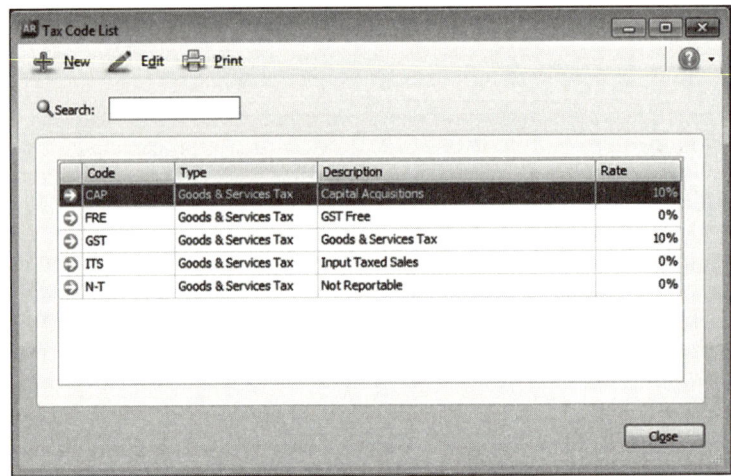

Figure 15-3:
A typical
Tax Code
List with
only five
codes.

Picking the Right Code

The secret to producing an accurate Business Activity Statement is to get the Tax Codes right on every transaction. Fortunately, this is pretty easy when you know how, as I explain in the next few sections.

Guaranteeing perfection, every time

Every account in your Accounts List is linked to a Tax Code. To see what I mean, go to your Accounts List and click the Expenses tab. Can you see how each account is linked to a different Tax Code, similar to what I show in Figure 15-4? (If every Tax Code on your Accounts List shows as N-T, this means that nobody has done the noble job of linking Tax Codes to accounts yet.)

Because every account is linked to a Tax Code, the correct Tax Code comes up as the default code every time you select an account on a transaction. For example, if the Tax Code for your Advertising Expense account is GST, every time you allocate a Spend Money transaction to Advertising Expense, GST pops up automatically as the Tax Code.

To change the linked Tax Code for an account, go to your Accounts List, double-click the account in question, and then click the Details tab. Change the Tax Code here. (For suggestions as to what Tax Code to choose, skip ahead to the following section.)

The implications are huge: If you set up the Tax Code for every account in your Accounts List correctly, right from the start, you're almost guaranteed of coding all your transactions right, every time. Perfection and nirvana are but moments away.

To compare your default Tax Codes for each account against what you've previously chosen as Tax Codes for individual transactions, check out the Transaction Tax Codes report under the GST tab of your Reports menu.

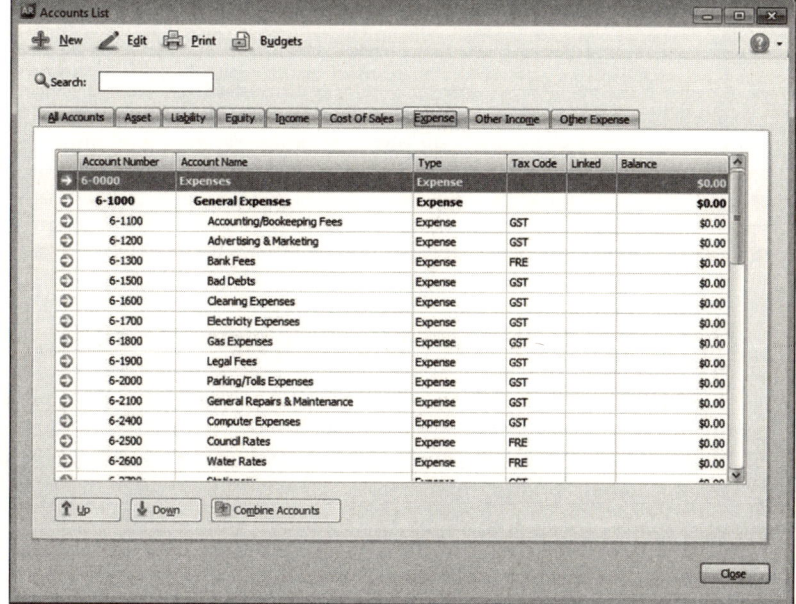

Figure 15-4:
Every account has a corresponding Tax Code listed in the Tax Code column.

Setting up Tax Codes in your Accounts List

As I explain in the preceding section, the secret to coding transactions correctly is to set up the linked Tax Codes in your Accounts List correctly. To change the linked Tax Code for an account, go to your Accounts List, double-click the account in question, and then click the Details tab. Change the Tax Code here.

Here's an indication of which codes to use for each account, although I do suggest you double-check all of these settings with your accountant before you begin:

✔ **Accounts with GST as the Tax Code:** Use GST as the Tax Code for most expense accounts, including things such as advertising, commercial rent, electricity, merchant fees, postage, telephone and travel within Australia.

- ✔ **Accounts with FRE as the Tax Code:** Use FRE as the Tax Code for accounts relating to bank charges (with the exception of merchant fees), government charges, interest expense, medical supplies, motor vehicle registration, rates, residential rent and stamp duty.

- ✔ **Accounts with CAP as the Tax Code:** Use CAP as the Tax Code for all fixed asset accounts, such as furniture and fittings, motor vehicles and tools.

- ✔ **Accounts with N-T as the Tax Code:** Use N-T as the Tax Code for all asset and liability accounts (with the exception of fixed asset accounts), private drawings accounts, superannuation and wages.

- ✔ **Accounts with QUE as the Tax Code — the query code:** Use QUE as the Tax Code for all hire purchase expense accounts, insurance expense, lease payments and subcontractor expense accounts. Then, ensure you double-check the correct GST treatment with your accountant or supplier.

Keeping everything squeaky-clean

I mention earlier in this chapter that the secret to producing accurate Business Activity Statements is to select the right Tax Codes for all transactions. I'm going to take this a step further now and talk about the most common coding mistakes.

And guess what? Because they're so common, these are the mistakes the ATO will be watching out for in any audit:

- ✔ **Bank fees and merchant fees:** Bank fees are almost always GST-free, but merchant fees (for credit cards and hire of EFTPOS machines) are not.

- ✔ **Government charges:** Council rates, filing fees, land tax, licence renewals, motor vehicle rego and stamp duty are all GST-free. So don't be tempted to claim back 10 per cent!

- ✔ **Insurance:** Insurance is tricky because almost every insurance policy has a mixture of taxable and GST-free items (for example, stamp duty doesn't have GST on it). Don't get caught out. Instead, double-check the exact amount of GST on every single insurance payment.

- ✔ **Overseas travel:** Overseas travel is GST-free.

- ✔ **Personal stuff:** You can't claim the full amount of GST on expenses that are partly personal — motor vehicle and home office expenses are the obvious culprits.

- ✔ **Petty cash:** Another trap for the unwary, petty cash is usually a mixed bag. Coffee and tea are GST-free, biscuits and sticky-tape aren't.

- ✔ **Small suppliers:** Watch out for small suppliers who have an ABN but aren't registered for GST. Record these purchases as GST-free.

Table 15-1 also provides a quick reference guide to selecting the right tax code.

Table 15-1	What Tax Code to Pick When	
Situation	*Examples*	*Tax Code*
Sales where you charge GST	Regular sales of most items	GST
Sales that are GST-free	Sales of childcare, medical supplies or unprocessed foods	FRE
Sales made to overseas customers	Export sales	EXP
Sales that are input-taxed	Interest income, residential rental income	ITS
Non-reportable transactions	Transfers between bank accounts, loan repayments, personal drawings, superannuation	N-T
Purchases of tax-free items	Purchases of unprocessed foods, bank charges, some medical items, or purchases from a supplier who isn't registered for GST	FRE
Purchase of taxable items	Most purchases and business expenses	GST
Capital acquisitions that have GST on them	Purchase of new equipment, motor vehicles or tools over $1,000 (exclusive of GST)	CAP
Capital acquisitions that have no GST on them	Purchase of new medical equipment, or a purchase of a vehicle from a private individual who isn't registered for GST	CGF
Purchases related to input-taxed sales	Expenses relating to a residential real-estate investment	INP

Knowing what not to touch

You've probably noticed an extra code you can't delete or change that sits in your Tax Code List. This code is called N-T and stands for non-reportable. (Yes, I know that logically the code should be called N-R, but it isn't!)

The distinction between the FRE Tax Code and the N-T Tax Code is that transactions coded FRE are reported on your Business Activity Statement, whereas transactions coded N-T are not.

Use N-T as the Tax Code for any transactions you allocate to an asset, liability or equity account — such as tax payments, loan settlements, private drawings or transfers between bank accounts. (The only exception is when you purchase new capital items, in which case you need to use the CAP code, as I explain earlier in this chapter.)

Also, use N-T as the Tax Code for all wages and superannuation payments. (Although you do report wages on your Business Activity Statement, they appear separately from other expenses.)

Dealing with transactions when GST isn't 10 per cent

Okay, let me get one thing straight. GST is *always* 10 per cent. That's the rate set by Australia's wonderful federal government (well, at least at the time of writing). However, sometimes you come across a transaction that seems like the GST *isn't* 10 per cent. Then, when you look closer, you find that the transaction is actually a combination of taxable items (which, of course, are 10 per cent) and non-taxable items (which are 0 per cent).

An example may help. You get an insurance bill for $550 and you enter the payment. MYOB calculates the GST to be $50 but when you look at the bill, you notice that GST is actually $49.09. That's because the bill includes $10 stamp duty and stamp duty is GST-free.

What some people do when faced with this icky situation is zoom in on the arrow next to the GST amount and then edit it. 'No, no, no!' I cry. Why? Because although MYOB lets you do this (why, I'm not quite sure), if you edit the GST amount, the figures MYOB produces on your Business Activity Statement are going to be incorrect.

The solution to this kind of situation, although a bit convoluted, is this: You record the insurance bill in Spend Money or Purchases, but you split the transaction over two lines. With the insurance example (assuming you've ticked the Tax Inclusive button), that means you'd allocate $540 to Insurance Expense with GST as the Tax Code, and then allocate $10 to Insurance Expense with FRE as the Tax Code. Clear as mud? My illustrious Figure 15-5 shows how it all works.

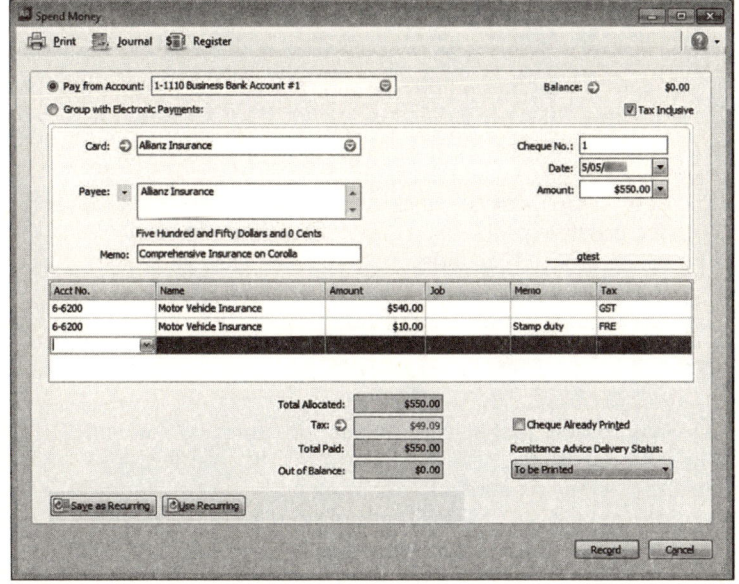

Figure 15-5:
Recording
a payment
when GST
doesn't
equal
10 per cent.

Getting personal

If your business purchases goods or services that you use partly for private purposes, be careful not to claim the GST on the private component. For example, if you run your motor vehicle as a business expense but your log book shows that 20 per cent of use is actually personal, then only claim 80 per cent of the GST when you record the transaction.

An example may help. Imagine you have motor vehicle repairs on your new Mercedes sports car (you wish) that cost $1,000, and your personal use of this vehicle is 20 per cent. To record this transaction, you allocate $800 to Motor Vehicle Maintenance on the first line, with GST as the Tax Code, and then allocate $200 to Owner's Drawings or a Director's Loan account on the second line, with N-T as the Tax Code.

Doing the Groundwork for Your Activity Statement

Before plunging into the ugly business of producing your Activity Statement for the Australian Taxation Office, take a few moments to check that the figures behind the scenes are as perfect as can be.

Auditing your own accounts

Want to give yourself an audit? Sounds kinda scary, but much better that you're trawling through your stuff, rather than some anonymous pale-faced chap from the tax office.

The most thorough way to check your work is to use the Company Data Auditor to scan for possible problems. I devote all of Chapter 18 to using this feature, the last stage of which includes an in-depth review of all your tax codings.

Checking your opening balances

Unless you're only just setting up your business, chances are that on the day you start entering transactions in MYOB, you already owe some GST to the tax office. For example, if you start entering transactions from 1 July, you almost certainly owe GST for the month of June, if not April, May and June (depending on whether you report monthly or quarterly).

Here's how to calculate your opening balances for GST:

1. **Look up how much GST you collected from customers in the period before your conversion date.**

   You find this figure next to box 1A in your June Business Activity Statement. (I assume here that you're starting to use MYOB from July 1.)

2. **Look up how much GST you paid to suppliers in the previous period.**

   You find this figure next to box 1B in your June Business Activity Statement.

3. **Go to your account opening balances and check that the opening balances for GST Collected and GST Paid match the amounts in Steps 1 and 2.**

   To view opening balances, go to Setup⇨Balances⇨Account Opening Balances. (I give the whole rave about opening balances in Chapter 3.) GST Collected should show as a positive figure, GST Paid should show as a minus figure.

4. **If you report for GST on a cash basis and you were owed money from customers on your conversion date, add the value of GST on these outstanding debts to your opening balance for GST Collected.**

   For example, if you are owed $11,000 from customers and GST makes up $1,000 of this amount, add $1,000 to your opening balance for GST Collected.

5. **If you owed money to suppliers and you report on a cash basis, add the value of GST on your outstanding accounts to your opening balance for GST Paid.**

That's it! In writing this step-by-step guide to opening GST balances, I'm aware that I've ventured deep into technical accounting land and that I may have lost you on this journey. If so, don't hesitate to ask your accountant for assistance.

Reviewing your final reports

Before generating your GST reports and Business Activity Statement, remember to reconcile your bank account right up to the last day of the period you're reporting for. Here are the reports I suggest you generate, along with why they're important:

✔ **GST [Summary–Accrual] or GST [Summary–Cash] report:** Choose either the GST [Summary–Accrual] report or the GST [Summary–Cash] report, depending on your reporting basis. (To find these reports, click the GST tab on your Reports menu.)

✔ **Profit & Loss Statement:** Your Profit & Loss Statement is a vital reference. Read this report and ensure it makes sense! (You can find the Profit & Loss Statement on the Accounts tab of your Reports menu.)

✔ **Balance Sheet report:** Your Balance Sheet is the litmus test for determining whether your GST accounts reconcile. (You can find the Balance Sheet report on the Accounts tab of your Reports menu.)

✔ **Employees Register Summary report (MYOB versions that include payroll only):** This report is important because it provides a double-check for Questions W1 (total wages) and W2 (total PAYG tax) on your Business Activity Statement. (You can find this report on the Payroll tab of your Reports menu.)

TIP

Cash is king

Lots of people ask me whether they can use accrual accounting for their finances, but cash accounting for GST. The answer is yes, of course. It's fine to record supplier invoices as Purchases and to record customer invoices as Sales (that's what I mean by *accrual accounting*, in case you're wondering). But then, when you're ready to report for GST, you ask for the GST [Summary Cash] or the GST [Detail Cash] report. (I'm assuming here that you've registered for GST on a cash basis; if you're unsure, ask your accountant.)

How does this work? Imagine you only had two transactions during a quarter, one being a sale to a customer and the other being a bill from a supplier, and that by the end of the quarter, the customer still hasn't paid, nor have you paid the supplier. On your Profit & Loss report, MYOB still shows both the income and the expense (in other words, reporting on an accrual basis). However, your Business Activity Statement comes up blank, because this statement (assuming you've selected to report for GST on a cash basis) only includes transactions when your customers pay you or you pay your suppliers.

Setting Up Your Activity Statement

Set up correctly, MYOB generates a report that looks almost identical to the Activity Statement form you receive from the ATO (except that your version comes complete with the correct figures, of course). In this section, I explain how to configure your Activity Statement and generate your GST worksheet.

Configuring your statement

The first step in preparing your Activity Statement is to tell MYOB what kind of taxes you pay on your statement — every business is a little different — and also how often you report to the ATO, as follows:

1. **From your Accounts command centre, click the BASlink button.**

2. **Click the BAS Info button.**

   You find this button in the top-left corner.

3. **Select your GST reporting frequency, accounting basis and GST option.**

   If you're not sure about these settings, refer to your most recent Activity Statement (you know, the form that the ATO sends you every month or quarter) or ask your accountant.

   Selecting Cash as your GST accounting basis when you're actually registered to report on an Accruals basis — or selecting Accruals when you should select Cash — can result in figures that are drastically incorrect. If you are at all unsure about what to select as your GST accounting basis, contact your accountant.

4. **Unless your accountant advises otherwise, check that Calculation Worksheet is selected as the Calculation Method.**

5. **If you pay PAYG Instalments, select your reporting frequency, accounting basis and instalment option.**

   Again, if you're unsure of your settings, seek advice from your accountant. If you're part of a partnership, you'll have a separate Activity Statement just for reporting PAYG Instalments.

6. **If you have employees, select either Monthly or Quarterly as the Withholding Reporting Frequency under PAYG Withholdings.**

   Alternatively, if you don't have employees, select Not Registered here.

7. **If you have to cough up for FBT, WET or LCT, tick this box.**

   By now, your BAS Information window should look similar to Figure 15-6.

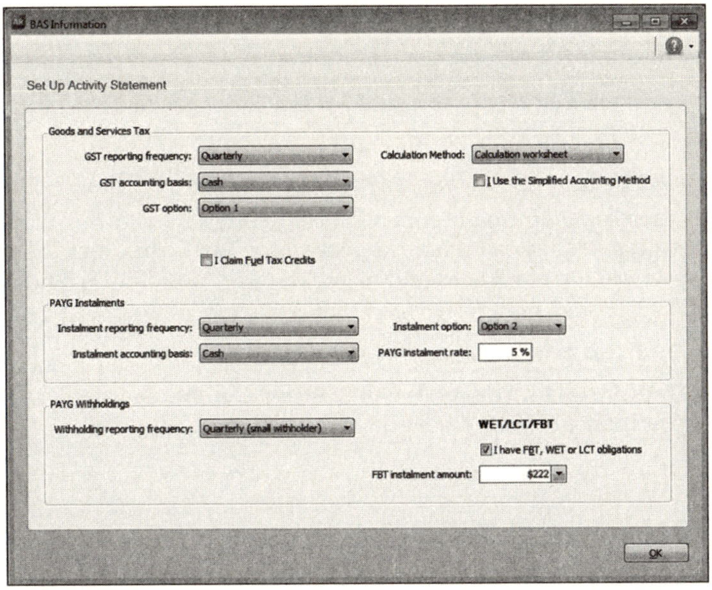

Figure 15-6:
Configuring
your Activity
Statement.

Matching codes and accounts

To set up the Activity Statement itself, go to the Accounts command centre and click the BASlink button, select a month, and then click Prepare Statement. You arrive at a window that looks comfortingly similar to the form itself.

This window divides into three tabs: GST Worksheet, Front Sheet and Back Sheet. Your job is to work through each tab, linking Tax Codes and accounts to every field (G1, G2, G3 and so on). This rite of passage gets a tad technical, but be comforted that you only need to endure it once.

GST Worksheet

To determine which tax codes belong in each box, click the grey Setup button that appears next to the amount field for each one. You arrive at the Field Setup window, shown in Figure 15-7.

Here are some hints on which Tax Codes to select and when:

✔ **Question G1:** You report all sales in this question, so select every Tax Code you ever use for sales. Usually, this is simply GST, ITS and FRE, but if you export goods overseas or sell liquor wholesale, you also require the EXP or WET codes.

✔ **Question G2:** You report all export sales here, so use the EXP code.

✔ **Question G3:** You report all GST-free sales here, so use the FRE code.

✔ **Question G4:** Here's the spot for any input-taxed sales, such as residential rental income. ITS is the code to select here.

✔ **Question G10:** You report all capital acquisitions here. CAP is the code.

✔ **Question G11:** You report all other expenses (with the exception of capital acquisitions) here. Select every Tax Code other than CAP that you use for purchases and expenses, such as FRE, INP and GST.

✔ **Question G13:** You report all purchases that relate to input-taxed sales here. INP is the darling that you're looking for.

✔ **Question G14:** You report all GST-free purchases here. FRE is your code.

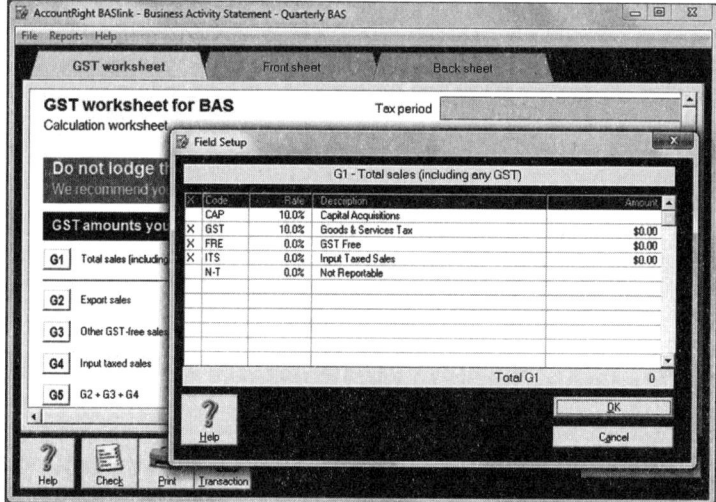

Figure 15-7:
Configuring each field on the GST worksheet.

PAYG tax withheld

How you configure the PAYG tax section, which appears on either the Front Sheet or the Back Sheet tab of your Activity Statement, depends on your version of MYOB:

✔ **If you use a version of MYOB that includes payroll:** Click the Setup button next to W1 and check out the list of payroll categories. Mark off all Wages categories, with the exception of Employee Advances. All done? Now, click the Setup button next to W2 and select PAYG Withholding.

> ✔ **If you use a version of MYOB that doesn't include payroll:** You can manually type in figures for total wages and total PAYG tax.

Remember the following:

> ✔ MYOB reports *gross wages* at W1 (in other words, wages before tax), not net wages.
>
> ✔ Unless you withhold amounts from investment distributions or you withhold tax from suppliers who don't provide an ABN — both unlikely scenarios — W3 and W4 will always be blank and W5 will be the same as W2.

PAYG income tax instalments

Don't get muddled with the terminology here. PAYG Withholding tax is the tax you deduct from employees' pays; PAYG Instalment tax is the tax you pay on income (whether or not you have to cough up PAYG Instalment tax depends on how much profit you made last year).

To set up your Activity Statement for PAYG Instalment tax, click the Setup button next to question T1 — which usually appears on the Back Sheet tab of your Activity Statements — and select all your income accounts, including the accounts that start with the number 8, as well as the accounts that start with the number 4.

Next, find the PAYG income tax instalment summary field on your Activity Statement (box 5A), and click the Link button that appears to the right of the amount. If you're a sole trader or partnership, select 'Drawings' or 'Drawings – Tax' as the account. If you're a company, select a liability account called Provision for Income Tax as the account.

Other taxes

How you configured your Activity Statement (when you clicked the BAS Info button) affects what taxes show up on the form itself. If you pay Fringe Benefits Tax, Luxury Car Tax or Wine Equalisation Tax, you need to click the Link button next to these fields and select the relevant account, such as Fringe Benefits Expense or Luxury Car Tax Expense. Ask your accountant if you're not sure which account to select.

Saving your settings (don't forget)

To save your settings, click Save Setup & Exit. Clicking this button automatically saves your configuration. To save the data itself, first click Save Setup & Exit, and then click Yes to the prompt that asks you if you want to back up. Alternatively, click No to close without saving your data.

Finalising Your BAS

After you've endured the brutal initiation rite of configuring your Activity Statement (thankfully, a one-off process — refer to the preceding section), printing only takes a few minutes. After printing your statement, you need to follow through by checking that everything balances, and then record the payment (or refund) in MYOB.

Printing your statement

So you're ready to do the deed? Get ready, set, go:

1. **Navigate to the Accounts command centre and click the BASlink button.**

2. **Select the period you want to report on.**

   Select the last month of your reporting period. So, if you're reporting for the period July to September, select September as the month.

   Be extra careful to select the correct financial year as well as the correct month. I've seen many clients spend hours trying to figure out why their Activity Statement figures don't balance, only to finally realise that they had clicked the Next Year button rather than the This Year button, or the other way around.

3. **Click Prepare Statement and then press OK to continue.**

   You should arrive at a screen that looks similar to the one shown in Figure 15-8.

4. **Review the figures that MYOB offers. Do they make sense?**

   For more on checking these figures, see the next section.

5. **Click the Check button on the bottom left.**

   The Check button double-checks that every field on your statement has either Tax Codes or Accounts linked to it. It also prompts you to complete the Document Identification Number, Contact Name and Time Taken. I often don't worry about completing these fields, because I only have to record this info again on the form that I submit.

6. **Click the Print button, and then either lodge the information online or copy the information onto the printed form that the ATO sent you.**

   If you lodge your Activity Statement online, log onto your business portal at www.ato.gov.au, click the Activity Statement side menu, and complete the relevant figures when prompted.

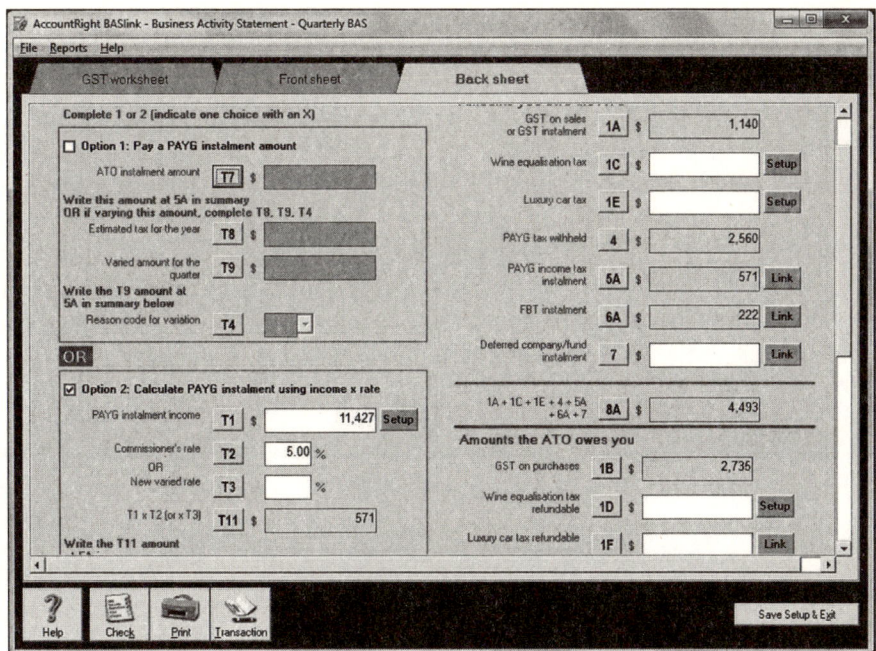

Figure 15-8:
Your Activity
Statement,
ready to go.

If you still lodge your Business Activity Statement by filling out a form
and posting it, note that you can't lodge the form that MYOB prints
out. Instead, copy the figures onto the form provided by the Australian
Taxation Office.

7. **Click Transaction and then Print to find out how to record your tax
   payment or refund.**

   This step produces a handy help-sheet, showing you how to record
   your tax payment or refund. The transaction is often quite complex and
   split across several accounts, so store this help-sheet carefully — you're
   going to need it all too soon!

8. **Click Save Setup & Exit, and back up when prompted.**

9. **Make sure that the amount of GST that you are about to pay balances
   with your Balance Sheet.**

   Need more info? For more info about reconciling GST against your
   Balance Sheet, skip ahead to Chapter 18.

Lodge online

For some unknown reason, I procrastinated about creating an online account for my business, and it was only recently, when I heard a rumour that the ATO are soon going to insist on all businesses lodging online, that I got my act together.

Afterwards, I felt silly about having dilly-dallied for so long. Lodging my Activity Statements online is not only super straightforward, but also takes a fraction of the time that filling out

a form by hand and posting it requires. And if I want to look up previous Activity Statements, I can do so at the click of a button, rather than having to do combat with my less-than-ideal filing system.

So if you haven't yet made the move, now is the time. Go to www.ato.gov.au, head to the Online Services menu and register for an account.

Checking your BAS is correct

I recommend you take a few moments to check that the information on your Activity Statement is correct. Here's my five-step checklist from hell:

1. **Check that GST Paid and GST Collected on your Activity Statement match with the totals on your GST Summary report for the same period.**

    For example, if 1A (GST Collected) on your BAS says you collected $1,350 in GST on sales, you would expect this exact figure to appear on your GST Summary report. You can find the GST Summary report under the GST tab of your Reports menu. (If you report for GST on a cash basis, ensure you use the GST [Summary Cash] report.)

2. **Check that the amounts against GST-free sales and GST-free purchases (G3 and G14 on your worksheet) make sense.**

    One of the errors newbies to MYOB make is to count non-reportable transactions as GST-free transactions. The idea of non-reportable transactions is that they are non-reportable, and so don't appear anywhere on your Activity Statement. (Refer to 'Knowing what not to touch', earlier in this chapter.)

3. **If relevant, check that T1 on your BAS matches with total income according to your Profit & Loss report.**

    If you pay PAYG Instalment tax and pay tax on a percentage basis, check that the total for T1 (found on the Back Sheet tab) matches with total income in your Profit & Loss report. (If you report for GST on a cash basis, ensure you refer to the Profit & Loss [Cash] Report.)

Don't be anxious if total sales in G1 on your Activity Statement don't equal total sales in T1. That's because G1 includes GST, but T1 doesn't!

4. **Check that W1 and W2 on your BAS match with your Payroll Register Summary report.**

   You can find the Payroll Register Summary report under the Payroll tab of your Reports menu.

5. **If you have time, compare the amounts for GST Collected and Paid on your BAS against your Balance Sheet.**

   I explain much more about verifying the balances in GST Collected and GST Paid in Chapter 18.

In the preceding list, I explain how to check your Activity Statement is correct, but fail to explain what to do if it isn't! However, knowing that you have a possible error is certainly 90 per cent of the battle and if you can't find a ready solution to any of the problems in the list, don't hesitate to ask your accountant.

Catch that train before it leaves

So what's the deadline for lodging your Business Activity Statements?

If your business reports monthly, the deadline is 21 days after the end of each month. Alternatively, if your business reports quarterly or annually, the deadline is 28 days after the end of each quarter, except for the second quarter of the year (October to December) when the deadline is extended by four weeks. Note that if you lodge Business Activity Statements electronically, these deadlines are usually extended by two weeks.

Most importantly, if you think you (or the business you're working for) won't have enough money to pay your Business Activity Statement on time, do lodge the form anyway. The Tax Office only issues fines for lodging forms late; it doesn't issue fines for paying late. The only punishment administered is an interest charge for late payments.

For most businesses, the Tax Office doesn't take any action or impose penalties so long as payment is made within a couple of weeks of lodgement. If you know that you still won't be able to pay within a couple of weeks, I suggest you contact the Tax Office and request a payment extension — the folks there are usually surprisingly obliging and keen to help.

Recording your payment or refund

After you've completed your Business Activity Statement, you need to record your payment or refund. In Step 7 in the section 'Printing your statement', earlier in this chapter, I explain how to print a help-sheet for recording this transaction.

The whole idea is this: When you send in your BAS, you report on a whole range of taxes: GST Collected, GST Paid, PAYG Withholding tax and PAYG Instalment tax, to name but a few. Therefore, when you pay your tax (or receive a refund), you need to allocate this payment or deposit to all the different tax accounts, as I do in Figure 15-9. Note that I allocate PAYG Withholding tax to a Payroll Clearing account — I explain this logic in the following section.

One last pearl of wisdom. No matter how miraculously everything balances, you always end up with a few stray cents because you always round every figure to the nearest dollar when you complete an Activity Statement. Simply allocate these few cents to your Bank Charges account and everything will be just fine.

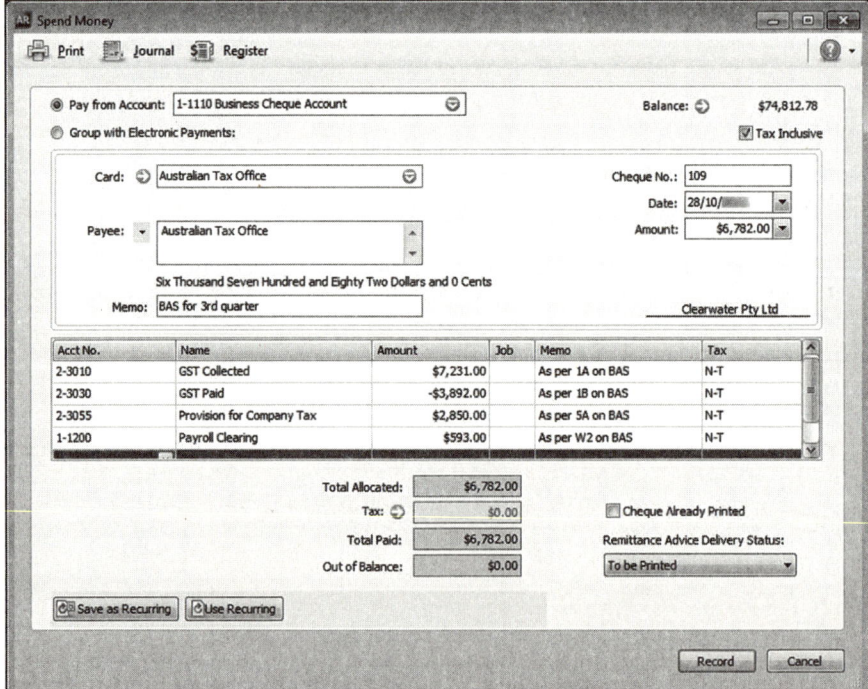

Figure 15-9:
Recording
your
Business
Activity
Statement
payment.

Including PAYG tax on your BAS payment

MYOB expects you to record the payment of PAYG Withholding tax in the Pay Liabilities window of the Payroll command centre. That's okay, but things become tricky when you have PAYG Withholding tax as part of your Activity Statement.

The trick to getting everything to come out clean in the wash is to create a special account called Payroll Clearing, and use this account as your bank account to record the payment of PAYG Withholding tax. Here's how:

1. **Go to your Accounts List and create a new asset account called Payroll Clearing, selecting Bank as the Account Type.**

2. **When you record your Activity Statement payment, allocate the PAYG Withholding tax component to this new Payroll Clearing Account.**

3. **Go to Pay Liabilities in the Payroll command centre and record the PAYG Withholding tax part of your Activity Statement payment, as if you're paying it a second time, but for the Bank Account select your new Payroll Clearing Account.**

   Hopefully, this suggested payment amount is exactly the same as what you paid on your BAS.

4. **Go to your Payroll Clearing Account in your Accounts List and check that this account now has a $0.00 balance.**

   The idea is that when you record your Activity Statement payment, you *credit* this clearing account. When you record paying the PAYG Withholding tax component using Pay Liabilities, you *debit* this clearing account. If all goes smoothly, this account always returns to zero.

Making Up for Your Mistakes

I remember being ditched by a boyfriend once who, listing my failures, recounted that I could never admit to my mistakes. He looked surprised as I replied that I'd made one with him.

And in this spirit of confession, you'll be delighted to know that I now readily admit to my mistakes, especially when it comes to accounts. It's so easy to muddle debits with credits, choose the wrong expense account or enter a payment twice. I freely admit it. And, assuming that you're not perfect either, I now discuss what to do when this happens to you.

Fixing mistakes

Don't despair if you find you've made a mistake with GST on an Activity Statement that you've already lodged. Usually, the easiest approach is to simply reverse the offending transaction (I talk more about reversing transactions in earlier chapters), dating your reversal in the current period, and then re-enter your transaction, recording it correctly this time! That way, the impact of your mistake comes up in the current BAS and you end up adjusting it automatically.

Be aware there are time and dollar limits on what corrections you're allowed to make in your current Activity Statement for mistakes made in a previous period. If you're not sure what these limits are, ask your accountant for the latest info. (See also my free online article on this topic, available as part of *Bookkeeping For Dummies*, 2nd Australian and New Zealand Edition. Just go to www.dummies.com/extras/bookkeepingau.) Also, regardless of what method you use to make adjustments, remember to keep notes about when mistakes were made as well as when they were corrected.

By the way, if you're not eligible to make an adjustment on your existing Activity Statement, your only option is to revise your earlier statement. Contact the ATO or your accountant and ask for help walking through this process.

Safeguarding against accidents

One way to protect yourself (or others) from accidentally changing transactions belonging to a previous month or quarter is to use the Lock Periods feature. After a period has been locked, you can't inadvertently add or change any transactions that belong to that period, or earlier.

To lock a previous period, go to the top menu bar, select Setup⇨Preferences, followed by the Security tab. Click against Lock Periods and select the date up to which you want to close off the accounts. Click OK and you're done!

Chapter 16

Managing Your Company File

• •

In This Chapter

▶ Finding your file, wherever it may be

▶ Shifting to the cloud — the pros and the cons

▶ Checking files in and out, and getting the speed you need

▶ Backing up, backing up, backing up

▶ Saving yourself from the clutches of death

• •

*E*very time I do a new edition of this book (and spare me a moment of pure pity — eight editions multiplied by 120,000 words a pop means close to a million words that I've written and rewritten about MYOB), I'm surprised by how much has changed.

This chapter is no exception. The processes for locating, opening, closing, backing up and restoring company files have all transformed with the new versions of MYOB, and the option to work in the cloud provides an added complication (as well as an added benefit, of course).

Although this chapter is one of the driest and most technical in this book, behind the geek-speak lies lots of good stuff. Find out how to make MYOB run faster, work online or offline, how to work in more than one file at a time, and much more besides.

Getting In and Getting Out

If you're a bookkeeper, you're probably an expert at complex journals, tricky calculations and obscure reconciliations. What's likely to trip you up is the behind-the-scenes technology, such as finding files, moving files from one computer to another or logging on from different computers. Never fear, help is here.

Opening your company file

In this section, I assume that you've already installed MYOB on your computer and that you (or someone else) have already created a company file. The day has dawned, new and sparkling, and you're ready to work on your accounts once more:

1. **Open up the MYOB application.**

   When you install MYOB on your computer, you find that a neat little icon complete with the letters AR (as in AccountRight) appears on your computer's desktop. Simply double-click this shortcut to fire up your MYOB application.

   You arrive at a list of recently opened files, similar to Figure 16-1.

2. **If you can see your company file in the list of recently opened files, double-click the company file name to open this file.**

   Just this week, a tech-support guru at MYOB gave me a great tip about this list: If a file name has the letters 'myox' at the end, your file is stored locally on your computer; if a file name doesn't have these letters at the end, this file is stored in the cloud.

3. **If you can't see your company file in this list, click the Open button to view a list of all files in your MYOB library.**

   When you click Open, MYOB displays a list of all company files in your AccountRight library, not just recently opened files. If you can see your company file in this list, double-click the file name to open this file.

   If you've never opened your company file on this computer before, but you have a copy of this file on another drive or device, see 'Adding a file from a memory stick or another location', later in this chapter.

4. **If you store your company file in the cloud, click the Online button, enter your email and password, and click Log In.**

   The email address and password is whatever email and password you used when you registered with MYOB or accepted the invitation to work on this company file. Once you're logged in, highlight your file from the list that appears and click Open.

5. **Enter your User ID and password.**

   If you haven't yet set up user roles and passwords (a topic I explain in more detail in Chapter 1), enter Administrator as your User ID and leave the password blank. Click OK and you're in.

For more details about logins, User IDs and passwords, skip ahead to the next section.

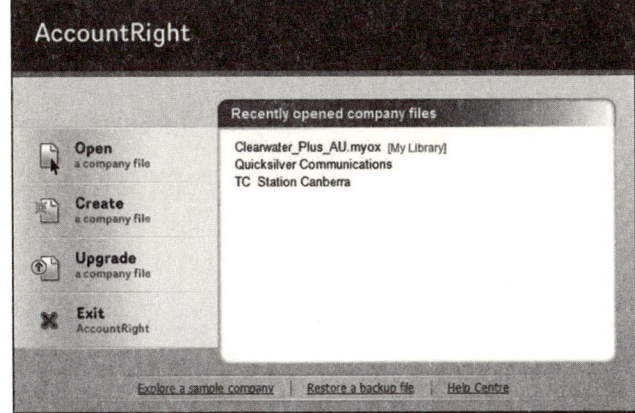

Figure 16-1:
When you first open up MYOB, you see a list of recently opened files.

Getting your head around the different logins

Do you have a squillion different passwords and have trouble remembering each one? I know I do, and the need to remember more than one login and password was something that caused me grief when I first started working with the newer versions of MYOB.

The confusion sets in when you move your company file to the cloud (a topic I discuss in more detail later in this chapter). This is because MYOB now requires that you log in twice:

1. **The first stage of the log-in process involves logging into the cloud, as shown in Figure 16-2. For this stage, you need the email address and password you used when first registering with MYOB.**

   Can't remember? You can always wing it by entering your email address and clicking the 'Forgot Your Password' link.

2. **The second stage involves logging into your company file itself, as in Figure 16-3. For this stage, you need the User ID and password that either you or somebody else has created within the company file itself.**

   Of course, many businesses choose not to add passwords, and simply log on by entering 'Administrator' as the User ID, leaving the password blank.

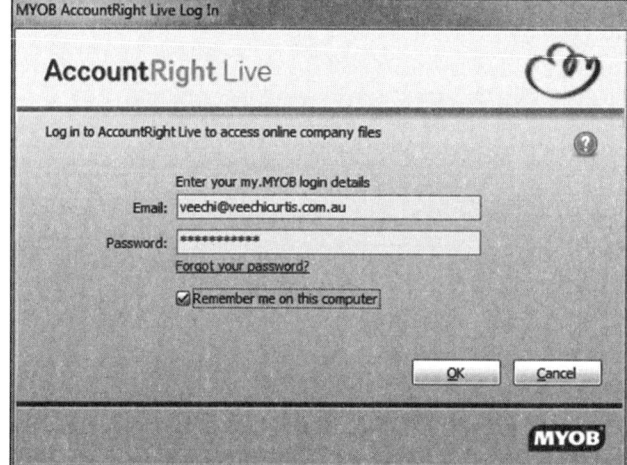

The User ID you use when opening your company file is almost certainly different from the email address you use when logging into the cloud. Similarly, the password for opening your company file *may* be different from the password you use when logging into the cloud. To make life easier, I suggest that when logging in you click the option to Link this User ID to your my. MYOB account (you can see how this option is circled in Figure 16-3).

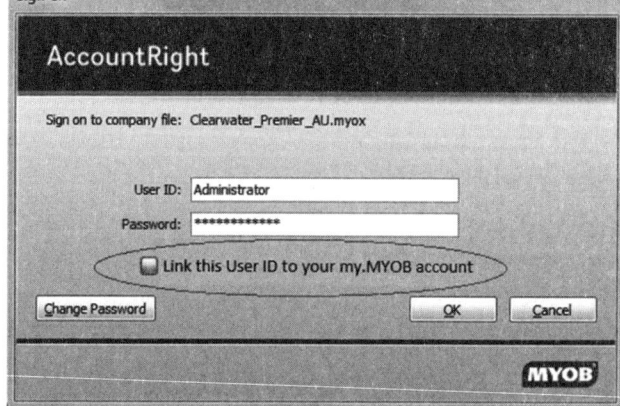

In the ideal world, I suggest you use the same User ID and password for both logins (in other words, use your email address as your User ID when opening your company file). However, just before you get too relaxed, here's a little pitfall to keep you on your toes:

Take the short way

Want to get started in a hurry? I can't be bothered minimising other programs just to get to my desktop, so I prefer to add MYOB to my taskbar. (Your taskbar is the list of programs that appears when you click your Windows Start button.) Want to give this a go?

In Windows 8, go to the Start screen, right-click the MYOB program icon, and select Pin to Taskbar. In Windows 7, go to your desktop, right-click the MYOB program icon and select Pin to Taskbar. Done.

The password for logging into the cloud is *case-sensitive* (meaning you have to get the CaPitAls correct), but the password for logging into your company file isn't.

Adding a file from a memory stick or another location

If your company file is located on a USB drive or external hard drive — maybe you recently upgraded computers, or maybe you want to work on a client's or a colleague's company file — you need to first add this file to the AccountRight library on your local computer.

Here's how:

1. **Double-click the MYOB AccountRight icon on your desktop to fire up MYOB.**

2. **From the Welcome window, click Open.**

3. **Click Add a Company File.**

   You find this command at the bottom of the Open a Company File window.

4. **Navigate to the location (memory stick, hard drive or whatever) where the company file is stored, highlight the file, and click Open.**

   All done. MYOB now adds this file to your 'library' where you'll be able to locate it easily next time.

MYOB Libraries? What about those cardigan-wearing revolutionaries?

I remember watching a comedian tearing apart the Clinton administration's Patriot Act, delighting in the fact that the real opposition against this Act hadn't come from students or card-carrying activists, but from cardigan-wearing, bespectacled librarians, who led a groundswell of protest defending First Amendment rights and stonewalling the request to provide the government with records of patrons' borrowing records. The skit was funny and the basis for it was true. I've never felt the same way about libraries (or librarians) since.

But onto more mundane topics, specifically the way MYOB refers to libraries. Free from

radicals — more's the pity — an AccountRight library is a specific location where you store your AccountRight company files. You get two types of AccountRight libraries: Local libraries and network libraries. A *local library* means company files are located on your computer; a *network library* means company files are located on a different computer that you access across a network.

The neat thing about working with libraries in this way is that you have a single location for all your company files. Because AccountRight knows where your file is, you don't need to navigate to your file when opening or upgrading it.

Finding your company file

Although MYOB tries to make life as easy as possible by organising files into libraries, you may, for whatever geeky techno reason, want to know exactly where your company file lives.

If MYOB is installed on a server, the file path should be C:\Users\Public\Public Documents\MYOB\My AccountRight Files. If MYOB is installed on a single PC, the file path should be C:\Users\<user.name>\My Documents\MYOB\My AccountRight Files (by <user.name> I mean whatever name you use when you log into your computer).

One quick way to identify the location of your file is to go to the Company Data Auditor in the Accounts command centre, where the Company File Overview lists the exact location.

Logging on, more than one at a time

As your business grows, you may find you want to have more than one person working on your accounts at a time. Maybe you want someone to be able to record invoices and another person to enter expenses and generate reports.

With the new generation of AccountRight products, the only way to have more than one person working simultaneously is to shift your file to the cloud. You can work in this way with any AccountRight product, from AccountRight Basics up. The only extra step you need to take is to set up each person with their own User ID and password.

Don't be confused by the network library option that appears when you go to open a company file. All this option does is make it easier for you to find your company file if it's living on a network — that is, on a location somewhere other than your own computer. Regardless of where you locate your company file, unless you store your file in the cloud, only one person can access the data at one time.

The requirement to store your file in the cloud if you want to have more than one simultaneous user is a deal-breaker for many businesses that still use the 'classic' version of Premier, but would like to upgrade to the latest version in order to access key features such as bank feeds, SuperStream compliance and improved reporting. I talk about the speed issue later in this chapter (see 'Aaargh! A tortoise could go faster') but the bottom line is that if you have a slow internet connection, the new version of Premier may simply not run fast enough to do the job. If you're not sure whether the new version is going to run fast enough, but you'd really like to upgrade, I suggest you make a backup, run the upgrade and then work for a couple of days in the new version. If the new version runs so slow you feel like you're stuck in a Fellini movie, you can ditch it, restore your backup, and return to the old version.

Working in more than one company file at a time

Lots of people run more than one business using MYOB, and often these businesses are related to one another in some way. For example, you may have a partnership that owns the building that you work from, but you use a company structure for your trading business. Or you may import goods into Australia via a family trust, but distribute these goods via an incorporated company.

When I'm working with businesses that are interrelated, I like to be able to have more than one MYOB company file open at a time so that I can flip from one to another. This helps me balance intercompany loan accounts and compare reports between different files, all of which helps to make me feel rather smug and very clever. (Dubious character traits indeed.)

To view more than one company file at a time, start by opening your first file in the normal way. Then, to open a second or a third file, return to your MYOB shortcut (usually on your desktop or your taskbar) and fire up MYOB again. Open up the next file in the normal way and before you know it, you have two files open at once. You can now alternate happily between the two files.

If you work on more than one company on a regular basis, and you have the physical space to do so, I suggest you set up two monitors side by side. This way you can view transactions for one company file on one monitor, and transactions for the second company file on the other monitor.

Moving to the Cloud

In the next section of this chapter I talk about whether or not to shift your company file to the cloud, and how to make this move first time around. If you're skim-reading this chapter looking for juicy plot turns and something interesting, you may be feeling slightly desperate by now. However, please don't skip past the stuff about synchronising your file. If nothing else, read this bit.

Deciding whether to shift to the cloud

Are you wondering whether to shift your accounts to the cloud, or not? I can understand that the idea of storing confidential financial information in some remote (and unknown) location via the internet may seem a rather risky strategy. However, here are just some of the reasons you may want to make the change:

✔ **You can access your data from wherever and whenever.** No matter whether you're out on the road selling to customers or stuck on a train, working in the cloud means that you can always access your accounts, wherever you are (so long as you have an internet connection, of course).

✔ **Your accounting data is arguably way more secure in the cloud than it is on the hard drive in your office.** Many small businesses have patchy backup systems, or forget to take backups offsite. Most cloud software providers invest far more in data security than any business will on its own.

✔ **Working with your company accountant is much easier.** Instead of having to make a copy of your accounting company file and sending this to the company accountant, you simply set up a separate User ID for your accountant so that they can log in and view your data at any time.

✔ **More than one person can work on the accounts at one time.** With the latest generation of MYOB software, your file must be in the cloud for more than one person to access your accounts at one time.

Now that I've elaborated on the good things about shifting to the cloud, I can share the not-so-good things. Two reasons that you may be best to avoid working in the cloud include:

✔ **Slow or unreliable internet access:** If the connection to the internet is slow or drops out frequently, storing accounts in the cloud is going to do nothing but cause grief.

✔ **A need for speed:** Even with a fast internet connection, the latest versions of AccountRight run slower than the classic versions, particularly if you make heavy use of inventory features. See 'Aaargh! A tortoise could go faster', later in this chapter, for more details regarding the speed issue.

One of the big misunderstandings people have regarding MYOB and the cloud is that you need to shift your file into the cloud in order to enable bank feed features. Not true. You can have bank feeds without shifting your file to the cloud, and vice versa.

Shifting to the cloud, first time round

So you're working locally, but you want to try shifting your company file to the cloud? Read on for all-singing, all-dancing instructions of what to do:

1. **Check you've paid your dues and you have the right to make the change.**

   Before you can move your company file online, you need to have a current AccountRight subscription for each company file that you want to access online. You also need to either be the company file *owner* (usually the person who set up the AccountRight subscription), or an Administrator.

2. **Open the company file that you want to shift online.**

   Refer to 'Opening your company file', earlier in this chapter, for more details.

3. **Go to the File menu and choose Go Online (Upload This File), logging in as an AccountRight Administrator if prompted to do so.**

   A message appears explaining that the file may take some time to upload, depending on the size of the file and the speed of your internet connection.

4. Click Upload now.

Now's the time for a cup of tea and a snooze until MYOB obligingly confirms the job is done.

5. Click Sign on to open the online company file.

Refer to 'Getting your head around the different logins', earlier in this chapter, for more on User IDs and passwords.

In theory, at this point you've done everything you need to do in order to shift your company file online. In practice, however, I suggest you take things a couple of extra steps further:

1. Add an exception for MYOB to your anti-virus software.

The tech support guys at MYOB tell me that over-enthusiastic anti-virus software is one of the main reasons for MYOB running slowly in the cloud. Skip ahead to 'Adding an exception to your virus software' to find out what to do.

2. Manually synchronise your company file so that if the internet goes down in the future, you have a local copy to fall back on.

For me, synchronising your company file is like putting on the handbrake when you park on a hill. Such a hugely important thing, and yet heaps of people don't realise they have to initiate the process first time around. Skip ahead to the next section about syncing files for what to do.

3. Check that no possible confusion can arise about which version to open.

Like Eeyore in *Winnie the Pooh*, I can be terribly full of doom and gloom. But one of the things that often goes wrong when people shift data to the cloud is that the company file that was stored locally (or usually an old backup or copy of this file in fact) still appears in the list of recently opened files. (Hark back to Figure 16-1 to see what I mean by this list.) An easy mistake is to accidentally open the local copy rather than the cloud copy, and end up with two different versions of the same company file. Yuck.

To avoid this possible confusion, go to your list of recently opened files and, if a non-cloud copy appears in this list (all locally stored files have the letters 'myox' at the end), gently right-click the name of the file and select Remove From List.

4. Invite others to join the fun.

Part of the benefit of working in the cloud is that you can invite as many people as you like to download MYOB software onto their own computer, so that they can log into your company file. MYOB doesn't charge for others to purchase the software — the download itself is free, because the monthly subscription relates to your company file, and not the software itself.

So make hay while the sun shines and invite anybody you like, such as other staff members, your accountant or business adviser. The easiest way to invite other users is to log on as Administrator into your company file, go to User Access from the Setup menu, and click New User. Enter a User ID and Password for this new user (they can change their password later on), assign a role to this user, and click Save. When prompted, click Log In to send an invitation to this person to work online. (You can see the User Access window in Figure 16-4.) Remember that if you want to keep certain information confidential, you can use the roles feature to restrict what each user can see.

Figure 16-4:
You've shifted to the cloud? Then invite others, such as your accountant or other staff members, to view your company file.

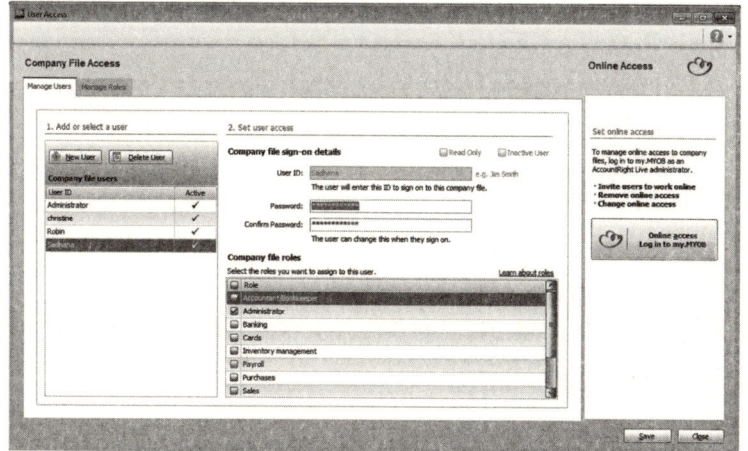

Syncing your file (and other excellent ideas)

Synchronisation is a very clever feature unique to MYOB. The idea is that even though you store your company file in the cloud, MYOB also keeps a copy of your data on your local machine. Every 20 minutes or so, MYOB synchronises the data in the cloud with the data on your machine. This way, if the internet goes down, you can revert to the local copy on your machine, and keep working. Neat, don't you reckon?

The only teensy fly in the ointment is that MYOB doesn't start synchronising your file automatically. Instead, you have to initiate the request to synchronise your file the first time around. MYOB only starts synchronising automatically after this first time. (The reason? Some people who work on your company file, such as your accountant, don't necessarily want to make a copy of your data on their local machine. With this in mind, MYOB waits for you to initiate the process.)

If you haven't done so already, synchronise now. Otherwise, if you ever have a problem with internet access at some point in the future, you won't have a local copy.

Enough of the whys, here's the how:

1. **Open the company file you want to synchronise.**

2. **Go to the File menu and select Sync Company File.**

   The Ready to Synchronise message appears.

3. **Click Synchronise.**

   You can continue working on the file while it's being synchronised; when synchronisation is complete, you get a comforting confirmation message.

4. **Click Close.**

   So easy.

Adding an exception to your virus software

When you store your company file in the cloud, one of the most frequent causes of MYOB running slowly is that the virus software goes into overdrive, monitoring all the data going from your computer to the cloud and back again, slowing everything down hideously in the process.

The solution is simple: Tell your anti-virus software that MYOB is friend not foe. The technical term for this process is to *add an exception* for MYOB and the actual procedure for adding exceptions varies depending on what software you use.

If you can't readily see how to add an exception to your anti-virus software, go to Google (or your favourite search engine) and type 'MYOB add exception' followed by the name of whatever anti-virus software you're currently using.

Working in the Cloud, Day-to-Day

In the next section of this chapter, I assume that you've shifted your company file to the cloud, either for all or some of the time. I address some of the challenges that can come with shifting to the cloud, such as what to do if you need to work offline or if the internet goes down, and how to address problems with speed.

Checking out (shifting your file offline)

Just because you've shifted your company file to the cloud doesn't mean you have to work online all the time. If you know you're going to be in an area with patchy internet or you're going to be on a long flight somewhere, you can choose to 'check out' your file and work locally on your own computer.

When you check out your company file, MYOB locks the version of the file that's currently living in the cloud and prevents this version from being changed by others. For example, if I decide to check out my company file onto my local computer because I'm travelling, my admin assistant is still able to log on from her computer and view data (looking up customer details or whatever). However, because the file is locked, she can't make any changes or add any transactions.

To check out your company file, here's what to do:

1. **Go to the green menu in the bottom-right corner, which should show Online as the status.**

2. **Select Work Offline (Check Out).**

   You get a message saying that when you check out, the company file that's online is going to become read-only. This is fine.

3. **Click Check Out.**

   Wait while MYOB does its stuff. If you have a really large company file, or you've never synchronised your company file, checking out can take a few minutes.

4. **All done? Observe how the words in the bottom-right now say Offline (Checked Out).**

   The band of colour in the bottom-right also changes from sea-green to a tranquil burnt-orange colour.

Can you spot the difference between checking out and synchronising? (I talk about synchronising a little earlier in this chapter, in 'Syncing your file (and other excellent ideas)'. With *checking out*, MYOB not only makes a copy of your company file on your local machine but also changes the copy that lives in the cloud to a read-only version. With *synchronising*, MYOB makes a copy of your company file on your local machine but the copy that lives in the cloud is unchanged, and remains the 'live' version that you, or anyone else, can use.

Checking in (shifting your file online)

In the previous section, I explain how you can check out your company file so that you can continue working offline. When you're ready to work online again, checking in is easy:

1. **Go to the orange menu in the bottom-right corner, which should have the words Offline (Checked Out).**

2. **Select Work Online (Check In).**

   You get a message saying that when you check in, the online company file is going to be updated with the changes you've made offline. All good.

3. **Click Check In.**

   Because upload speeds are slower than download speeds, the process of checking in usually takes longer than the process of checking out.

4. **See how the words in the bottom-right now say Online.**

Before you start uploading your company file, make sure you're using a reliable internet connection. If you have poor upload speeds (MYOB defines 'poor' as being less than 0.5 Mbps) or you have intermittent dropouts caused by wireless connections, the upload can end up taking forever or simply not work at all.

Not sure what your upload speed is? Run your own mini-athletics trial and test your upload speed at www.speedtest.net. And if you're not a city dweller and suffer the kind of connection that I do, write a seething letter of protest to your nearest politician while you're at it.

Making a read-only copy

Imagine you know you're going to be without the internet but you want to make a copy of your file so you can look up information and generate reports. However, you don't want to check out your file, because others need to keep working.

The solution in this scenario is to view a read-only copy. To do so, go to your list of recently opened files (as per Figure 16-1), right-click the company name you want to view, and select View a Read-Only Copy (Offline). *Note:* Opening a read-only copy in this way is only possible if you have already synchronised your company file.

Aaargh! A tortoise could go faster

I'm going to call a spade a spade: When MYOB released the 'new generation' of AccountRight in 2011, the speed (or lack of) was a disgrace. For the first time ever, I had clients ringing me up asking how they could downgrade, and revert to the old version.

Fortunately, with every new update, things run a little faster, and at the time of writing (early 2015), AccountRight buzzes along at a completely acceptable pace. However, I still come across people with issues regarding speed, particularly those people who work exclusively in the cloud.

So, if you find you can make a pot of tea in the time it takes to record a transaction, I suggest you take action:

✔ **Have you downloaded the latest version?** For example, version 2014.9 is light years faster than version 2011.1. (To check which version you're using, open up MYOB and select About MYOB AccountRight from the Help menu.)

✔ **Have you added an exception for MYOB to your anti-virus software?** Refer to 'Adding an exception to your virus software' earlier in this chapter for more details.

✔ **Is your internet connection slow as a wet week?** For two people using the same connection, the tech guys at MYOB say that a stable 1 Mbps for both upload and download speeds is the minimum. Of course, if you are doing a bunch of other things online at the same time this speed may still not cut the mustard.

✔ **Is your computer up to the job?** Don't even try to leave home without at least 4 MB of RAM and 2.1 GHz of processing power.

> ✔ **Have you checked for viruses or malware?** If your computer is running slow generally, not just with MYOB, you may have a problem virus or some malware.
>
> ✔ **Do you have enough free disk space on your computer?** Whatever the capacity of your hard drive, you should always have at least 10 per cent of this capacity as free space.

If you do all of these things, and find that the MYOB still runs too slowly when in the cloud, you may need to accept defeat and shift your company file out of the cloud again.

Oh no! The internet is down

Earlier in this chapter I talk about synchronising your company file so that even when you work in the cloud, you always have a local copy. What this means is that you can still view your data even when the internet goes down.

Using my fictitious buddy Tim, here's how this whole concept works in real life:

1. **Tim has his company file stored in the cloud. He's happily working away, analysing sales reports, when a thunderstorm strikes and the internet goes down.**

2. **Tim cusses only briefly, then goes to his list of recently opened files, right-clicks on his company file and selects View a Read-Only Copy (Offline).**

   Tim grizzles a little because he has to work on a read-only copy and can't record any new customer invoices, but he accepts his fate with relative good grace.

   Note that Tim can only open a read-only copy because he synchronises his data. (Refer to 'Syncing your file (and other excellent ideas)' earlier in this chapter.)

3. **The power eventually returns, Tim logs back on as normal, and continues with his work.**

Are you reading my contemporary fable wondering what if Tim wasn't happy with working on a read-only copy? Maybe it's Christmas Eve and Tim has to pay 15 hungry employees by the late afternoon.

Isn't the whole point of having a synchronised copy that you can work on this file if you need to? The answer is both yes and no. To work on a synchronised file, Tim would first need to open a read-only copy, back up this file locally, restore this file locally, and then inform any other people who normally work on his company file that they can't do any work in MYOB. Then later, when the internet came back on, he would have to restore his company file online. This whole process is fairly tricky for ordinary mortals without IT geek credentials, and may indeed be too hard for Tim.

So my answer to Tim, if he absolutely had to record transactions in MYOB, would be to go find an internet connection that's working, whether this means using the wi-fi at a local cafe, tethering to his smartphone or calling in favours with a friend. Tim could use the connection just for long enough to check out his file (refer to 'Checking out (shifting your file offline)' earlier in this chapter), and then continue working offline until the internet returned.

Backing Up Is Easy (You Just Have to Do It)

What does all this talk about backing up mean? Put simply, you create a backup when you make an extra copy of your business data and store the copy somewhere other than on your computer, usually on a USB stick, CD, external hard drive or in an online location. This extra copy is important in the event that something happens to your computer, such as a corrupted hard drive, a lightning strike, fire or theft.

Deciding how often to back up

How often should you back up?

- If you work locally (that is, not in the cloud), you should back up every time you do more than a couple of hours' work on your accounts.
- If you work in the cloud, you only really need to back up at the end of financial year, or if you need a point-in-time backup. For more info, see 'Backing up when in the cloud', later in this chapter.

To receive a backup reminder every time you quit out of your company file, go to Setup⇨Preferences, go to the Security tab and click Prompt for Data Backup When Closing.

Doing the deed

So you want to back up your company file? What an excellent idea. Here's how:

1. **Choose File from the top menu bar and then select Back Up.**

   I'm assuming you have your company file open at this point. If not, open up your company file without another moment's delay.

2. **Think about where you want to store your backup, changing the drive or folder location if necessary.**

   For me, desirable locations include Scotland, the Australian outback and Cuba. Sadly, my computer offers no such exotic locations, so I'm left with the more mundane decision of which drive or folder to select.

   On my computer, my CD drive shows as the D: drive and any external hard drives show up as the E: drive or F: drive. I've also set up Dropbox (which is an online location) so that Dropbox appears as a folder on my hard drive, as per Figure 16-5. (I suggest that if you want to store your backup on a CD or a USB drive, you're best to back up to a folder on your hard drive first, and then copy this backup file from the hard drive to the CD or USB.)

   Always choose a drive or online location different to the location where you currently store your company file.

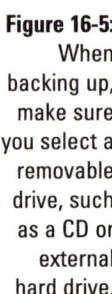

Figure 16-5:
When backing up, make sure you select a removable drive, such as a CD or external hard drive.

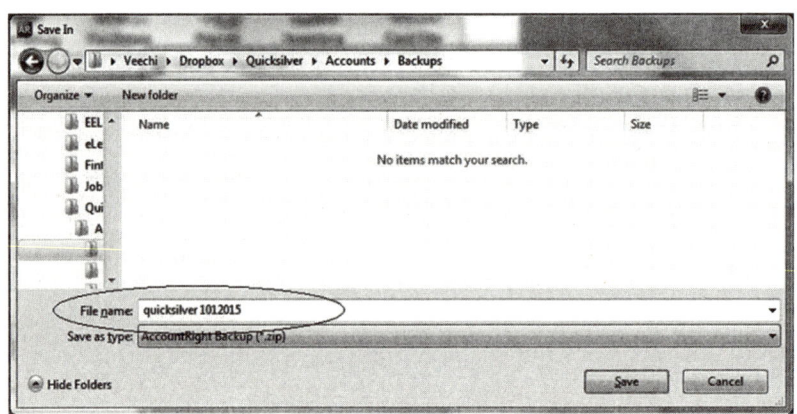

3. Check the file name, clicking Save to change this name if necessary.

The file name that comes up automatically is always something like MYOB12302015.zip. The numbers stand for the date in a warped, back-to-front kind of way (for example, 1230 stands for 30 December) and the extension 'zip' means that your information is compressed so that it takes up the least room possible. Usually, this file name is fine and you can leave it as is.

If you're backing up more than one company file, change the file name so that it includes the company name, as I do in Figure 16-5. Otherwise, when you back up more than one company file on the same backup drive, each new backup overrides the one you did last.

4. Add a password (optional).

You can add a password to protect this backup in case it falls into the hands of industrial pirates, aggrieved employees or rampant garden pixies. I confess to not being entirely convinced about the necessity of adding this additional password, because most people already have a password for opening their company file.

5. Click Back Up.

You know the deed is done when you return to your regular MYOB command centre.

6. Check that the file actually copied into your backup folder.

I always like to go into My Computer and check that the file is sitting on my backup drive.

7. If your backup is a physical backup (as opposed to being stored online using a service such as Dropbox), label your backup and store it in a cool, dry place away from the office.

If you want your backup to live a full and healthy life, don't store CDs or flash drives on the dashboard of your car, underneath the rabbit cage or, worse still, on top of the computer. Take backups away from the office and put them somewhere they won't be disturbed.

Backing up when in the cloud

If you store your company file in the cloud, you may wonder why you should even bother backing up. After all, part of the benefit of working in the cloud is that MYOB as a company takes the responsibility for ensuring that your data is as safe as Fort Knox, held with top security protocols by Microsoft Azure (Microsoft's cloud application platform).

Truth or dare

If you're making an archival backup (such as an end-of-year backup), consider writing your password on the backup label (or, if storing your file online, incorporating the password into the filename). That way, if you need to restore this backup several years later, maybe in the event of an audit, you won't be scratching your head trying to remember what password you used all those years ago.

Even if you're working in the cloud, I still reckon it pays to keep a local backup of your data in a couple of situations, as follows:

✔ **Every time you import data:** If you're importing data such as new items, customer lists or price updates, backing up beforehand is crucial. (Why? Importing data can be a risky business, and if you accidentally mismatch the mapping of data, you can easily do a lot of damage to a company file in a matter of seconds.)

✔ **Before you start a new financial year:** Sure, the latest versions of MYOB no longer purge data when you start a new financial year, but I like to keep an archival record of my data nonetheless, labelling each year and storing the backup in a safe place for seven years. (Also, you can only generate reports for the most recent three years, regardless of how many years' worth of data is stored in your company file.)

Backing up in this way is what you call a *point-in-time backup*, where you capture a snapshot of your company file at a certain point in time. However, other than in the special situations outlined in the preceding list, when you store your company file in the cloud, and so long as you synchronise your data regularly, you don't need to worry about creating a backup routine.

Storing your backups — no fibs now

Okay, tell me truthfully: Where do you store your backups? If your answer is that you store them in the office somewhere (or if you work from home, they're in the house somewhere), then my reply to you is that you may as well not bother making backups. Why? Because if you store your backups anywhere near the computer, and you're not working in the cloud, you're not protected against fire or theft.

If your company file is stored on your office computer (as opposed to being located in the cloud), you must take your backups off-site, away from where you work. If you work from a home office, ask a close relative or friend to store your backups. If you're based in a regular office, take your backups home, ideally every night.

If you find that despite your best intentions, you don't manage to get it together to take your backups offsite, I suggest you consider shifting your company file to the cloud and working online.

Resurrecting Data

From time to time, you may want to retrieve a backup — maybe you've had a computer disaster, or maybe you want to look at data from a previous financial year. When restoring data, you want to be careful you don't overwrite your current data unless you're absolutely sure that the data you're restoring is the information you need.

I explain how to restore a backup in the following section. Then — because I'm nothing if not a realist — I leap to your aid and tell you what to do if restoring your file fails.

Restoring your company file

It may be that you never worry about using the backup or restore commands, and that to back up, you simply copy your company file onto an external drive using My Computer. This way of working is just fine, and means you don't have to do anything special in order to 'restore' your data. If you need to restore data, you can simply drag your copy from the external drive back onto your computer.

However, if you choose to back up using the special backup commands in MYOB, you have to use a specific restore routine in order to bring your data back to life. Here's how:

1. **Fire up your MYOB application.**

2. **From the Welcome window, click the link to Restore a Backup File.**

   Can't see this command? Look for the underlined words in a small, pale-grey font at the bottom of this window.

3. **Click Browse to navigate to the drive where your backup is stored and click Open.**

Unless you renamed your backup file when you saved it, your backup will be called something like 'MYOB' followed by the date, with the date in back-to-front US-format, with the month first, followed by the day. For example, if you made a backup on 12 December 2014, the name of your file would be 'MYOB12012014', as seen in Figure 16-6.

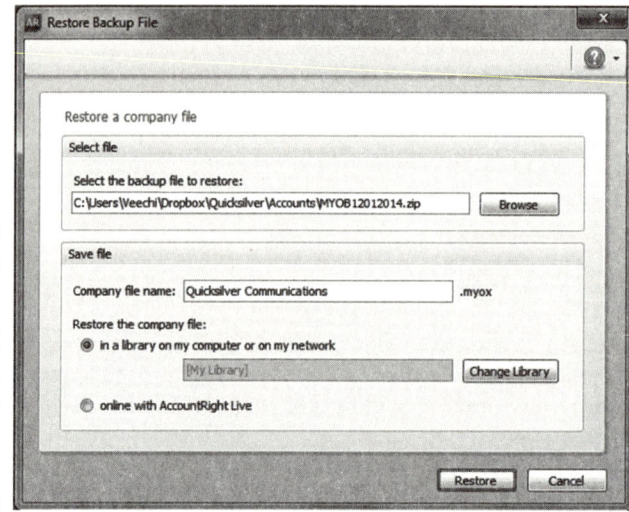

Figure 16-6:
Not keen
on living
dangerously?
Then choose
the location of
your restored
file carefully.

4. **If prompted, enter a password.**

When you backed up this file, you may have been asked if you wanted to protect the file with a password. If you did so, now you have to enter this password in order to retrieve your data.

Unless you consciously named it so, the backup-protection password isn't the same as the password you use to log into MYOB. (Incidentally, this potential for confusion is just one of the reasons I don't usually bother adding additional passwords to backups.)

5. **Change the name for this restored file in the Company File Name field.**

This step is important. If the company file you're restoring already exists on this computer (which it will, unless you're restoring the backup onto a completely new computer), I strongly suggest you change the company file name. (If you don't change the file name, your restored file will overwrite the existing file, which may be ultimately what you want to do. However, until you actually restore your backup, you can't be sure it's the file that you need.)

I usually simply add the current date to the name of the file. For example, if my company file is called 'Dream Gardens' and I'm restoring a file on 31 May, I name my restored file 'Dream Gardens 31 May'.

When you restore an online backup, you don't have the option to change the company file name — MYOB simply replaces the current online company file with the backup file you're restoring and all changes made to the online file since that backup was taken will be lost. Be super careful at this point: Are you absolutely sure you want to overwrite the current file that's online? If you're at all unsure, make a fresh backup of your online company file first.

6. **Choose whether you want to restore your file to a library on your computer or whether you want to restore your file online, into the cloud.**

You can only restore a backup file to the cloud if the backup was taken from the same company file when it was already online. This rule may seem restrictive at first but in actual fact prevents you from getting yourself into a dreadful pickle.

7. **Click Restore followed by your login details, and then click OK.**

Depending on whether you're restoring to a local drive or to the cloud, this process can take anywhere from a few seconds to several minutes.

8. **Open your restored file and check that everything is cool.**

Whenever I restore a backup, I like to browse through a few transactions to make sure I have the right file.

Panic! The black hole beckons

So, your computer died, you've tried to restore a file from the backup and, for one reason or another, the restore process didn't work. Or maybe — could this possibly be true? — you never had a backup in the first place.

Stay cool — you don't need to flee into exile quite yet. A few things you can try before packing your suitcase include:

- ✔ **Search for a backup.** Even if you think you may have no other backups, dig around for one that you or someone else may have made in the past. Even if they're a couple of months old (the backups, not your co-workers), they're better than nothing.

- ✔ **Call the MYOB Technical Support team.** If you think your backup is alright, but you can't get your head around how to restore your file — I can't imagine how this could be the case after you've read my flawless instructions — phone MYOB Tech Support and get them to walk you through the process, step by step.

- ✔ **Look on your hard drive.** It's possible that either you or someone else has accidentally backed up onto your hard drive sometime in the past. Go to My Computer and do a search for all files that end in the letters 'myo', 'myox' or 'zip'.

- ✔ **Fix the original cause of the error message.** If you were restoring a backup because your existing file had come up with error messages, and your restore hasn't worked, it's possible that the MYOB Company File Repair team can repair your file (for a modest charge, of course). Call 1300 555 123 for help.

✔ **Look for your most recent synchronised file.** If you used to store your company file in the cloud previously, have a look to see if you have a synchronised file on your hard drive. Search on files ending with the letters 'sync'.

Unintelligible scary messages

So everything is going along swimmingly. You have money in the bank, the weather is glorious, even your relationship is kind of okay at the moment. And then one day, you go to open your MYOB company file and you get one of those really scary but completely incomprehensible error messages. (What were those programmers thinking? As if terms such as 'error -47', 'missing chain' or 'index 32' mean anything to ordinary mortals like you and me.)

Sometimes, error messages appear out of the blue and then disappear like a stranger in the night, never to be seen again. Sometimes, however, error messages persist, causing problems when opening files or generating reports. What should you do?

If you subscribe to MYOB Technical Support or MYOB Cover, your easiest solution is to call the support phone number. (Why struggle when there's an expert waiting to help?) Alternatively, go to Google (or any other search engine) and type in the error message, word for word. I almost always find a forum or a helpful website with info about the error, and what to do about it.

Chapter 17

Understanding Your Business

- -

In This Chapter

▶ Analysing how profitable you are, day by day and month by month

▶ Tracking jobs and projects to find out how profitable they are

▶ Managing your finances better with budgets and cashflows

- -

*B*efore accounting software gave people the ability to analyse information with such ease, many businesses led a precarious existence where optimism and intuition played a bigger part than the analysis of facts and figures. To some extent this still happens, especially in smaller businesses.

Without information at their fingertips, many businesses operate in the dark. For example, a builder knows that only some jobs make money, but he's not sure which ones; a hairdresser suspects that one of her branches is profitable, while the other isn't; and a guesthouse owner wonders whether the expenses from the restaurant eat into the profits made by accommodation.

What if you could switch the light on? If the builder knew for certain which jobs brought in the money, he'd probably be more selective with his clients; if the hairdresser could see just how much she was losing in her second shop, she'd probably close it down; and if the guesthouse owner could really analyse the restaurant figures, he'd make some big changes, and quick.

Fortunately, MYOB gives you the ability to cast as much light on any situation that you could ever wish for. In this chapter, I explain how you can use MYOB to analyse where you make money, and where you don't.

Understanding Financial Statements

In this chapter, I explain how to generate Profit & Loss reports and Balance Sheet reports using MYOB. I don't have the space in this book to explain how to interpret and understand these reports, but if you do want to explore this topic in more detail, I suggest you get hold of a copy of *Bookkeeping For Dummies*, 2nd Australian and New Zealand Edition, written by my good self and published by Wiley Publishing Australia.

Checking out your bottom line

I'm always amazed at the number of clients who work on their books for hours every week without taking the time to generate financial reports. In this next section, I show you three easy ways to view your Profit & Loss report.

Grab a business insight

The easiest way to analyse your profitability quickly is to go to your Business Insights menu (on the bottom-right corner of all windows) and select Profitability Details. You arrive at a four-panel profitability analysis (as shown in Figure 17-1), where you can see the following:

- ✔ Total income and expenses, month by month, as a bar chart
- ✔ Profit margins on all the items you sell
- ✔ Cumulative income, expenses and profit, as a line graph
- ✔ Your top 10 expenses

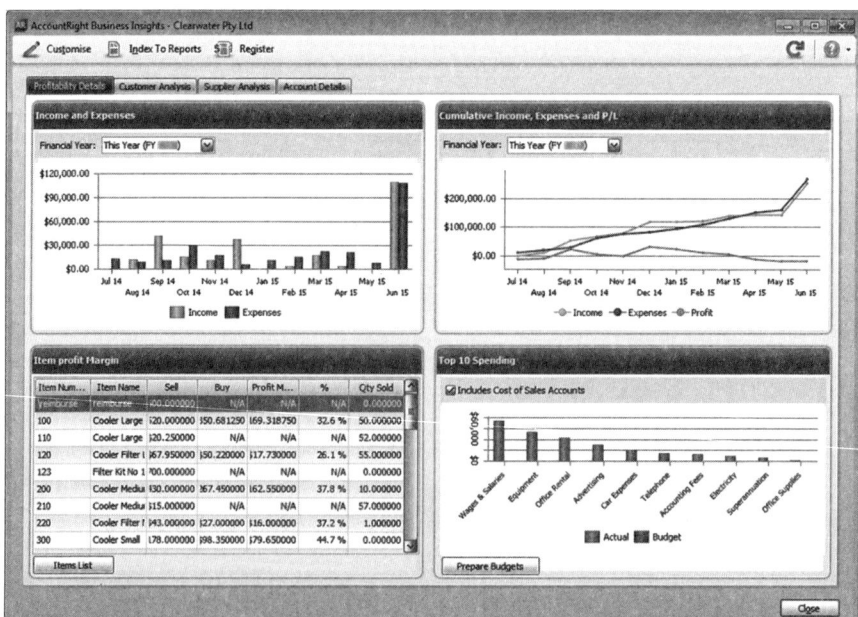

Figure 17-1: Analyse your business performance, month-by-month.

I also like to click the Customer Analysis and Supplier Analysis tabs, and check out the following:

✔ Aged receivables, showing how much customers owe me

✔ Aged payables, showing how much I owe to suppliers

Although you can't manipulate the graphs in the Profitability Analysis, what you can do is right-click on any of the four images and save the image as a jpg file. You can then insert the image into management reports.

Also, if you find that your data relates to last financial year and not to your current year, all this means is that you haven't started a new financial year yet. You can find out more about starting a new financial year in Chapter 20.

Go digging for the detail

For more detail or specific date ranges, I make my way to the main Reports menu and click the Accounts tab:

✔ The simple Profit & Loss Statement shows how much you sold and how much you purchased for any date range. For a less detailed report, go to your Report Filters and as the Report Level select Level 2 or Level 3.

✔ The Profit & Loss [Cash] report is similar to the standard Profit & Loss Statement report, except the income only shows up on this report when you get paid and, likewise, expenses only appear when you part with the cash. I use this report if I'm wondering why I've got no cash (a perennial event), but my Profit & Loss Statement shows a profit. (Can't find this report? Look under the Small Business Entity heading in the Accounts tab of your Reports menu.)

✔ The Profit & Loss [With Year to Date] report shows how your business is faring for any date range and compares these figures with the year so far.

✔ The Profit & Loss [Multi-Period] report is great for sending into Excel. Click Customise to select a whole year as your reporting period, display this report to screen, and then select Export followed by Excel from the blue drop-down menu in the top-left corner. Your monthly income and expense figures appear in Excel, with the figures for each month listed in a separate column, making an ideal starting point for budgets or cashflow reports.

✔ The Profit & Loss [Last Year Analysis] report compares how you're doing this year with how you did last year. I like to highlight a few months at a time to make this report more meaningful.

If you're responsible for reporting to management or a board of directors, make sure your Profit & Loss report is as smart as can be by adding logos, changing colours and inserting comments. I explain these reporting features in detail in Chapter 14.

Giving your Balance Sheet a health check

Think of your Profit & Loss as a story of what goes on in your business over any period of time, and your Balance Sheet as a photograph. A Balance Sheet is really a picture of how much you own and how much you owe at any point in time, and the difference between how much you own and how much you owe is your stake in the business. (The Americans love to call this your net worth, but personally I prefer to calculate my net worth using other values as a yardstick.)

Even though most people find Balance Sheets hard to understand, that doesn't mean they're not really important. A Balance Sheet is the first report I look at when I want to check out if the Profit & Loss reports are accurate, because this is where mistakes are easiest to spot. In other words, if you want to be able to rely on your Profit & Loss reports, you have to be sure your Balance Sheet is correct.

You can find the standard Balance Sheet report on the Accounts tab of your Reports menu. I usually select the last day of the reporting period I selected when generating my Profit & Loss as the date. To check that your Balance Sheet makes sense, work through the following points:

✔ Ask yourself whether every single line on your Balance Sheet makes sense. A simple idea, but it works.

✔ Check that every bank account shows the right balance. Savings, credit card and loan accounts are the most prone to neglect, so check the amount showing on the Balance Sheet against the latest bank statements.

✔ Consider the balances of your fixed assets. Do they make sense? Perhaps you have an old bomb that barely scrapes through rego, but Motor Vehicles shows up as a $50,000 asset in your Balance Sheet. In this case, something has gone astray.

✔ All accumulated depreciation accounts should be minus figures. They're not? Something is definitely crook.

✔ All liability accounts should be positive figures. They're not? Again, something is almost certainly wrong. (GST Paid on Purchases is an exception to this rule!)

✔ Your Historical Balancing account should always be zero.

Seeing Where the Money's Made

One of the fascinating facts about small businesses is that so many of them are really a collection of businesses bundled under the one name — like the newsagency that doubles as a post office and dry-cleaning agent, or the handyman who fixes your cupboard doors and also mows the lawn. The secret of success in these kinds of businesses is to find out which part of the business is bringing in the dough, and how much profit it's making.

MYOB's ability to help you find out where your business is making money is one of its best-kept secrets. It's a cinch! You simply use the Jobs List.

The Jobs List can be used for lots of different things: Cost centres, profit centres, projects, ventures, locations or any other identifiable arm of your business. I talk lots about this in the following sections.

Finding out how jobs work

Every transaction you record includes the following information:

- **A name:** The name of the customer, supplier or employee.

- **An allocation account.** This information is an account number or name in your Accounts List and refers to the type of income or type of expense it is. A payment for electricity may be allocated to Electricity Expense, and a payment for rent may be allocated to Rent Expense.

- **A job (optional).** Ah, here we are! This is where you can record a job code, if you like, selecting what part of your business (whether it's a project, a location or an arm of your business) this income or expense belongs to.

- **A tax code.** Select the GST code that applies.

The Spend Money window shown in Figure 17-2 illustrates how you refer to jobs when recording a transaction (you can see that the job code for this transaction is 'Sinclair' and the Memo reads as 'Special drill hire for Sinclair Crescent job'. In addition, the Card field shows the name of the supplier, the Account Name field shows the type of expense it is, and the Tax column shows the tax code.

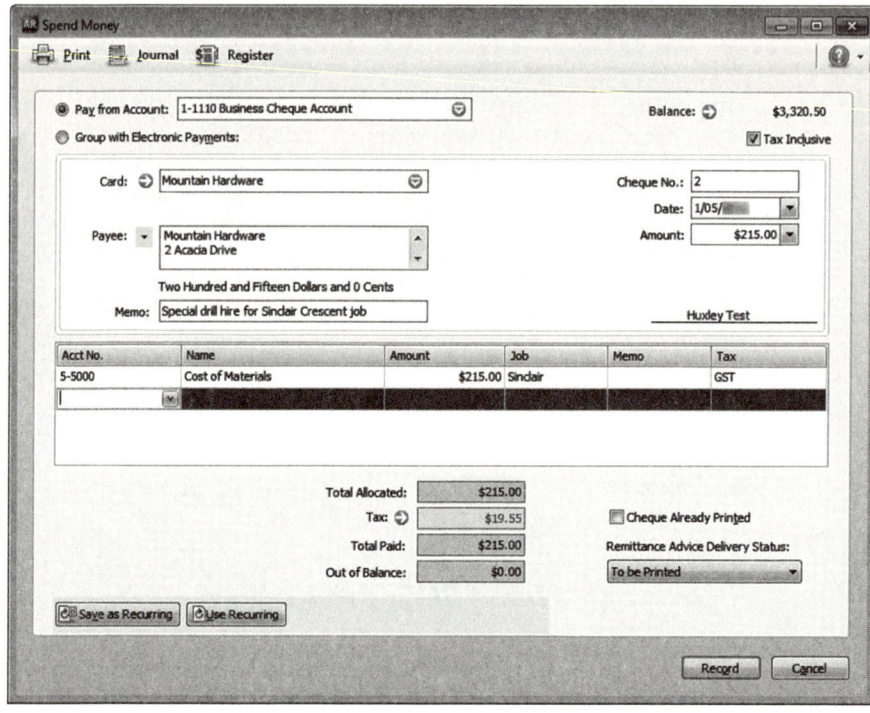

Figure 17-2:
Use the
Jobs
feature to
track where
you make a
profit.

Figuring out how job reporting can work for you

Make yourself a drink, sit back and have a think about how your business could use the jobs feature in MYOB. Contemplate the different projects you do, and consider whether your business is made up of different enterprises.

In case all this navel gazing doesn't make sense to you, here are a few of my own examples, which show how I've set up jobs for different clients:

✔ One client has a guesthouse that offers both accommodation and dining facilities. All accommodation income and expenses are given the job code A and all dining income and expenses are given the job code D. This allows my client to produce a monthly Profit & Loss for the accommodation business, a Profit & Loss for the restaurant and a Profit & Loss for the combination of both.

✔ A hairdresser friend has two salons in different suburbs of Sydney — one in Paddington and one in Rose Bay. She codes the income and expenses from each salon with a different job code

(P for Paddington and R for Rose Bay) so that she can print a Profit & Loss for each salon separately, as well as a Profit & Loss for the two salons combined.

✔ My neighbour is a builder who builds several houses every year. He creates a new job code for every house and codes all income and expenses with these codes. This allows my neighbour to see how much profit (or sometimes how much loss) he makes on each house.

When working with jobs, the reports you rely on are the Jobs Profit & Loss reports tucked away on the Accounts tab of the Reports menu. Another place to look up job info on the run is to go to your Lists menu and click Jobs.

Creating a new job

After you've got your head around jobs and how they work, you're ripe to create your first new job. Here's how:

1. **From the main menu, choose Lists⇨Jobs, and then click New.**

2. **Decide whether the job is a Header Job or a Detail Job.**

   Header jobs are the headings under which detail jobs are grouped. For example, a builder may have a header job called Renovations. Then, under Renovations, he lists separate detail jobs for each renovation job that he's doing.

3. **Enter a Job Number and, if desired, select a header job in the Sub Job field.**

   If you only have a few jobs, avoid using numbers — use letters of the alphabet instead. Numbers are hard to remember and you're more likely to make a mistake with them. I like to make job numbers short (a single letter is often fine), because the fewer keyboard strokes I have to type the better.

   If you want this job to sit under a particular header, select its header in the Sub-job field.

4. **Insert a Job Name.**

   Enter the name of the job in the Job Name field. This may be the name of a job, a project, a location or an arm of the business.

5. **Optional: Enter a Job Description and a Contact.**

   These two fields are entirely optional and to be honest, hardly ever useful. Feel free to ignore them!

6. **Optional: If you've already started the job, enter the Percent Complete.**

   Another optional field, the Percent Complete box is only meaningful if you want to enter budgets for this job and track actuals against budgets as the job progresses. Entirely up to you.

7. **Fill in some other fairly unnecessary details (again, optional).**

   If you're feeling incredibly enthusiastic, complete the Start Date, Finish Date and name of the Manager. (I usually find most businesses are too busy doing the job to spend time recording all these details.)

8. **If you want to track expenses for reimbursement, complete the Linked Customer field.**

   If you're likely to incur job-related expenses that you want to on-bill to a particular customer, you need to specify the customer's name in the Linked Customer field. You also need to click the Track Reimbursables check box in the top-right corner of the New Job window.

9. **Click OK.**

   This adds the job to your Jobs List, as shown in Figure 17-3 — my, that was quick!

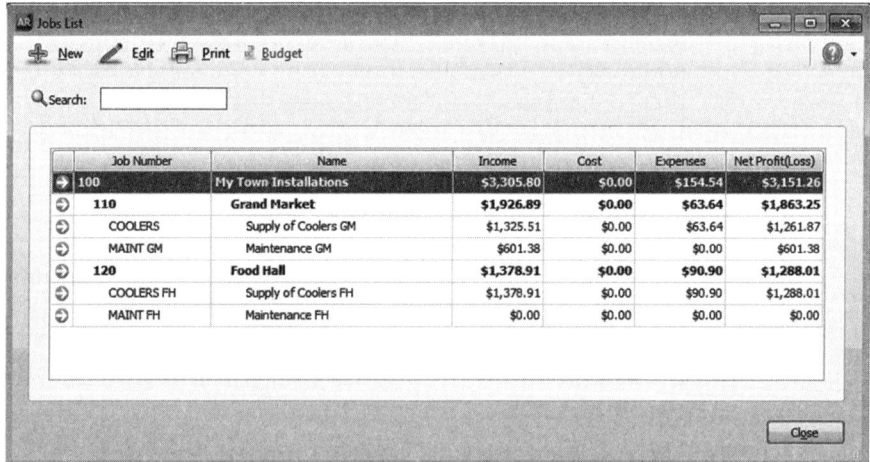

Figure 17-3:
A completed
Jobs List.

Did you know you can sort your Jobs List in any manner you like? For example, to sort by Job Name, click the Name column label. Or, to sort according to income — with the job that generates most income listed first — click the Income column label.

What's that thingy?

When you're working with jobs, sooner or later you'll come across expenses that are difficult to allocate to any one particular job. Things such as accounting fees, bank charges, legal fees, merchant fees and even telephone bills are often hard to pigeonhole. I've got a neat solution to this dilemma: Create an additional job called Admin and use this job for all expenses that don't belong to a particular job. Then, you can generate a Profit & Loss report for each job, as well as a Profit & Loss report that shows all shared overheads.

Getting rid of jobs

Jobs tend to come and go, and from time to time it's good to give your Jobs List a good spring-clean.

Here's how to delete a job:

1. **Go to your Jobs List and double-click the job you want to remove.**

   A dialogue box appears showing information for that particular job.

2. **From the main menu, choose Edit⇨Delete Job.**

   If you still have current transactions relating to this job, a warning may pop up. If you're sure you want to proceed, ignore the warning and continue.

3. **Gloat!**

   Incidentally, you can exclude finished jobs from your Jobs List report, without having to delete these jobs from your Jobs List. Just enter 100% in the Percent Complete field in the Job Information window for finished jobs and then click Exclude 100% Complete Jobs in the report filters.

Setting up job budgets

When you get the hang of how jobs work, you'll probably want to set up job budgets so that you can ensure everything stays on track.

To set up a job budget, go to your Jobs List, highlight the job in question and then click the Budget button. A list of all income, cost of goods sold and

Where categories fit into the picture

If you have several business divisions, you may prefer to analyse your cost centres using categories rather than jobs.

Categories work in almost the same way as jobs, but with two important differences. The first difference (and here's the good news) is that you can generate a Balance Sheet report for each category (which you can't do for jobs), making categories ideal for businesses with distinct divisions. The second difference (and this is the bad news) is that you can't split a single transaction across more than one category, whereas you can split a single transaction across several jobs.

So, if your business has individual payments that need to be split across more than one cost centre, you're better off using jobs to analyse your cost centres, rather than categories. On the other hand, if you have separate bank accounts and business divisions that operate relatively independently, category tracking is your best bet.

To switch on category tracking and see how it works, go to your Setup menu, select Preferences and click the System tab. Tick the option to Turn On Category Tracking and select Required if you want it to be compulsory for every single transaction to have a category allocated to it. Finally, go to your Lists menu, select Categories and click New to create your category names.

---

expense accounts appears on your screen. (By the way, you can't set up budgets for header jobs, only for detail jobs.) Work your way down the list of accounts, entering income and expense budgets one by one.

After you've set up your job budgets, you're ready to produce some reports. One of the reports I find really handy is the Jobs [Budget Analysis] report, which you can find under the Accounts tab in your Reports menu. However, for this report to make any sense, you must first specify the Percent Complete for the job. To do this, go first to your Jobs List, edit the job in question and change the Percent Complete field there.

Here's where a trick of the trade comes in. To generate a budget report that shows how much you've spent on the job so far and compare this against what you budgeted for the job in total, enter 100% as the Percent Complete, regardless of how far along the job actually is.

Budgeting for jobs by the month or by the year

One drawback with job budget features is that you can only set up budgets for the entire duration of a job, meaning that you can't set up monthly or annual budgets. For builders who use jobs for single one-off projects, this limitation isn't a problem. However, if you use jobs for cost centres, locations or departments, then this limitation renders the job budget features within MYOB virtually useless.

If you do lots of work with jobs and job budgets, your best bet is to purchase an add-on product called Calxa. With Calxa, you can create monthly or yearly budgets for each job, copy budgets from one job to another, generate a current budget automatically using last year's actuals as a basis, and lots of other stuff. I've used Calxa for a couple of my clients and have been delighted with how quickly and easily my clients are able to create and review their budgets. Visit www.calxa.com.au to find out more.

Working with Budgets and Cashflows

Part of getting intimate with your financials is deciding what you want the figures to be (as opposed to just looking at what they are) and figuring out how you're going to get there. In order to do this, you need to get your hands dirty and draw up a few serious budgets — not to mention a cashflow prediction to boot.

Deciding whether it's gruel for dinner tonight

Creating budgets is a piece of cake. Simply go to your Accounts List, highlight the account you want to create a budget for and click the Budgets button. You see a window similar to the one shown in Figure 17-4. Some comments:

✔ Don't forget to select your Financial Year at the top of the Prepare Budgets window. This way, you can keep going with budgets into the next year even if you haven't yet finalised last year's accounts.

✔ For an injection of realism, start the budget preparation process by clicking Copy Previous Year's Actual Data. If you increase an income account or decrease an expense account by more than 10 per cent when compared to last year, you'd better have a really good reason!

✔ If an expense is the same every month (like rent or insurance), save time and click the Copy Amount to Following Months button.

✔ If a few people work in your business, ask for input into the budget. The more involved everyone is, the more realistic the budget.

Remember that some expenses are irregular, such as quarterly electricity bills (rather!) or one-off annual payments. Also, keep an eye out for months with five pay weeks, rather than four. (Usually, if you pay employees weekly, every third month has five pay weeks, not four.)

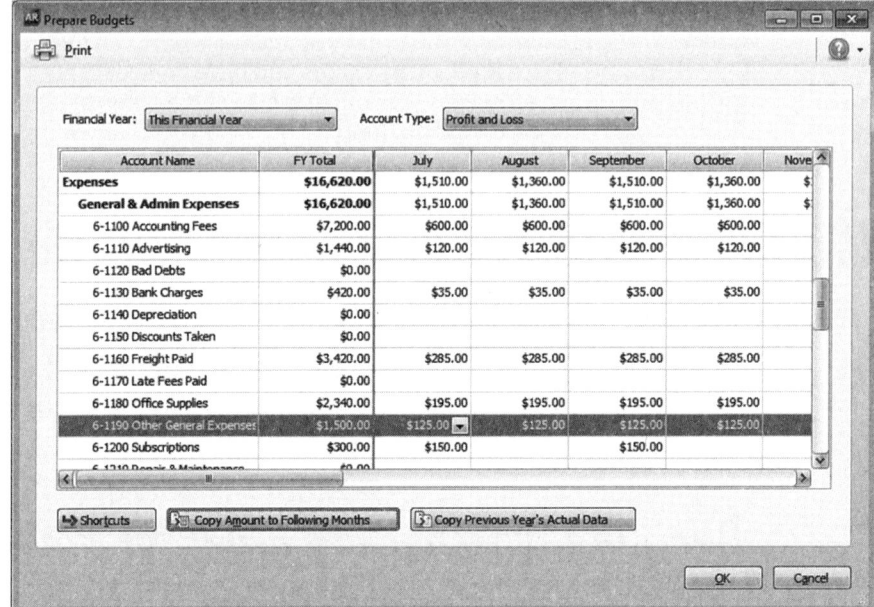

Figure 17-4:
Setting up budgets in your accounts.

Generating cashflow reports

You get two different types of cashflow reports: A statement of cashflow report or a cashflow projection report.

Statement of cashflow reports

A *statement of cashflow* report examines the money that has flowed in and out of a business during the previous financial period (usually the previous year). This report often goes a long way towards explaining the mystery of why a business has a handsome profit but no cash, or vice versa. To view this report, go to the Banking tab of your Reports menu.

Many people think that a cash-based Profit & Loss report does the same job as a statement of cashflow report. Not true. A statement of cashflow includes a lot of information that you don't get on a cash-based Profit & Loss, such as details about bank loans, owner's drawings or new equipment purchases.

Cashflow projection reports

A *cashflow projection* report predicts future cash coming in (not income) and your cash going out over a certain period, and produces a projection of your final bank account balance.

Although budget reports are often very similar to cashflow projections, you may find that for your business, your cash position varies greatly from your profit position. For example, you may make a huge profit just before Christmas (as planned in your budget), but not actually receive the cash until February (as shown in your cashflow).

Although MYOB doesn't have a cashflow projection report, you can create your own by first setting up budgets in MYOB and then sending these budgets to Excel. Here's what to do:

1. **Set up your budgets for all your income and expense accounts.**

   For more details, refer to 'Deciding whether it's gruel for dinner tonight', earlier in this chapter.

2. **Go to the Accounts tab of your Reports menu and highlight the Profit & Loss [Multi-Period Budget] report.**

3. **As the date range, select from the current month up to the end of the financial year.**

4. **Click Export to Excel to view this report in spreadsheet format.**

Now all you have to do is adapt this budget to become a cashflow projection, adding extra lines to the bottom of the report to forecast how much money you'll have left in your bank account at the end of each month, and adding any cash amounts that don't relate to either income or expenses, such as loans, purchases of new equipment or personal drawings.

I make this process sound relatively straightforward but, in fact, creating a cashflow projection report can be a very technical process, depending on the size of your business. If you need more help, I explore cashflow reporting in way more detail in *Creating a Business Plan For Dummies*, published by Wiley Publishing Australia. Alternatively, a great tool that can generate cashflows with a few clicks of the mouse (as opposed to spending hours setting up complex formulas in Excel), and hooks up with MYOB so that you don't have to rekey any data is a product called Calxa. Visit www.calxa.com.au for details.

Chapter 18

Keeping Your Company File in Top Shape

Staying healthy is such an effort sometimes: Working out at the gym, submitting to the dentist's chair, trailing off to the health clinic for one of those gruesome annual checks, keeping tabs on your blood pressure and much more besides. So much to do, so little time.

You have to go through the same healthcare shenanigans with your MYOB company file. In this chapter, I explain how to scan your company file for ailments, administer first aid where required, and keep both MYOB's blood pressure, and your own, under control.

Lining Up for a Health Check

Most of the common disorders that lie dormant in your MYOB company file can be detected by running the Company Data Auditor. To run this nifty little feature, go to the Accounts command centre and click the Company Data Auditor button.

Figure 18-1 shows the Company File Overview window, the first thing you see when you fire up the Company Data Auditor. The Company File Overview focuses on those boring but vital health maintenance activities, such as maintaining current versions, backing up and applying locked periods.

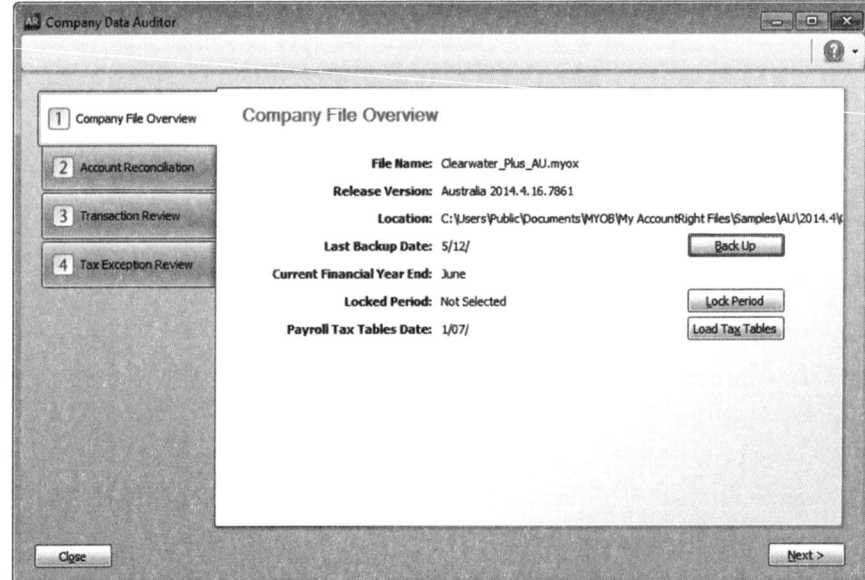

Figure 18-1:
The
Company
File
Overview
window.

If you're managing a business but you aren't the bookkeeper, the Company File Overview enables you to spot-check that your bookkeeper has data and file maintenance under control.

Keep your eyes open for the following:

✔ **Last Backup Date:** Here you see the date you last backed up or, if you've never backed up before (perish the thought), you see the message Never Backed Up. Unless you store your company file in the cloud, if this backup date is more than a week old, it's time to take action. (For more on making backups, refer to Chapter 16.)

Just because the Company File Overview says you've backed up, that doesn't mean you can sleep easy. Unless you store your company file in the cloud, you still need to ensure you've backed up onto an external drive (not onto your hard drive!) and that this backup is stored off-site, away from the office. (And, actually, even if you do store your company file in the cloud, making a regular backup on your local machine provides that extra peace of mind.)

✔ **Locked Periods:** I recommend you lock periods every time you complete a Business Activity Statement, and every time you finalise a financial year. So, if the date shown here harks back to the dinosaur era, or the date displays Not Selected, don't waste a second. Click that Lock Period button and bolt that door.

✔ **Payroll Tax Tables:** Got a bunch of employees? Then the Payroll Tax Tables Date should be the first day of the current financial year. If your tables are out of date, click Load Tax Tables. If the tables are still out of date after you've loaded them, you probably need to upgrade to the latest version. Phone MYOB Customer Service, bare your soul (and your credit card details) and they'll offer a helping hand.

Taking your Temperature: Account Reconciliations

Earlier in this tome (Chapter 9, to be precise), I devote an entire chapter to the scintillating topic of bank reconciliations. Bank reconciliations form the guts of the whole accounting business, because until you're sure all bank accounts balance, you can't rely on a single report.

The second step in the Company Data Auditor (shown in Figure 18-2) checks how recently each bank account was reconciled.

Sometimes the Account Reconciliation Review lists accounts that haven't been reconciled for years. Surprisingly, unreconciled accounts aren't always a problem. In the next couple of sections, I tell you about the different kinds of bank accounts that appear in this review, and explain why some need reconciling and others don't.

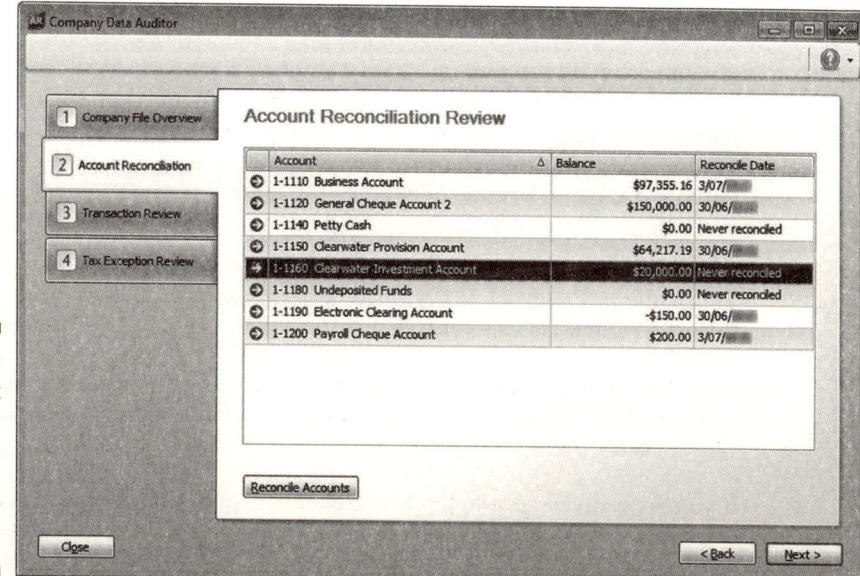

Figure 18-2:
The Account Reconciliation Review forms part of the Company Data Auditor.

Balancing the scales

When you go to the Account Reconciliation Review in the Company Data Auditor, you see a whole list of accounts, along with the dates each one was last reconciled. The most important account in this list is your main business cheque account. Make sure that the listed Reconcile Date falls within the last few weeks. (Even the smallest of businesses shouldn't go more than a month or so without reconciling their business cheque account.)

Other accounts

You also see a few other accounts listed in this Account Reconciliation Review window, not just your business cheque account. Whether these accounts need reconciling depends partly on the nature of the account and on how you structure your business. Read on to find out more.

Undeposited funds

Your undeposited funds account isn't a real bank account. Instead, undeposited funds represent all money you've received but haven't banked yet.

Although you don't need to waste precious time reconciling this account, I recommend you take a moment to double-check that no dead wood has washed up here. Click Prepare Bank Deposit from the Banking command centre, enter the current date and check that no old deposits are listed (say, anything more than a week or two old).

If a deposit is showing its age, show no mercy. Every old deposit is a mistake waiting to cause trouble. Figure out why this deposit was never banked. Maybe you pocketed the cash (oh, sweet cash), or maybe you entered a payment twice? Whatever the source of the problem, fix it now.

Petty cash

In Chapter 6, I suggest either using a petty cash tin or recording petty cash expenses using general journal entries.

If you use a petty cash tin, I suggest you balance the tin every time you top it up. If you don't do this, reconciling the Petty Cash account becomes an unnecessary palaver.

If you record your out-of-pocket expenses using general journal entries, you don't allocate transactions to your Petty Cash account. This means that the balance of your Petty Cash account should always be zero (just like in

Figure 18-2). If it isn't, you've made a mistake somewhere along the line. Go to Find Transactions, select your Petty Cash account and reallocate any transactions sitting in this account.

Investment and savings accounts

My savings accounts are always so pitiful — you know, the 10 cents twice a year kind of scenario — that I don't bother reconciling them so often. At the end of the financial year, though, I record the interest and reconcile the account, all in one hit.

Of course, if things are a little flusher around your way, you probably want to record interest income and reconcile the account every time you get a statement. In Figure 18-2, however, you can see that one savings account has been reconciled (the Clearwater Provision Account) but the other one hasn't been (the Clearwater Investment Account).

The quickest and easiest way to ensure all bank accounts are reconciled and up to date is to sign up for bank feeds for each one. Assuming you have a current MYOB subscription, bank feeds are a free service, regardless of how many accounts you have.

Clearing accounts

What's a clearing account, you ask? Clearing accounts include Payroll Clearing, Electronic Clearing, Cash Drawer and the like. A clearing account isn't a real bank account; rather, it's a holding account where you allocate transactions for a wee while before you shift them to somewhere else.

You know a clearing account is in rude health when its balance shows as zero. If the balance doesn't show as zero, you may have a problem and it may be worth taking the time to try to reconcile this account. (For example, in Figure 18-2, both my Electronic Clearing Account and my Payroll Cheque Account may have issues, because neither account shows a nil balance.)

You reconcile clearing accounts the same way you reconcile any other bank account. Simply go to Reconcile Accounts, select the account number and date, and mark off all cleared transactions. Total deposits should always equal total withdrawals, and the New Statement Balance should always be $0.00.

If this account has never been reconciled, you'll probably discover unreconciled transactions reaching way back to the mists of time. Here's what you can do: Start by marking off all the deposits and withdrawals that cancel each other out, reconciling one week or one month at a time. Ignore any weeks or periods where deposits don't equal the withdrawals.

With this task complete, only the transactions that *don't* balance show up in the Reconcile Accounts window.

Loan accounts

If you choose not to reconcile loan accounts, such as business loans or motor vehicle loans, that's okay. After all, you've got to leave something for your accountant to do. On the other hand, you can save accounting fees and generate more accurate Profit & Loss reports if you do the hard yards and reconcile these loans.

When you make payments against a business loan, I suggest you allocate these transactions directly to the loan account itself (not to Interest Expense). Then, when the loan statement arrives, do a separate journal entry (go to the Accounts command centre and click Record Journal Entry) for each month's interest. Debit Interest Expense and credit the loan account, as shown in Figure 18-3.

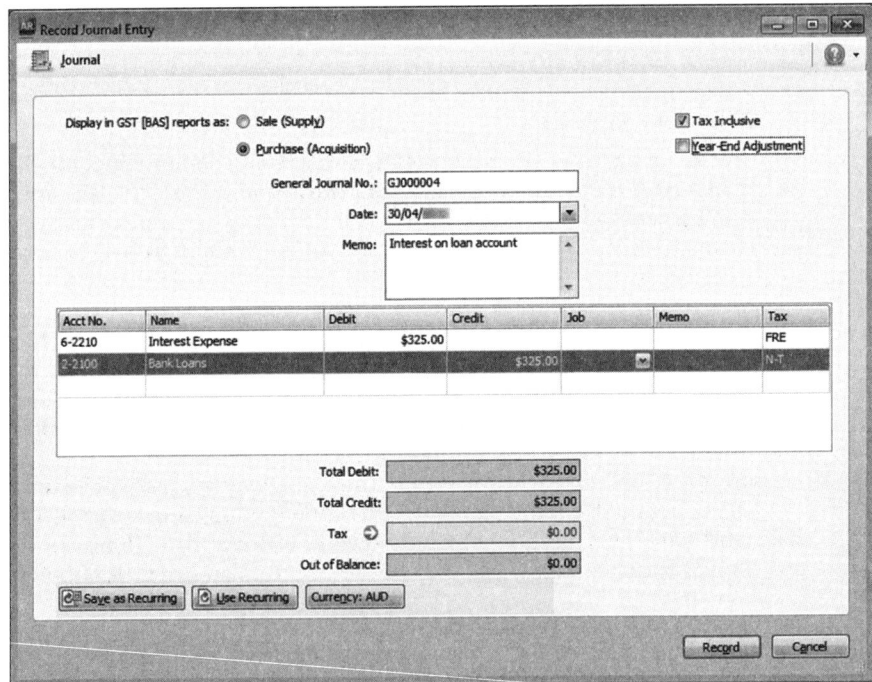

Figure 18-3: Recording interest on loan accounts.

Next, go to Reconcile Accounts, select your loan account, and reconcile this account the same way you reconcile any other bank account.

Hunting for hidden ailments

When I'm giving a company file a thorough once-over, I don't reckon it's enough just to check that the bank reconciliations are up to date. Instead, I go hunting for trouble, double-checking that no bank accounts have any unreconciled transactions more than a couple of months old.

To do this review, click Reconcile Accounts from the Account Reconciliation Review window (within the Company Data Auditor) for every bank account, and enter the current date as the Bank Statement Date. Assuming you've reconciled this account fairly recently, investigate any unreconciled transactions that are more than eight weeks old and figure out why these transactions still haven't cleared. Unreconciled transactions are often duplicated entries — if you enter something twice, the duplicate shows as uncleared.

Going in Deep: The Transaction Review

The third step of your health check is what some accountants call *balancing control accounts*.

To run this review, go to your Company Data Auditor, click Transaction Review and select your date range (the beginning of your current financial year right up to the current date is usually your best bet). Click Run Review. You'll see a column showing either green ticks (meaning all is sweet) or red question marks (meaning it's time to investigate further), similar to Figure 18-4.

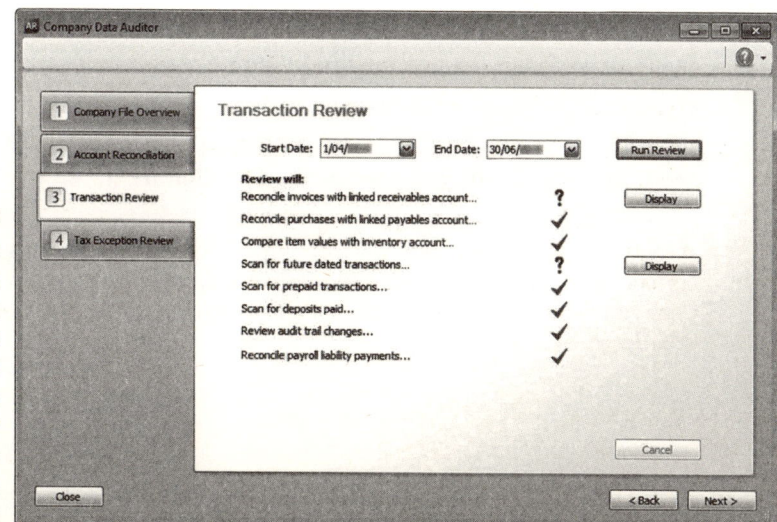

Figure 18-4: The Transaction Review is the third step in the Company Data Auditor.

In the next couple of sections I describe what each error message means and provide some hard-core troubleshooting tactics.

Reconciling invoices and purchases

Within the Transaction Review, the first two reviews reconcile invoices with linked receivables, and purchases with linked payables.

The main culprits that cause receivables or payables not to balance include incorrect opening balances (I explain how to set up opening balances in Chapter 3) or any transactions allocated directly to your Trade Debtors or Trade Creditors accounts. The other possible culprit is a sale or purchase with a payment date that falls before the invoice date.

In this step-by-step guide, I help you diagnose what's causing the out-of-balance malaise and explain how to administer the cure. To keep things simple, this set of instructions explains how to reconcile invoices and receivables. However, if you're troubleshooting payables, you can still follow these instructions, but instead substitute the word 'purchases' for 'sales', the word 'payables' for 'receivables' and the words 'Trade Creditors' for 'Trade Debtors'.

To work through the reconciliation, follow these steps:

1. **Click the Display button next to the red question mark to display your Receivables Reconciliation Exceptions report.**

   I'm assuming that the question mark has appeared next to the first item in your Transaction Review of the Company Data Auditor (the one entitled 'Reconcile Invoices with Linked Receivables').

2. **Look through the list of Possible Causes of Exceptions.**

   If you don't see any exceptions listed here, skip to Step 4.

3. **For every exception listed, drill down into the transaction itself and see if you can identify the problem, and then fix it.**

   Usually, the exception will be a transaction that has been allocated directly to your Trade Debtors account (maybe a spend money transaction, a general journal or a service sale). The solution is to change the allocation account, seeking advice if you're unsure where it should go.

4. **If your receivables are still out of balance, return to your Transaction Review and see whether you have a red question mark next to the item called 'Scan for Prepaid Transactions'.**

   If you do, turn up the heat on this little sweetheart first, because prepaid transactions are often the cause of receivables not balancing. Skip to 'Looking to the future, burying the past', later in this chapter, before going any further.

5. **If your receivables are still out of balance, go to your Reports menu, click the Sales tab, and select the Receivables Reconciliation Summary report.**

6. **As the date Filter, select the first day of your financial year as your Receivables date.**

   If you're not sure which date to choose, go to Setup⇨Company Information, and subtract a year. So, if the Current Financial Year is 2016, enter the first day of July 2015 as your date.

7. **Click Display and confirm that the Out of Balance Amount is nil.**

   If the Out of Balance Amount *isn't* nil, you're up the creek without a paddle, because your problem relates to the previous financial year. My suggested solution? Have a deep-and-meaningful session with your accountant.

8. **Assuming your Out of Balance Amount was nil at the beginning of the financial year, change the date Filter again, but this time move the date forward a month. Run the report again. Repeat this action, moving the date forward a month at a time until an Out of Balance Amount appears.**

   Eyes on the prize? Well done.

9. **Try to narrow this Out of Balance Amount to a particular day of the month.**

   Using elimination and your death-defying powers of logic, keep narrowing down the date until you identify the exact day when the Out of Balance Amount first appeared.

10. **Note down the date that this Out of Balance first appeared as well as the Out of Balance Amount.**

11. **Go to the Find Transactions menu, select your Trade Debtors account and enter the date that things went wrong as both the From and the To date.**

    Usually the offending transaction sticks out like the proverbial dog's you-know-whatsies.

12. **Fix the transaction.**

    Sadly, teleporting myself out of the pages of this book into your office isn't possible, so I can't tell you exactly what to do. However, the problem is almost always that the transaction has been allocated directly to Trade Debtors. The solution is simply to change the allocation account to something else.

13. **Cross your fingers, return to your Receivables Reconciliation Summary report and check that the problem is fixed.**

    It is? Wicked.

14. **Continue displaying your Receivables Reconciliation Summary report, moving forward month by month, right up to the current date.**

    If you encounter other errors, fix them up. Work forward until you arrive at the current date, hopefully with an Out of Balance Amount of zero. You did it!

Giving inventory a clean bill of health

The third step in the Transaction Review (part of the Company Data Auditor) is a sexy little number called Compare Item Values with Inventory Account. If you get a question mark here, grab your stethoscope and take some emergency action:

1. **Click the Display button next to the red question mark.**

   I'm assuming you're already deep in the guts of the Company Data Auditor at this point. Ah, this is so exciting, my pulse is racing at the very thought!

2. **Scroll down to the bottom of this report where, if you're lucky, you see a list of Possible Causes of Exceptions.**

   If you don't see any exceptions listed here, skip to Step 4.

3. **For every exception listed, drill down into the transaction itself and see if you can identify the problem, and then fix it.**

   Most often, the exception is a transaction that has been allocated directly to your Inventory asset account (maybe a cheque, general journal or a service sale). The solution is to change the allocation account, seeking advice if you're unsure where it should go. If the transaction is an item sale or item purchase, double-check the linked account codes for each item listed. (Your inventory account should only ever be used as the Asset Account and never as the Cost of Sales or Income Account.)

4. **After you've dealt with every possible cause of exception, redisplay the report and check that the Out of Balance amount is zero.**

It is? Then your work is done. If it isn't, keep reading …

Troubleshooting inventory when it's sick

So you can't get a green tick for inventory in your Company Data Auditor? Time to give your company file a triple bypass:

1. **Go to the Inventory tab of your Reports menu and display the Inventory Value Reconciliation report, selecting the first day of your financial year as the date.**

2. **If the Out of Balance Amount is nil, breathe a sigh of relief and skip to the next step.**

If the Out of Balance Amount isn't nil, the problem with your inventory relates to last financial year and you should talk to your accountant.

3. **Keep redisplaying the report, moving the date forward a month at a time, until an Out of Balance Amount crops up on the report.**

Aha! You're now one step further to solving the mystery.

4. **Now try to narrow down the date range, and identify the exact date when the Out of Balance Amount first arose.**

For example, if inventory balanced on 1 Aug but didn't on 1 Sept, run the two reports for 5 Aug, 10 Aug, 15 Aug and so on, and using a process of elimination, identify the date when things went astray.

5. **Go to your Find Transactions menu, click the Account tab and enter your Inventory account as the account.**

In the From and To date fields, enter the date when you know the problem arose.

6. **Scan every transaction in your inventory account for that date and see if you can spot the culprit.**

Transactions that cause trouble are purchases or general journals that have your inventory account as the Allocation Account.

7. **Reallocate the transaction, correctly this time.**

If you're not sure how to reallocate a transaction, ask your accountant or allocate it to Historical Balancing (usually 3-9999).

8. **Regenerate the Inventory Value Reconciliation report. Hopefully all is now well!**

Of course, if you have more than one problem in your company file, you may have to continue moving forward, month by month, fixing transactions as you go.

Looking to the future, burying the past

The fourth, fifth and sixth reviews in your Transaction Review (part of the Company Data Auditor) scan for future-dated and prepaid transactions, as well as transactions where deposits have been paid.

Future-dated transactions

This review picks up any transactions with a date later than the End Date you enter in the Transaction Review. Given that you're usually best to select the current date as your End Date, any future-dated transactions that do show up are almost always mistakes, such as someone dating a transaction 31/12/2025 instead of 31/12/2015.

Prepaid transactions

This review identifies any sales or purchases where the payment date falls before the invoice date. The easiest solution is to drill down into each transaction and change the date of the sale or purchase so that it's the same as, or falls before, the payment date.

What should you do if the customer really did pay before you did the work? In this situation, the more correct accounting treatment for this transaction is to record a sales order for the customer first, applying the customer's payment as a deposit. Later, when you complete the job, you convert the order to an invoice. Although this method involves extra work, prepaid transactions can be a nightmare for your accountant — and, therefore, very expensive in fees for you — if they span financial year-ends.

Deposits paid

This review lists any sales or purchase orders that have a deposit applied. Of course, transactions with deposits against them aren't necessarily a problem, and you may review this list and think everything's hunky-dory. However, if you see a really old deposit, take a minute to investigate. You probably completed this sale or purchase long ago, but forgot to convert the order into an invoice or bill.

Employing a forensic expert

The seventh review in your Transaction Review (part of the Company Data Auditor) displays any audit trail changes. Getting a red question mark against this review doesn't usually indicate a problem, but if more than one person works in your MYOB company file, I recommend you click the Display button and take a quick stickybeak at the Audit Trail report.

The Audit Trail report looks for quirky or strange things in your company file, including changes to tax codes, linked accounts, preferences or transactions. You can also view deleted transactions, as well as see who deleted this transaction, and when.

The Journal Security Audit report can be found independently of the Company Data Auditor, under the Security and Audit section of the Accounts tab of your Reports menu.

I've conducted a few investigations in businesses where a manager suspects that an employee is fiddling the books. I've used the Journal Security Audit Trail report to uncover many grievous sins, such as receptionists deleting invoices after customers pay in cash — and pocketing the cash, of course — and bookkeepers changing their own pay transactions to boost their entitlements.

Knowing a red herring when you see one

The last step in the Transaction Review indicates whether your Payroll Liabilities reconcile.

If you use the Pay Liabilities window to record payments for tax and super, troubleshooting is a cinch. Go to Pay Liabilities in the Payroll command centre and select either Superannuation or Taxes as the Liability Type. In the Dated From field, select 1 July. In the Dated To field, select the current date. See if any payroll liabilities for previous months appear. If they do, chances are you missed these payments and that's why the balance of this account isn't returning to zero.

If you still record payroll payments using Spend Money rather than using the Pay Liabilities feature, you'll always get a red question mark indicating that your payroll liability payments don't reconcile, even if these accounts are perfectly in balance. Don't worry. You can take a different tack to ensure everything is in order:

1. **Go to the Find Transactions menu and click the Account tab.**

2. **Select your payroll liability account and enter 1 July as your From date and 31 July as your To date.**

   For example, if you're reconciling superannuation, select Superannuation Payable as the account. If you're reconciling PAYG Tax, select PAYG Tax Payable as the account.

3. **Note down the Total Credits.**

4. **Repeat this month by month, until you have a figure for Total Credits for each month up to the current date.**

5. **Now note down how much you've paid each month (or each quarter if you pay quarterly).**

   Stay in the Find Transactions window to look at Total Debits for each month so that you can see how much you've paid.

6. **Compare what you should have paid (Total Credits) with what you actually paid (Total Debits) each month or quarter.**

   The two should match! In Figure 18-5, for example, the opening balance on 1/02/2015 is $876.00 and this is the amount paid later on in February.

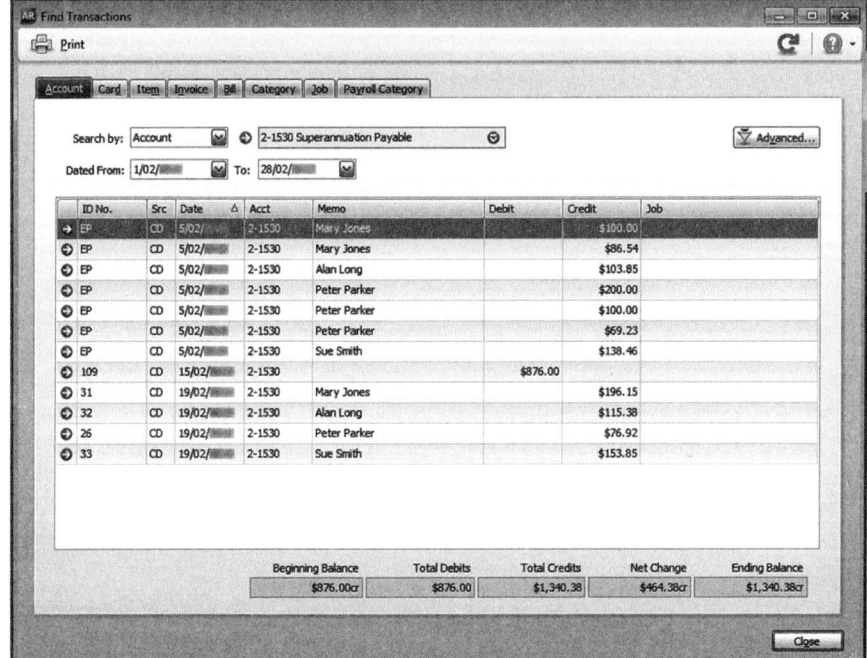

Figure 18-5:
The Find Transactions window helps you to balance payroll liabilities.

Every time you pay super or PAYG Tax, look up the Ending Balance of Superannuation Payable or PAYG Tax Payable for the month just gone. This balance should always be equal to your payment.

Dishing Out Medicine: The Tax Review

The last step of the Company Data Auditor is the Tax Exception Review. Contrary to the overwhelming dullness implied by the name, this review is actually quite a nifty wee beastie, surprisingly efficient at highlighting mistakes and inconsistencies.

Splitting hairs

The first two reviews in the Tax Exception Review check for tax variances and highlight if you (or anyone else) changed the default tax calculations on a transaction. If any transactions come up with tax amount variances, zoom in and fix 'em up. This may require splitting the transaction across two lines: One line for the taxable bit and another line for the tax-free bit.

Taking exception

The third and fourth reviews in the Tax Exception Review identify any transactions with the Tax Code for an account that differs from the Tax Code on the transaction. For example, if you have GST as the Tax Code for Telephone Expense, but you record the payment of a telephone bill with the FRE code, then this transaction comes up as a tax code exception.

Just because something appears as a tax code exception doesn't mean to say you've made a mistake. For example, you may have GST as the Tax Code for Staff Amenities Expense, which makes sense, because most of these expenses include GST. However, every now and then you buy coffee and tea and these beverages, defined by the powers-that-be as a necessity (how wise for once), are GST-free. The fact that you allocate this purchase to Staff Amenities and code this transaction as GST-free doesn't mean you got it wrong.

What I generally do with the Tax Code Exceptions review is display the associated report and look through for mistakes. If I zoom in on a transaction and I can see that it really is a tax exception, I stick an asterisk (*) in front of the memo. That way, if myself or anyone else displays a Tax Code Exceptions report in the future, they know that all transactions with an asterisk in front of the memo are okay and have been checked.

One more thing. You may find that the problem is that the Tax Code for the account itself is wrong in your Accounts List. To fix this up, go to your Accounts List, double-click on the offending account, click the Details tab and change the Tax Code. Easy as pie.

Reconciling yourself

The last step in the Tax Exception Review reconciles Tax Code details against linked accounts in an attempt to see if the GST accounts in your Balance Sheet are correct. The review looks at the total debits or credits in your GST Collected and GST Paid accounts, and compares these figures with the balances of GST Collected and Paid on your Balance Sheet.

If you report for GST on an accruals basis and this report generates an Out of Balance amount, all is not well. Do not pass Go. Instead, check out the following section for the lowdown on how to balance your GST Collected and GST Paid accounts.

If you report for GST on a cash basis, the Tax Exception Review report will always chuck a wobbly and say you're wrong. Maybe you are, but maybe you aren't. Don't waste time trying to figure out the whys and wherefores of this report; instead, reconcile your GST Collected and GST Paid accounts using the method outlined in the next section.

Making sure the whole deal is spot on

Every time you record a transaction that includes GST, the transaction impacts on your GST liability accounts. Therefore, the balance of your GST liability accounts is a running balance of how much you owe.

The correct technique for ensuring that your GST accounts balance depends on whether you report for GST on an accruals basis or a cash basis.

If you report for GST on an accruals basis, here's what to do:

1. **Print a Balance Sheet for the last day of the reporting period on your most recent Business Activity Statement.**

   For example, if your most recent Business Activity Statement was for the month of June, print a Balance Sheet dated 30 June.

2. **On your Balance Sheet, look at the balance of your GST Collected and GST Paid accounts.**

3. **In your most recent Business Activity Statement, look up the amounts you declared for GST Collected and GST Paid.**

   Not sure where to look? Check out boxes 1A and 1B on your statement.

4. **Compare the figures from Step 2 against the figures from Step 3. Guess what? They should match.**

   If the two figures don't match and the difference is more than $100 or so, take further action. I suggest you go right back to the beginning of the financial year, and do this health check for each GST period so that you can pinpoint where the rot set in. If the problem goes further back to before the beginning of the financial year, usually the best approach is to talk to your accountant.

If you report for GST on a cash basis, things take a much trickier turn, because you have to allow for the GST that you haven't paid yet (because you haven't received payments from customers for outstanding invoices or you haven't paid suppliers for outstanding accounts). I'm a little hesitant sharing this procedure with you, because the whole deal is unashamedly tricky, but if you can master reconciling GST on a cash basis, you're already truly ahead of the pack.

1. **Look up the amounts you declared for GST Collected and GST Paid on your most recent Business Activity Statement.**

   You're looking at boxes 1A and 1B on your statement.

2. **Print a Receivables with Tax report and a Payables With Tax report, and calculate how much GST is included in the totals of each of these reports.**

   For example, if I'm owed $11,000 and I charge GST at a rate of 10 per cent and I charge GST on all my sales, I can calculate that my receivables include $1,000 in GST.

3. **Add the amount of tax on receivables (see Step 2) to GST Collected (see Step 1), and add the amount of tax on payables (see Step 2) to GST Paid (see Step 1).**

   Figure 18-6 shows this whole drama in action.

4. **Print a Balance Sheet for the same period, and look at the balance of your GST Collected and GST Paid accounts.**

   For example, if your most recent Business Activity Statement was for the month of June, print a Balance Sheet dated 30 June.

⧄	A	B	C
1			
2		**GST Reconciliation, Cash Basis**	
3			
4		**GST Collected**	
5	Step One	GST Collected shown on Business Activity Statement as at June 30	$ 2,500.00
6	Step Two	Amount of tax as per Receivables with Tax report as at June 30	$ 320.10
7	Step Three	GST Collected as per Business Activity Statement plus tax on receivables	$ 2,820.10
8			
9	Step Four	Balance of GST Collected as per Balance Sheet as at June 30	$ 2,805.00
10	Step Five	*GST Overpaid*	$ 15.10
11			
12		**GST Paid**	
13	Step One	GST Paid shown on Business Activity Statement as at June 30	$ 2,390.00
14	Step Two	Amount of tax as per Payables with Tax report as at June 30	$ 210.20
15	Step Three	GST Collected as per Business Activity Statement plus tax on payables	$ 2,600.20
16			
17	Step Four	Balance of GST Paid as per Balance Sheet as at June 30	$ 2,430.10
18	Step Five	*GST Overclaimed*	$ 170.10
19			
20		*Combined GST discrepancy*	-$ 155.00
21			
22			

Figure 18-6:
Reconciling
GST on a
cash basis.

5. **Compare the figures from Step 4 against the figures from Step 3. If the stars are in your favour, these figures should match.**

If the two figures don't match and the difference is more than $100 or so, take further action. I suggest you go right back to the beginning of the financial year, and do this health check for each GST period. This way you can hopefully see where the problem began. If the issue relates further back to before the beginning of the financial year, your best approach is to talk to your accountant.

Heading to the Beach

So you've made it to the end of this chapter, enduring an accounting marathon that's resulted in a complete audit of your company file. You are awesome.

Only one thing left to do. Head to the Rewards command centre, click the Gone Surfin' button and highlight the preference Do Not Disturb.

Part V
The Part of Tens

the part of tens

In this part ...

- ✔ Discover ten very handy — and delightfully easy — ways to speed your work.

- ✔ Find out what's involved with starting a new financial year, and make life as easy as can be for you and your accountant.

Chapter 19

Ten Tricks to Speed Your Work

In this chapter, I talk about a few tricks to make your bookwork as speedy and efficient as possible. None of these tricks is essential to doing your bookwork — your accounts will still balance and your accountant will still be quite happy even if you ignore every single one.

But if you like to live life to the full and spend as little time in front of a computer screen as possible, this chapter is for you.

Get Bank Feeds Up and Running

Bank feeds are such a huge innovation and timesaver that I devote all of Chapter 5 to explaining how to set up bank feeds and work with 'em. In short, if you haven't already signed up for bank feeds, do so now.

Wait a moment, I hear you cry! What about the fees? (You can't get bank feeds unless you shell out for the monthly subscription to MYOB, which at the time of writing is at least $30 per month.) While I agree that every penny counts, pause for a moment and ask yourself:

> ✔ Do you currently pay for someone else to do your books? If your answer is yes, and this person currently takes more than a couple of hours per month to do your books, chances are that the cost of bank feeds more than cancels out the money you spend on bookkeeping.

✔ Do you do your own books and, if so, could you be earning money elsewhere during the time that you normally spend bookkeeping? Again, if your answer is yes, and bookkeeping takes more than a couple of hours per month, subscribing to MYOB and getting bank feeds can save rather than cost you money.

Tune Up Those Bank Rules

If you already subscribe to bank feeds, take the time to configure bank rules so that MYOB automatically codes as many transactions as possible. Think of bank feeds as being the motorised transport that enables you to get around quickly, and bank rules as the fuel that keeps this transport on the move.

I talk about bank rules at length in Chapter 5, but here's a quick overview of the essentials:

✔ **Look for the unique, but identifying, element in each transaction.** If any transaction has a unique name or number that distinguishes it from other transactions, create a rule to match. For example, a transaction containing the word 'Caltex' is almost certainly fuel, or a transaction containing the word 'Vodafone' is almost certainly phone or internet.

✔ **Don't be too pedantic.** For example, you may occasionally buy something that's not petrol when at the Caltex station, but you can always edit individual transactions. The idea of rules is to create defaults that work most of the time — you can override these rules whenever you need to.

✔ **Keep your business and personal transactions separate.** Rules and bank feeds work best if you don't muddy the waters with a heap of personal transactions. So open a separate bank account for personal stuff, and only hook up bank feeds to your business account.

✔ **When paying bills over the internet, think about the bank rules you've created and enter consistent payment descriptions.** For example, if you only include invoice numbers in payment descriptions, you can never create rules to automatically allocate payments, because invoice numbers change with each transaction. So, instead include a few initials to indicate the supplier name, followed by an invoice or account number. The supplier name can then be the unique 'chunk' of information that allows you to create a rule to automatically allocate all payments made to this supplier.

Integrate Everything

Every time you (or someone else) enter the same bit of information more than once, this duplication costs both time and money. For example, maybe you write invoices by hand because you're on the move, and then rekey these invoices into MYOB when you return to your home office. Maybe you add customer names and addresses into your mailing list in Excel, and then once again into your Cards List in MYOB. Or maybe you receive orders from your website that you then rekey as sales into MYOB.

Be merciless and try to eliminate duplication wherever possible. Load the MYOB OnTheGo app on your smartphone and issue invoices to customers wherever you are; get rid of your Excel mailing list and work instead direct from MYOB; hook up your website so that orders go straight from your website to appear as orders in your MYOB sales register.

To find out more about off-the-shelf apps and utilities that connect with MYOB, visit the MYOB Add Ons page at www.myob.com.au/addons.

Use All Ten Fingers

I don't think there's any other activity in the world that people spend so much time doing quite so badly. The average person on the street wouldn't consider using a Swiss army knife to chop down a tree, nor use nail scissors to cut the lawn. However, many people persist in using a computer, hour after hour, without learning how to touch type.

It's basic. If you spend more than half an hour a day keying information into a computer, you should know how to type properly. The average speed of a non-typist is about 15 words a minute — and that's for a pretty hot two-fingered typist. But by *touch typing* (using all ten fingers), you can easily expect to key in 60 words a minute. That's four times faster!

So, if you're a non-typist and you usually spend just four hours a week in front of the computer and you learn to type, you'll save about three hours a week, every week, from now until you die. And, guess what? Learning how to type takes about an hour a day, every day, for six weeks. That's not so long.

Even if you can type properly, consider your employees. If they're spending time in front of the computer every day and they can't touch type, think about paying for them to learn.

Play Memory Games

Want to go to Spend Money? You don't have to quit out of wherever you are, navigate to the Banking command centre and then click Spend Money. No, you're much more intelligent than that. Instead, simply type Ctrl+H and, in two shakes of a lamb's tail, you arrive at the Spend Money window.

Typing Ctrl+H means finding the Ctrl key (usually at the bottom left of your keyboard) and holding it down. Keep holding it down and then press the letter H. Let go and you're there.

Spend Money isn't the only place you can go to using shortcuts. Ctrl+J takes you to Sales, Ctrl+E to Purchases, Ctrl+D to Receive Money and so on. I summarise these shortcut keys on the Cheat Sheet for this book, available from www.dummies.com/cheatsheet/myobsoftwareau.

Hurl Your Mouse Out the Window

Want to move faster? Then grab your mouse, kiss it a fond farewell and hurl it out the window.

This may sound radical but you can do just about every transaction without using your mouse. To see how this works, go to the Sales command centre and look at the Sales Register button. Can you see how the letter **g** is underlined? This means that instead of clicking the Sales Register button using your mouse, you can press down the Alt button and the letter **g** at the same time. (If you find that some commands in the newer versions of MYOB don't have any letters underlined, don't worry. Press the Alt key down and the underscore marks will appear.)

When entering sales or payments, keep working without your mouse. Press the Tab key to go forwards, or the Shift key plus the Tab key to go backwards (the Tab key sits next to the letter **Q** with the arrows pointing in either direction). After you get the hang of working this way, you'll notice that you can do most tasks without even touching the mouse.

Create Cards Wherever Possible

Have you noticed that when you go to Spend Money, you can skip typing anything into the Card field? I find that beginners often do this, ignoring the Card field and instead just completing the Payee field. This may seem speedy the first time you do it, but in the long run it's not.

The first reason skipping the Card field isn't a time-saver in the long run is this: If you create a card every time you pay someone, the next time you record a payment for that person you only need to type the first few letters of the name into the Card field; MYOB software gets psychic, guesses the name you're after and fills in the rest. You can even get MYOB to complete each person's address details and the allocation account (see 'Tell Suppliers Where to Go', later in this chapter). The second reason? If you complete the Card field every time you record a transaction, you can use the Find Transactions menu to list every cheque, deposit, purchase or payment that relates to a business or individual.

The Card field makes it easier to complete transactions and to refer to them again later. Only ignore the Card field when completing a transaction if you think you'll never pay this person ever again.

Move On to Advanced Searches

When looking for a transaction, instead of browsing through endless transaction journals take a shortcut and perform an advanced inquiry.

Imagine you're looking for a payment for $85.50. You can't remember the exact date of the payment, nor which account you allocated it to. What you need to do is search for every transaction in your company file for this amount.

Here's how:

1. **Go to Find Transactions and click the Account tab.**

   The Find Transactions menu is on the bottom of every command centre.

2. **Click the Advanced button.**

   This button is in the top-right corner and has a magnifying glass next to it. I hope you're feeling clever already — the word Advanced alone makes me feel smart.

3. **In the Search By field, change the option from Account to All Accounts.**

   You can choose to search by one specific account or by All Accounts. All Accounts may take a couple of seconds longer, but it's usually your best bet.

4. **Enter a date range in the Dated From and To fields.**

   When you're not sure of the date, pick a wide range.

5. **Enter the amount you're looking for in the Amount From and To fields.**

   Type the amount you're looking for twice — in the Amount From and Amount To fields. (See Figure 19-1 for an example.)

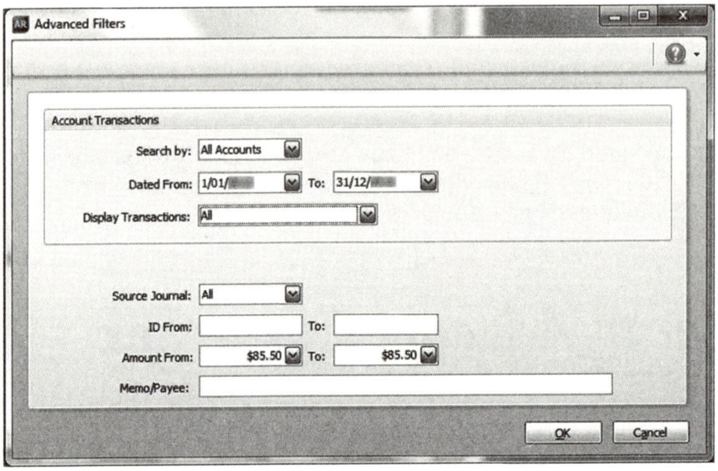

Figure 19-1:
Using
Advanced
Filters
to find
transactions
and search
by an
amount.

6. **Click OK.**

   In the blink of an eye (well, almost), up pops every transaction that has the dollar amount you're searching for. It's so cool.

Tell Suppliers Where to Go

Did you know you can set up your supplier cards so that every time you record a purchase from this supplier, the correct expense account pops up automatically? This innocuous little trick can save you hours of time when it comes to recording supplier invoices or payments and, as an extra bonus, makes for more reliable data entry as well.

Here's the lowdown:

1. **Go to your Cards List and double-click on a supplier card.**

   Pick any old card for the moment. I just want to show you how the whole idea works.

2. **Click the Buying Details tab.**

3. In the Expense Account field, enter the expense account that payments for this supplier would normally go to.

For example, if you pick Telstra as your supplier card, the Expense Account is likely to be Telephone Expense, as shown in Figure 19-2.

4. Click OK to save your changes.

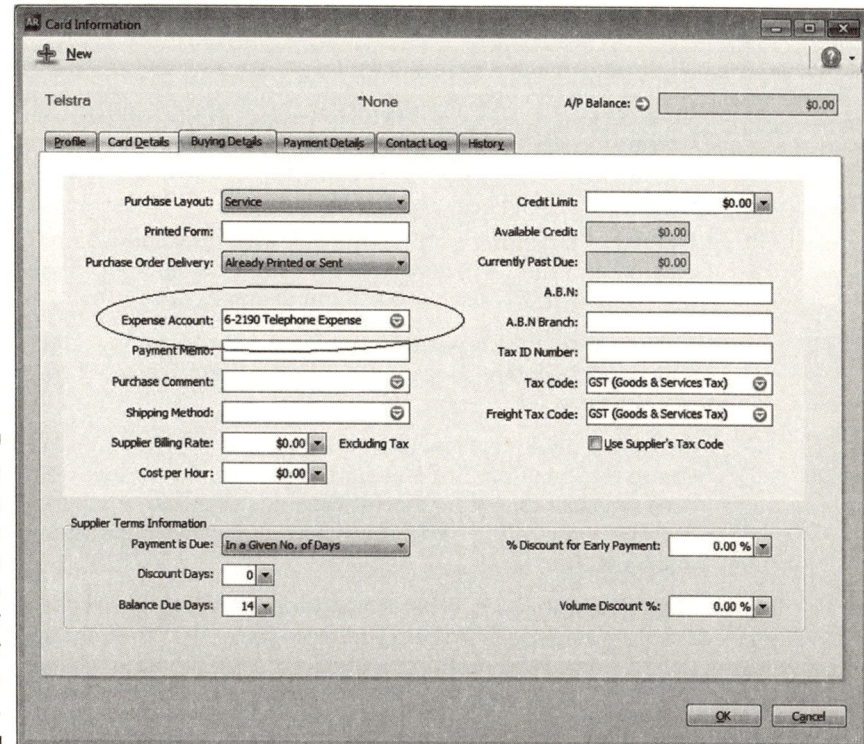

Figure 19-2:
Linking expense accounts for each supplier makes for speedy data entry.

5. Go to Enter Purchases and experiment, entering a payment to this supplier.

In the Enter Purchases window, enter the supplier's name as normal, and then tab through the transaction as you normally would. When you get to the Allocation Account, instead of entering an account number, simply press the Tab key and marvel as the allocation account pops up automatically. Yippee! Life doesn't get much easier than this.

Get Creative with Lists

Kind of like the magnificent sorting hat in *Harry Potter*, one of the ingenious things about MYOB is the way you can view information and sort stuff.

The best place to check out these nifty sorting powers is in the Cards List. Go to your Cards List right now, and try the following:

- **Sort the wheat from the chaff.** Click the Name column label and see how this simple flick of the wrist sorts every card alphabetically, so that cards starting with the letter **A** appear at the top. Click a second time, and cards starting with the letter **A** appear at the bottom. Now repeat this trick with the other column labels. (I like to click the Current Balance column so that customers who owe me the most appear at the top.)

- **Get rid of irritating guff.** Right-click with your mouse on the Card ID column and then left-click Remove This Column. Before you know it, this (usually fairly useless) column disappears.

- **Change your mind.** Want that column back? Right-click on any column and select Column Chooser. Drag the column you want to revive back to your main list.

- **Become a groupie.** Now right-click on the Type column label and select Group By This Column. This action groups like by like, so that every card that has Customer as the Type sits together. Click the little plus button on the left to expand any one of these groups and view the details within.

- **Make Russian dolls.** What if you want to create a group within a group? Try grouping cards first according to Type, and then by the Current Balance owed. To do this, right-click on any column label and select Group By Box. Then drag the Type column over into the grey area in the top-left, just above the first column label. Next, drag the Current Balance column over to the left also. Last, click the plus button to the left of the Type: Customer label to view your excellent handiwork. Figure 19-3 shows this group work in action. Neat, huh?

- **Feel free to be fickle.** Don't like the result? Then right-click with the mouse and left-click Clear Grouping to return to your original view.

- **View customers from the smartest state in Australia.** To view customers in NSW only, click the Advanced button, and against Postcode, select 2000 as the From range and 2999 as the To range.

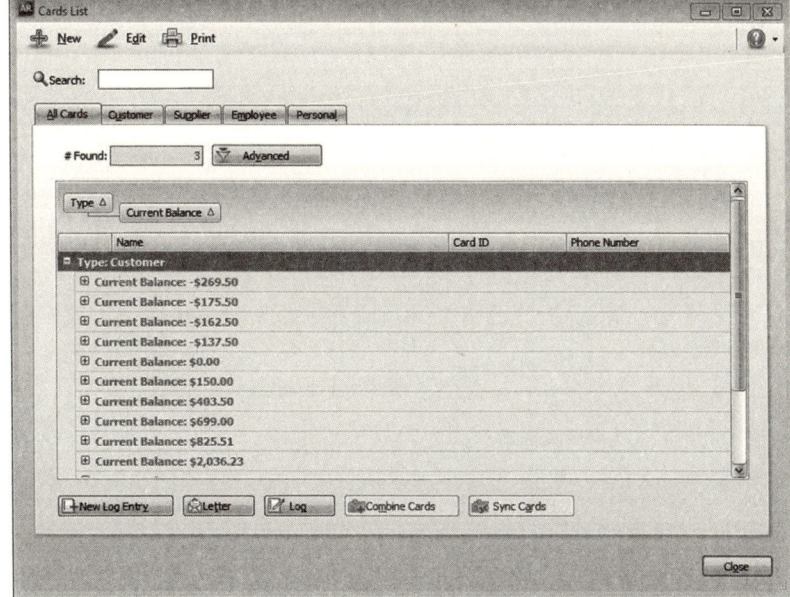

Figure 19-3:
You can sort and group lists in many different ways.

Is this the best fun you've had in ages? (If your answer is 'yes', then I suspect you need to get out more.) Well, more merriment is yet to be had. Go to your Bank Register and then your Sales Register to try these tricks on a different audience.

Chapter 20

Ten Tricks (Nine, Actually) to Starting a New Year

Being a person of Scottish descent, I'm used to associating the words 'New Year' with raucous drinking parties, freezing cold winds and the warbling refrains of 'Auld Lang Syne'.

By contrast, starting a new *financial* year with MYOB (which just happens to be the subject of this gloriously fascinating chapter) is a time when you want to be as sober as a judge. It's a pretty involved process that no kind of liquor will make easier.

Give Your Company File the Once-Over

The morning of 1 July dawns and with a vague sense of misgiving you slowly stir, bleary eyes focusing on the calendar. No need to fret. A new financial year may have begun, but you have a few weeks — if not months — before you need to get your company file ready for the accountant. In that time, I suggest you take advantage of every quiet moment in the office to make sure your accounts are absolutely shipshape. Remember, the more that you (or your bookkeeper) can tidy up your accounts, the less work for your accountant.

Not sure where to begin? Turn back to Chapter 18, where I walk you through the company file health check from hell, explaining everything from fixing up GST codes to balancing inventory accounts.

With this under your belt, go to your Reports menu and print a Profit & Loss report for the year just passed, and a Balance Sheet report for June. Read through these reports carefully, checking any amounts that look strange or don't make sense. (If in doubt, make your way back to Chapter 17, which covers these two reports in more detail.)

Become an Irritating Pedant

Follow this step-by-step guide on how to prepare your file for your accountant and finalise the year:

1. **Complete every transaction up to 30 June, including payments, deposits, sales and purchases.**

   You don't have to finish recording transactions on the last day of June. In fact, it may be months later by the time you've finished recording everything for the previous year.

2. **Run a health check on your company file to check that your work is as accurate as can be.**

   For more information on completing this step, refer to 'Give Your Company File the Once-Over', earlier in this chapter.

3. **Print a copy of your Profit & Loss Statement for the financial year, along with a Balance Sheet for 30 June, and store these reports somewhere you can find them later on.**

   However much you trust and respect your accountant, the reality for most businesses is that the grunt work of preparing your tax returns and final reports is done by a clerk in the back office who knows nothing about your business and who has never worked on your accounts before. For this reason, I like to have a reference of what the financial figures look like before the accountant starts doing their stuff. This way I have more of a chance of understanding what adjustments have been made and checking that no mistakes have occurred.

4. **Either invite your accountant to view your company file or send your accountant a copy of your company file.**

    If you're working in the cloud, all you have to do is ensure you add your accountant as an adviser, and then tell your accountant that they can view your data whenever they're ready. Or, if you're like me and you tend to work both in the cloud and locally, depending on where you are and the internet speed, tell your accountant that you're ready

whenever they are, but they just need to let you know a day or so before they want to start work on your data, so that you can make sure you shift your data back into the cloud before they begin work.

If you don't store your company file in the cloud, you need to provide your accountant with a backup or copy of your data (I explain more about backups in Chapter 16). You can copy this file onto a CD or flash drive, or, if your company file is small enough, you may be able to send it to your accountant via email.

5. **Lock periods so that you can't accidentally post transactions to last year.**

   When you lock the period you've just completed — usually June of the current financial year — you can't accidentally post stuff to the year you've just finished. For more information on completing this step, see the section 'Lock Yourself Out', later in this chapter.

6. **Wait until your accountant provides you with completed financial reports and tax returns.**

   Most accountants provide you with financial reports using their own specialist taxation software. I suggest you compare these financial reports against what your reference reports (refer to Step 3 of these instructions), and play spot the difference. Ensure you understand, and agree with, the differences between your original figures and the final figures in your accountant's reports.

7. **If necessary, enter your accountant's adjustments.**

   If you're working in the cloud, hopefully your accountant has already entered their adjustments in your company file. (However, don't count on this — double-check your company file to make sure!)

   If you're not working in the cloud, you need to ask your accountant for a list of journal entries so that you can get your figures in MYOB as at the end of the financial year to match your accountant's. You may want to ask your accountant or an MYOB Certified Consultant for help to do this.

8. **Do a final backup and name it Final End of Year.**

9. **Gaze at your navel and seriously consider the possible consequences of what you're about to do.**

   What happens now depends on what version you're using. With the 2015 version of MYOB, the process of starting a new year doesn't actually purge any data, and you can roll back the year-end if you need to. With AccountRight 2011 to 2014, starting a new year doesn't purge any data but the process itself is irreversible: After you close a year, you can never re-open that year to enter a new transaction, nor can you edit existing transactions for that period.

   With MYOB 'classic' versions, the process can be even more drastic. Not only are you unable to return to a previous year to enter or edit transactions, but depending on your selections, you may also end up purging the previous year's transactions altogether.

10. Go to the File menu and follow the commands to start a new year.

Go to File⇨Close a Year⇨Close a Financial Year, and click the Next button. Look carefully at what year you're about to close, as shown in Figure 20-1, and double-check that nobody else has already closed off the year. (If you store your company file in the cloud and your accountant works in the file, you may find that they have already initiated the new year process on your behalf.) If all looks okay, click Next one more time followed by Close the Financial Year.

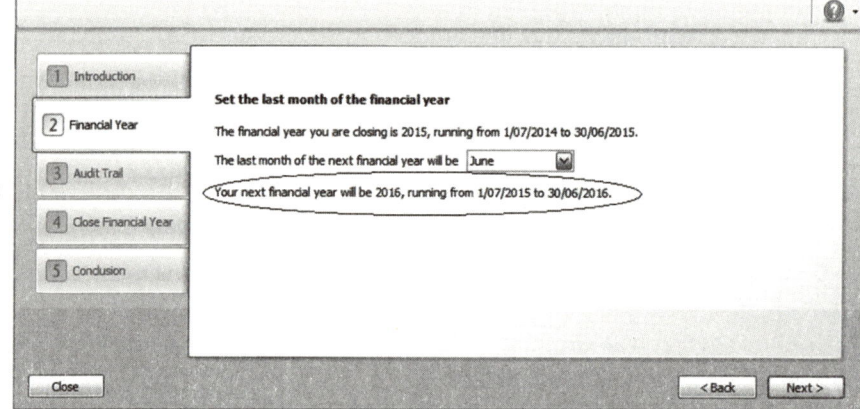

Figure 20-1:
Look carefully at what year you're about to close.

11. Be patient. Write a poem. Tell your husband/wife/workmate/cat you love them.

This end-of-year process can take anywhere between a few minutes to a few hours, depending on the size of your file. (Declarations of love can vary in how long they take too.)

12. Pop the champagne bottle — you're done!

Preferably a Moët, darling.

Tell Your Accountant about Your Good Work

If this is the first year that you've worked with MYOB, or if you recently switched to a new accountant, you want to instil confidence in your accountant that you've done your part of the deal. After all, you don't want to pay someone to rehash the work you've already done.

The best approach is to write a simple letter to your accountant and list everything that you've completed (bank reconciliations, debtor reconciliations, payroll reconciliations and so on). You can even refer to the health check in Chapter 18, and list all the items you've managed to work through. Add to this list everything that you know needs extra attention, such as particular transactions you don't know how to allocate, or things you're not sure you've recorded correctly.

If your accountant asks for copies of bank statements and you know that you've reconciled these bank accounts, tell your accountant they don't need to go through each statement. Instead, provide your accountant with a copy of your bank statement as at June 30, along with your Bank Reconciliation Report for this date, so that your accountant can be reassured that you have this end of things under control.

Jump the Gun

Earlier in this chapter, I recommend you wait for your accountant's year-end adjustments before starting a new year. The only hitch with this method is if your accountant takes months to produce final accounts. Having two years open can be a hassle, because many reports aren't available for the current year until the old year is closed.

An alternative approach is to send your file to your accountant, back up carefully and then start a new financial year without waiting for your accountant's adjustments. Much later, when your accountant produces final accounts, you can do a journal entry to adjust your opening Balance Sheet so that it matches the accountant's closing Balance Sheet (you'll need to date this journal entry 1 July and avoid recording any other transactions on that date). Such journals are pretty technical stuff and you may want to ask either your accountant or an MYOB Certified Consultant to help you out.

Lock Yourself Out

At Step 5 in the section 'Become an Irritating Pedant' earlier in this chapter, I mention locking periods so that no-one can create or edit transactions that belong to the previous year.

To lock a period, go to Setup⇨Preferences and, with a delicate flick of your little finger, press the Security tab. Select Lock Periods and then enter the first date of the new financial year. For example, if I want to lock the 2014/15 year, I enter 1/7/2015 as the Lock Period date. This means I can't enter any transactions with a date of 30/6/2015 or earlier.

Later, when your accountant comes back to you with adjustments, it's easy to return to your security preferences and unlock this period. All you have to do is remove the tick from Lock Period and you're away.

Switch Off Auto Confirmation

Every now and then when you go to open up MYOB, you'll be prompted to confirm your software. If you're always connected to the internet and you've set your preferences for automatic confirmation, chances are you're hardly even aware of this process. Every few months a message pops up, you click OK and that's it.

However, if your accountant is working with a copy of your file (as opposed to working online in the cloud) and a confirmation message falls due when the accountant is connected to the internet, your file will end up being confirmed twice. This can cause confusion and ultimately 'use up' the number of company files you can have activated. However, an easy solution is available:

1. **Make a copy of your company file, ready to give to your accountant.**

2. **Open up this copy and select Preferences from the Setup menu.**

3. **Click the Security tab.**

4. **Unclick the option I Prefer to Use Automated Online Company File Confirmation.**

In addition to changing your preferences, tell your accountant not to confirm your company file if prompted by a message to do so. Instead, ask your accountant to click the option Confirm Later.

Anticipate the Obvious

Make things easy for yourself by anticipating the questions your accountant has to ask you every year.

Here are a few things I suggest you consider:

- **Your motor vehicle percentage:** If you use a motor vehicle for part-business, part-personal use, you either need to tell your accountant the percentage split or apportion each transaction as you go (I explain how to record part-business, part-personal transactions in Chapter 6.) You may also need to do one of those mind-numbingly bureaucratic log books at least once every five years.

- **Your home office percentage:** If you claim home office expenses such as rent, rates or mortgage interest, provide your accountant with a record of how you've calculated your home office percentages. Also, tell your accountant how you've dealt with these expenses in your company file.

- **The number of your dependants:** Always a tricky and contentious question. If only my dog were eligible for the family tax benefit.

- **Interest or dividend income:** You need to tell your accountant about any interest or dividend income that you didn't bank in your business account (and, therefore, isn't showing in your company file).

Beware of Unwanted Upgrades

Sometimes accountants ask that you don't work on your company file while they're working on it, with the idea that once they've finished doing their stuff, they can return the file to you, complete with adjustments. (Incidentally, I discourage this way of working because errors often occur when moving company files around, and instead recommend shifting to the cloud whenever possible.)

If you do find yourself in the situation that your accountant has your company file and plans to return it to you after they've worked on it, be careful that your accountant doesn't then inadvertently upgrade your company file to a newer version, or a version that's 'higher up' the family tree (for example, upgrading to AccountRight Premier when you only have AccountRight Plus).

If an accountant or external bookkeeper upgrades your company file to a newer version, you can't 'downgrade' it back again. In other words, if they upgrade your file and do a whole lot of work in your file ready to give back to you, you'll have to upgrade to the version that they were using in order to be able to view your data.

Communicate More, Communicate Better

The biggest key to any relationship, whether with your accountant, your lover or your cat, is communication. MYOB makes communicating with your accountant easier than ever, so long as you know a few tricks of the trade:

- ✔ **Ask your accountant to provide a list of adjustments.** I talk about end-of-year adjustments earlier in this chapter, in the section 'Become an Irritating Pedant'. I explain that your accountant often makes adjustments using their own software, with the result that the final Profit & Loss report they create is quite different from yours. Pre-empt future confusion by asking your accountant for a list of year-end adjustments for you to record in MYOB.

- ✔ **Ask for criticism.** Don't be too laissez-faire about your accounts, relying on your accountant to fix all your mistakes every time your tax falls due. Paying good money for your accountant to fix the same mistakes, year in, year out, is a waste! A much healthier scenario is to ask your accountant to explain what you're doing wrong and ask what you can do better next year.

- ✔ **Become more informed.** Now that you and MYOB are lifelong partners, you can produce your own Profit & Loss and Balance Sheet reports whenever you want. Ask your accountant to look through these statements with you, explain to you what they mean and analyse how your business could perform better.

- ✔ **Double-check you send your accountant the most recent version of your company file.** Not sure? Open up your company file, go to the Accounts command centre, click Company Data Auditor, and look at the File Location listed in the Company File Overview. Navigate to this folder on your computer and make a copy of your company file from here. (Of course, if you work in the cloud, you don't need to worry about sending your company file — instead, you simply send your accountant an invitation to log in.)

- ✔ **If you store your company file in the cloud, ask your accountant to make the change as well.** Depressingly, I come across a few accountants who aren't making a genuine transition to the cloud. Instead they log on to their client's company file, print reports, and continue working in their own specialist practice software. If you've made the shift to the cloud, explain to your accountant that you would prefer them to work directly in your company file, so that you can be confident that your financial reports are accurate.

- ✔ **Plan ahead for tax.** Don't wait until June has come and gone before worrying about your tax bill. Get your accountant to give your company file the once-over in April or May and ask for help minimising your tax, before it's too late.

Index

• *J* •

• *K* •

• *L* •

Q

R

About the Author

Veechi Curtis loves to teach and communicate with others (just try to stop her talking!). She's passionate about small business, and loves helping people realise their dreams and succeed.

Born in Scotland, Veechi attended university in Bathurst, New South Wales, where she completed her degree in Accountancy and Business Management. She has been an MYOB Certified Consultant for more than 20 years, training hundreds of businesses in how to make MYOB software work for them. As a journalist, she has written for many publications and has also been a columnist for the *Sydney Morning Herald*.

Veechi is also the author of *Small Business For Dummies*, *Bookkeeping For Dummies*, *QuickBooks For Dummies* and *Creating a Business Plan For Dummies*.

Veechi has three children and lives with her husband in the beautiful Blue Mountains of NSW. Feel free to send Veechi a message, or ask a question about this book, via her website at www.veechicurtis.com.au.

Author's Acknowledgements

Veechi would like to thank David Wilson from MYOB Australia, for his technical review of this manuscript. His sharp eyes and technical expertise have contributed immeasurably to this book. Thanks also to the John Wiley editorial team: Charlotte Duff, Dani Karvess and Kerry Laundon.

Publisher's Acknowledgements

We're proud of this book; please send us your comments through our online registration form located at dummies.custhelp.com.

Some of the people who helped bring this book to market include the following:

Acquisitions, Editorial and Media Development

Project Editor: Charlotte Duff

Acquisitions Editor: Kerry Laundon

Editorial Manager: Dani Karvess

Production

Graphics: diacriTech

Technical Reviewer: David Wilson, MYOB

Proofreader: Jenny Scepanovic

Indexer: Veechi Curtis

The author and publisher would like to thank the following copyright holders, organisations and individuals for their permission to reproduce copyright material in this book:

- Cover Image: © MYOB, 2015. MYOB® is a registered trademark of MYOB Technology Pty Ltd.
- Screen captures from MYOB® reproduced with permission. Copyright © 2015 MYOB Technology Pty Ltd. MYOB® is a registered trademark of MYOB Technology Pty Ltd and its affiliates.
- Microsoft Excel screenshots used with permission from Microsoft.

Every effort has been made to trace the ownership of copyright material. Information that enables the publisher to rectify any error or omission in subsequent editions is welcome. In such cases, please contact the Legal Services section of John Wiley & Sons Australia, Ltd.

Business & Investing

978-1-118-22280-5
$39.95

978-0-73031-945-0
$19.95

978-0-73031-951-1
$19.95

978-0-73031-065-5
$19.95

978-0-73030-584-2
$24.95

978-1-11864-126-2
$19.95

978-0-73031-949-8
$19.95

978-0-73031-954-2
$19.95

978-0-730-31069-3
$39.95

978-0-730-31937-5
$39.95

978-0-73031-534-6
$39.95

978-1-118-64122-4
$39.95

Order today!

 Available in print and e-book formats.

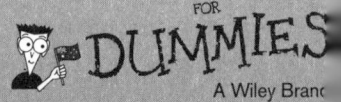